D1526570

THE **AZTEC CALENDAR STONE**

THE AZTEC
CALENDAR
STONE

**Edited by Khristaan D. Villela
and Mary Ellen Miller**

Introduction by Khristaan D. Villela, Matthew H. Robb, and Mary Ellen Miller

PUBLISHED BY THE GETTY RESEARCH INSTITUTE

The Getty Research Institute Publications Program
Thomas W. Gaehtgens, *Director, Getty Research Institute*
Gail Feigenbaum, *Associate Director*

The Aztec Calendar Stone
Diane Mark-Walker, *Manuscript Editor*

© 2010 J. Paul Getty Trust
Published by the Getty Research Institute, Los Angeles
Getty Publications
Gregory M. Britton, *Publisher*
1200 Getty Center Drive, Suite 500
Los Angeles, CA 90049-1682
www.getty.edu

14 13 12 11 10 5 4 3 2 1

Front cover: *Aztec Calendar Stone,* Mexico (Tenochtitlan), ca. 1502–19 (detail). See p. 151, pl. 1
Back cover: Left, Masonic commemorative medal, struck in Mexico, 1945. See p. 27, fig. 12. Top, *Aztec Calendar Stone,* engraving by Francisco de Agüera (Mexican, act. 1779–1820), ca. 1792. See p. 54, fig. 2. Bottom, front cover of Alfredo Chavero, *Historia antigua y de la conquista,* 1888. See p. 159, pl. 13
Cover background: Detail of *Codex Borgia,* fol. 43, tracing by Eduard Seler (German, born Prussian, 1849–1922)
Frontispiece: *Aztec Calendar Stone,* ca. 1839 (detail). See p. 20, fig. 7
Title page: Title page of Alfredo Chavero, *Historia antigua y de la conquista,* 1888. See p. 160, pl. 14
Copyright page: Tonatiuh image (*ixiptla*) featured in 4 Ollin ceremony, Bernardino de Sahagún, *Florentine Codex,* vol. 1, bk. 2, fol. 135r, ca. 1575–77. See p. 270, fig. 8
Facing pp. 1, 300: Skeletonized Huitzilopochtli and Tezcatlipoca inside of the Earth-jaguar, drawing by Ariane Fradcourt after Beyer 1965g, fig. 1 (detail), modified by Kurt Hauser (American, b. 1954). See p. 286, fig. 11

Library of Congress Cataloging-in-Publication Data

The Aztec Calendar Stone / edited by Khristaan D. Villela and Mary Ellen Miller ; introduction by Khristaan D. Villela, Matthew H. Robb, and Mary Ellen Miller.
    p. cm.
Includes bibliographical references and index.
ISBN 978-1-60606-004-9 (hardcover)
1. Aztec calendar. 2. Aztecs—Antiquities. 3. Aztec cosmology. 4. Aztec sculpture. 5. Inscriptions—Mexico. 6. Mexico—Antiquities. 7. Mexico City (Mexico)—Antiquities. I. Villela, Khristaan. II. Miller, Mary Ellen.

F1219.76.C35A98 2010
972'.01—dc22

                2009032142

Contents

Acknowledgments

We first discussed an *Aztec Calendar Stone* anthology in early 2005 and lamented that for such a key monument in Pre-Columbian and world art so many of the main sources were available only in Spanish or were buried in obscure or rare publications. It was difficult for our students to find and read the history of *Calendar Stone* studies. Outside of large university libraries, most of the sources that explain the *Calendar Stone* can hardly be found. In Mexico in the last fifteen years, Eduardo Matos Moctezuma, Leonardo López Luján, and the late Felipe Solís have published articles and two books on the *Calendar Stone* and related monuments; a few of these works appeared in Spanish in the popular journal *Arqueología mexicana.* But these important efforts notwithstanding, we felt the need for a comprehensive anthology that would publish long excerpts of the most important writings on the *Calendar Stone,* or the *Piedra del Sol,* as it is known in the Spanish-speaking world, from its discovery in 1790 to the present day. A considerable number of these works are published here in English for the first time.

Many friends and colleagues have helped make this book possible. Thanks are due to Thomas W. Gaehtgens and Gail Feigenbaum, both at the Getty Research Institute (GRI), and to Barbara Anderson, formerly at the GRI, who encouraged us to assemble, edit, and translate all the constituent elements of the book and the Getty to publish it. Julia Bloomfield, former head of the GRI's Publications Program, and the GRI publications staff—Diane Mark-Walker, Michele Ciaccio, Genevieve Gonzalez-Turner, John Hicks, Alicia Houtrouw, Daniela Loewenthal, Rachelle Okawa, and Jannon Stein—gave careful attention to every phase of the manuscript's editing process. Jobe Benjamin, Christine Nguyen, and John Kiffe contributed expert photographic services. Kurt Hauser and Stacy Miyagawa were responsible for the book's striking design and production, respectively. We are grateful to the authors who have been gracious about the necessary revisions and (in some cases) shortening of their texts: Ariane Fradcourt, Michel Graulich, Cecelia Klein, Eduardo Matos Moctezuma, Carlos Navarrete, Richard F. Townsend, and Stacie Graham Widdifield. Emily Umberger not only allowed us to reprint her article on the dates carved on the *Calendar Stone* but also aided the project with many helpful comments. We were saddened to learn of the death in April 2009 of Felipe Solís, longtime director of the Museo Nacional de Antropología, whose article in 2000 on the *Calendar Stone* in *Arqueología mexicana* brought a clear interpretation to a large reading audience.

We would like to thank Frank Comparato and his team at Labyrinthos Press for allowing us to reproduce selections from their English-language edition of Eduard Seler's *Collected Works.* Richard Kristin and Logan Wagner reviewed the translations of some excerpts and provided helpful comments. Thanks go to the staff at the American Philosophical Society, who allowed us to adapt their manuscript translation of 1818 of Antonio de León y Gama's *Descripción histórica y cronológica de las dos piedras* of 1792. We also owe thanks to the staff at Dumbarton Oaks Research Library, Washington, D.C.; the Center for Southwest Research, Zimmerman Library, University of New Mexico; and the Fray Angélico Chávez History Library, Santa Fe, New Mexico.

At Yale University, Cesar Rodríguez, librarian of the Latin American collections, helped us find obscure sources.

Many others have offered encouragement, suggested sources, and directed us to *Calendar Stone* reproductions, including Dennis Carr, Leonardo López Luján, Diana Magaloni, Elisa Mandell, Barbara Mundy, and Megan O'Neil. Thanks are also due to Jorge Gómez Tejada for biographical research on the chapter authors. Most of all, we would like to thank Matthew H. Robb, without whose aid this book would not have been published in its present form. Robb joined the *Aztec Calendar Stone* team in the fall of 2008 and, in addition to cowriting the introduction, edited many of the chapters and contributed to their introductions. Villela and Robb ran the last lap of the project, checking details and tying up every loose end.

To my wife, Jennifer, and son, Octavio, who was born as we finished the manuscript
—Khristaan D. Villela, Santa Fe, New Mexico

With thanks to my Yale students of the last twenty years
—Mary Ellen Miller, New Haven, Connecticut

Note to the Reader

Assembling a collection of writings on the *Aztec Calendar Stone* from 1581 to the present day in one volume presented many challenges. We reviewed dozens of works for inclusion, and we believe that the twenty-one works selected represent a fair history of the monument's interpretation, with several published for the first time or published in English for the first time. As is often the case with anthologies, the texts in this collection are presented in a slightly altered form. We have reduced the length of certain texts and excised some basic information that, although important, would make the book unduly repetitious as a whole. This was particularly true of the earliest works on the *Calendar Stone*. Only a third of Antonio de León y Gama's treatise deals with the *Calendar Stone;* the works of Alfredo Chavero, Enrique Juan Palacios, and Hermann Beyer include many pages of description; and, in the case of Eduard Seler, we excerpted segments of several longer articles that touch only peripherally on the *Calendar Stone.* The texts written after 1950 generally are more focused and consequently are reprinted here with little or no alteration, although they, too, are condensed in some cases. Richard Townsend's discussion of the *Calendar Stone* takes place within the context of a larger book on Aztec sculpture; only about half of Stacie Graham Widdifield's unpublished master's thesis has been included.

Places where portions of the original version have been omitted are indicated by ellipses. Editorial interpolations appear in brackets. The few selections that have been lightly revised from an English-language original are so noted in the source footnotes. The remaining works that were first published in English retain their original language here, and so the reader can expect to find variant spellings of key terms among the reprinted excerpts. Some of the illustrations that accompanied the original editions are not reproduced in these pages. Figure numbers have been changed to reflect the current order of illustrations, and all figure captions have been standardized. Slight technical changes in the citations have been made to conform references to the bibliography at the end of this volume, and incomplete citations have been augmented according to modern citation standards where possible. Unless otherwise noted, Khristaan D. Villela made all of the translations from Spanish and also translated any Spanish passages in the English-language contributions.

Piedra del Sol
un sauce de cristal,
un chopo de agua,
un alto surtidor que el viento arquea,
un árbol bien plantado mas danzante,
un caminar de río que se curva,
avanza, retrocede, da un rodeo
y llega siempre:

Sun Stone
a crystal willow, a poplar of water,
a tall fountain the wind arches over,
a tree deep-rooted yet dancing still,
a course of a river that turns, moves on,
doubles back, and comes full circle,
forever arriving:

—Octavio Paz[1]

Khristaan D. Villela, Matthew H. Robb, and Mary Ellen Miller

Introduction

The *Aztec Calendar Stone* is one of the most famous objects in world archaeology, art history, and visual culture. Since its rediscovery in the Zócalo, or main plaza, of Mexico City on 17 December 1790, the *Piedra del Sol* (*Sun Stone*), as it is generally known in the Spanish-speaking world, has played a key role in the history of Pre-Columbian studies and in Mexican history and cultural politics. The *Calendar Stone* has been nearly always both inescapable and ineffable: as proof of the astronomical and mathematical skill of indigenous Americans, as the centerpiece of Mexico's Museo Nacional de Antropología, and as a symbol that has outpaced the Mexican (and equally Aztec in its origins) state seal of the eagle alighting on a cactus. It also has appeared as a decoration on innumerable items of official and popular culture in every medium and at every scale, from currency to screen prints on clothing; been depicted in prints and photographs; been reproduced in sterling silver, bronze, plaster, and etched glass; and even taken the form of food items such as chocolates and cakes. "Who does not know the *Aztec Calendar Stone*?" Leopoldo Batres asked rhetorically in 1888 (Batres 1888, x). The afterlives of the *Aztec Calendar Stone* suggest levels of "knowing" that span a spectrum in which the object moves from being almost entirely drained of meaning to being elevated as a recondite, mysterious, and impenetrable repository of the secrets of the universe. Despite its ubiquitous, almost numinous, presence, the full meaning of the monument remains just beyond our grasp. It has been on display as an object of study and curiosity in our world for more than two centuries—but in all likelihood the Aztecs knew it for less than twenty years, leading to an uncanny circumstance: it has developed a richer and more varied biography among moderns than among those who carved it. Those sculptors left behind only the object—no contemporary accounts of its design and creation are known to us. Everything written about the *Calendar Stone* has always been refracted through the lens of modern inquiry, forever departing and forever arriving.

The *Calendar Stone* is an irregular basalt slab weighing roughly twenty-four and one-half tons, with a raised disk measuring eleven feet and five inches in diameter emerging from a planed flange (see pls. 1–11). Aztec sculptors carved both the top face and the rim of the disk with mythological and historical imagery consistent with the needs of its patron, Motecuhzoma II (1466–1520), and its place in the constellation of sculptures made in Tenochtitlan in the last years before the conquest of 1519–21. A series of concentric circles organizes the symmetrical composition, radiating out from a central image depicting either the Aztec sun god Tonatiuh, the earth deity Tlaltecuhtli, or some hybrid entity. Claws grasping human hearts flank this face. What is usually thought to be a string of beads below the face may be gouts of blood, rendered unevenly along a neckline, and could indicate that the *Calendar Stone* deity is shown as a sacrificial victim, decapitated and perhaps dismembered. Several authors in this book argue that the sun god on the

Calendar Stone is the dead, night sun, consumed by or combined with the earth deity. The stone seems to confirm that the sun was sacrificed, but we cannot say whether that means it was a dead or reborn deity (Taube 2000, 320–21). Many other large Aztec sculptures that we presume were sited close to the Templo Mayor also show chthonic deities dismembered or otherwise sacrificed, including the Coyolxauhqui disk, the *Coatlicue,* and the so-called *Coatlicue of the Metro.* The head sunk in the center of the *cuauhxicalli* of Motecuhzoma I, usually identified as the sun god Tonatiuh (e.g., Matos Moctezuma and Solís Olguín 2004, 120), also appears to be decapitated.[2] All of the imagery at the monument's center is enclosed by the glyph for the date Nahui Ollin, or 4 Motion. The "arms" or "wings" of the Ollin glyph contain the names of the previous world creations, or suns, according to the order used by the Aztecs. Each is named by the date when it ended, beginning in the upper right and proceeding counterclockwise: Nahui Ocelotl, or 4 Jaguar; Nahui Ehecatl, or 4 Wind; Nahui Quiahuitl, or 4 Rain (this sun ended in a rain of fire); and finally Nahui Atl, or 4 Water. Four Motion is the date in the Aztec 260-day calendar when the Fifth Sun—the sun of our world—is to end. Four smaller glyphs carved within the central circle surrounding Nahui Ollin are the dates 7 Monkey, 1 Rain, and 1 Flint and a headdress glyph now recognized as the name of Motecuhzoma II.

The next ring contains the twenty days of the 260-day calendar, beginning with the first day, Cipactli, or Alligator, to the left of the "pointer" above the central face, and proceeding counterclockwise until reaching the last day, Xochitl, or Flower.[3] The next ring contains a repeated five-part motif, sometimes called a quincunx, which was the symbol of the *chalchihuitl,* representing precious greenstone or the concept of preciousness in general.[4] The eight large symmetrically disposed points in this zone are usually interpreted as sunbeams, although the four lesser points may also represent perforators, used to draw blood, since the six square forms with which they alternate have been described as the decorated end of a blood-letter, like a knife handle. Beyond the quincunxes are three closely spaced rings of imagery, including rounded squares in groups of ten, usually interpreted as feathers, a triple line punctuated by fourteen circles, representing greenstone beads, and twelve groups of four toothlike forms that Hermann Beyer thought were drops of blood. In the outermost zone of the *Calendar Stone,* two large dragons, called *xiuhcoatls,* or fire serpents, bind the whole scene, with tails above and heads below. Their segmented bodies enclose fire-butterfly symbols and similar fire signs erupt from their backs. Their noses curl back and are decorated with star symbols. At the "top" of the monument, their tails frame the date 13 Acatl, or 13 Reed, while at the bottom, their mouths open to reveal the faces of Tonatiuh on the left and the fire god Xiuhtecuhtli on the right.

Although it is rarely reproduced, the profile of the *Calendar Stone* is carved with imagery identifying it as the sky, either day or night. The flange is smooth but uncarved, save for about fifty small circular depressions. The irregularly shaped flange has led many writers to argue that the *Calendar Stone* was unfinished, or perhaps that it was broken, either during its manufacture before the conquest or in the general iconoclasm of native sculptures after 1521; few other large-scale Aztec stone monuments that we presume were finished show similar breakage or even this kind of border around the principal subject. Even this cursory description of the monument and its contents would not have been possible without the accumulated efforts of more than two centuries of patient, thorough, passionate, and occasionally tendentious scholarship. This volume is a chronicle of those works that have made major contributions to our understanding of this singular object.

Although exact identification of the central face has been contested for two hundred years, the monument as a whole presents some key themes in Aztec cosmology; the previous creations; the "present" creation of Aztecs, Nahui Ollin; and the deities that they believed were key players in the creation and destruction of the universe—the sun god, the earth deity, and the fire god. Much of the remainder of the imagery and the smaller calendrical glyphs either establish the sacred context of the central scene or connect it to events in Aztec history and mythology. Although it features the twenty days of the 260-day calendar, the *Calendar Stone* does not function as any kind of "calendar" that would be familiar to us. Neither can it be used to tell the time or predict the solstices, equinoxes, solar zenith passages, or any other similar periodic event.

Most writers today agree that the *Calendar Stone* was a *cuauhxicalli,* or "eagle vessel," and that perhaps also it was a *temalacatl,* a circular stone used in the gladiatorial sacrifice. Both object classes are attested and known in many examples, including extant large-scale stone sculptures, painted representations in the codices and other pictorial sources, and prose descriptions. The problem for present-day students is that in central Mexico before the conquest many objects that to us seem so different were considered to be members of these sculpture classes. *Cuauhxicallis* can be both basins and flat objects; *temalacatls* were supposed to be pierced so that a captive could be tied to the stone, and not all examples have the expected ring shape. Although only stone examples survive today, *cuauhxicallis* and *temalacatls* likely were made in various media and at many scales, from monumental examples such as the *Calendar Stone,* the *Stone of Tizoc,* and the *Stone of Motecuhzoma I,* to small-scale *cuauhxicallis,* measuring about five by seven inches, which horrified Hernan Cortés in Veracruz when Motecuhzoma II's emissaries offered one to him filled with blood.[5] The ancient Mexicans equated all of these varieties of *cuauhxicallis,* and to a lesser extent, *temalacatls;* all were sacrificial vessels and ritual equipment, some were flat and some were basins, and others were more conceptual "containers."[6]

The *Calendar Stone* began to accrue its present-day repertory of meanings in the decades after the conquest, a process already in progress when Archbishop Alonso de Montúfar ordered it buried, probably in the second half of the sixteenth century. Studies of the *Calendar Stone*'s iconography have dominated the past century of scholarship on the monument, particularly the identity of the damaged face at the center of its multiple rings, but this has not always been the case. In the beginning, *Calendar Stone* studies centered on questions of function, placement, and patronage. Was it a calendar or other timekeeping device? How should the calendrical glyphs carved on the work be interpreted? Was it not a calendar at all but rather a *cuauhxicalli,* a metaphoric sacrificial vessel or altar? Which Aztec ruler commissioned the monument? Where was the monument originally placed, and was it mounted horizontally or vertically?

Many of the eighteenth- and nineteenth-century authors were not especially interested in what we would call iconography but instead focused on the object as an illustration of the calendar, notions of timekeeping, the indigenous understanding of the movement of celestial bodies, and how the ancient Mexicans corrected their calendars to account for the true length of the solar year. These were, after all, the questions that had vexed the sixteenth century itself, when Pope Gregory XIII corrected the old Julian calendar. Since the late eighteenth century, writers have commented on the apparent geometric and mathematical precision of the *Calendar Stone* composition. Not until the work of Isaac Newton in the mid-eighteenth century did the Catholic Church approve the notion that the earth revolved around the sun. So it is little wonder that these scholars expended minimal effort on the identity of the central face: the driving intellectual questions of the day were big-picture notions of cosmology. In contrast, modern scholars have seen little reason to use the *Calendar Stone* as a key to ancient timekeeping and focused instead on the ideology it conveys. This may be because professional academics today consider the Mesoamerican calendar systems to be more or less transparent. Mathematical, astronomical, and geometric interpretations now occupy the periphery of *Calendar Stone* studies; perhaps the cycle will reverse itself in the future as new eyes view the sculpture and new monuments come to light. For all that has been written on the *Calendar Stone,* we can be sure that it has not yet fully revealed its secrets.

CALENDAR STONE RESEARCH

The historiography of the *Calendar Stone* begins about thirty years after the conquest, when Fray Diego Durán seems to have seen the work lying in the Zócalo of Mexico City (Diego Durán, this volume). Dim memories of its function had apparently persisted decades after the death of Motecuhzoma II; Durán recalls that Montúfar had the monument buried on account of the murders that had been committed on its surface.[7] Thus, the object was removed from view, hidden for more than two centuries. But it reappeared in December 1790, the second in a series of three extraordinary works of monumental Aztec sculpture that emerged from the Zócalo beginning in August 1790: first, the *Coatlicue* (see p. 53, fig. 1a–e), then the *Calendar Stone,* and finally, the *Stone of Tizoc* a year later (see p. 242, fig. 2). These were not the only ancient works known in the colonial capital of New Spain, but their monumental scale and complex imagery were unequaled.

During a project to level the Zócalo, workers found the *Calendar Stone* in its southeast corner, about three feet deep and about eighty yards west of the southernmost doorway of the Palacio Nacional and about twenty-eight yards north of the Portal de las Flores (eventually replaced by the Palacio del Ayuntamiento). Originally, the plan was to place the stone as a step in front of the Catedral Metropolitana de la Asunción de María. Thanks to the joint intervention of Viceroy Juan Vicente de Güemes Padilla Horcasitas y Aguayo (the count of Revillagigedo), some church officials, and—most notably for *Calendar Stone* studies—Antonio de León y Gama (a *criollo*[8] trained as an astronomer at the Colegio de San Ildefonso), the object was spared this indignity and subsequently was mounted on the west side of the southwest tower of the cathedral (see pl. 12).

Publication of the *Calendar Stone* began soon after, when the royal halberdier José Gómez recorded seeing the work in the Zócalo, and its discovery was reported in the Mexico City press.[9] Antonio de León y Gama, who had also been a student of ancient Mexican culture since the 1760s, published the first study of the monuments: the *Descripción histórica y cronológica de las dos piedras,* with engravings by Francisco de Agüera, in 1792 (see p. 53, fig. 1; p. 54, fig. 2; p. 55, fig. 3). His treatise on the *Calendar Stone* was less of a description of the object as such and more a point of departure for his theories on the ancient Mexican calendar and astronomy. As might be expected, he made major discoveries and left somewhat surprising lacunae. León y Gama thought the Aztecs used the monument, rigged with gnomons and strings, to track the progress through the annual festivals, the solstices, and the zenith passages of the sun during half of the year. The other half of the year clearly required, he thought, another similar stone. Although the months of the 365-day calendar do not appear on the *Calendar Stone,* he correctly ordered them and discovered how the Lords of the Night series functioned. In the stone's center, he recognized the names for the previous world creations, or suns, as described in the so-called *Codex Zumárraga,* a sixteenth-century manuscript he owned, but does not discuss them at length. Based on this work and on images in the hieroglyphic *Aubin Codex,* León y Gama also identified the whole center image as the year sign for Nahui Ollin Tonatiuh—the so-called Fifth Sun of our world—and discussed how the entire object related to sun worship. But he never explicitly identified the central face as the primary Aztec solar deity, Tonatiuh.[10] León y Gama's seemingly evasive circumlocution may have resulted from caution, a desire to avoid appearing partial to or even curious about pagan gods in a time and place where such interest might attract the attention of the Inquisition (Gutiérrez Haces 1995). Additionally, although León y Gama owned manuscript copies of Fernando Alvarado Tezozómoc's *Crónica mexicana* and several other colonial-era histories, he never connected the numerous large-scale sculptures they describe with the *Calendar Stone;* neither did he attempt to historicize the monument or otherwise place it in an Aztec chronology.

León y Gama was successful at publishing on the *Calendar Stone* and other Mexican antiquities during his lifetime, but he was far from the only student of ancient Mexico in the colonial capital. José Antonio Alzate y Ramírez, another *criollo* scientist equally engaged with a larger international scientific community at the end of the eighteenth century, also wrote about the *Calendar Stone* soon after its discovery and mounted a baseless and irrelevant attack on the interpretations advanced in León y Gama's work. The two had a long-standing antagonism that stretched back to a disagreement over one of León y Gama's pamphlets on astronomical matters, and Alzate y Ramírez also considered himself an antiquarian, having carried out the first archaeological reconnaissance of the ruins of Xochicalco in 1777.[11] León y Gama and Alzate y Ramírez exchanged heated letters in the Mexico City press, and their dispute must have attracted more attention to the *Calendar Stone.* Though they argued over the monument and the ancient Mexican calendar, both recognized the object's potential importance. How prescient they were to focus on it, and how like their successors in arguing about its very identity.

More significant than this academic dispute for *Calendar Stone* studies during these years was the visit of Alexander von Humboldt to Mexico in 1803, after the death of both León y Gama (d. 1802) and Alzate y Ramírez (d. 1799). Humboldt, duly dismissive of Alzate y Ramírez's cartographic talents, introduced León y Gama's ideas and Agüera's engravings to European audiences. He also said what León y Gama could not: that the central face was an image of the sun god Tonatiuh, thus initiating one of the lines of inquiry about the monument that has persisted to the present day. Although their motivations differed, both León y Gama and Humboldt saw the *Calendar Stone* as ammunition in the battle against negative images of the Pre-Columbian world promoted by Georges-Louis Leclerc de Buffon, Guillaume-Thomas Raynal, William Robertson, and other eighteenth-century European Enlightenment writers who viewed the Aztecs and other New World peoples as hopelessly superstitious and barbarous.[12] The *Calendar Stone* provided evidence of advanced astronomy and mathematics and was proof that civilized people existed in the Americas before the conquest. The iconography of the monument entered León y Gama's and Humboldt's works only insofar as it could be tied to these indices of civilization.

After the generation of León y Gama and Humboldt, *Calendar Stone* studies paused until after Independence in 1821, when Mexican scholars again had the opportunity to think about their antiquities as the country opened to curious travelers. While the histories of the Aztecs and other central highland peoples dominated works printed in Mexico in the first half of the nineteenth century, ancient Maya sites in southern Mexico played an increasingly important role in foreign publications. Although some of these works were written by men in the employ of the Spanish colonial government, all were first published outside Mexico, beginning in 1787 with Antonio del Río's description of Palenque (1822), then moving on to Guillermo Dupaix's explorations (1831–48; Dupaix, Lenoir, and Warden, 1834–44), and reaching a high point with the popular works of American lawyer John Lloyd Stephens (1841, 1843). Dupaix, a former army officer, was exceptional in discussing both the Maya area and central Mexico. Stephens neither mentioned nor illustrated the *Calendar Stone*. In contrast, the German expatriate Carl Nebel (1836) discussed the *Calendar Stone*, El Tajín, and Xochicalco, but not the Maya ruins.

In the decades after Independence, foreigners penned both popular and scholarly descriptions of the *Calendar Stone*. The monument was a must-see for every visitor to Mexico City, and it figures in period travelogues, such as those written by William Henry Bullock (1824b), Joel Poinsett (1825), and Frances Calderón de la Barca (1843). Bullock's visit to Mexico in 1823 and the subsequent exhibitions he organized in London in 1824 were key events in *Calendar Stone* historiography.[13] Bullock's cast of the *Calendar Stone*, the first of many, introduced European audiences to the physical scale of an object they previously knew only in book illustrations (fig. 1). As will be discussed below, the mass of images of the *Calendar Stone* in all media produced between this time and the present is part of the key to its notoriety.

In 1832, Carlos María de Bustamante edited a new edition of León y Gama's *Descripción*, together with previously unpublished studies of several other Aztec sculptures. Thus began a new era in *Calendar Stone* studies, since the first edition was by then very rare.[14] Bustamante identified the *Calendar Stone* as the sculpture described in Alvarado Tezozómoc's *Crónica mexicana* that Motecuhzoma II ordered brought from a quarry in Chalco and whose weight triggered the collapse of a causeway as it was brought into Tenochtitlan (León y Gama 1832, pt. 1:112–14). He is also the first to suggest that Motecuhzoma II commissioned the *Calendar Stone*. William H. Prescott followed this attribution in his *History of the Conquest of Mexico* of 1843; the broad reach of Prescott's work prompted many nineteenth-century writers to describe the sculpture as "El relox de Montezuma," or "Montezuma's watch."[15]

During the French Intervention (1862–67), Emperor Maximilian reopened the Museo Nacional in the old mint on Calle de la Moneda (1864) and appointed as its director José F. Ramírez, also his minister of foreign affairs. Ramírez had previously served as the director of both the Academia de San Carlos and the museum (when it was in the university).[16] In the same spirit as the *Description de l'Egypte* (1809–28) of an earlier generation, French scientists and writers surveyed Mexican natural history, exploitable resources, history, and antiquities and published their results in continental scholarly journals, reports, and books.[17] Somewhat oddly, it seems no French author wrote a dedicated study of the *Calendar Stone* during this period. But a cast was made for the Paris Exposition universelle of 1867 and was placed outside the Mexican building at the fair (fig. 2). Although this was not the first reproduction, from 1867 forward, casts became an important vehicle for disseminating the image of the *Aztec Calendar Stone* internationally.

After Maximilian's execution in 1867 and the collapse of the empire, the liberal Benito Juárez returned to power. Ramírez fled into European exile, leaving the study of antiquities in Mexico to younger figures, like Alfredo Chavero (1841–1906), Francisco del Paso y Troncoso (1842–1916), Antonio García Cubas (1832–1912), Manuel Orozco y Berra (1816–81), and Antonio Peñafiel (1831–1922). Chavero began the late nineteenth-century chapter of *Calendar Stone* research in 1875, when he published the first of a series of studies on the monument. At the same time, with the support of President Porfirio Díaz, the Museo Nacional began publishing its

Fig. 1.
William Henry Bullock
(English, ca. 1773–1849)
Cast of the central section of the *Aztec
Calendar Stone,* 1823, plaster painted
gray, diam.: 74.9 cm (29½ in.)
Edinburgh, National Museum of
Scotland

Fig. 2.
Mexican building, Exposition universelle, Paris,
with cast of *Aztec Calendar Stone* at right
1867, albumen print
From Pierre Petit, "Exposition universelle de
1867," unpaginated album
Los Angeles, Getty Research Institute

Anales, and further articles by Chavero and Spanish translations of *Calendar Stone* studies were published elsewhere by Philipp J. Valentini and Konrad T. Preuss.[18] These interpretations not only made more effective use of the colonial accounts of Alvarado Tezozómoc and Juan de Torquemada but they also mined the works of Durán and Fray Bernardino de Sahagún, which had been rediscovered and published in the decades since León y Gama and Humboldt. Chavero objected to the *Calendar Stone* appellation and suggested that—since it could in no way be used to track the hours, days, months, seasons, or years—it would be better called the *Piedra del Sol,* or *Sun Stone.* Attempting to understand the object in Aztec terms, he collected references in the colonial-era sources to large sculptures like the *Calendar Stone* and concludes that the best possibilities were sacrificial altars the Aztecs called *cuauhxicallis* and *temalacatls.* Both were sometimes used for sacrifices to the sun, which for Chavero proved that the central face was the sun and the sun god Tonatiuh. He also established that León y Gama was in error that the stone was one of a pair of objects, each of which tracked the movements of the sun; the *Calendar Stone* never had gnomons and strings to track shadows. The colonial accounts describe how participants in sacrificial rituals involving *cuauhxicallis* would sometimes climb on top of the monument, which Chavero took as evidence that the *Calendar Stone* was originally mounted horizontally rather than in a vertical position.[19] This last assertion was a major shift in how most writers approached the *Calendar Stone,* and not everyone was convinced. Indeed, Zelia Nuttall agreed that the *Calendar Stone* originally was displayed horizontally but instead thought that its celestial and directional imagery made sense only if it were mounted on a ceiling or slanted wall, to be viewed from below, like a lintel, and not to be looked down upon, like an altar, as Chavero argued (Nuttall 1901, 250). Chavero's argument failed to affect the display of the *Calendar Stone* in the three times it has moved since 1885; the object is still mounted vertically (López Luján 2008a).

Although Chavero was never an employee of the Museo Nacional and was essentially an amateur, his influence in late nineteenth-century Mexican archaeological circles cannot be overestimated. He wrote many official or quasi-official treatments of Mexican history and antiquities, notably in his *Historia antigua y de la conquista* (1888), the first volume in the quasi-official historical survey *México a través de los siglos.* With the *Calendar Stone* adapted for both the cover and the title page, Chavero's work surveyed Mexico before Cortés, beginning with mammoths and prehistory (see pls. 13, 14). As Stacie Graham Widdifield discusses in her essay in the present book, Chavero separated the Mexica from the Aztecs, the former being the whole group of tribes that departed from Aztlan, wandered for hundreds of years, and practiced a nature-based religion with no human sacrifice. The Aztecs, in contrast, were the group that settled at Tenochtitlan and later became despotic, superstitious, bloodthirsty rulers. Chavero's Aztecs were not an admirable people and almost seem to deserve to have been conquered by the Spanish. We can also read his Mexica and Aztecs as equivalent to the liberals and conservatives of late nineteenth-century Mexico, where liberals (like Chavero) were peace loving, tolerant, agrarian, and above all governed by reason, whereas the conservatives represented reactionary forces, the Catholic Church, superstition, and tyrannical powers (such as the French). Chavero's historical reconstruction also clearly derives from the theories of Lewis Henry Morgan and Adolph Bandelier, who in the 1870s and 1880s advanced a negative and oversimplified image of the Aztecs.[20]

Much new literature appeared in the last decades of the nineteenth century, and it might be said that Mexican scholars of this period leverage the *Calendar Stone* as a counterweight against the increasing popularity of the ancient Maya. National and international interest in the Maya had been steadily growing since the 1840s; the arrival in Mexico City of the Chacmool discovered by Augustus LePlongeon at Chichén Itzá in 1875, as well as the center panel from the Palenque *Tablet of the Cross* in 1884, created an alternative to the archaeological past of the Aztecs of Tenochtitlan. Scholarly treatments like Bandelier's *Report of an Archaeological Tour in Mexico in 1881* (1884) and those of Chavero joined travelogues and tour guides written to introduce Mexico to tourists and potential investors.[21] Peñafiel may have been the first to refer to the *Calendar Stone* in print as "art," in his *Monumentos del arte mexicano antiguo* of 1890, which published José María Velasco's accurate drawing of the monument (fig. 3). The Velasco drawing, exhibited in the Palacio Azteca at the Exposition universelle held in Paris in 1889 and also at the Exposición Histórico-Americana in Madrid in 1892 (Paso y Troncoso 1892–93, 2:234), joined a growing corpus created during this period, including most notably those by Hesiquio Iriarte (Batres 1888) and Francisco Abadiano (1889) (figs. 4, 5).

Elements of archaeological heritage like the *Calendar Stone* played an important role in the image Mexico projected to the world about itself during the Porfiriato.[22] As president, Díaz was keenly interested in crafting a national image that would be perceived by the world as both modern and civilized, and museums and other proofs of high culture like the *Calendar Stone* were used and promoted wherever an unmistakably national symbol was required. His government oversaw Mexico's participation in the world's fairs in 1889, 1892, and 1893, among others, and archaeological monuments always figured prominently in these displays.[23]

At the same time that Chavero, Valentini, Bandelier, and Abadiano were arguing about the *Calendar Stone,* the monument was itself in transition, from the cathedral to the Museo Nacional. In August of 1885, Batres engineered the difficult transfer of the *Calendar Stone* from

Fig. 3.
Aztec Calendar Stone, lithograph by José María Velasco (Mexican, 1840–1912), before ca. 1889

Fig. 4.
Aztec Calendar Stone, lithograph by Hesiquio Iriarte (Mexican, ca. 1820–ca. 1897), 1888

Fig. 5.
Aztec Calendar Stone, lithograph by Francisco Abadiano (Mexican, act. 1880s–1890s), 1889

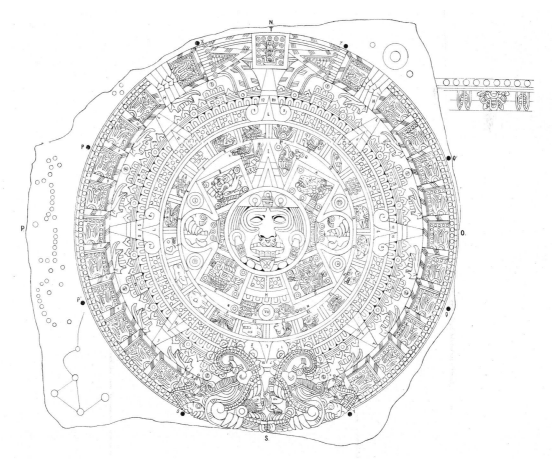

the cathedral to the patio of the Museo Nacional and eventually indoors to the Salón de Monolítos, inaugurated on 16 September by Díaz (Batres 1888).[24] While still on the cathedral tower, the *Calendar Stone* could be considered a curiosity of pagan religion, its history linked less to the ancient past and more literally to the long centuries of colonial New Spain. But from this point forward, the *Calendar Stone*'s placement in a context where national history and leitmotifs were manufactured led to its thorough integration as a state symbol and placeholder for the preconquest past in the emerging narrative of the country's history. One mystery of the object's material properties was solved by the engineer and geologist Ezequiel Ordóñez, who determined that the stone was olivine basalt, almost certainly from the southern part of the Valley of Mexico.[25] By the end of the century, with the *Calendar Stone* in its new home, and likely in response to the great number of guidebooks, the Museo Nacional published its own catalog, written by Gumesindo Mendoza and Jesús Sánchez. The *Calendar Stone* would be item no. 1 in their catalog. Although its canon of Pre-Columbian Mexican objects was substantially formed by the 1820s, the Museo Nacional produced guidebooks, displays, catalogs, and international exhibitions in the later nineteenth century that firmly established the *Calendar Stone* as the undisputed central object.[26] The German anthropologist Eduard Seler closes this period of *Calendar Stone* research at the turn of the twentieth century with a series of articles on sun imagery, the Malinalco wooden drum, the Ollin day sign, and Batres's excavations on Calle de las Escalerillas (in the 1970s, these would be confirmed as the site of the Templo Mayor). Seler's approach to the *Calendar Stone,* shared by American anthropologist George G. MacCurdy, was to analyze the iconography by comparing its details with those found on other monuments and in the pictorial manuscripts.[27] Seler's knowledge of Aztec sculptures in European collections dramatically expanded the corpus of known objects related to the *Calendar Stone.*

Beyer's study of 1921, entitled *El llamado "Calendario Azteca"* (*The So-Called "Calendario Azteca,"* this volume), established iconography as the primary means of interpreting the monument. This analysis is one of the most influential, and it dominates *Calendar Stone* studies between the turn of the twentieth century and the removal of the *Calendar Stone* to the new Museo Nacional de Antropología in 1964. Beyer wrote in response to a study in 1918 by Enrique Juan Palacios that he thought lacked a thorough understanding of the imagery of the *Calendar Stone.* Building upon the solid foundation established by Seler a generation earlier, Beyer reaffirmed the identification of the central face as Tonatiuh and added important new data on the *xiuhcoatls* and the quincunxes found on the monument. Several other *Calendar Stone* studies were published in the 1930s, including Rubén García's annotated *Calendar Stone* bibliography (1934), works by Erwin P. Dieseldorff (1930) and Preuss (1931) and, perhaps most significantly, Alfonso Caso's proposal in 1928 that a geometric modulus—one-thirty-second of the diameter of the circular section—organizes the composition. Caso was Beyer's student at the Universidad Nacional Autónoma de México, and although he was a leading figure in Mexican archaeology for fifty years, he made no further advances in *Calendar Stone* research.[28]

In the mid-twentieth century, the *Calendar Stone* began to take its place in the survey texts then emerging for more general audiences. New voices toward the end of this period included the art historians José Pijoán and Salvador Toscano.[29] These years also saw increased cultural and economic ties between the United States and Mexico, contributing to a burgeoning interest in Mexico's artistic past and present.[30] As World War II seemed to bring the world closer to a cataclysmic end, archaeologist George C. Vaillant published a popular book on the Aztecs, one of the first written by a scholar since the nineteenth century. He reiterates the identification of the central face as the sun god, noting that the *Calendar Stone* represents the history of the world and its prior destructions and that its relief presents "a finite statement of the infinity of the universe."[31] Interestingly, although early survey texts discuss the *Calendar Stone*, they tend to illustrate the *Coatlicue*, perhaps owing to the prominent display of a cast of the latter sculpture in the Museum of Modern Art's sweeping exhibition of 1940, *Twenty Centuries of Mexican Art*. This visual imbalance began to be redressed when the *Calendar Stone* was included in the third edition of the classic survey text written by Helen Gardner in 1948.[32] More recent surveys of Pre-Columbian art rarely omit the *Calendar Stone*, even if it is mentioned only in passing.[33] Although the work has never traveled abroad, except as a reproduction, exhibition curators and writers often register its presence virtually, in catalogs.[34]

The decades after Beyer's essay also saw two reproductions of the original colors of the *Calendar Stone*—the first by Roberto Sieck Flandes in the late 1930s and the second by Miguel Covarrubias in the 1950s. Although not the first attempt at documenting the object's color scheme, the proposal Sieck Flandes presented at the International Congress of Americanists in 1939 has come to dominate the popular image of how the Aztecs painted the *Calendar Stone* (see pl. 15).[35] Near the end of this period, Caso published a general book on the Aztecs that includes Covarrubias's color reconstruction of the central face of the *Calendar Stone* (see pl. 16), which differs from Sieck Flandes's version only in minor details (Caso 1953, 1958). Covarrubias of course included the *Calendar Stone* in his panorama of ancient Mexican art (1957), yet as an *olmecquista,* or specialist and partisan of Olmec art, he seems resistant to its charms, seeing Aztec art in general as almost always derivative of everything that had come before it. Raúl Noriega (1954, 1955, 1959) and José Avilés Solares (1957) also wrote on the *Calendar Stone* during this period but did not challenge the sun god identification, although they did differ on how the imagery could be translated into calendrical, mathematical, and astronomical cycles. These texts all contributed to a growing sense of certainty and completion: the meaning of the object was well understood, and few, if any, questions remained to be asked of it. In June of 1964, the *Calendar Stone* was transferred to the newly inaugurated Museo Nacional de Antropología in the Bosque de Chapultepec, where it continues to preside magisterially over the Sala Mexica.

Perhaps inspired by the sculptures discovered in the Mexico City Metro subway excavations that began in 1967, the next phase of *Calendar Stone* research continued the iconographic focus of previous decades, with major contributions by Cecelia Klein, Richard Townsend, and Carlos Navarrete and Doris Heyden, all published during the 1970s.[36] But unlike earlier writers, these scholars all argue that the long-accepted identification of the central face on the *Calendar Stone* as the sun god Tonatiuh should be revised in favor of either the night sun; Tlaltecuhtli, the earth god; or a hybrid sun and earth deity. Their revisionist identifications proceed from an attempt to explain aspects of *Calendar Stone* iconography that do not match the known characteristics of Tonatiuh. The four authors point out that the central face's flint-blade tongue and the claws gripping human hearts flanking it are features associated with aspects of the earth god Tlaltecuhtli, as seen in manuscript illustrations and other sculptures, including the *Coatlicue of the Metro.* Although the exact details of each interpretation varied, all reasoned that the earth god imagery on the monument must in some way refer to the sun at sunset or during the night, when it is swallowed by the earth god and becomes a night jaguar sun. This was one of the most significant shifts in scholarship on the object, and one that remains contested today.

Fig. 6.

El adiós y triste queja del gran Calendario Azteca (The farewell and sad lament of the great *Aztec Calendar Stone*)

Front and back sides of broadside published August 1885 by A. Vanegas, Mexico City, and bound in a copy of León y Gama 1832, zinc or copper-plate etching

Paris, Musée du Quai Branly

Although most studies during this period focused on identifying what is shown on the *Calendar Stone,* Townsend has argued that whatever the exact meaning of its iconography, the object was intimately linked to the needs and interests of the Aztec empire and those who ruled it. Townsend's step toward historicizing the monument opened a new avenue of inquiry in *Calendar Stone* studies. Earlier writers had very little to say about the historical context of the *Calendar Stone,* preferring to assert no more than that its 13 Reed date corresponded to 1479, a year during the reign of the Aztec emperor Axayacatl. This, along with the statements of Durán and Tezozómoc that Axayacatl had commissioned a *cuauhxicalli,* seemed to firmly identify him as the patron of the *Calendar Stone.* Townsend raised the possibility that this attribution, too, might not be as secure as earlier scholars (with the notable exception of Bustamante) thought and provided an opportunity to consider Aztec sculpture in historic terms.

Since the "Tlaltecuhtli decade," iconographic studies have continued to dominate the discourse about the monument, and several writers have reaffirmed the sun god identification. New studies address the dates carved on the monument, and others examine its style and patronage. Emily Umberger has discussed the five dates carved on the *Calendar Stone,* the 13 Reed glyph, and the four others carved above and below the central face.[37] She places the work during the last phase of Aztec monumental sculpture and argues that the dates, rather than being linked to

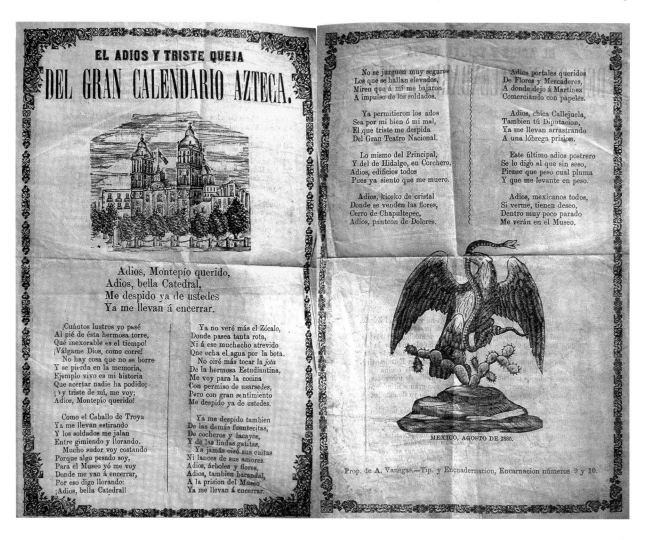

aspects of general mythology or to the cardinal directions, as Seler and Beyer think, had been carefully selected to refer to deities and events of special interest to Motecuhzoma II, whose name she identifies among one of these "dates." The central face continues to be an important issue for writers during this period, with Ariane Fradcourt and Michel Graulich asserting that it is an image of the skeletal sun after midday, when it begins its journey toward dusk, and H.B. Nicholson rejecting all interpretations since Beyer and advocating for a return to the Tonatiuh identification.[38]

The most recent studies of the *Calendar Stone* have been synthetic treatments by Felipe Solís and Eduardo Matos Moctezuma, combining histories of the *Calendar Stone* with a photographic facsimile of León y Gama's first study and a thorough and copiously illustrated study of other solar monuments of the Aztecs, including the *Stone of Motecuhzoma I*.[39] The works of these two experts on Aztec archaeology and sculpture embrace the dispute over the central face and offer a full-throated defense of the Tonatiuh identification. Solís also published a new reconstruction of the original colors of the *Calendar Stone*, based on investigations led by Víctor Manuel Maldonado (see pl. 11). This new version differs dramatically from the previous versions, with much of the relief colored red. Although it has been published for a decade—and a large color rendering of it is installed near the *Calendar Stone* in the Sala Mexica at the Museo Nacional de Antropología—there is little evidence that it has replaced the Sieck Flandes version in the popular imagination. Leonardo López Luján wrote an article on the travels of the *Calendar Stone*, from its original Pre-Columbian context to the Museo Nacional de Antropología, accompanied by newly discovered or less well-known images of the sculpture. He published a previously unknown illustrated broadside from 1885, printed by Antonio Vanegas (later the publisher of folk artist and engraver José Guadalupe Posada) (fig. 6). The poem, entitled "El adios y triste queja del gran *Calendario Azteca*" (The farewell and sad lament of the great *Aztec Calendar Stone*) is an ironic valedictory, putatively authored by the *Calendar Stone* itself, on the occasion of its transfer from the cathedral to the Museo Nacional on Calle de la Moneda (López Luján 2008a).

Paraphrasing Batres, it seems apt to ask: who *did not* write about the *Calendar Stone*? Among the major Euro-American students of ancient America who do not either mention the monument or illustrate it or who cover it only in the barest detail are Desire Charnay (1885, 1887), J. Eric S. Thompson (1950; 1937, 273), Pál Kelemen (1943), and George Kubler (1943; 1962a). It is not immediately clear why this would be the case—perhaps these authors shared a weary sense of the object's overexposure. Writing about the *Calendar Stone* often entails a rehearsal of the monument's interpretation that can be so long and exhausting that it can threaten to overwhelm the argument or new materials in books and articles; in the case of survey texts, *Calendar Stone* historiography seems capable of filling all the available space.[40] To be fair, Kubler does give it more than a paragraph in his massive survey, but it seems particularly telling—and almost deliberately contrarian—that he does not include the object in his essay on metropolitan Aztec sculpture. Perhaps these scholars gloss over the *Calendar Stone* because they think its cosmological content is obvious and their efforts are better spent on lesser-known works, such as the *Temple of Sacred Warfare*, commonly called the *Teocalli de la Guerra Sagrada*. But as we hope this survey of *Calendar Stone* research makes clear, the monument still raises more questions than it answers. Among the most important unresolved issues are the original location of the stone, how it was buried in the sixteenth century, the damage to the face, why it was mounted on the Catedral Metropolitana, questions of its style, and how to describe and interpret the thousands of reproductions of the sculpture.

WHENCE IT CAME AND HOW IT WAS BURIED

After the Aztecs surrendered to Cortés in August 1521, the *Calendar Stone* was apparently visible for some time. Durán reports seeing it near the acequia, or small canal, that crossed the Zócalo from east to west, and we wonder why such a monument was left relatively undamaged and uncovered for so many years, within sight of the cathedral then under construction. But the chaos of those early years is not easily reconstructed. Both Bernal Díaz del Castillo and the indigenous authors of book 12 of the *Florentine Codex* describe the horror of the final defeat of the Aztecs at Tlatelolco; both dwell on the aftermath of war.[41] Hiding from rapacious Spaniards, emaciated women covered their bodies with mud and fled to swampy marshes where dead bodies rotted; the smallpox epidemic that had killed more persons than the war continued to devastate the country. Crops had been destroyed, and the victors requisitioned any remaining supplies. Spaniards rounded up survivors and branded them on the face to mark their ownership, even though slavery was officially forbidden.

Under such conditions—and we cannot imagine the full scope of the dislocation and despair that attended the Spanish invasion—workers presumably hauled the *Calendar Stone* to the location where it would eventually come to light in 1790, almost certainly anticipating that it would be hidden forever. Did they sense an aura and numen emanating from this object? Did they consider a face-down burial to be entirely appropriate, somehow akin to the images of Tlaltecuhtli so often carved on the undersides of objects? If the features on the *Calendar Stone* that overlap with earth god imagery are now fairly obvious to us, they were likely even clearer to people living two hundred years closer to the conquest than we do. Or was it understood as an apposite rejection of the past at a time when the gods of Mesoamerica had failed them?

The monument was finally turned face down and buried sometime between 1554 and 1572, by order of Archbishop Montúfar. And although Durán ascribes the action to anxiety over the potential resurgence of idolatry, perhaps there was also a sense that such a large piece of masonry could serve a practical function. The low-lying plaza flooded often; the first afterlife of the *Calendar Stone* may have been as a stepping-stone in the mud, flipped over, slowly sinking along with the rest of the city. Monolithic sculptures like the *Calendar Stone* were often hauled out of the rubble of Tenochtitlan and recarved to provide stable pavements in new colonial spaces, even as the buildings were knocked down and ruthlessly excavated time and again in the search for treasure.

Mesoamerican scholars will doubtlessly continue to debate the identification of the central face for years to come. But the discovery in 2006 of the Tlaltecuhtli monument during the renovation of La Casa de las Ajaracas, a colonial-era palace next to the Templo Mayor, provides an opportunity to shift our attention away from this detail and offer a tentative proposal about its original placement as part of a larger sequence of monumental sculpture somewhere in the sacred precinct of Tenochtitlan. According to early colonial sources, *cuauhxicallis* and *temalacatls*—large monuments like the *Stone of Tizoc,* the *Stone of Motecuhzoma I,* and the *Calendar Stone*—were placed on platforms in a courtyard near or on the platform of the Templo Mayor.[42] Other sources mention that the Aztecs worshiped the sun in the Cuauhxicalco, the Eagle House, located inside the Templo Mayor precinct (Torquemada 1723, 2:148). Given the solar themes of the object, as well as its formal and functional connections to the larger class of *cuauhxicallis,* we wonder if the *Calendar Stone* was originally mounted in front of the Templo Mayor, in close proximity to the Ajaracas monument. This massive Tlaltecuhtli stone (larger than the *Calendar Stone* by about nineteen inches) was placed on a platform at the base of the Templo Mayor; colonial-era accounts record that three Aztec rulers were buried in or near a platform called the Cuauhxicalco, which also happens to be where the *cuauhxicallis* were located (Matos Moctezuma and López Luján 2007). That the *Aztec Calendar Stone* also may have been located in this area of the sacred precinct comes from a suggestive passage in chapter 31 of book 12 of the *Florentine Codex.* The block-by-block urban warfare that gripped Tenochtitlan in the summer of 1521 reached a turning point as the Spanish passed the Eagle Gate and numerous monumental sculptures. After firing their cannon to clear warriors hiding in the shadows, "they brought the cannon up and set it down at the round stone (of gladiatorial combat) [*temalacatitlan*]" (Lockhart 1993, 194). In the translation by Arthur Anderson and Charles Dibble, the Spanish placed the cannon *on top* of the *temalacatl* and there they soon abandoned it (Sahagún 1950–82, 12:88–89).[43] The parallel Spanish text specifies that this "large round stone was in the square of Huitzilopochtli," locating the scene near the Templo Mayor. Subsequent descriptions of soldiers climbing the temple steps to kill some Aztec drummers confirm this proximity. Although the term *temalacatl* could apply to any number of monuments, the possibility that this zone was conceived as a place for objects dedicated to both the sun and the earth is reinforced by another sculpture made late in Motecuhzoma II's reign.

The *Teocalli de la Guerra Sagrada,* also called the *Temple Stone,* may hold the key to understanding the original context of the *Calendar Stone.* As soon as the work was excavated in 1926 from the foundations of the south tower of the Palacio Nacional, it was clear that it was in dialogue with the *Calendar Stone,* as it appears to depict that work, or a similar monument.[44] The *Teocalli* is both a small-scale temple model and a throne, and many authors now consider that the work was commissioned by Motecuhzoma II, since it records a date in his reign (the last pre-conquest New Fire ceremony in 1507), was discovered in the foundations of what was his palace, and also bears his name glyph.[45] The sun disk on the *Teocalli* was carved in vertical orientation, serving as a throne back, or perhaps reflecting an Aztec artistic convention deployed to avoid foreshortening. Vaillant notes that the *Teocalli* might explain the original position of the *Calendar Stone,* a point reiterated by Toscano, who adds that although the work was perhaps originally intended as a horizontal disk, its breakage necessitated a different treatment than the other stone disks (Vaillant 1941, 164; Toscano 1944, 291–92). If this is the case, might the *Teocalli* show *the Calendar Stone*? Emily Umberger writes that the *Teocalli* is part of a group of works similar in style that includes the *Calendar Stone,* although it is not clear if it precedes or postdates that monument (Umberger 1981a, 236–41). The *Teocalli* shows an eye at the center of the Ollin, not a face and claws; this and other simplifications may have resulted from reducing the composition. If and when Motecuhzoma II sat on the *Teocalli,* his body was literally between the sun and the earth goddess (Pasztory 1983, 168), perhaps making manifest his supporting role in keeping the sun from falling on the earth (Miller 2006, 229). The *Teocalli* may refer to an actual place, a platform with two large sculptures, the *Calendar Stone* and the image of the earth god Tlaltecuhtli. It and the Ajaracas monolith are among a handful of relief sculptures that show the image of Tlaltecuhtli on an upper or visible surface; too, the skeletal gods on the sides of the *Teocalli* are visually below the Tlaltecuhtli, as the remains of Ahuitzotl may be below the Ajaracas monument. The *Calendar Stone* combines the sun and earth images that are split on the *Teocalli.*

Large-scale Aztec sculptures differ from most other kinds of Mesoamerican sculpture by being technically movable. Like their Olmec ancestors, the *tlatoanis,* or rulers of Tenochtitlan, could manipulate objects into tableaus to convey particular narratives (albeit with great effort).

Unlike Maya stelae or the Danzante stones of Monte Alban in Oaxaca, Aztec sculptures tend to be carved so that they need not be engaged or otherwise fixed to either architecture or the earth. The later Huastec people, whose territory overlapped that of the ancient Olmec, probably gave the Aztecs their penchant for freestanding deity effigies (Townsend 1979, 23). Perhaps this approach also extended to other sculpture classes, such as large stone disks; they could be moved. But if the flange on the *Calendar Stone* meant that the work was originally mounted, then perhaps both it and the new Tlaltecuhtli goddess were unlike other Aztec sculptures and immovable.

THE CALENDAR STONE AS SCULPTURAL ANOMALY
IN COLONIAL NEW SPAIN

The *dos piedras* that formed the pretext for León y Gama's treatise—the *Calendar Stone* and the *Coatlicue*—both began their afterlives in the modern world in 1790, when they were discovered four months apart in Mexico City's Zócalo. The similarities end there. In marked contrast to the reverential treatment of the *Calendar Stone,* with its installation on the south tower of the cathedral, the *Coatlicue* was taken to the old Real y Pontificia Universidad Nacional de México (1551–1867), just a few hundred yards away, and subjected to burial, exhumation, reburial, reexhumation, and burial for a third time before being permanently exhumed sometime after 1830. Their different fates can be directly correlated to their form, content, and whether they could be compared to any other class of sculpture in colonial New Spain. Although León y Gama makes passing reference to Greco-Roman sculpture and to its canons of representation in his *Descripción,* and although art students at the Academia de San Carlos (founded in 1781 and in full operation in 1785) sometimes drew from the most "classical" Aztec sculptures, the interpretive lens of Mediterranean antiquity was applied neither to the *Calendar Stone* nor to the *Coatlicue.*[46]

There were few if any secular sculptures in the streets of New Spain's capital during the last years of Spanish domination. The most famous such sculpture was the so-called *Caballito* (Little horse), the equestrian bronze of the Spanish king Charles IV, cast thirteen years after the discovery of León y Gama's stones by the Valencian artist Manuel Tolsá in 1803.[47] There was much religious art, with images of Jesus Christ, the Virgin Mary, and the saints found in quantity and in diverse media in every church. Like the *Caballito,* many of them were characterized by their human scale and more or less naturalistic proportions. But these works were found almost exclusively indoors or on architectural facades on churches or elsewhere. When the *Coatlicue* was discovered in August 1790, there was no appropriate place for her in the visual landscape. Although monstrous and outsized, she clearly had human proportions (the same rough proportions that allow viewers to see the human form in Mark Rothko paintings). These proportions, the serpent heads emerging from her wounded neck and hands, and the skulls on her waist signaled danger to the Spanish colonial authorities, religious and secular. They knew what an idol looked like. *Coatlicue* was an idol, and an aggressively female one at that. León y Gama may have been mistaken in his identification of the image as the goddess Teoyamiqui, but he correctly recognized her gender. Mexico City's subjugated native people also immediately recognized her numinous qualities, and when they began leaving candles and offerings at her feet, the friars at the university quickly buried the *Coatlicue* in the corner of the patio, where she remained for more than thirty years, notwithstanding her exhumations by Humboldt in 1803 and Bullock in 1823.[48]

Why was the *Calendar Stone,* an object so clearly from the not-so-distant Aztec past, mounted on the Catedral Metropolitana, the seat of Roman Catholic authority in New Spain?

With respect to Pre-Columbian objects known in 1790, the *Calendar Stone* was an anomalous object. It emphatically lacked the *Coatlicue*'s threateningly quasi-human proportions. It did not fit the category of "idol," although anyone can see a humanoid face at its center. There were no other large disk-shaped Aztec sculptures in Mexico City in 1790, and only the Chapultepec cliff carving could be compared to its scale. León y Gama ascribed the decision to save the *Calendar Stone* to the viceroy, who wished it to be preserved as an "appreciable monument of Indian antiquity."[49] And it has often been suggested that, unlike the *Coatlicue,* the *Calendar Stone* was not reburied because it was understood to be an astronomical or calendrical device and hence simultaneously acceptable to the Spanish colonial authorities (who wished to be perceived as enlightened) and not threatening to the church (which did not see these scientific functions as dangerous).[50] But actually incorporating it into the structure of the cathedral? Matos Moctezuma (2002b, 30; 1993, 96) has argued that the *Calendar Stone* was mounted to the cathedral because it might aid Spain against its enemies—by proving that ancient Mexico had a civilized past—as part of the ongoing intellectual battle against Raynal, Robertson, and others. Soon after its installation, the *Calendar Stone* became as much an attraction as the cathedral itself. Throughout the nineteenth century, the sculpture threatened to overwhelm the cathedral, like a symbiote outgrowing its host.

Like the *Coatlicue,* the *Calendar Stone* was an anomalous sculpture when compared to other objects in the visual culture of colonial New Spain. The similar circular, pictorial objects included coins, some of which also had a face, the king of Spain in profile. There were also the *escudos de monjas* worn by Mexican nuns, usually copper disks painted with saints, the Virgin Mary, and other devotional scenes. On architectural sculpture, there were stone medallions and heraldic devices—emblems of the mendicant orders or the monograms of the Virgin Mary. These were also rendered in relatively large scale on church and convent exteriors. And finally, there were clocks and sundials. The only circular Pre-Columbian–related objects known in New Spain during this time were the various calendar wheels published in many seventeenth- and eighteenth-century books on ancient Mexico by authors such as Giovanni Gemelli Carreri, Francisco Saverio Clavigero, and Mariano Fernández de Echeverría y Veytia.[51] But none of these is quite like the *Calendar Stone.* In mounting it on the cathedral, the authorities made the stone an official part of the building's decorative program. In effect, they rendered it an engaged sculpture, a category of visual culture that could be understood and observed by any city dweller on the facades of religious and secular buildings.

DAMAGE TO THE CALENDAR STONE

Although the *Calendar Stone* relief is generally well preserved, probably because the large flange acted like a protective frame, the face in the center is clearly damaged. Other sections, especially on the viewer's right edge of the circular relief, show what seems to be erosion. León y Gama noted that three of the day glyphs—Itzcuintli, Cuauhtli, and Cozcacuauhtli—were already damaged when the stone was discovered (1792, 101n). Did the other damage occur before 1790, or was it the result of actions since then? If the monument was exposed to the elements for several decades after the conquest, as Durán recalled, it might have weathered or been otherwise damaged at that time. Many Mesoamerican images display patterns of damage to the face, particularly the eyes, and it has been suggested that this was not simple vandalism but a serious effort to defuse the power of these monuments, to ritually "kill" them by destroying precisely those features where identity and likeness reside.[52] The eyes of the central face on the *Calendar Stone* are not gouged, and the nose appears to be abraded;[53] perhaps the object was dragged face down across the ground over the flagstones that can still be seen at the base of the last phase of the Templo Mayor. Since León y Gama's time, writers have commented that vandals threw rubbish and rocks at the *Calendar Stone* relief. Nineteenth-century writers like Batres also wished for the *Calendar Stone* to be moved indoors, out of the weather. There are also persistent stories of various armies occupying Mexico City using the *Calendar Stone* for target practice, evocative of similar legends about the Great Sphinx.[54] Although the engravings of 1792 do not show damage to the face, it may be that León y Gama asked Agüera to "restore" the nose and other effaced features. In the history of *Calendar Stone* images and even casts, there are just as many examples of renderings where damaged or eroded features were restored as there are of the more strictly documentary variety. The early nineteenth-century travelogues do not describe the face as damaged. Bullock's cast of 1823 shows no damage (see fig. 1), although he may have repaired the face. The first daguerreotype of the *Calendar Stone,* made about 1839, shows the damage, as does Nebel's lithograph of 1836, so if there was active vandalism, the responsible parties were not soldiers from France or the United States, who were in Mexico City in the 1840s and 1860s, respectively. If soldiers did practice their marksmanship on the central face of the *Calendar Stone,* they must have been excellent shots, since the area immediately surrounding the nose of the central face is relatively undamaged (figs. 7, 8).

STYLE

As editors of the present anthology, we were struck by the lack of discussion of the style of the *Calendar Stone,* or even of much discussion of the work as an object. The vast majority of attention focuses on its iconography and function, connecting it with comparable monuments, or treating it as a bridge or window to other bodies of knowledge. Umberger (1981a, 193–208, 236–41) makes a convincing case for considering the *Calendar Stone* as one of several monuments commissioned by Motecuhzoma II (r. 1502–20) characteristic of the last group of Aztec metropolitan sculpture, beginning at the end of Ahuitzotl's reign (1486–1502) and lasting until the conquest. It is hard to imagine a sculptural studio of less than a half dozen individuals working on an object the size of the *Calendar Stone,* and their talents must have been used elsewhere as well. Although the scale of the objects is radically different, close examination of the features shared by the *Stone of the Five Suns* (Chicago Art Institute), the *Relief of the Five Ages* (New Haven, Conn., Peabody Museum, Yale University), and the *Altar of the Cosmogonic Suns* (Mexico City, Museo Nacional de Antropología) suggests that the last is the closest stylistic analogue of the *Calendar Stone.* On the *Calendar Stone* and the Chicago piece, the Ehecatl profiles have eyes formed in the usual manner, and each has a short beard. On the *Box of the Sun* and the Peabody work, the Ehecatl profile has an extruded or projecting eye and lacks a beard. Similar differences and parallels can be seen in

Fig. 8.
The Zodiac, lithograph by Jean-Baptiste Arnout (French, b. 1788) (or Jules Arnout) and Émile Lassalle (French, 1813–1871) after drawing by Carl Nebel (German, 1805–1855), 1836

Fig. 9.
Agostino Aglio (Italian, 1777–1857)
Interior of exhibition of ancient
Mexico at the Egyptian Hall, Piccadilly,
1824 or 1825, drawing and lithograph,
21 × 41 cm (8¼ × 16 in.)
Los Angeles, Getty Research Institute

the other profiles—the head of Chalchiuhtlicue in a U-shaped basin rather than a splashing water motif, the four fangs of Tlaloc embedded in a small panel, the proportion and slight curve of the borders between elements. The *Box of the Sun* has a very level, planed relief layer; the Peabody altar shows cross-hatching on the *itzpapalotl,* or obsidian butterfly, motifs carved on its sides, traits lacking on the *Calendar Stone.* Much more work of a Morellian variety could be done in this regard to identify the lithic workshops, if not the individual hands, that created these monumental sculptures.

The *Calendar Stone*'s large and irregular flange make it an unusual work when compared to much Aztec monumental sculpture. Beyer (this volume) and others think that it was intended to be a disk, like the *Stone of Tizoc,* but the stone fractured during carving. If it should be considered a *cuauhxicalli* (or perhaps also a *temalacatl,* as Solís argued) the *Calendar Stone* is unusually thin, especially when compared to the *Stone of Tizoc* or the *Stone of Motecuhzoma I.* There are depressions scattered around the join of the disk and the flange where the stone might have been laboriously separated.[55] Their presence, and Beyer's invocation of process, raises questions about design, execution, and oversight that careful inspection of the monument could help answer. Faced with the possibility of losing such a monumental object, did the sculptors develop a strategy for its preservation? Or perhaps the flange resulted not from the stone breaking as it was carved but because it was always intended to be integral to architecture, mounted into the Cuauhxicalco platform, with the flange functioning like a jewelry setting. If this were the case, then the marks on the flange that Abadiano first noted may be incidental, or even graffiti made by the stonemasons, rather than the constellations suggested by Nuttall (1901) and Anthony F. Aveni (2001).

REPRODUCING THE CALENDAR STONE

As Aztec myth attributed four hundred (i.e., countless) sons to Coatlicue, so too does the *Calendar Stone* have numberless progeny in the form of almost infinite reproductions of its imagery, in part and in whole. From the moment when León y Gama hired Agüera to make the first engraving of the monument, these derivative images have played key roles in the historiography of the *Calendar Stone*. There is now such a plenitude of images and adaptations of the *Calendar Stone* in every fine art, craft, and industrial medium that it cannot be encompassed or even merely described by any single book or writer. The sheer volume of the *Calendar Stone*'s image raises a potentially tautological question: is the object famous because it has been so often reproduced, or is there something intrinsic to the object that demands such copious reproduction?

Ambiguous works like the *Calendar Stone* often present this kind of conundrum. Nonetheless, it is arguably the *image* of the *Calendar Stone* and the varied uses to which it has been applied over the past two centuries—and not the object itself—that has raised its status as a metonym and allegory in our world. This image serves as a bridge to destinations as disparate as the Aztec past, New World civilization before Cortés, Mexican nationalism, and modern-day Latino cultural pride, especially in the United States. We search for anchors in this visual ecology, reminded of Walter Benjamin's assertion that the mass of reproduced images withers the aura of the original but equally of Kubler's invocation of the Prime Object and "the entire system of . . . reproductions, copies, reductions, transfers, and derivations" that came after it (Kubler 1962b, 39). In practical terms, there is no way of fully evaluating the importance of the *Calendar Stone* separate from its reproductions; it thus becomes critical to better understand both the contexts through which this image has moved and the contexts it has created. We can roughly classify *Calendar Stone* images by the ends to which they have been directed: scholarly interpretation, travelogues and tourism, representations of Mexico as a whole, Mexican history and antiquities, and adaptations of the sculpture's imagery.

Key writers on ancient Mexico, among them Edward King, usually known as Lord Kingsborough, and William Prescott, knew the *Calendar Stone* only through reproductions. Even some of the monument's portraitists made their images from other images, as did Agostino Aglio, who includes the *Calendar Stone* cast in a lithographic installation view in 1824 of Bullock's *Ancient Mexico* exhibition at the Egyptian Hall in London (fig. 9).[56] Although Aglio usually worked directly from the works he copied, most famously the Mexican pictorial manuscripts published by Kingsborough, he made his own drawing of the *Calendar Stone* from the cast Bullock made in Mexico City in 1823, itself probably the first copy of the work at scale (see fig. 1). Few of the artists who made the hundreds of *Calendar Stone* engravings and lithographs in Europe or the United States saw the monument in person; they usually worked either from sketches made on site by the authors of books they were hired to illustrate—such as Humboldt, Bullock, and Nebel—or from other prints and, later, from photographs.

Although documentary or "scientific" images form the smallest class of *Calendar Stone* renderings, they have played a disproportionately large role in *Calendar Stone* studies, since we tend to believe that increasingly accurate depictions imply ever-greater knowledge about the sculpture. But whether drawing, painting, engraving, lithograph, or photograph, these renderings are only as "accurate" as the artist could manage or as was necessary for the image's intended function. In contrast to the decipherment of Maya hieroglyphic writing, where photographs and drawings published by Alfred Maudslay led to major advances, better drawings and photographs of the *Calendar Stone* generally did not result in important shifts in the understanding of the monument.[57] Instead, *Calendar Stone* historiography has always been driven by better and expanded use of prose sources and greater familiarity with comparable Aztec sculptures and painted images on the other. But despite the fact that the object has not changed, the images of it have—some filling in details of the central face, and others leaving it obscured; some including the rough flange, and others excluding it; some showing the profile view, and others neglecting it. The image as reproduced is not simply steps removed from the original—it has often left out critical visual information.

Documentary images of the *Calendar Stone* tend to be frontal views, frequently with blank surroundings or otherwise lacking contextualization, a means of representation that may disassociate the disk's imagery from the fact that it is part of a three-dimensional stone sculpture. Agüera initiated this approach in 1792 with his two engravings of the monument. Whereas the first image shows the irregular contours of the stone around the circular design, the second reduces the outer edge of the monument to an easily ignored outline (see p. 53, fig. 1; p. 54, fig. 2; p. 55, fig. 3). The tendency to decontextualize the *Calendar Stone* continued with the advent of photographic views. The earliest photograph of the image, dated circa 1839, shows the irregular shape around the central circular form, but its status as a daguerreotype limited its distribution (see fig. 7). Although later photographs and lithographs of the *Calendar Stone* showing it in place at the cathedral do include the flange, many photographers actively chose to remove it, or published images where the context of the monument has been trimmed, as for example in Charnay's albumen print of circa 1855 (fig. 10). Likewise, early drawings of the sculpture ignored the pecked holes in the flange, first noticed and drawn by Francisco Abadiano in 1889 (see fig. 5).[58] These were mostly forgotten in later scholarship and, in fact, we generally ignore the reality that the work *has* a flange (and also a profile with carved relief). Those who reproduce the work in two-dimensional media generally work only with the disk, rehearsing and reinforcing the disjunction between the object and its iconography.[59]

León y Gama initiated another enduring way of seeing and documenting the calendar by assigning letters to those portions of the relief he wished to describe in detail (see p. 55, fig. 3). The method continues to the present day, with other significant examples published by Albert Gallatin (1845), Chavero (1875), Batres (1888), Abadiano (1889), Caso (1928), Noriega (1954), Carlos Chanfón Olmos (1978), and Solís (2000), who provides a new interpretation and segmentation of the imagery (Felipe Solís, this volume). Is this done simply because the *Calendar Stone* iconography is complicated and can most easily be digested by labeling, decomposing, or otherwise defeating the intent of its patron that it be perceived as a whole? We label complicated monuments not only to draw attention to those features we wish to discuss but also to exclude those we will not discuss; León y Gama did not consider the identification of the central face and accordingly placed no letter on or next to it.

Gallatin's diagram, published in his "Notes on the Semi-Civilized Nations of Mexico" (1845), is a good example of this way of understanding the *Calendar Stone* by analyzing its components (fig. 11). In spite of the fact that Nebel had published a more accurate image in 1836, Gallatin published a new lithograph, redrawn by G. and W. Endicott of New York from the Bustamante edition of León y Gama, with all of the inaccuracies introduced by Agüera.[60] But instead of republishing the entire image, Gallatin deleted those parts that he considered decorative or otherwise unrelated to the stone's astronomical and timekeeping functions, as then understood. Rather like

Fig. 10.
Desire Charnay (French, 1828–1915)
Aztec Calendar Stone, ca. 1855,
albumen print
Los Angeles, Getty Research Institute

THE CALENDAR STONE.

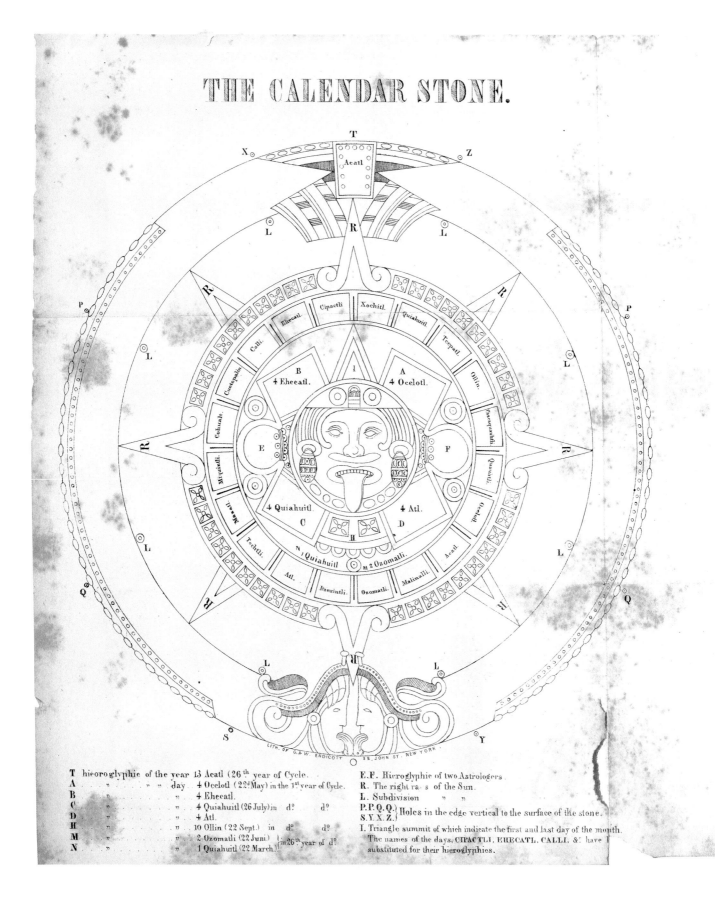

T hieroglyphic of the year 13 Acatl (26th year of Cycle).
T A   „   „ day 4 Ocelotl (22d May) in the 1st year of Cycle.
B   „   „   4 Ehecatl.
C   „   „   4 Quiahuitl (26 July) in do   do
D   „   „   4 Atl.
H   „   „   10 Ollin (22 Sept.) in   do   do
M   „   „   2 Ozomatli (22 Juni) in 26th year of do
N   „   „   1 Quiahuitl (22 March).

E.F. Hieroglyphic of two Astrologers.
R. The right rays of the Sun.
L. Subdivision   „   „
P.P.Q.Q. } Holes in the edge vertical to the surface of the stone.
S.Y.X.Z. }
I. Triangle summit of which indicate the first and last day of the month.
  The names of the days, CIPACTLI, EHECATL, CALLI, &c. have been substituted for their hieroglyphics.

early books on ancient Maya writing, like Sylvanus G. Morley's *Inscriptions at Copan* (1920) and *Inscriptions of Petén* (1937–38), which reproduced only those sections of inscriptions that could be read at the time, Gallatin simply erased half of the *Calendar Stone*'s iconography, and replaced many other details with captions, for greater "legibility."

Beginning with Bullock's cast in 1823, three-dimensional reproductions of the *Calendar Stone* in plaster, bronze, and other media and at all scales have played essential roles in *Calendar Stone* historiography. The *Calendar Stone* was a key work in the first exhibition of Mexican antiquities—but as a *cast*. *Calendar Stone* casts have been common features of museum installations on ancient Mexico since then. Although art museums frequently displayed casts next to real objects in the nineteenth century, especially in displays of Greco-Roman antiquities, few do so today. Yet many natural history museums still display *Calendar Stone* casts next to real Pre-Columbian objects, among them the American Museum of Natural History in New York and the Field Museum in Chicago.[61] Full-scale *Calendar Stone* replicas, too, usually include only the disk, suggesting their derivation is not from the original object but from its edited version. They can be found in many contexts outside of the museum, such as those on Calle Tulum in Cancún, Mexico; at the Aztec Theater, San Antonio, Texas; and at Forest Lawn Memorial Park in Hollywood Hills, California. In every case discussed above, except at the Aztec Theater, the *Calendar Stone* cast or copy is mounted vertically, as if the gesture entails replicating not only the sculpture but also how the work has always been displayed since the eighteenth century.

Fig. 11.
Diagram of the *Aztec Calendar Stone,* lithograph by G. & W. Endicott after drawing by Albert Gallatin (American, 1761–1849), 1845

Fig. 12.
Masonic commemorative medal Struck in Mexico, 1945, silver, diam.: 3.1 cm (1⅕ in.) Collection of Khristaan D. Villela, Santa Fe, New Mexico

Giving a representation of the *Calendar Stone* has long been an important act of diplomatic and commercial performance, for example, the offering in 1871 by the United States minister to Mexico of an Abadiano cast to the governor of Indiana; the gift in 1952 of a copy from Mexico's state-owned oil company, Petroleos Mexicanos (PEMEX), to the city of El Paso, Texas; the gift by the Instituto Nacional de Antropología e Historia of a scale replica to the Soviet Union in 1946 (*New York Times,* 22 September 1946); or the vase with its image given to Charles Lindbergh in 1927.[62] Although a ceramic vase and a full-sized cast are not entirely comparable, we might ask, *what exactly* is being gifted?[63] Of course, in Mexico the *Calendar Stone* has long had many uses on media of exchange, including coins and paper money, not to mention on stamps and other exonumia, like *arras* wedding tokens or commemorative medals (fig. 12).[64]

Appropriating or taking the image of the *Calendar Stone* has also been a gesture repeatedly associated with foreign invasions of Mexico or with incorporating ancient Mexico into hemispheric historical narratives. During the Mexican-American War (1846–48), United States soldiers carried copies of Prescott's *History of the Conquest of Mexico,* racing toward the Zócalo as they enacted their own narrative of Mexican conquest. Nebel memorialized the moment when Winfield Scott's troops arrived in downtown Mexico City, with the Catedral Metropolitana and the *Calendar Stone* in the background (fig. 13). Taking authority over Mexico entailed controlling not only the country's political epicenter but also its symbols, especially the *Calendar Stone.* In the historical murals he created for the United States Capitol rotunda in 1878–80, Constantino Brumidi painted the *Calendar Stone* behind Cortés and Motecuhzoma (fig. 14). By embracing and appropriating the best-known monument of American antiquity, the mural incorporates the *Calendar Stone* into the history of the United States, a visual reminder of our

Fig. 13.
Adolphe-Jean-Baptiste Bayot (1801–66)
after drawing by Carl Nebel
(German, 1805–1855)
*General Scott's Entrance into Mexico City,
September 15, 1847,* 1851, hand-colored
lithograph heightened with gum arabic,
30 × 40 cm (11¾ × 15¾ in.)

Fig. 14.
Constantino Brumidi
(American, born Italian, 1805–80)
"Cortés and Montezuma Meet,"
section of the *Frieze of American
History,* 1878–80, fresco
Washington, D.C., United States
Capitol Rotunda

imperial ambitions no less potent today than the invocation of the "Halls of Montezuma" in the first line of the "Marines' Hymn," the official song of the United States Marine Corps. This, five years before the real *Calendar Stone* would be moved to the old Museo Nacional on Calle de la Moneda, a building connected to the Palacio Nacional in Mexico City (fig. 15).

France also incorporated the *Calendar Stone* into its national narrative. During the French Intervention, the *Calendar Stone* was cast and sent to Paris to represent Maximilian's (and Napoleon III's) New World empire at the Exposition universelle in 1867 (see fig. 2). The work was mounted vertically outdoors in front of the Mexico building, a confection modeled after the Pyramid of the Feathered Serpent at the ruins of Xochicalco. Like their Yankee counterparts twenty years before, French soldiers considered the *Calendar Stone,* the *Coatlicue,* and other Mexican antiquities as intellectual war booty, worthy of being taken back to France in miniatures, engravings, photographs, and tracings pasted into souvenir albums.

At the Exposition universelle in Paris in 1889, Mexico represented itself in a Pre-Columbian–inspired pavilion, the Palacio Azteca, designed by Peñafiel and Antonio de Anza and decorated on the exterior with bronze sculptures of Aztec emperors and other ancient Mexican figures by Jesús Contreras (fig. 16). A medallion that resembled the *Calendar Stone,* based on the so-called *Humboldt Disk* (see p. 128, fig. 18), greeted visitors above the main doorway and recalled a similar feature on the Mexican building at the Paris Exposition universelle of 1867. Inside was a special bronze *Calendar Stone* cast made from the Abadiano cast of 1871 (fig. 17).[65] Although the same could not be said for Francisco Abadiano's drawing, Dionisio Abadiano's cast was well regarded in its day for its accuracy. In a roundabout manner, the cast later played an important role in the first three color reproductions of the *Calendar Stone,* published between 1916 and 1958, because he found many traces of original pigment while making the mold.[66] Mexico also sent *Calendar Stone* casts to the Exposición Colombina in Madrid in 1892 and the Louisiana Purchase Exposition, held in 1904 in St. Louis, Missouri. In Madrid, when the case that held the *Calendar Stone* was opened, the cast was discovered to have melted away; the papier-mâché did not survive the voyage or the Spanish climate.[67]

Reproductions that show people, animals, or other sculptures form another important class of *Calendar Stone* images. Unlike the more documentary images, these contextualize the sculpture, showing its scale and location on the cathedral (1791–1885), in the patio of the old Museo Nacional (1885–87), in the Salón de Monolítos at the same institution (1887–1964), and, since 1964, in the Sala Mexica in the Museo Nacional de Antropología. Among the richest images in this group are those showing Mexicans of all races and classes posed next to the stone, updates of eighteenth-century *casta* paintings, and a large group of photographs of both unknown and famous people posed with the monument, including Díaz, the politician Venustiano Carranza, the performer Cantinflas, the writer Carlos Fuentes, and almost every twentieth-century Mexican president (figs. 18, 19). Images like that published in Manuel Rivera Cambas's *México pintoresco, artístico y monumental* (1880–83), which shows both an Indian child and a middle- or upper-class Mexican couple posed next to the *Calendar Stone,* seem to establish the monument as history, heritage, and national symbol for all Mexicans, no matter their race or class (see pl. 17). Having one's photograph taken in front of the *Calendar Stone* is practically a rite of passage for tourists to Mexico City, as though they, like the American and French soldiers who occupied Mexico in the mid-nineteenth century, could return home with some of the *Calendar Stone*'s numinous power.

Fig. 15.
Salón de Monolítos, Mexico City,
Museo Nacional de Antropología
Ca. early 1940s, postcard,
8.9 × 13.3 cm (3½ × 5¼ in.)
Collection of Khristaan D. Villela,
Santa Fe, New Mexico

Fig. 16.
Palacio Azteca, Exposition
universelle, Paris
1889, albumen print, album:
31 × 50 cm (12¼ × 16⅝ in.)
From "L'Exposition, 1889," album
Los Angeles, Getty Research Institute

Fig. 17.
Aztec Calendar Stone, cast by
Dionisio Abadiano (Mexican, act.
1880s–1890s), 1871, albumen print
From Abadiano 1889, foldout after p. 22
Los Angeles, Getty Research Institute

Fig. 18.
Porfirio Díaz during a visit to the Museo
Nacional de Antropología, Mexico City,
ca. 1905

Fig. 19.
Cantinflas during the filming of *El signo
de la muerte*, Mexico City, 1939

The largest class of *Calendar Stone* images might be called the adaptive reuse category and, like the other types, it includes works in a variety of media and scales. This group encompasses the great mass of *Calendar Stone* objects in world visual culture—murals, mosaics, tattoos, calendar art, and images emblazoned on mass-produced items (figs. 20–22; see pls. 18, 19). Many of these material goods related to the *Calendar Stone* make one wonder if the image, now almost completely divorced from its physical referent, is no more than a cipher, a placeholder emptied of all specific meaning. No matter what archaeological site one visits in Mexico—Palenque, Chichén Itzá, Monte Alban, Teotihuacan—one can buy a T-shirt with the site name printed below an image of the *Aztec Calendar Stone,* as though the Aztec Empire still (or ever) held these sites under its sway. Some images in this group are quite accurately rendered, at least with regard to the details of the central disk, such as we imagine the small-scale copies that hung in the homes of the Mesoamericanists Nuttall and Alfred M. Tozzer.[68] We should add to this group the magnificent sterling silver and garnet tray made by Tiffany and Company for its corporate exhibit at the World's Columbian Exposition in 1893 in Chicago (fig. 23).

The growth of tourism to Mexico during the Porfiriato likely led to the creation of numerous forgeries based on the *Calendar Stone,* as well as small-scale souvenirs of the work,

Fig. 20.
Maurio Muñoz
Cat Eyes–Aztec Calendar Stone, 1996,
cotton handkerchief (*paño*) with ink
drawing, 40.65 × 40.65 cm (16 × 16 in.)
Private collection

Fig. 21.
Lalo Alcaraz (American, b. 1964)
Pochteca Calendar of Raza Pop Culture,
1998, drawing, diam.: 23 cm (9 in.)

Fig. 22.
Anatol Kovarsky (American,
born Soviet, act. 1940s–1970s)
New Yorker cartoon, 1960, drawing,
12.7 × 19 cm (5 × 7½ in.)

"No, no, no! Thirty days hath September!"

such as those for sale at the Mexican Art and Curiosity Store in El Paso, Texas, where for $2.50 one could buy plaster "Copies of the *Calendar Stone*" eight and one-half inches in diameter with a wire loop for hanging. For the less solvent (or those with less wall space), cabinet photographs of the monument could be had for twenty-five cents.[69] On the other side of the fine line between souvenir and forgery were a host of fake antiquities embossed or otherwise elaborated with the *Calendar Stone* design. In one case, a woman in New York purchased for $3,500 a black terra-cotta *Calendar Stone* a foot in diameter and was told it was the original monument. (Given the number of copies at all scales, how would one know the true scale of the work without seeing it?) The famous anthropologist Franz Boas at Columbia University had to tell her that the *Calendar Stone* she purchased was worth thirty-five cents! And the *Calendar Stone* figures prominently in the earliest works on Pre-Columbian forgery, written by William Henry Holmes and Leopoldo Batres, who both discussed ceramics made in Mexico, at Teotihuacan in the case of Batres.[70]

Fig. 24.
The *Aztec Calendar Stone,* deconstructed
to highlight its geometric organization,
drawing by Carlos Chanfón, 1978

Altogether the quantity—not their quality—of images of the *Calendar Stone* has been critical to the work's notoriety. If we can find meaning in such images (what is the meaning of depicting the *Calendar Stone* in a tattoo or on the label of a tequila bottle?), we might say that they are all acts of appropriation, large or small. Determining *what* exactly is appropriated is the challenge: Is it the idea of the Aztecs? Ancient Mexico? Mexican nationalism? Chicano or Latino pride? New Age spiritualism? We wonder if the Aztecs thought of the many objects with imagery similar to the *Calendar Stone* as "copies." Was the *Teocalli de la Guerra Sagrada* a "copy" of the *Calendar Stone?*

METHODOLOGY

In assembling this anthology of *Calendar Stone* sources, we selected only those works that dealt with the monument in such a way that produced scholarly progeny. Even so, this book could easily have been twice as long as it is, and we wished to include some works for which there was simply no space. We made a conscious decision to exclude works that were less productive in the overall historiography of the monument or that presented interpretations too far outside the general consensus of the fields of art history, archaeology, anthropology, and the history of religions. In particular, we have avoided most works where the primary methodology entailed counting iconographic elements of the relief and subjecting the resulting sums to mathematical calculations to arrive at numerologically "significant" numbers, such as 13, 25, 52, 104, 260, 365, and so forth. León y Gama initiated this approach, and it was continued by Chavero and many others down to the present day. But its twentieth-century iterations have, we feel, added little to our understanding of the object. This "counting methodology" has often led writers to reconstruct content that is not found on the stone and has even necessitated proposing duplicate monuments, as when León y Gama thought that there were two *Calendar Stone*s and Batres imagined there were four.[71] We do not doubt that numerology played an important role in ancient Mexican thought and that the *Calendar Stone* and similar works of state-sponsored art would have been carefully planned—pictorial elements were neither disposed nor duplicated on the relief at random. The designers of the *Calendar Stone* did so according to precise repeated and regular numerical units, but whether it was thirty-two segments of the circumference, as Caso proposes in 1928, or the more complicated geometric figures favored by Chanfón (1978), awaits further confirmation (fig. 24).

CONCLUSION

The Mexican writer Enrique Krauze calls the *Calendar Stone* a "petrified symbol of the past" (1997, 39). Although history as we practice it does in some ways seek to fix or petrify the past, historiography is the stratigraphy of history, revealing the layered sequences of ideas over time and demonstrating that they have never been so fixed or certain as we presumed. The documents presented in this anthology show that, far from being an ossified allegory of Aztec splendor, the monument has been one of the most fertile in world art history. Despite its size and prominence, it remains a remarkably, almost painfully, opaque monument. Paradoxically, its meanings were almost certainly clear for those who made it, recalling Claude Levi-Strauss's admonition that although we may constantly seek the true messages of these objects from the distant past, we must remind ourselves that these messages were not meant for us.[72]

Notes

1. Epigraph from Octavio Paz, *Sunstone,* trans. Eliot Weinberger (New York: New Directions, 1991), 10–11.

2. We note that the Aztec fascination with depicting their own deities sacrificed can be traced deep in Mexican antiquity; human heads in sacrificial plates or bowls were common offerings among all ancient Mesoamerican peoples. They can be seen, for example, in the many Classic Maya depictions of the maize god's head in a bowl or plate. The Maya did not call these vessels *cuauhxicallis,* but the structural parallel illuminates the heads at the center of the *Calendar Stone* and the Motecuhzoma I stone. At Teotihuacan, the so-called Great Goddess at Techinantitla appears as a decapitated head with flanking claws (Miller 2006, 85). As on the *Calendar Stone,* the deity has been sacrificed, and blood and symbols of preciousness—greenstone beads—scatter and pour from its neck. See also Klein 2008 for a new interpretation of the various *Coatlicue* sculptures as female deities who sacrificed themselves to enable the last creation of the sun at Teotihuacan.

3. The *Calendar Stone* contains no explicit references to the 365-day calendar used by the Aztecs and other peoples of ancient Mesoamerica.

4. Several writers have noted that there may be fifty-two quincunxes, if one imagines that they continue behind the four large points at 0°, 90°, 180°, and 270°. See Enrique Juan Palacios, this volume; and Michel Graulich, this volume.

5. The Cortés story is related in an account of the conquest recorded in Nahuatl about 1528 by unknown informants from Tlatelolco. The manuscript survives in the Bibliothèque nationale, Paris (MS 22, "*Unos anales historicos de la nacion mexicana*"). See León-Portilla 1992, 128. Examples of the small *cuauhxicalli* survive at the National Museum of the American Indian, Washington, D.C. (6 × 17 cm, cat. no. 163405A), the Museum für Völkerkunde, Kunsthistorisches Museum, Vienna (6.4 × 15.5 cm, cat. no. MVK 59.896), and the Museum für Völkerkunde, Berlin (14.5 × 23.8 cm, cat. 4 Ca 1). All three are illustrated in Matos Moctezuma and Solís Olguín 2004, 129–30; see also p. 109, fig. 5; and p. 121, figs. 7, 8.

6. It is possible that we do not yet understand these object classes well enough to distinguish their varieties and uses according to ancient Mexican classifications.

7. See Diego Durán, this volume. Riley (1997, 18) suggests that it was buried in 1559; part of that year would have coincided with the New Fire fifty-two-year ceremony. The year 1559 would have been five years after Archbishop Montúfar arrived in Mexico City.

8. A Spanish colonial subject born in the New World, as opposed to in Europe.

9. See José Gómez, this volume; and Antonio de León y Gama, this volume.

10. See León y Gama 1792, sec. 61, 96; 1832, 93.

11. See Antonio de León y Gama, this volume; and Alzate y Ramírez 1791.

12. See Antonio de León y Gama, this volume; and Alexander von Humboldt, this volume. See also Keen 1971 for a good summary of this dispute.

13. In a well-known episode, Bullock also had the *Coatlicue* sculpture exhumed from the patio of the university in order to make a cast. See Bullock 1824b; and Graham 1993.

14. There are just seventy-two names on the subscriber list at the end of the edition of 1792, and even owing for a few dozen additional copies, León y Gama's work was exceedingly rare.

15. The English-language sources use "Montezuma's watch," not "clock." Earlier writers refer to the *Calendar Stone* as such, e.g., Bullock, both in his travelogue (1824b) and in the catalogs for his exhibition of 1825 at the Egyptian Hall, Piccadilly, London (Bullock 1824a). See Prescott 1843, 1:142–43, 2:115. Aside from publishing Bustamante's attribution in English, Prescott closely follows the interpretations of León y Gama and Humboldt, emphasizing, to Chavero's later distress, the monument's use as a sundial, hence "Montezuma's watch." The "Montezuma's watch" appellation, widely applied to the *Calendar Stone* in the nineteenth century, had little to do with scholarly opinions about the patronage of the *Calendar Stone.* Although Bustamante (Sahagún 1829–30, 2:xxx–xxxii; see also León y Gama 1832, pt. 1:112–14n) suggested as early as 1829 that Motecuhzoma II commissioned the *Calendar Stone,* writers both before and after his time called it Montezuma's watch, even when they advanced an alternate history, most often that it was carved in 1479, during the reign of Axayacatl (r. 1469–81).

16. This structure was on the south side of the Palacio Nacional, set back about a block from the line of the Zócalo, just to the south of the Plaza del Volador. It was demolished in 1935, and the Suprema Corte de Justicia de la Nación now stands on the site of both the Volador and the university.

17. See the *Archives de la Commission scientifique du Mexique* 1865–67.

18. See Chavero 1877a, 1882, 1886, 1903; P. Valentini 1877; Preuss 1931, 426–34; and García 1934.

19. We note that León y Gama's idea that the *Calendar Stone* was mounted vertically during Pre-Columbian times likely determined its position on the side of the Catedral Metropolitana tower. Otherwise would it not have been left in a horizontal position, like the *Stone of Tizoc,* which was discovered just months afterward?

20. Morgan believed that all the world's societies could be placed in the categories of savagery, barbarism, or civilization, depending on their level of advancement along a continuum that ended with modern Western Europeans. Native American peoples were fixed in one of the stages of savagery or barbarism. He thought the sixteenth-century Spanish accounts by Cortés and others, describing Motecuhzoma II as the emperor of a civilized kingdom, were fabulous inventions of the superstitious or gullible. Being Native Americans, the Aztecs could not possibly have advanced to civilization, and they were better described in terms Morgan observed firsthand in New York among the Iroquois: Motecuhzoma was a "sachem," and the palaces and temples of Tenochtitlan were "longhouses." See Morgan 1876; and Keen 1971 for a useful summary of this argument and its era.

21. There are too many to list, but see Tylor 1861; Manero 1878; Zaremba 1883; Conkling 1884; Ober 1884; Charnay 1885, 1887; Janvier 1886; Blake 1891, 1906; Baedeker 1893; Campbell 1895; and Terry 1909. Most of the guides had numerous later editions.

22. The Porfiriato refers to the presidency of Porfirio Díaz, from 1876 to 1910, with a brief interruption from 1880 to 1884.

23. Although Mauricio Tenorio-Trillo does not discuss the *Calendar Stone,* see his work of 1996 for a discussion of the image Mexico projected of itself at the world's fairs.

24. Given Mexico's interest in and connections to France at this time, we should also cite the opening in 1882 of the

Musée d'ethnographie du Trocadéro in Paris as an impetus for moving the *Calendar Stone* and establishing a formal gallery of Pre-Columbian sculpture.

25. See Ordóñez 1892. López Luján (2008a, 79) notes that similar basalt deposits are found both in the Pedregal de San Angel and to the south and southeast of Xochimilco.

26. It should be noted that earlier attempts to catalog the Pre-Columbian objects in Mexico City and (after 1827) in the Museo Nacional include the unpublished manuscript by Guillermo Dupaix (1794), two works by José F. Ramírez (1844–45, 1857), and the brief and incomplete catalog by Isidro Ignacio de Icaza and Isidro Rafael Gondra (1927). See Dupaix 1794; Ramírez 1844–46, 1857; and Icaza and Gondra 1927.

27. See MacCurdy 1910; the American expatriate, antiquarian, and bookseller William Wilberforce Blake published a small, competent treatise on the *Calendar Stone* in 1906 to almost no notice in later years, perhaps owing to his political sympathies to the Porfiriato.

28. In the mid-1930s, Caso attacks the proposals of Frederick S. Dellenbaugh in the *American Anthropologist*, see Dellenbaugh 1933, 1935; Caso 1934; and Hermann Beyer, this volume. Although Caso's short essay in *Thirteen Masterpieces of Mexican Archaeology* (1938) mentions his geometric investigations, it largely reiterates Beyer's interpretations.

29. See Pijoán 1928, 1931, 1952; and Toscano 1944.

30. See Oles 1993; Delpar 1992; and Barnet-Sánchez 1993.

31. See Vaillant 1941, 163. Paperback editions were published in 1944.

32. Neither the *Calendar Stone* nor any other Aztec object is illustrated in the first edition of 1926.

33. For example, José Alcina Franch, after discussing the *Coatlicue* sculpture, concludes, "Aztec relief art, on the other hand, is sorely lacking in originality: Toltec models were slavishly copied. Types of works of this kind are the Stone of the Sun and the Stone of Tizoc" (1983, 287).

34. See, for example, Nicholson and Quiñones Keber 1983, 18; Matos Moctezuma and Solís Olguín 2002, introduction; and Solís Olguín, ed., 2004, 37.

35. As Beyer (1921, 16) mentions, there was an earlier color reconstruction, based on the research of the Abadiano brothers, published in *Acción mundial* (29 January 1916). We have not seen this. The latest color reconstruction, published by Solís in 2000 (and in Felipe Solís, this volume) differs dramatically from the earlier proposals.

36. We note that the Mexican government minted a medal with the *Calendar Stone* to commemorate the opening of the first section of the Metro in 1969.

37. See Umberger 1981a; and Emily Umberger, this volume.

38. See Fradcourt 1982, 1988a (republished 1993; see also Ariane Fradcourt, this volume), 1988b, 1991, 1992; Michel Graulich 1992 (this volume), 1997b; and H.B. Nicholson 1993 (this volume).

39. Matos Moctezuma 1992; and Matos Moctezuma and Solís Olguín 2004.

40. Hermann Beyer (this volume) and Frederick Starr (Enrique Palacios, this volume) both mention that they wished to write a history of the *Calendar Stone*'s students and their approaches to the work but were unable to do so.

41. Sahagún 1950–82, vol. 12; and Díaz del Castillo 1908–16, or any of the later editions.

42. See Durán 1967, 1:98; and Alvarado Tezozómoc 1975a, 415–16.

43. Gordon Whittaker (personal communication, 2009) supports Lockhart's version, noting that the specified term, *temalacatitlan,* is either a place-name or a reference to "at or by the *temalacatl*," whereas "on the *temalacatl*" would be *temalacapan* or *temalacaticpac.* Whittaker also notes that firing even a small cannon atop the *Calendar Stone* likely would have resulted in more damage than is visible.

44. The *Teocalli* was discovered in 1831 but not removed for almost a century. See Caso 1927, 7. Other important treatments of the *Teocalli* include Mena 1928; Palacios 1929; Townsend 1979, 49–63; Umberger 1981a, 172–92; Pasztory 1983, 165–69; Graulich 1997b; and Matos Moctezuma and Solís Olguín 2004, 108.

45. Ramón Mena (1928) first made this identification.

46. See Gutiérrez Haces 1995. The Academia de San Carlos art students drew the *Standard Bearer* (*Indio triste*), found in Mexico City in the early nineteenth century; the *Dead Man* (*Cabeza del hombre muerto*); and the *Eagle Warrior* (*Cabeza de caballero aguila*), probably from Tetzcoco, Mexico (Leonardo López Luján, personal communication, 2009). (All three are now in the Museo Nacional de Antropología, Mexico City.)

47. Although there are many sources on Tolsá and the *Caballito,* the most relevant for *Calendar Stone* studies is Humboldt's discussion of how he was in Mexico City when the work was cast. See Humboldt 1814, pt. 1:50–51; and Alexander von Humboldt, this volume.

48. The history of the reburials of the *Coatlicue* is well known. The description of native Mexicans leaving flowers and candles at the foot of the sculpture in the university is from a letter of 1805 by Benito María de Moxó (1839, 189–90). Humboldt noted that the university professors, who were Dominican friars, had the work buried. We recall that the Dominicans directed the Inquisition in colonial New Spain. He writes that he was able to see the work only because the bishop of Monterrey, one Feliciano Marín, was passing through Mexico City at the time and prevailed upon the university rector to have the *Coatlicue* exhumed (1814, pt. 2:47–48). Bullock had the sculpture exhumed again in 1823, for the purpose of making a cast, and mentioned that just as they had done years prior, the native Mexicans left flowers before the statue. He also mentions that she was reburied after a week (1824b, 337–42). See Graham 1993 and Costeloe

2006 for more on Bullock in Mexico. We do not know when the *Coatlicue* was finally exhumed for good. She was still underground in a work published in 1830 (Conder 1830, 259; note that Conder never actually visited Mexico). It must have been by the early 1840s, since she is visible in the corner of the patio in Pedro Gualdi's lithograph of 1841 and in an oil painting of the same subject. See Gualdi 1841 for the lithograph. The oil painting is reproduced in *El escenario urbano de Pedro Gualdi, 1808–1857* (1997, 91, cat. no. 10). Matos Moctezuma suggests that native Mexicans made devotions to the *Coatlicue* precisely because they knew it would upset the Spanish colonial authorities, since they had already moved her out of sight, into the university, where only "qualified" people could view her (1993, 96).

49. León y Gama 1792, 12; and Antonio de León y Gama, this volume.

50. See Gutiérrez Haces 1995 for more on León y Gama's categories of objects and how they affected how he wrote about the sculptures.

51. Emily Umberger suggests that these calendar wheels were key to León y Gama's conceptualization of the *Calendar Stone,* as though the discovery of the *Calendar Stone* actualized what had previously appeared only in manuscript or printed form. She and others note that the portrait of Lorenzo Boturini Benaduci published on the title page of his *Idea de una nueva historia general de la América septentrional* (1746) shows him holding prints of a calendar wheel and the Virgin of Guadalupe, epitomizing his obsessions (Emily Umberger, personal communication, 2009). The three varieties of colonial-era calendar wheels visualize the 260-day calendar, the 365-day calendar, and the fifty-two years of the so-called Calendar Round, or Mexican "century." The wheel in the *Durán Codex,* unknown to León y Gama and unpublished until the late nineteenth century, shows the fifty-two-year cycle with a sun face at its center. Although the image seems derived from European renderings of the sun, we wonder if it might not also derive from the central face of the *Calendar Stone,* which Durán saw.

52. For the Maya, see Houston, Stuart, and Taube 2006, 76; for the Olmec, see Diehl 2004, 119; and for Teotihuacan, see López Luján et al. 2006, although the latter is not solely about face damage.

53. Although they may be damaged in the sense that they have lost their inlaid obsidian or other material. See Hermann Beyer, this volume.

54. For example, in Solís Olguín 2000.

55. Matos Moctezuma and Solís Olguín 2004, 12, 29—although many images of the *Calendar Stone* show these at about the 5, 7, 8, and 10 o'clock positions.

56. The central thirty-six inches of Bullock's *Calendar Stone* cast still survives, in the National Museum of Scotland, inventory A.1956.703. The exhibitions *Ancient Mexico* and *Modern Mexico* opened on separate floors of the Egyptian Hall in April 1824, were combined in November, and closed in September 1825. The exhibition contents were sold at public auction. See Costeloe 2006, 288; and Graham 1993, 63.

57. See Maudslay 1889–1902; Coe 1992; and Stuart 1992.

58. These holes, found on the lower left side of the *Calendar Stone* flange, have been thought to be rough representations of constellations of the night sky. See Nuttall 1901; and Aveni 2001, 32–37.

59. For example, the book in which H. B. Nicholson published the contribution (Cordy-Collins and Sharon 1993), excerpted in the present volume, has the Sieck Flandes color reproduction on the cover but without the profile reconstruction, which he published in 1942. Sieck Flandes omits the stone flange, and so do the designers of the volume of 1993.

60. Gallatin based his image on the edition of 1832 of León y Gama, for which it seems the original plates were used.

61. At the American Museum of Natural History there was also a color floor mosaic of the *Calendar Stone* in the Hayden Planetarium. For the opening of the Hall of Mexican Archaeology, with its cast, see the *New York Times,* 17 December 1899. Other museums with *Calendar Stone* casts include the Smithsonian Institution; the Florida Museum of Natural History, Gainesville; and the Natural History Museum of Los Angeles County. The Blackmore Museum, Salisbury, England, has (or had) small wax models of the *Calendar Stone,* the *Coatlicue,* and the *Stone of Tizoc;* see Stevens 1870, 308–11. The British Museum and the Haslemere Museum also have small wax models of the *Calendar Stone* (British Museum) and Tizoc stones (British Museum and Haslemere Museum). We note that at the exhibition of 1940, *Twenty Centuries of Mexican Art,* at the New York Museum of Modern Art, the *Coatlicue* was represented by a cast, though the exhibition catalog makes no mention of this fact. See the *New York Times,* 7 April 1940.

62. A copy of the Abadiano cast was sent to the governor of Indiana by Thomas Nelson. There is also documentation of a couple of casts made under Maximilian and sent abroad, which were not as accurate as Abadiano's (*New York Times,* 13 August 1871). The El Paso copy is discussed in Little 1996, 204. For the vase given to Lindbergh, see the *New York Times,* 24 December 1927.

63. PEMEX gave the *Calendar Stone* reproduction to a Mexican-majority neighborhood in an effort to promote *mexicanidad* in a United States city (Rex Koontz, personal communication, 2009).

64. *Arras* tokens are exchanged by brides and grooms in some traditional Latin American weddings. They may be made of gold, silver, or other metals and are a symbolic currency, usually the same size as the smallest circulating coins. See Matos Moctezuma 1992, 134–35, for the better-known coins, stamps, and paper money with images of the *Calendar Stone.*

65. See Abadiano 1889, 202. Perhaps it was pulled from the mold, if it still existed. We note that copies of works of art officially were excluded from display at the Exposition universelle. Apparently the *Calendar Stone* cast did not register as such (reported in the *Diario oficial del Supremo Gobierno de los Estados Unidos Mexicanos,* 6 March 1888; cited in Díaz y de Ovando 1990, 112).

66. Nuttall mentions the Abadiano cast and how the process revealed some of the original colors (1901, 251). See also Hermann Beyer, this volume; and Roberto Sieck Flandes, this volume.

67. See Stacie Graham Widdifield, this volume; and *El monitor republicano,* 22 October 1892, reprinted in Lombardo de Ruiz 1994. For St. Louis, see *Catálogo oficial de las exhibiciones* 1904, 295. Also on display were Chavero's book on the *Calendar Stone* (the version of 1886) and Peñafiel's *Monumentos del arte mexicano antiguo* (1890), which itself had been prepared for an earlier world's fair, with its José María Velasco drawing of the *Calendar Stone.*

68. See Nuttall 1901, 12. Tozzer's was a wooden copy, mounted over the fireplace in his study. See Willey 1988, 270.

69. See *Illustrated Catalogue of Mexican Art Goods and Curiousities* 1888, 55. See also the *New York Times,* 1 January 1903, for mention of the *Calendar Stone,* reproduced as a paperweight in onyx, for sale in New York.

70. Forgeries based on the *Calendar Stone* are reproduced in Holmes 1889. The fake *Calendar Stone* ceramic is reproduced on p. 325. For reproductions of several terra-cotta fake *Calendar Stone*s, see Batres 1910. For the $3,500 forgery, see the *New York Times,* 18 May 1921.

71. León y Gama thinks that one stone marked the festivals, solstices, and equinoxes for one half of the year, and the other, similar stone marked those for the other six months. Batres (1888, 13) argues that each of four *Calendar Stone*s represented one of the *tlalpillis,* or thirteen-year periods of the fifty-two-year Mexican "century."

72. Levi-Strauss 1990.

FRAY DIEGO DURÁN

History of the Indies of New Spain (1581)

Editor's Commentary

Although much of the historiography of the Calendar Stone *postdates its rediscovery in 1790, some Europeans likely saw the sculpture during and after the conquest of Mexico. The Dominican Fray Diego Durán may even have seen it himself fifty years later and recorded the circumstances of its burial. Durán's works are today among the best known of the sixteenth-century accounts of life in Mexico before the conquest. His* Historia de las Indias de Nueva España y islas de tierra firme *(1581), the* Libro de los ritos y ceremonias en las fiestas de los dioses y celebración de ellas (Book of the Gods and Rites) *(1576–79), and* El calendario antiguo (The Ancient Calendar) *(1579), collectively called the* Durán Codex *and found today in Madrid's Biblioteca Nacional de España, include many pertinent references to stone sculptures commissioned by the Aztec rulers. But Durán's writings present many difficulties, owing especially to their relationship to other sources, like the writings of Fernando Alvarado Tezozómoc and the* Crónica X, *a lost source by an unidentified writer. Unknown native Mexican artists illustrated several stone monuments in the* Durán Codex *(Couch 1981; Umberger 2003). These images also present challenges because they seem to be based both on the text and on sculptures that could still be seen in Mexico City in the late sixteenth century. The central questions are which sculptures were still visible in Durán's day, and how do they relate to the sculptures mentioned in the text?*

Durán's Historia de las Indias de Nueva España *and Alvarado Tezozómoc's* Crónica mexicana *and* Crónica mexicayotl *(both ca. 1598) relate the history of the Aztecs, from their mythological departure from Aztlan to the Spanish conquest. Both works likely derive from the mysterious* Crónica X *and form part of a group of related histories that includes the works of Juan Tovar and Joseph de Acosta (Barlow 1945; Bernal 1994; Horcasitas and Heyden 1971; Durán 1994).*

Although the Durán and Alvarado Tezozómoc histories differ only in certain details, their importance to Calendar Stone *studies has varied relative to their availability and the interests of the writers who mined them. Both works describe in several chapters how the Aztec rulers Motecuhzoma I, Axayacatl, and Motecuhzoma II commissioned large-scale round stone sculptures like the* Calendar Stone. *Carlos Sigüenza y Góngora owned the manuscript of Alvarado Tezozómoc's* Crónica, *which survived in both Spanish and Nahuatl versions, and donated it to the Jesuit Colegio de San Pedro y San Pablo in Mexico City upon his death in 1700 (Moreno 1971, 253–54). Lorenzo Boturini Benaduci acquired the manuscript by about 1740, and the Nahuatl-language version appears in the catalog of*

Excerpted from Diego Durán, *The History of the Indies of New Spain,* translated, annotated, and with an introduction by Doris Heyden (Norman: Univ. of Oklahoma Press, 1994), 263–64, 477–81. Published with permission. Introductory text by Khristaan D. Villela.

his famous collection (1746, pt. 2, sec. 8, no. 2), the Museo Histórico Indiano *(the catalog of which forms the final portion of his* Idea de una nueva historia general de la America Septentrional*). Antonio de León y Gama used a copy in his work on the* Calendar Stone *(1792) but only in a discussion of how the dates of historical events illuminated the workings of the Mexican calendar. Alvarado Tezozómoc's* Crónica *was first published by Lord Edward King Kingsborough in the ninth volume of the* Antiquities of Mexico *(Kingsborough 1831–48, 9:[1]–196), and a French-language version appeared five years later (Alvarado Tezozómoc 1853). The* Crónica *was finally published in Spanish in Mexico in 1878 in an edition by José Vigil, annotated by Manuel Orozco y Berra.[1] By this time, the first section of Durán was published, and Alfredo Chavero had realized that the two histories were more pertinent to* Calendar Stone *studies because of their treatment of the types of Aztec stone monuments for their discussions of the Mexican calendar.*

The Mexican statesman and antiquarian José F. Ramírez discovered the Durán Codex *in Madrid. He had it copied in 1854 and the illustrations traced and lithographed in Paris. As he published the first seventy-one chapters in early 1867, Maximilian's empire was collapsing, and Ramírez, who was minister of foreign affairs, fled Mexico for Europe.[2] The second half of the Durán text and the atlas of plates were seized by the Mexican government (Sabin, Eames, and Vail 1868–1936, 6:33) and were thought lost until Chavero found them in a damp storeroom in the Colegio de Minería (Chavero 1876, 164). Chavero and Gumesindo Mendoza, director of the Museo Nacional de México, convinced the Mexican government to underwrite the publication of the rest of the Durán manuscript and the atlas of plates in 1880. In addition to the first publication, there have been several other editions of Durán, notably the Porrúa publication edited by Ángel María Garibay (Durán 1967) and three English versions by Doris Heyden and Fernando Horcasitas.[3] The latter authors published Durán's* History of the Indies of New Spain *separately from his writings on the calendar and rites of the Aztecs. They are published together in all the Spanish-language versions.*

Durán wrote when there were still large Aztec stone sculptures visible on the streets of Mexico and when native historians still knew the histories of the Aztec kings. References to commemorative stones, especially temalacatls *and* cuauhxicallis, *punctuate Durán's* Historia *from the beginning to the end, and they also figure in his works on the calendar and the gods and rites of Mexico. Detailed discussions of the use of these monuments and how they were commissioned, carved, and dedicated can be found in chapters on the reigns of Motecuhzoma I (Durán 1994, chaps. 20, 22, 23), Axayacatl (Durán 1994, chaps. 35, 36, 38), and Motecuhzoma II (Durán 1994, chap. 66). It seems that in addition to the battles that cemented and maintained Aztec dominance, the stones literally embodied these historical narratives; it is almost as if the history of the Aztecs, in semaphoric form, may be reassembled from the stones that almost every ruler ordered carved. Both* temalacatls *and* cuauhxicallis *were associated with sacrifices, either for the feast of the Flaying of Men, Tlacaxipehualiztli, or for the sacrifice of war captives.*

Among the writers on the Calendar Stone, *Chavero (1875, 1876, 1877a, 1882, 1886, 1903), Hermann Beyer (1921), and Emily Umberger (1988) have made the most use of Durán. But it was the discoverer of the* Durán Codex, *Ramírez, who observed (Durán et al. 1867–80, 1:272) that one section of the text seems to describe the* Calendar Stone:

> *Chapter XXXV Which treats of how the people of Tenantzinco asked the Aztecs for aid against Toluca and Matlatzinco. With a description of how this help was sent and how those cities were destroyed. (Durán 1994, 263)*

…After Tezozomoctli had departed for Tenantzinco, King Axayacatl turned his attention to the building of a place for the Sun Stone that had been carved, at his orders, by the sculptors. Upon it the master craftsmen had painstakingly wrought images of the heroic Aztec dignitaries of the past, scenes of the wars in which they had conquered lands and the remote coastal provinces they had subjected, in which wars they had suffered greatly. They had already brought men from those conquered regions, who had been sacrificed upon this stone. In the center were represented the rays of the sun radiating from a round depression where the victims' throats were slit and from which ran a channel to carry away the blood.

The king was also occupied in the making of the great and finely worked stone upon which were represented the months, years, days, and weeks, all so splendidly carved that it was an amazing thing to behold. Many of us were able to see this stone in the Great Square of Mexico City, next to the canal, before the most illustrious Don Fray Alonso de Montúfar, Archbishop of Mexico, of happy memory, ordered that it be buried because of the criminal acts, such as killings, that had been committed upon it.

Axayacatl had these two stones carved as a kind of altar for sacrifices and offerings and he was in the process of constructing bases for these stones at the summit of the temple.… (Durán 1994, 263–64)

The first object would seem to be the sculpture now called the Stone of Tizoc. *The second stone—described as carved with the signs of the months, days, years, and week—may be the* Calendar Stone. *Both Ramírez and Chavero (Chavero 1876, excerpted in this volume) noted that the find site of the* Calendar Stone *accords with where Durán says he saw the work in the main square of Mexico City. Since this chapter in Durán deals with events in the reign of Axayacatl, Ramírez and Chavero attributed the* Calendar Stone *to the patronage of that ruler. But the error may originate with Durán, rather than from his sources. Alvarado Tezozómoc has no equivalent passage, and we believe Durán added these details because he had seen sculptures that matched those described in the Aztec histories. Ramírez's identification of the* Calendar Stone *in Durán's text has been barely acknowledged in the historiography of the work because most writers now accept that Motecuhzoma II, and not Axayacatl, commissioned the sculpture. Durán's text would seem to give us the approximate date when the* Calendar Stone *was buried since Alonso de Montúfar was archbishop of Mexico between 1551 and 1572.*[4]

The Durán and Alvarado Tezozómoc manuscripts were illustrated with images painted by native artists, placed at the beginning of many chapters and scattered throughout the text. It is difficult to gauge how relevant these images might be to the study of Pre-Columbian objects because they were probably painted at the end of the 1570s. The images are based upon the content of the text and, in some cases, upon whatever examples of costume, architecture, and sculpture may have been seen, known, or remembered more than fifty years after the conquest (Umberger 2003; Couch 1987). Aztec sculptures that Durán saw on the streets of Mexico City likely also affected the illustrations found in the Durán Codex. *The* Calendar Stone, *or another similar but lost work, was likely the model for the illustrations Durán's painter made for chapters 23 and 35 of the* Historia *and chapter 10 of* El calendario antiguo.

Chapter 23 of the Historia *relates how Motecuhzoma I dedicated a* cuauhxicalli *in Tenochtitlan with the sacrifice of prisoners from Coaixtlahuaca (see pl. 20). The illustration shows a man sacrificed on a stone that resembles the* Stone of Tizoc, *or the* Calendar Stone, *or the recently discovered* Stone of Motecuhzoma I, *with the sun rays arrayed in a circle on its upper surface. In Durán's*

Libro de los ritos *and* El calendario antiguo *the illustration for chapter 10, a depiction of the feast in honor of the sun, called Nauholin (i.e., Nahui Ollin), features a prisoner of war standing upon a large disk-shaped sculpture carved or painted with the Ollin sign in its center (see pl. 21). The sun in the sky above is also rendered as an Ollin sign with emanating rays. The* Calendar Stone *would seem to be the model for this illustration, as its center is also occupied by an Ollin sign with the same dart form passing behind it and the same nodules to the side, which frame the claws on the sculpture.*

The image for chapter 66 shows men pulling a wagon loaded with a large square stone. Both Durán and Alvarado Tezozómoc discuss in detail the workmen and the ropes necessary to move the stone from its quarry. Of course, the Aztecs had no wagons, and the wheel was used only in toys, so this image is less relevant than the others for understanding sculptures before the conquest.

Durán's Historia *and Alvarado Tezozómoc's* Crónica *discuss only one sculpture commissioned by Motecuhzoma II, to whom most writers now attribute the* Calendar Stone. *We reproduce this chapter below from Durán, noting any significant differences between the Durán and Alvarado Tezozómoc versions, and have left the discussions of monuments commissioned by Motecuhzoma I and Axayacatl in the respective works by Chavero, Beyer, and Umberger excerpted in the present volume. These other chapters are relevant to the* Calendar Stone *as a class of object, not to the sculpture per se.*

Chapter 66 of Durán's Historia *discusses why Motecuhzoma II wished to have another stone carved, as well as the process of identifying and moving the work to Tenochtitlan. Durán details the sacrifices and rituals required by the Aztec religion to move such a stone. The priests wrapped the stone with paper, sacrificed quail, and sang and danced in its honor. As discussed below, the stone spoke to the workmen and the emissaries of Motecuhzoma II and refused to be taken to the capital. No one doubts that the* Calendar Stone *was taken to Tenochtitlan, and Umberger (this volume) notes that in Juan de Torquemada's version (1969, 1:214–15), the stone was retrieved, carved, and set up as a sacrificial stone in the tenth year of Motecuhzoma II's reign, in 1511 or 1512. Ramírez commented (Durán et al. 1867–80, 1:509) that from this episode forward Durán's text includes many omens of doom for Motecuhzoma II. Umberger adds that this must have been a postconquest elaboration in the* Crónica X, *that it was adopted by both Durán and Alvarado Tezozómoc, and that it should be understood as a retrospective effort to portray Motecuhzoma in a negative light (personal communication, 2008). Perhaps the reference is to another sculpture. Whatever the case, this episode relates details that either are not found in other sources or elaborate on what is known elsewhere about how the Aztecs viewed sculptures: they were living beings that could speak and interact with humans. The discussion of the rites undertaken at the quarry also complements how Durán, Alvarado Tezozómoc, and other writers describe the dedication of these sculptures in Tenochtitlan* after *they were completed.*

✳　　　　　✳　　　　　✳

History of the Indies of New Spain

Chapter LXVI Which treats of how Motecuhzoma ordered that the largest stone that could be found be brought for the sacrifice of the Flaying of Men and of what occurred while it was being brought to Mexico-Tenochtitlan.

Motecuhzoma was always anxious to have his accomplishments well known throughout the entire land, and all the feats of earlier kings seemed of minor importance to him, from his own point of view of grandeur and fame. He considered that the sacrificial stone his grandfather had set up was too small and banal and that it did not conform to the magnificence and authority of his city. Therefore, he called a meeting of the chieftains of his council and spoke to them of making another stone, the widest and largest that would be found in the entire region, for the feast of the Flaying of Men.[5] Having heard their agreement in this matter, he summoned the stone sculptors of the city and told them of his decision, requesting that they search for the largest and finest stone in all the province, with all the diligence possible. This was to be carved carefully and made into a great *temalacatl,* which means "round stone," to be used in the sacrifice of the Flaying of Men, since the present stone no longer pleased him.

The stonecutters, obeying his orders, went off to different places where they knew good stone existed and in the province of Chalco, at a site called Aculco near Tepepulla, next to the river that flows down from Amequemecan, they found on a hill a great rock that seemed suitable for what the king desired. When he had been notified of this, Motecuhzoma ordered that the men of Xochimilco, Cuitlahuac, Itztapalapa, Colhuacan, Mexicatzinco,[6] and Huitzilopochco bring ropes and stout poles so that all together they could carry the stone. They were told where to go and Motecuhzoma ordered that all the stone workers be provided with food for the entire time it would take to convey it. They were thus given ample provisions.

The stonemasons went to the indicated site, scraped the rock clean, and prepared to pull it out from the place in which it was stuck. When it was ready to be removed, Motecuhzoma was notified so he could send his men. A great number of these men arrived, together with more people from the above-mentioned towns, all carrying ropes, poles, and other instruments they might need. Anxious to have propitiatory rites performed [that we call] superstition and idolatry, Motecuhzoma ordered that the priests of the temple go to that place with their incense burners, paper, incense, little balls of rubber, and many quail. Together with them were to go chanters of the temples to sing and dance in front of the stone when it began to be moved along the road. Jesters and clowns were also sent to perform buffooneries before it, celebrating it and rejoicing, since it was a sacred thing to be used for divine rites.

A great number of men who were to drag the rock arrived and the priests, having donned their sacerdotal garments, took the paper they had brought and covered the whole rock with it. Going around it many times, they incensed it with much ceremony, pouring molten incense and rubber upon it, killing quail, and splashing the blood upon the stone. The chanters began to sing pleasant, joyful songs and the clowns and jesters performed little skits and buffooneries, all of which provoked laughter and pleasure. While this was being done, the Xochimilcas tied a long, stout rope around the stone and the same was done by the men from Cuitlahuac, Mezquic, Colhuacan, Itztapalapa, Mexicatzinco, and Huitzilopochco. With great enthusiasm, these men began to pull with so much shouting and yelling that the noise went up to the heavens. After having persisted a long time, trying to wrench the stone from its bed but without success, the ropes snapped as if they had been made of tender cotton. The officials in charge of the operation, seeing that the stone refused to move, sent word of this to Motecuhzoma. He then begged the king of Tezcoco to give him more men to help bring in the monolith. This was done and, when the priests again had performed the same rites as those of the day before, new ropes were tied to it by the Tezcocans. At last the stone began to budge, and the men managed to drag it as far as Tlapechhuacan. They rested there, and at dawn the next day the men again went back to work, tying new ropes while conch shells and other instruments were played, the priests performed their ceremonies, and the singers sang while quail were killed. Shouting, the men began to pull at the ropes with all their strength, but for two days they were unable to make it move from that place. Our chronicle says that it seemed to have sprung deep roots and had no intention of moving. In spite of enormous efforts by so many men, even the stoutest ropes snapped. When Motecuhzoma heard this, he summoned the Otomis of the province of Cuauhtlalpan and they, with their strong ropes and poles, went to help those who were struggling with the rock. These Otomis also tied their ropes around the stone, on top of those that already were there, and as they began to pull, shouting and howling all the time, a voice was heard coming from within the stone. It spoke: "O wretched people, O unfortunate ones! Why do you persist in your desire to take me to the city of Tenochtitlan? Behold, your work is in vain for I shall not go there, it is not my will. But since you insist so much, pull me and I shall go as far as I wish, but it will be to your misfortune!"

The voice was then silent and everyone was bewildered and frightened by this extraordinary event, something never before heard or seen. The men began to pull again, and the stone moved with such ease that they barely felt its weight. In that way it was carried that afternoon as far as Tlapitzahuayan. From this point messengers were sent to Motecuhzoma to inform him of the amazing things that had taken place and what the stone had said. When the king heard this, he had the messengers thrown into jail, for he felt they were joking. He then sent one of his officials to inquire of the people there in Tlapitzahuayan if this information was correct. When the official saw that it was true, he told this to Motecuhzoma and informed him that everyone at the site had heard the stone speak. So the king released those men he had incarcerated. He then sent a message to the ruler of Azcapotzalco requesting men from there to help move the stone. When they arrived with ropes and devices to do this work and tried to move the stone, it refused to budge but spoke these words:

> Poor wretches! Why do you labor in vain? Have I not told you I shall never reach Tenochtitlan? Go, tell Motecuhzoma that it is too late. He should have thought of this before, it occurred to him too late. Now he no longer will need me; a terrible event, brought on by fate, is about to take place. Since it comes from a divine will, he cannot fight it. Why does he want to take me? So that tomorrow I be cast down and held in contempt? Let him know that his reign, his power, has ended. Soon he will see what is to come upon him, and this will happen because he has wanted to control things more than the very god who determines everything. Therefore, leave me. If I go farther it will cause you harm.

All this was told to Motecuhzoma, and although it filled him with fear he did not really believe it. He was angry with the messengers, he was furious with them, he threatened them and commanded them to return and bring the stone, thus fulfilling this obligation. So the men again pulled at the ropes, and the stone moved so easily and so rapidly that it seemed that at least twenty were tugging at it. That day it arrived at a place called Techichco, next to Itztapalapa, and the following morning the men pulled it so easily that they were most contented. They were accompanied by people who sang and danced, by the music of conch shells and whistles, by the buffoons who acted out farces, and by the priests who burned incense and sacrificed quail. When the stone reached Tocititlan—which is the place where today there stands the first cross as one leaves the city of Mexico—Motecuhzoma was informed of its arrival. He ordered everyone in the city to go out and welcome the stone with quantities of flowers and with incense and to adorn and honor it as much as they could. This was done with all the care, solemnity, and festivity that is correct for a divine thing. Motecuhzoma remembered what the stone had said to the masons and other officials, its bad omen, that it would never reach Tenochtitlan, but since the king was obstinate, insisted on having his own way, he again ordered that great ceremonies, sacrifices, and offerings be made in the stone's honor in order to calm its ire, if it still was angry. After these ceremonies had been performed, Motecuhzoma ordered that the stone be taken into the city. When the men pulled it, it moved with such ease and speed that it reached the place that is now the irrigation gate of San Antón, where Motecuhzoma had built a strong bridge with many stout beams especially for this occasion. When it reached the middle of the bridge, with a tremendous crash the stone broke all the beams, falling into the water—which then was very deep—and carrying with it numerous men who had been attached to it by the ropes. Most of these drowned, while others were severely wounded.

The people were terrified by this accident and because the words the stone had spoken, that it would not enter the city, had turned out to be true. Motecuhzoma, informed of the events, went with his officials to the place where the stone had fallen. When he saw the destruction of the bridge and heard of the death of so many men, he immediately called for divers from Xochimilco, Cuitlahuac, and Mezquic. These divers were brought to Tenochtitlan and were ordered to go into the water without delay and seek the stone. If it was in the place where it had fallen, Motecuhzoma wished to try to pull it out again, all because of his stubbornness and stern will. The divers went into the water and searched all over for it, from noon until night, but, unable to find it, they went to the king and informed him that they had not been able to locate it in all that water, not even in the very bottom of the canal. They wondered if it was not there at all, since it had said that it was being moved against its will, and perhaps it had gone back to its original place. Motecuhzoma, considering that this was possible, sent some of his people to go seek it where it had first been extracted. The envoys found it there, all covered with paper and with signs of the sacrifices it had been offered. It was still bound by the ropes just as it had been when it fell. The bewildered and frightened envoys returned in great haste and told Motecuhzoma of the astonishing thing they had seen. Terrified, the king went in person to see the rock, accompanied by all the lords of his court. The king made offerings to it, prayed, and sacrificed some slaves. Having done these things, he returned to Tenochtitlan and spoke the following words to his principal followers: "Truly, O brothers, I now believe that our labors and afflictions will be great and that our lives are about to end. And I am determined to allow death to come just as my brave ancestors did. Let the will of the Lord of all Created Things be done!"…

Notes

1. See also Alvarado Tezozómoc 1944, 1975a, and 1975b.

2. Ramírez left Mexico on 20 January 1867 to exile in Europe. Unpublished letter to Joaquín García Icazbalceta, cited in Bernal 1994, 566. He never returned and died in Bonn, Germany, in 1871. Maximilian was executed on 19 June 1867 in Queretaro, Mexico.

3. Durán 1964; Horcasitas and Heyden 1971; and Durán 1994. See also Boone 1988 and Umberger 2003.

4. Montúfar did not arrive in Mexico until 1554. See Lundberg 2002.

5. Alvarado Tezozómoc's *Crónica* treats this incident in chapter 52 (Alvarado Tezozómoc 1878, 662–67). All of the details are as in Durán, including how the stone returned to its quarry after crashing through the bridge and falling into the water outside Tenochtitlan. However, he adds that the dimensions of the stone were to be one *braza* (fathom, about six feet) wider and two *codos* (cubits) higher than the stone that was already in the Temple of Huitzilopochtli (Alvarado Tezozómoc 1878, 662).

6. Doris Heyden: I am indebted to Jorge de León, official historian of the city of Itztapalapa, for having called my attention to a line in Torquemada stating that before the Spanish conquest Mexicatzinco was called Acatzintitlan (Torquemada 1975, 1:132).

JOSÉ GÓMEZ

<h1 style="text-align:center">Curious Diary and Notebook of the Memorable Events in Mexico during the Government of Revillagigedo (1789–94)</h1>

Editor's Commentary

A halberdier from Granada in the service of the viceroy, Count Revillagigedo II, José Gómez (1732–1800) kept a diary in Mexico during the 1790s. Portions of the work have been published three times since it was written, but it has only recently entered the corpus of Calendar Stone *studies (Matos Moctezuma 1992; Matos Moctezuma and Solís Olguín 2004; López Luján 2008a). The diary survives as two handwritten manuscripts in the Biblioteca Nacional de México (Gómez 1854, 1947). Although Gómez was a laconic writer, his manuscript contains important references to the* Coatlicue, *the* Calendar Stone, *and the* Stone of Tizoc. *Most significant for* Calendar Stone *studies is his observation that the monument lay in the Zócalo for six months after its discovery, until the beginning of July 1791.*

*　　　　*　　　　*

Curious Diary and Notebook of the Memorable Events
in Mexico during the Government of Revillagigedo

On the day 4 September 1790, in Mexico City, in the main plaza [*plaza principal*], in front of the royal palace, while excavating some foundations, they found a heathen idol, whose form was a deeply carved stone, with a skull on its back, and in front another skull with four hands [and] forms on the rest of its body, but with neither feet nor a head. This was when the Count Revillagigedo was viceroy.[1]…

On the day 2 July 1791, in Mexico City, they moved the stone that was in the great plaza [*plaza grande*] (which was a calendar [*almanaque*] of the heathen Indians) to the cemetery of the cathedral; we do not know where they will put it.[2]…

On the day 3 September 1793, in Mexico City, they moved the stone that was used for sacrifices in heathen times, to the place where the Holy Cross was in the cemetery of the cathedral [facing the Empedradillo].[3]

Notes

1. [The *Coatlicue* was discovered on 13 August, not 4 September, 1790.]

2. [Gómez made no mention of the discovery of the *Calendar Stone* on 17 December 1790.]

3. [As Matos Moctezuma and Solís (2004, 14) noted, the object described must be the *Stone of Tizoc;* the location is the street now called Republica de Brasil, on the west side of the Catedral Metropolitana de la Asunción de María.]

Excerpted and translated by Khristaan D. Villela from José Gómez, *Diario curioso; y, Cuaderno de las cosas memorables en México durante el gobierno de Revillagigedo (1789–1794)*, ed. Ignacio González-Polo (Mexico City: Universidad Nacional Autónoma de México, 1986), 25, 40, 82. Published with permission. Introductory text by Khristaan D. Villela.

"A Historical and Chronological Description of Two Stones, Which Were Found in 1790 in the Principal Square of Mexico during the Current Paving Project" (1792)

Editor's Commentary

Antonio de León y Gama published the first detailed discussion of the Calendar Stone *in his* Descripción histórica y cronológica de las dos piedras *of 1792. To this work and to its author we perhaps owe the very survival as objects of both the* Calendar Stone *and the* Coatlicue *sculptures. Although it has been considered a foundational document of American antiquarian studies since its publication, and has been reprinted in Mexico at least three times, the* Descripción *has never appeared in English.[1] León y Gama (1735–1802) was a native of Mexico City who for more than forty years served as a bureaucrat in the Real Audiencia of the viceregal government.[2] With interests in fields as disparate as astronomy, mathematics, chronology, linguistics, and natural history, León y Gama epitomized the Enlightenment spirit in New Spain.[3] His publications include astronomical almanacs (1769, 1770) and works on a solar eclipse and an aurora borealis in Mexico (1778, 1790) and on a lizard cure for cancer (1782, 1783). Among the many manuscripts unpublished during his lifetime are a work on the image of the Virgin of Guadalupe, descriptions of the bishopric of Michoacán (1927b) and of Mexico City (1927a), and a practical treatise on perspective in painting and drawing (Moreno 1970, 126). León y Gama became interested in Mexican antiquities as early as 1768 and began writing his first work on the subject in 1780, the unpublished* Historia antigua de mexico *(Moreno 1981, 58). He wrote eight works on ancient Mexico, although by the time of his death on 12 September 1802, only his treatise on the* Calendar Stone *and the* Coatlicue *had been published (León y Gama 1792).[4]*

León y Gama was a leading member of a group of criollo *intellectuals in late eighteenth-century Mexico. José Antonio de Alzate y Ramírez (1737–99) was his most notable peer, but the group also included Mariano Fernández de Echeverría y Veytia (1718–ca. 1780), the Jesuits exiled by King Charles III in 1767, Francisco Saverio Clavigero (1731–87), Pedro Márquez (1741–1820), and Andrés Cavo (1739–1803). Alzate undertook one of the first archaeological expeditions in New Spain when he visited the ruins of Xochicalco in 1777 (Alzate y Ramírez 1791). He also both planned a Spanish-language edition of Clavigero and proposed a history and geography of America (Moreno 1972, 1981). Veytia collected the remains of Lorenzo Boturini Benaduci's library and wrote a history of ancient Mexico (1836). At his death in 1803, Cavo was preparing a Latin edition of León y Gama's* Descripción *and had begun a work containing Alzate's description of Xochicalco and an account of Diego Ruíz's visit in 1785 to the ruins of El Tajín (Márquez 1832, viii; López Luján 2008b, 75). Márquez finished the work on El Tajín and Xochicalco and published an Italian version of León y Gama's*

Excerpted and slightly revised from Antonio de León y Gama, "A Historical and Chronological Description of Two Stones, Which Were Found in 1790 in the Principal Square of Mexico during the Current Paving Project," manuscript of a previously unpublished translation made by William Hulings and donated to the American Philosophical Society, Philadelphia, in 1818. Introductory text by Khristaan D. Villela.

Descripción.[5] *Although he never mentions them, León y Gama may also have known of the earliest expeditions to the ruins of Palenque, undertaken by José Antonio Calderón and Antonio Bernasconi in 1784 and Antonio del Rio and Ricardo Almendáriz in 1787.*[6]

León y Gama's unpublished history of ancient Mexico was one of many similar projects undertaken during the eighteenth century in Europe and New Spain that all required collecting native-language documents. Clavigero's Storia antica del Messico *(1780–81) was the most influential history of a group that included works by Boturini (1746) and Veytia (1836). To these works should be added the life of Hernan Cortés published in 1770 by Francisco Lorenzana, archbishop of Mexico; Juan Muñoz's* Historia del Nuevo-Mundo *(1793); and a new illustrated edition of Antonio de Solís's* Historia de la conquista de México *(1783–84). The Americans in this group wish to redress the negative image of ancient Mexico advanced in the works of European writers like the encyclopedist Georges-Louis Leclerc de Buffon (1749–1767) and William Robertson (1777).*[7]

When the Coatlicue *and* Calendar Stone *were discovered in 1790, León y Gama was lobbying the Spanish government for support to finish and publish his history of ancient Mexico (Moreno 1981, 60).*[8] *His request was denied, and he instead incorporates into his description of the Aztec sculptures much information from that history and also from a treatise on ancient Mexican chronology. He notes that he was motivated to write about the newly discovered sculptures by the excavations of Pompeii and Herculaneum (1792, 4). He uses the term* antiquity *to refer to both works throughout the* Descripción, *a choice that underscores his opinion of their similarity to Greco-Roman sculptures (Gutiérrez Haces 1995, 130–31). Considering the works as valuable documents rather than "idols," León y Gama carefully avoids creating any impression that he is sympathetic to either ancient Mexican religion or their astrological practices. He deals with the* Coatlicue *sculpture by changing its classification from a fearsome female deity to an illustration of the calendar and almost the entire Aztec pantheon, including Teoyamiqui, Quetzalcoatl, Tlaloc, Mictlantecuhtli, Coatlicue, and other deities.*[9]

The Descripción *was announced in the* Gazeta de Mexico *of 16 August 1791*[10] *and was printed in early June 1792. Alzate immediately published two attacks on the work and its author in his* Gacetas de literatura.[11] *León y Gama responded in the Mexico City press*[12] *and began writing a longer rejoinder that prefaced a work on several more ancient sculptures that he began in 1794.*[13] *This manuscript was unfinished at León y Gama's death and remained in the hands of his executor, José Pichardo, and Pichardo's own executor, Dr. José Vicente, until 1828, when Carlos María de Bustamante and Lucas Alamán forced Vicente to release the work (Bustamante 1832). Bustamante prepared the unpublished manuscript and the Mexican government published it in 1832 in a combined edition that also reprinted the* Descripción *of 1792.*[14]

Anyone reading the Descripción *will be struck by how little actual* description *the work contains. For León y Gama, both sculptures are little more than points of departure that confirm his theories about the ancient Mexican calendar (Gutiérrez Haces 1995, 139–40). His* Calendar Stone *is an ancient timekeeping device that employs strings and gnomons to mark the festivals, solstices, equinoxes, and solar zenith passages for half the year; he thinks that another as yet undiscovered and similar* Calendar Stone *tracks the events for the other half of the year. Like many other writers during both the colonial era and the nineteenth century, León y Gama is obsessed by the question of how the ancient Mexicans "corrected" their calendar, how and when they intercalated extra days to account for the difference between their year of 365 days and the true length of the solar year. In his favor, León y Gama is the first to correctly order the Mexican months and to decipher the workings of the nine Lords of the Night (the* acompañados). *He also recognizes that the hieroglyphs in the "arms" of the Ollin glyph at the center of the* Calendar Stone *refer to the four previous world creations (León y Gama 1792, 97).*[15]

León y Gama's conclusions are limited by the sources available to him in Mexico City at the end of the eighteenth century. The most important (then) unpublished sources for the Descripción *were the* Codex Aubin *of 1576,* Codex Azcatitlan, Codex Cozcatzin, Codex en Cruz, Codex Ixtlilxochitl, Codex Xólotl, Historia Tolteca-Chichimeca, Matrícula de Tributos, Aubin Tonalamatl, *and* Mapa Sigüénza. *He also had Hernando de Alvarado Tezozómoc's* Crónica Mexicayotl, *Cristóbal del Castillo's* Historia de los mexicanos, *the* Codex Chimalpopoca, *three works by Domingo Francisco de San Antón Muñón Chimalpahin, Fernando de Alva Ixtlilxóchitl's* Sumaria relación, *and fragments of the works of Fray Toribio de Benavente and Fray Andrés de Olmos, as transcribed by Juan de Torquemada.*[16] *For* Calendar Stone *studies, the most important sources León y Gama lacked were the works of Bernardino de Sahagún and Diego Durán and the pictorial manuscripts in European libraries.*[17]

Two images of the Calendar Stone *and one folded sheet with five images of the* Coatlicue *illustrate the* Descripción *(figs. 1–3). León y Gama (1792, 3–4) notes that he had an exact copy made of the sculptures and engravings produced, both to illustrate his report and as a safeguard in case the works were damaged by ignorant people or destroyed or their carvings otherwise lost. The* Calendar Stone's *carvings would have been lost if it had been used as a paving stone in front of the cathedral, as was planned.*[18] *Although León y Gama did make some drawings of Aztec sculptures and images in the codices,*[19] *he entrusted the* Calendar Stone *and* Coatlicue *renderings to Francisco de Agüera, who drew both monuments and made the copperplate engravings of the works for the* Descripción.[20]

Agüera was one of a group of engravers active in Mexico City in the later eighteenth century who mostly executed devotional prints, to be sold loose or printed as text illustrations (Mathes and Grañen Porrua 2001; Romero de Terreros 1948). The catalogs of eighteenth- and early-nineteenth-century Mexican imprints include many university theses, novenas, saint's lives, and other religious texts, usually illustrated with one engraving (Buxó 1994; Garritz Ruíz 1990). Among Agüera's engravings with religious themes are images of the Virgin of Guadalupe, Felipe de Jesus, and Ignatius of Loyola.[21] *Beyond devotional prints, he also made ex libris and book frontispieces.*[22] *His most influential works were his scenes of skeleton actors illustrating Joaquín Bolaños's* La portentosa vida de la Muerte *of 1792, which related the life of Death from birth to the grave.*[23]

Agüera's renderings of the Calendar Stone *and the* Coatlicue *were reasonably accurate and were disseminated to Euro-American readers through the works of Alexander von Humboldt, who had the images reengraved in Europe. Agüera also executed the engravings of Xochicalco in Alzate's work of 1791, published by the same firm that printed León y Gama's* Descripción. *He may have been hired for the* Descripción *engravings on account of a preexisting relationship with the printer rather than a demonstrated ability to render sculptures and architecture. Or perhaps he was the artist León y Gama hired to work in his house for more than a year copying manuscripts (Burrus 1959, 70–71). Although he was active until about 1820, there is no evidence Agüera published further archaeological engravings after 1792.*[24]

This translation was made by William E. Hulings (1765–1839) and presented to the American Philosophical Society in 1818.[25] *A Philadelphia physician, Hulings served as the United States vice-consul in Spanish Louisiana in 1798–99.*[26] *Four years later, when France surrendered New Orleans to the United States, he was the acting vice-consul. He corresponded with Secretary of State James Madison on several occasions, and a letter he wrote protesting the Spanish closure of the port*

Fig. 1.
Coatlicue, engraving by Francisco
de Agüera (Mexican, act. 1779–1820),
ca. 1792
Detail *f* is the profile of the
Calendar Stone

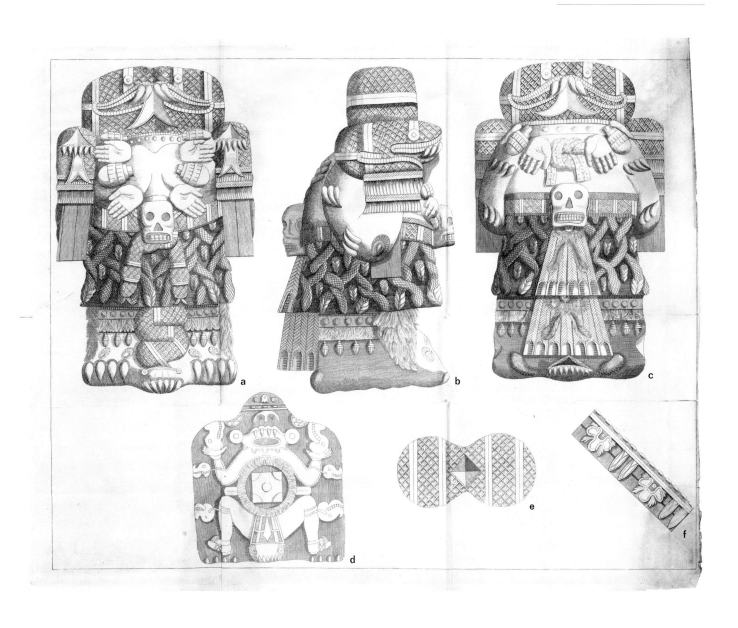

Fig. 2.
Aztec Calendar Stone, engraving
by Francisco de Agüera (Mexican,
act. 1779–1820), ca. 1792

Fig. 3.
Schematic illustration of the *Aztec
Calendar Stone,* engraving by Francisco
de Agüera (Mexican, act. 1779–1820),
ca. 1792

of New Orleans was published in 1803 in the National Intelligencer and Washington Advertiser.[27] *As a Spanish-speaking doctor and diplomat in New Orleans, Hulings gave advice that clearly was valued in Washington and was important for the successful conclusion of the Louisiana Purchase in 1803.*[28]

Hulings made the translation at the request of Benjamin Smith Barton (1766–1815), a Philadelphia physician, naturalist, and professor at the University of Pennsylvania. Barton was vice president of the American Philosophical Society (1802–15) and was one of the key figures in the development of science in the United States in the early nineteenth century. The first professional naturalist in the United States and the author of Elements of Botany; or, Outlines of the Natural History of Vegetables *(1803a), Barton was asked by President Thomas Jefferson to train Meriwether Lewis to identify and collect plants for the expeditionary group known as the Corps of Discovery, and he analyzed the specimens collected by them upon their return.*[29] *Humboldt must have known Barton's works on the origins of Native Americans (1797) and on comparative linguistics (1803b), and he adopts a similar methodology in his* Vues des cordillères *of 1810 and* Essai politique *of 1811–12 (Campbell 2000, 34). Barton met Humboldt in Philadelphia in 1804 and they corresponded afterward (de Terra 1958a, 139; 1958b, 563).*

In a letter to Jefferson, dated 14 September 1809, Barton writes that he has just received from Mexico a pamphlet on Mexican astronomy, "principally founded upon the discovery of the 'Mexican Century,' a vast stone monument, which was discovered in Mexico, in the year 1790." He continues that the work would overturn the theories of Robertson, Cornelius de Pauw, and other similar writers and that, intending to publish León y Gama's work in English, he has given it to a friend to translate. Barton concludes by offering to send the Spanish original to Jefferson (Jefferson 2004, 521). The editor of the Retirement Series of the Thomas Jefferson Papers identifies the work's author as León y Gama and also Hulings as Barton's "friend," based on the manuscript translation he gave the American Philosophical Society, the same manuscript published (in part) for the first time here. Hulings was a correspondent of Barton's and there seems no doubt that he is the friend in question.[30]

Jefferson responded to Barton on 21 September 1809:

> *I learn with pleasure of your acquisition of the pamphlet on the astronomy of the antient Mexicans, if it be antient & genuine, or modern & rational it will be of real value. It is one of the most interesting countries of our hemisphere, and merits every attention.*
>
> *I am thankful of your kind offer of sending the original Spanish for my perusal. But I think it a pity to trust it to the accidents of the post, & whenever you publish the translation, I shall be satisfied to read that which shall be given by your translator, who is, I am sure, a greater adept in the language than I am. Accept the assurances of my great esteem & respect. Th. Jefferson. (Jefferson 2004, 556)*

The bulk of the same letter to Barton deals with collecting word lists of Native American languages. Like Barton (and Humboldt), Jefferson is curious what language could tell about the origin of the Native Americans.[31] *Surely Humboldt discussed León y Gama's work with Jefferson in June 1804, when he visited Washington and Philadelphia (McCullough 1992, chap. 1), but the United States president did not own a copy of the* Descripción *(Gilreath and Wilson 1988).*

León y Gama's text is difficult to translate, with many dependent clauses and what today would be considered fragments. Hulings's translation runs to 113 manuscript pages. We have transcribed it, corrected the spelling and some punctuation, added bibliographic citations, and checked it against the original Spanish. We think it still preserves some of the feeling of Spanish of 1792 and English of 1818. Below we print only León y Gama's account of the discovery of the Calendar Stone *and the* Coatlicue *sculpture and his detailed discussion of the former. Lengthy sections on the workings of the calendar and on the* Coatlicue *are not included.*

✻   ✻   ✻

"A Historical and Chronological Description of Two Stones, Which Were Found in 1790 in the Principal Square of Mexico during the Current Paving Project"

…A Historical and Chronological description of the two stones, which by means of a new pavement were found in the principal square of the city of Mexico, in the 1790—The system of the Indian Calendar is explained, the method that they had of dividing time, and the use they made of it to equalize the civil year, which they used, or were regulated by, with the Solar tropical year: very necessary information to the perfect understanding of the second stone. To which are added other curious and instructive facts respecting the Mythology, Astronomy, rites and ceremonies of the Mexicans whilst they were heathens—By Don Antonio de León y Gama—Mexico. At the Printing Office of Don Felipe de Zuñiga y Ontiveros.

A Historical and Chronological Description of the Two Stones, Which Were Found in the Principal Square of the City of Mexico

Preliminary Discourse I have always been of opinion that in the principal square of this City, and in the quarter, or division of Santiago Tlatelolco, there would be found many precious Monuments of Mexican antiquity; because the first, containing a great part of the largest temple of Mexico, which was composed of 78 buildings, such as smaller temples, Chapels and dwellings for the Priests and Ministers; where were kept so many false Gods, which, in their blind idolatry they adored (These, as is certain, were of hard stone, and of excessive size and weight; and for this reason difficult to transport to other places); if not many other instruments, with which they carried on their arts and trades: Also Historical and Chronological Documents, or information, engraved on great tables of stone, by those same Priests, who had the charge of preserving the memory of the feats, or actions of their ancestors; Of the arrangement of time; of the festivals which they celebrated, and of everything else which conduced to their political and religious government.—And the second Place, the plaza of Tlatelolco, having been the last spot which the Indians retired to; and where they maintained themselves until the taking of the City. It is presumable that they carried there with them all their Household Gods, or light Idols; which they made of all kinds of materials (even of the most precious, according to the circumstances of the proprietors) and kept in their own houses, as well as all the jewels and treasures they possessed. Also those which served to adorn the said idols; and all the riches that the Spaniards lost on the night they fled fugitively from Mexico; and which they could never recover; although with much anxiety and diligence, they caused the whole Lake to be searched where the Indians said they had thrown them. It is then probable that all these, or the greatest part of them, are under the ground of Tlatelolco. If excavations were made, as has been done in Italy, to search for statues and fragments, which remain as monuments of ancient Rome; and as they are now doing in Spain, at the town of Rielves, three leagues from Toledo, where they have discovered various ancient Pavements.—How many Historical monuments would they not meet with of Indian antiquity? How many books and paintings hidden by these Priests of the Idols, and chiefly the *teoamoxtli,* in which were written with their proper character, their Origin, the increase of their Nation, from the time that they left Aztlan, to come to inhabit the land of Anahuac: The Rites and Ceremonies of their Religion; the fundamental principles of their Chronology and Astronomy, etc.? And how many treasures would be discovered?

We are indebted to Chance for light to discover what the Indians were in the time of their heathenism. It has given us two precious Monuments, which demonstrate their cultivation and instruction in the Sciences and arts. The one last found ought to be considered as a particular Prize, being an original and instructive document, which sets forth great part of the History of the Chronology and the exact method which the Mexicans had to measure time for the observance of their feasts,[32] and for their political government; the more especially, as the best of their Histories have perished in the flames, on account of the signification of the paintings being unknown.[33]—A lamentable loss; which has been felt by the Men of taste [*hombres de buen gusto*], who have dedicated themselves to the study of the Ancient literature of these Nations.

The Government having given orders to level and pave the great square, and to form works to conduct the waters by subterranean canals; they met, whilst digging for this purpose, at a small depth from the surface of the Earth, with a curiously worked statue of hard stone, and of an extraordinary size, which represented one of the Idols worshipped by the Indians whilst they were heathens [fig. 1a–e]. Few months had passed when they found another stone, much larger than the first, at but a small distance from it and at so little a depth that it almost appeared at the surface. The superior part was not at all carved; but on the portion that was sunk into the earth, various figures were seen [fig. 1f; figs. 2, 3]. Both stones being taken up, the first was carried to the Royal University; and the second remained where it was found for some time; but in its natural vertical situation, in which position, all the sculpture could be examined with facility. As soon as I saw [the *Aztec Calendar Stone*], I was filled with joy at having found in it a faithful testimony, which confirmed what I, after so much labor and study, had written on the system of the Mexican Calendars, against the false hypotheses, with which the writers of Indian History have disfigured and confounded them; pretending to explain them; as I demonstrate in my Indian Chronology: and I shall show in this paper their most palpable errors.[34]

As I had for a long time, collected Indian manuscripts and paintings in the Mexican tongue, as well as the works of Spanish authors, it was easy for me to comprehend the signification of most of the ornaments and figures engraved on this second stone, adjusting every day, by means of it the representations, or ideas which are found so confused, diffused, and mutilated in the writings of the Indians themselves; and nowise noticed by the Spanish authors. And with much labor I attained knowledge of other figures, of which, I before, knew nothing. Nevertheless, there remain some of its figures whose Hieroglyphics conceal many allegorical significations, yet to be interpreted.

Being exposed to the Public, there was no preventing rustic and childish people from injuring several of its figures with stones and other instruments, this in addition to what it suffered in raising it. Before they should do it more damage, or its destiny be changed; which was contemplated; I caused an exact copy of it to be drawn in my presence; to keep it in my power, as an original monument of antiquity; and I only made some notes of the signification of its ornaments. But several curious persons having obtained knowledge of what I had done, they pressed me to publish an explanation of it. And I knowing that if I failed to publish and not to give the print to the public (if by any accident it should be demolished, or the contemplated disposal of it, take place, the engraved, or sculptured work would be lost, and no copy or notice would remain of what so beautiful a monument contained) the ancient History of Mexico would suffer the like misfortune which has attended it for so many years. I determined to publish the description of both stones, in order to throw some light on ancient literature, so much encouraged in other countries; and which, our Catholic Monarch Charles III (who enjoys happiness), being King of Naples, promoted in the celebrated Museum, which, at an immense expense, he founded at Portici, from the excavations he commanded to be made in discovery of the ancient cities of Herculaneum and Pompeii; buried for so many ages under the ashes, stones and lava thrown out by the eruptions of Vesuvius.

Moreover I was induced to make known to the literary world a part of the great knowledge which the Indians of America possessed in the arts and sciences whilst heathens; that it may be shown how falsely they have been calumnied as irrational or foolish by our enemies.... From this narration and from the figures here given will be shown or manifested the excellence of the artificers who made the originals, who, not having any knowledge of iron or steel, of tempered chisels and steeled points, engraved or cut with such perfection the hard stone statues which represent their idols and executed other works of architecture.

On the second stone are depicted various parts of the mathematical sciences with which they were perfectly acquainted. Its bulk and weight give us an idea of their knowledge of mechanics and machinery, without whose fundamental principles they never would have been able to cut it and convey it from the quarry, to the spot where it was placed. By the perfection with which the circles are formed, by the parallels that are preserved amongst them, by the exact division of their parts, by the direction of the right lines to the center, and by other circumstances not found amongst persons who are ignorant of geometry; are known the clear lights possessed by the Mexicans on this science. Of astronomy and chronology, the use that they made of this stone, (which we are going to explain) will show us how familiar they were with the observations of the Sun and stars for the division of time; and the distribution of it into periods, which had a certain analogy with the movements of the Moon; from which they formed a lunar-solar year that served them to regulate their festivals to certain determined days, which could not vary from the time prefixed for its rites more than 13 days in the long space of 52 years, at the end of which they reformed their civil year.[35]

The variety of opinions expressed by our Spanish historians respecting the magnitude and the matter of which the Indians made the statues of their false gods and the prejudices of the first ministers who preached the Holy Gospel to them, who supposed that every thing they saw engraved on stone, or painted on cloth or paper, were objects of their idolatry, occasioned the confusion which overwhelmed them, without being able to discover which were the figures that pertained solely to the worship of their gods, and those which related to their history. The latter were commonly engraved or sculptured on great tables of stone. On the portals of the palaces of their great men, the feats of their forefathers were emblazoned: there was no city or village that had not the year of its foundation cut on the stones of its walls or on the rocks of its hills; also the origin of its name; who were its founders, and their increase during their residence; [all] represented by symbols and characters, which were only understood by the Indians themselves, without whose interpretation it was not easy for the Spaniards to comprehend them. As they were ignorant of what such figures signified, they destroyed many monuments that pertained to history, thinking that they were objects of their superstitious rites. Some of the Indians, [although] fearful of being calumnied as apostates, returned to idolatry and hid as many of them as they could. Others maliciously concealed their true significance, and filled not only the heads of the Spaniards with fables and nonsense, but even those of their own nation who wished to become acquainted with them, as is set forth by D. Fernando de Alva Ixtlilxochitl at the end of the *Sumaria relación de todas las cosas que han sucedido en la Nueva España.*

This they did with respect to their historical and political events; but they kept a profound silence on whatever pertained to the things of their ancient religion. There are none of them who make any particular mention of all their gods in their writing, of the forms in which they painted them; of their diverse supposed attributes; of their transformations; of the titles by which they distinguished them; and of the mode of worship which they used. Although now and then some idea was given of it and some curates and priests knew much, yet so little, and so obscure was what was left in writing on this subject that a perfect conception of their mythology could not be formed from it. Notwithstanding, by combining some manuscripts of anonymous authors with their ancient paintings anterior to the conquest; along with what the monks and curates afterwards published about them, much may be known, although with considerable labor. In this manner I have obtained certain facts of their history, which have been so much misrepresented in the printed works of authors. The facts exposed on the two monuments, whose description we are about to give, have the good fortune, in great part, to be corroborated by the express relations and authority of persons of the most distinguished character; as well literary, as in respect to their circumstances; greater credit being due to them on account of their considerable antiquity (It is no small thing, in so obscure a subject as the history of the Indians, to find printed authorities, which confirm knowledge obtained with so much labor.)[36] The manuscript relations in Nahuatl, which I have also made use of, are the most faithful and true, as one does not meet with the contradictions in them that are found in others, as well in the substance, in the mode of describing the facts; for which they have always held due rank amongst the enlightened Spaniards who have possessed them.[37]

From these several writings, and from the ancient paintings, I have deduced the signification of the two stones; but to understand them, it is necessary to know all that pertains to the division which the Mexicans made of time and of their calendars and *tonalamatl,* principally to be able completely to comprehend the contents of the second stone. We shall divide the explanation into four parts. The first will contain a general idea of the method which was observed in distributing time into permanent [i.e., regular, *constante*] periods of cycles, years, months, and days; and into their aliquot [fractional] parts; with what pertains to their weeks, or rather *trecenas,*[38] of which their *tonalamatl* was composed, in which the first of the two stones that were found, had place. The second part will be an explanation of the first. In the third will be found minutely the account, by which they regulated the celebration of their feasts, their commerce; and for other uses, civil and political, dependent on the movements of the Sun and Moon.

The true system of their calendars will be established; and the other systems invested by certain authors, being entirely opposed to what is proved from the writings of the Indians themselves, and the nature, and invariable method which they observed in all things relative to their government; as erroneous and absurd. Their two kinds of calendars will be made to agree with each other, and with ours. The beginning of their year will be ascertained, with other particular information touching their chronology. And finally, the fourth part will contain as exact explanation of the works and figures contained on the second stone; and of the principal uses which the

Mexicans made of them. But having, since the conclusion of this paper (or discourse), been made acquainted with other facts and circumstances which will more amply satisfy the public curiosity; and that they may not be deprived of them, it has seemed convenient to insert them in the following supplement.

Addendum

When it was announced in the *Gazeta de México* of Tuesday the 16th of August in this year 1791 that this work was then finished, inviting curious persons to subscribe for it; I was ignorant of the steps that were taken by his Excellency the Lord Viceroy, Count of Revilla Gigedo; and by the Lord Corregidor Intendant, Col. D. Bernardo Bonavia y Zapata, conducive to the perpetual preservation of these statues, and for the permanency of their fame; as precious monuments, manifesting the lights which illuminated the Indian nation in times anterior to their conquest; of which they had taken no care in those immediately posterior to it; it being then proper to hide every thing from the Indians which might enable them to call their past idolatries to mind; by which means the ancient history of this nation has remained, if not totally, at least in greater part wanting in original documents, which should prove it to have been one of the best civilized and politic of the New World, and have defended it from the calumnies with which foreign nations have always branded it. The same day that the notice was published, the Lord Corregidor sent for me, and impelled by his great benignity, not only communicated to me all the precautions which had been taken, promoted by the zeal, anxiety [i.e., diligence, *solicitud*], and efficacy with which he proceeds in those cases under his charge; but also delivered to me the juridical researches [i.e., official reports, *diligencias jurídicas*] which were made respecting the discovery of the stones, that from them the public might be informed of the days, hours, and places in which they were found. His inclination for ancient literature, and the desire of illustrating the history of Mexico is sufficiently shown by the Official Note, by which he informed his Excellency, the Lord Viceroy, of this discovery, pointing out to him the means proper to be taken, in his opinion, to perpetuate, and keep the first statue in safety; which were approved by His Excellency in the same words expressed in the aforesaid note which read thus:

> Excellent Lord—In the cavities that [they] are making in the square of the Palace, for the construction of works; has been found, as is known, a figure of stone of considerable size, which shows marks of being anterior to the conquest. I consider it worthy of being preserved, for its antiquity, on account of the scarcity of monuments of those times; and for as much as it may be able to contribute to illustrate them. Persuaded that for this end it cannot be put in better hands than in those of the Royal and Pontifical University, it appears to me proper to place it there; not doubting that they will admit it with pleasure. I will take it upon myself, if Your Excellency approves of it, to have it measured, weighed, sketched and engraved, that it may be published with the information which the said body or corps may have or obtain, respecting its origin. God preserve Your Excellency many years. Mexico, 5th of September of 1790.

His Excellency, the Lord Viceroy, replied to the above note on the following day, being the sixth, showing his approbation, as denoted by these expressions:

> I heartily agree that the stone figure found in the excavations made in the square of this Palace be carried to the Royal and Pontifical University, and that it may be placed in such part of the edifice, as may be thought most proper; Your Excellency [León y Gama has V.S., "Your

Lordship"], taking care, as you have mentioned to me, to have it measured, weighed, sketched and engraved, that the same may be made public, together with the information which that illustrious corps may have or obtain respecting its origin.

Afterwards the lord Rector solicited the same thing; and His Excellency by a letter of the 22nd of the said month requested the Lord Intendant that he would communicate the authentic information of the discovery of the stone to the said Lord Rector, which was done by the following note.

> In compliance with the request of His Excellency the Lord Viceroy, made known to me by his note of the 22nd of last month I communicate to Your Lordship the testimony which authenticates the discovery of the stone figure, found in the excavation made in the great plaza, in appearance of heathen workmanship, that Your Lordship may take measures for its removal to the Royal University, to the end that it may be preserved; and that, with the assistance of the documents in the library, a dissertation may be written on it; remaining for me, when it shall be there, to have it weighed, measured, and engraved, that at the same time the public may have knowledge of the print, its weight and dimensions. God keep you, etc. Mexico the 29th of October 1790.

In consequence of this note it was carried to the Royal University, where it can be found today, in one of the corners of its atrium. But the taking of the dimensions, weight, sketching and engraving which the Lord Intendant undertook to have done, have not hitherto been performed, on account of the many and important affairs, which first claim his attention; and perhaps a knowledge of my taking the trouble to give a description of it to the public, might have suspended his intentions.

It is stated in the judicial [i.e., official] documents, that on the 13th day of August in the year 1790, a memorable date, being the same on which possession of the city was taken for the King of Spain, in the year 1521 (although two of the witnesses equivocally say that it was the 14th). In digging for the construction of a subterranean aqueduct in masonry, there was found close to the shops that are called the Lord St. Joseph's, at the distance of five yards (varas) north of the canal [acequia]; and 37 yards west, from the Royal Palace; the statue of stone, whose head was at the depth of a yard and one third; and the other extremity, or foot, at a little less than a yard. That on the 4th of September, at midnight, it was suspended and placed in a vertical posture, by means of a tackle and double pulleys; and that at the same hour of the night of the 25th, it was taken from that place and put in front of the second door of the Royal Palace; from whence it was afterwards carried to the Royal University.

But little time had passed from the moving of this stone, when on account of the new pavement, they were lowering the ancient pavement (piso) of the square or place. On the 17th December in the same year the rear face of the second stone was discovered at the depth of only half a yard, and at a distance of 80 yards west from the aforementioned second door of the Royal Palace, and 37 to the northward of the colonnade of flowers, according to the note which was sent by one of the chief masters of this very noble city, D. Joseph Damian Ortiz, to the Lord Intendant, dated 12th January 1791, thereby communicating to him the information of this discovery. This stone, which is the largest, the most particular and instructive, was requested his Excellency the Lord Viceroy, by the gentlemen D. Joseph Uribe, Doctor and Master, Penitentiary Canon, and Prebendary, and Doctor D. John Joseph Gamboa, Commissary of the building of the holy Cathedral Church, to be put in a public place, where it might be preserved as an invaluable monument of Indian antiquity and although this demand was not made in writing, or in any other juridical manner, nor any decree, or donation so made of it; it was delivered to them by the verbal order of His Excellency; as I have been informed by the Lord Corregidor Intendant.

But not only these two stones were found in the part of the great square that has been already paved; another ancient monument has been discovered, which not having been made public, as the others were, I knew nothing of it, until the Lord Intendant himself communicated information of it to me; giving orders to the Lieutenant Colonel of Engineers D. Michael Costanzo, that he should describe the contents of it to me; who did so, as will be seen by his letter hereafter. This new discovery confirms what I before remarked of the quantity of antiques that might be found in this great square or place; since, if in so small a place, and at so short a depth, three such valuable monuments of remote Indian antiquity have been met with; we have reason to believe that in the part that is yet unpaved, and at greater depths, others would be discovered which might give new light to their history. The last discovery was a sepulcher which contained the bones of an unknown animal; notwithstanding the head retained its teeth; and canine teeth, characters by which the kinds of quadrupeds are distinguished. With the animal were found various earthen pots, and other things of earthenware, neatly made; some large metal bells, and other like things. I was not able to get a sight of these, as they were in the possession of Capt. D. Antonio Pineda, who is at present at the city of Guanajuato; for this reason, I cannot undertake to say what they signify, only from inferences drawn from the following information given to me by the aforesaid Lieutenant Colonel of Engineers.

A laborer named Juan de Dios Morales, found in the month of January of this year 1791, almost in the middle of the new square, constructed in front of the Royal Palace, surrounded with pillars and chains, a sepulcher two yards long, and a little less than one yard wide, formed of square cut stones, of a kind called tezontle,[39] very handsomely worked. In the interior part, which was filled with very fine white sand, was found the entire skeleton of an unknown animal with various articles of earthen ware, like those of Quauhtitlan, of very handsome workmanship, which contained some bells of cast copper, of the form of pears; and other baubles of the same metal. Some infer from the long and strong canine teeth, which protrude from both jaws, that the animal was a wolf (or fox) ("coyote") of extraordinary size; but I do not know if this conjecture will be verified.

Combining the discovery of this animal, placed in a sepulcher so well made, situated within the bounds of the great temple, with bells, baubles, etc., etc., which were found interred with it, with what is related by Dr. Hernández and the Father Torquemada, describing the temples, chapels, and other parts which were contained within the great temple of Mexico, it is inferred that this animal was one of the gods that the Mexicans adored under the name of "Chantico," which according to the said Torquemada, signifies a Wolf's Head.[40] Having asked of the aforesaid Lieutenant Colonel if it appeared to him to have been a wolf, he replied that the make and arrangement of the canine teeth resembled those of that animal. We know that amongst the multitudes of ridiculous gods which the Mexicans worshipped, there were some animals, like the jaguar, by the name of Tlatocaocelotl; the eagle with insignias of the turkey cock, adorned with a rich plumage called Quetzalhuexôloquauhtli; the serpent, or Cihuacòhuatl [Cihuacoatl], and others. This god Wolf had a particular temple within the square of the great temple of Mexico, by the name of Tetlanman: in it was kept a festival, with sacrifices of captives, when the sign of Cexocitl

[Ce Xochitl] governed. He had for a companion a goddess called Cohuaxòlotl [Cohuaxolotl], according to Torquemada,[41] and Quaxolotl, according to Dr. Hernández; to whose honor also the same festival was kept. Various priests were allotted for the service and worship of this god Chantico. These had a separate abode in the form of a convent, which was called Tetlacmancalmecac. All of this is asserted by the aforenamed authors, although Hernández equivocally calls Chantico a goddess.[42] From this it cannot be doubted that the skeleton which was found, is of that animal, to whom, from some particular circumstance of which we are ignorant, they paid adoration, and placed it amongst the number of their gods. . . .

SECTION IV

Description of the Second Stone, Which Was Found in the Square of Mexico

47. Amongst the many false gods adored by the blindly idolatrous Indians, the sun was the principal one, to whom not only the Mexicans paid continual worship, but it was paid also by all the kingdoms and civilized provinces of both Americas. The people of this New Spain held it in such veneration that they were not satisfied with adoring it when it was visible, most splendid, beautiful and clear; and when they more immediately felt its effects in the burning rays of summer, and in the temperate and benign beams of winter. But they acknowledged it as the source of light, even amidst the shades of night; and when the moon, by her interposition, threw her shade upon the earth, veiling his fires. In all his movements, in all periods of the year, in every hour of the day; in his humiliation or eclipses; they worshipped him, and offered particular sacrifices, and burnt offerings to him. Its image (which, as Dr. Hernández says,[43] they made in a human form, like our painters and sculptors), had a particular temple, named Quauhxicalco, within the boundary of the great temple [Templo Mayor], besides the celebrated, and beautifully constructed one, which they built for him on an elevated mountain in Teotihuacan; of whose size and elegance, Torquemada, Boturini, and others, make mention. They kept several festivals for him during the year at all which, the king and nobility were present. The king retired to a beautiful edifice called, according to Father Torquemada (Torquemada 1723, 2:148), Hueyquauhxicalco, and according to Dr. Hernández, Quauhxico,[44] and remained in it the time of four days, fasting and doing other penance, in honor of the sun, to whom they sacrificed many captives, and among them four who were the principals; two of whom they called *Chachame,* which, according to Torquemada, signifies "dunces," and the other two represented the images of the sun and moon. This was one of the principal and solemn festivals which they kept to the sun, and was called Netonatiuhqualo, that is, the sun eclipsed, literally, "the unhappy sun eaten"; and this festival was kept every 200 or 300 days. . . .

58. They kept another particular festival to him, in the winter solstice, on the day when he reached the Tropic of Capricorn, although Father Torquemada attributes it to the gods of the water named Tlaloque. But this gentleman contradicts himself there, since he sets down that it was celebrated when the sun arrived, *at the height of its course* (these are his words), *or career, that, as everybody knows, at the 21st of this* (he speaks of the month of December) *he finishes his course, and turns to retrace his steps.*[45] They kept also another great festival for him, which lasted forty days, in the temple dedicated to Iztaccinteotl, or the god of the white maize grains (or harvests); in which they sacrificed leprous persons and those infected with contagious diseases whom, Torquemada says, they slew at the time, in which, they kept Lent to the sun.[46] But the greatest of all was that which they kept at the time that the sign Nahui Ollin Tonatiuh, governed by the sun in his

four movements,[47] accompanied by the galaxy [Milky Way], which they called Citlalinycue, or Citlalcueye, and which took place in the sixteenth *trecena*. Torquemada makes no mention of this festival; neither of the one kept on the day so called, which was the fourth of the second *trecena*. But the Indian historians and the doctor Hernández, who conversed with old men of his time, and who was acquainted with the writings which the first priests left who came to Mexico after the Conquest, speak of them, including a fragment written in the Castilian language; of which, I am of opinion, Cristóbal del Castillo was the author. For this reason, I say in the note of No. 16, the following is expressed:

> The fourth of this sign (he speaks of the second *trecena,* which begins with Ce Ocelotl) is called Ollin. They say that it was the sign of the sun. And the great men held it in much account, because they had it for their sign, and killed quails, and illuminated, and put incense before the statue of the sun, and dressed it with plumes, which they called Quetzaltonameyotl; and at noon they killed captives; and all of them, little and big [young and old], and the women, did penance, and cut their ears, and drew blood in honor of the sun, etc.

59. This statue, before which they performed the sacrifices on the day Nahui Ollin, bears the same image which is seen sculptured on the stone which we are going to describe. It is a monument which contains a great part of the Mexican calendars, as in it are pointed out several of the principal festivals kept by the people of that nation, and shows exactly the time of the year in which they ought to be celebrated. It was a monument which demonstrated the various movements of the sun in declination, in the period of 260 days of the lunar year; from the time he [the sun] left the equinoctial line, to go to the Tropic of Cancer, until his return to the said line. That is, in the interval of time, which the sun spent from the vernal to the autumnal equinox. This points to the four periods of the year, in which the most sensible effect of his rays was observed at the latitude of Mexico, being then nearest to us, until his twice coming to dart his rays vertically upon us. This stone also served as a sundial, by which the priests daily knew the hours in which they ought to perform their ceremonies and sacrifices. This knowledge was obtained by means of gnomons, or hands, which they fixed upon it, as we shall see hereafter. So that the half of the ecliptic, or the proper movement of the sun from west to east, according to the order of the signs, from the first point of Aries, to the first of Libra, was comprised in this stone, as was also his diurnal motion from east to west, from his rising to his setting. By this account this stone ought to be considered a valuable monument of Mexican antiquity, for astronomical, and chronological purposes and for sundialing—all without mentioning the other uses made of it by the heathen priests in their judicial astrology.

60. The figure of this stone must originally have been a parallelepiped rectangle, which is sufficiently evident (although some considerable pieces are wanting, and in other places it is much injured) from the angles which are preserved. Those which show the remaining extremities are least injured, as is seen in Figures 2 and 3. The principal superficie, and its corresponding one formed perfect squares, which measured on each side, four Castilian yards and a half; its thickness on the side where it appeared the greatest was one yard. On the principal plane arose a portion of a cylinder, whose center deviated towards the right, from the middle of the square, or the point where the diagonals intersected, almost half a yard; an equal quantity remains on the plane on the left; as is seen in the figure. The diameter of the circle, or portion of the cylinder, is a little more than four yards (Spanish) and its circumference almost reaches to the side of the square on the right hand, which shows that this stone was not solitary, but that there was another like it, which was joined to it at that part, and which perhaps may be at no great distance from the spot where this was found. The other Mexican calendars which are comprehended in the time which the sun takes in traveling with its movement in declination the other half of the ecliptic, going from the equinoctial line, to the Tropic of Capricorn, until it returns again to the said line; ought to be found represented on it [the mate to the Aztec Calendar Stone]. In the discovery of this single stone, the same is observed with respect to the Mexican calendars as was observed in respect of the Romans in the invention of only the six books of Ovid, which contain the half of the year. The manner in which this stone must have been placed, was upon a horizontal plane, elevated vertically, looking to the south, and with a perfect direction east and west.

61. The side of the circular projection, or portion of the cylinder, is about one-third of a yard in height, and is sculptured as is seen in figure 1f; which workmanship [i.e., the decoration on the sides] serves only as an ornament, and signifies nothing. But the figures which are within its circumference, sculptured in bas relief, are those which demand the full explanation we are about to give. And because the many figures and works contained in figure 2 would prevent the letters and numbers which ought to be put for references from being clearly seen, I have added figure 3, only in outlines, that the minute parts of some figures may the more easily be seen without confusion, where there is scarcely room for numbers. Within the inner circle is seen the image of the sun in the form in which the Indians were accustomed to represent him; his principal rays are the eight, pointed out by the letter R, of which four are seated entirely on the little houses,[48] [every fifth of which contains the numerical characters; the other four remain covered in part by the said houses (boxes)]. The letter L marks the other eight kinds of radii; or rays, with which they were accustomed to adorn his image, as appear in those found in the *tonalamatl*. Certain small bows (or arches) drawn uniformly, and like to those with which the radii terminate, are found all round the circumference which the little houses [boxes] of the numbers occupy, and which express the lights that surround it. To this image are joined the four squares A, B, C, D, which with the circular figures E, F, of the sides; the triangle I of the superior part, and the portion H of the inferior, form the complete figure I, B, E, C, H, D, F, A, with which the Indians expressed the symbols of hieroglyphic of the sun's movement; to which, if we join the numerical characters a, b, c, d,[49] in the form in which they were accustomed to make them (which, as has been said, was in small circles somewhat swelled), all the figure represents the sign Nahui Ollin Tonatiuh. Within each of the four squares, or parallelograms, one of the symbols of the days is respectively represented, marked also with the number four. That which is contained in the square A is the head of a jaguar, which with its numerical character four, represents the day Nahui Ocelotl. In the Square B is found the hieroglyphic of the air or wind, dedicated to the god Quetzalcoatl, whom they painted in the same manner, as was the door, or entrance into his temple; which, according to Torquemada,[50] was in the figure of a serpent's mouth; and with the number four, denoted the day Nahui Ehecatl. In square C, the day Nahui Quiahuitl, with the same number four, is represented. This symbol they applied to Tlaloc, whom they feigned to be the god of the rains. And finally in the square D is demonstrated the day 4 Water, Nahui Atl. The principal orb, the sun, is here reduced to the sign and day of the second *trecena* of the *tonalamatl*, to which the number 4 corresponds, and symbol of the solar movement, that is, to the day Nahui Ollin. The other planets and signs of the four squares belong to the days of the other *trecenas*, in which the number four, accords to them respectively.

62. This figure, thus represented, had its origin in the ridiculous fables, which the Mexicans related of the sun; and they preserved the memory of them in the symbols Nahui Ollin, as is set forth in an anonymous history in the Mexican tongue, which is found at the end of one, copied by D. Fernando de Alva Ixtlilxochitl, and is cited by Boturini in Section 8, no. 13, of his Museum (1746, pt. 2:17–18). They believed that the sun had died four times, or that there had been four suns which had come to an end in so many times, or ages; and that the sun which gave them their light, was the fifth. They counted 676 years for the first age, or duration of the first sun; at the end of which, in a year called Ce Acatl, the sun being in the sign Nahui Ocelotl; the men were destroyed, grain and other provisions failing them; they died, and were eaten by the tigers, or Tequanes, which were ferocious animals; the first sun being destroyed with them; which destruction lasted the time of 13 years. They feigned that the second age, and end of the second sun took place whilst he was in the sign Nahui Ehecatl, in which furious winds tore up the trees by the roots, demolished houses, and swept away the men; of which, some remained, and were converted into monkeys; and that the second destruction happened in the year Ce Tecpatl, 364 years from the first, and on the said day Nahui Ehecatl. In another year, also named Ce Tecpatl, 312 more having passed since the second destruction; they say that the third destruction, and end of the third sun took place in the sign Nahui Quiahuitl, in which they were destroyed by fire and converted into birds. Finally, the fourth time, in which they feigned the sun to have disappeared, was by the deluge, in which the men perished, being overwhelmed by the waves and whom they supposed were converted into fishes of the sea. And this catastrophe followed in fifty-two years from the third, in a year named Ce Calli; and in the day of the sign Nahui Atl. After these fictions, they invented the fable of the gods who assisted at the creation of the fifth sun, and of the moon, with the ridiculous expressions which Torquemada, Boturini, Clavigero, and others relate; who tell the fable of the Syphilitic One [Buboso], who threw himself into the fire, to be converted into a sun.[51]

63. Cipactonal and his wife Oxomoco, who were the inventors of the *tonalamatl,* exceedingly superstitious, and judicial astrologers, in memory of these four circumstances, or destructions of the sun, placed it in the *tonalamatl* itself, giving it place and dominion in one of the *trecenas,* with its proper title Nahui Ollin, besides the place and government which they attributed to it in the 4th day of the second *trecena,* as a celestial diurnal sign, as has before been said (No. 58); and the dominion, that, as the sun itself, and without any attribute, they gave him in every day of another *trecena.* He holds a place three times as a planet in the *tonalamatl,* one time as Sol, in the eleventh *trecena,* all of which they supposed him to govern, in company with Tlatocaocelotl and Tlatocaxolotl, or with Tepoztecatl, according to Castillo. Two other times, with relation to his movements, in the fourteenth and sixteenth, he governed with the title of Ollin Tonatuih, accompanied by Citlalinycue, or Citlalcueye, which is the Milky Way, another of the celestial signs. And as the diurnal sign, it is found only once in the 260 days, which the *tonalamatl* contains, reduced to the symbol and character Nahui Ollin; he also has a place, two other times as a celestial sign, but with other numerical characters; as may be seen in the space of the 260 first days of the calendar, which is given in No. 43 [not reproduced here].

64. The circular figures of the letters E, F, which unite the four squares, contain within a kind of claws which denote or have relation to the aforesaid inventors of the *tonalamatl,* Cipactonal and Oxomoco; whom they painted in it, like ugly faces, in the form of eagles or owls; as appears in Boturini Section 30, no. 2, of the Catalog of his Museum (1746, pt. 2:70–71)....

65. The angle I points out the first division of the 20 days of the month that are dedicated to the sun; this is the beginning, whence they should commence to count in inverse order, or from the right hand, to the left, (which is the method always observed by the Indians in their paintings; the Hebrew style, in the writing of their characters), as is shown in the series of the numbers 1, 2, 3, etc., in which No. 1 denotes the first symbol of the year, which is Cipactli,[52] a sign represented differently in the calendars; although all agreed that that it was a kind of fish, with a protuberance in front in the form of a sword; on which account, Torquemada and others call it a swordfish. But the figure which is found on the stone is as it ought to be. The symbol of No. 2 is Ehecatl, second in the order of the days of the month, which as has been said was the symbol of Quetzalcoatl; and they represented him in the same form and figure, which the door or entrance of his temple had. No. 3 shows the figure with which they designated House, Calli, third symbol of the days of the month. It also was one of the four with which they denoted the years of the cycle. The fourth is a Lizard, Cuetzpallin; the 5th a Snake, Coatl; the 6th represents Death, Miquiztli, sixth symbol of the days of the month. The 7th is a deer's head, Mazatl; The 8th, a rabbit's head, Tochtli, which was also one of the hieroglyphics of the year. The 9th, Water, Atl, is like to that of the square D; the 10th is a kind of dog, Itzcuintli;[53] the 11th, a monkey's head, Ozomatli. The 12th, a twisted herb, is Malinalli, which they designed in the form that is represented with allusion to one of their gods, whom they worshipped under the name of Macuilmalinalli. The 13th is the Reed, Acatl, which was also one of the symbols of the year. The number 14 is a tiger's head, Ocelotl, like that of square A. The 15th is the head of an Eagle, Quauhtli; the 16th, another head of a bird called Cozcaquauhtli. The 17th, the movement of the sun, Ollin Tonatiuh, drawn in the same form as it is, in the interior circle. In the *tonalamatl,* and in the histories where they point it out as a day on which some events took place, they draw it without the triangle, whence it is inferred that this triangle in the principal figure serves to denote the beginning of the account of the days of the month and first symbol of the year. The 18th, Tecpatl, Flint, was a symbol of the year and a celestial sign, which governed last *trecena* of the *tonalamatl.* The number 19 is Quiahuitl, Rain, represented with the device attributed to Tlaloc, another of their principal gods, whose figure is like to that of the square C. And finally the number 20 denotes a flower, Xochitl, the last symbol of the days of the month. But none of these figures have numerical coefficients. On the circumference which surrounds them are found the whole 260, which correspond to the twenty *trecenas* of the second calendar, or account of the moon; 200 of them in the forty houses [boxes] which are seen in the four portions of the circle marked mn, op, gr, and st., each one of them containing five numerical characters;[54] and the remaining 60 in the twelve houses [boxes] which are covered by the four principal rays; three of these being covered by each ray.

66. The vertical ray which is seated over the first and last symbol of the days of the month; that is, over Cipactli and Xochitl; terminates in the zone, or portion of the superior circle, pointing to the house [box] T, in which is seen the symbol Reed, with 13 little circles, which denote an equal number; not of the days of the month; but of the years of the cycle. Which is to say, that the state of the heavens, or movement of the sun represented on the stone, is not applicable to the whole fifty-two years; the declination of the sun varying in them; because of the deficiency of one day, which they lose in each quadrennium; as has been said before; and it only reaches to the middle of the said cycle, and year Matlactli Omey Acatl, 13 Reed;[55] where the second Indiction terminates;[56] in which the arrival of the sun at equinox, at the solstitial points, at the meridian, or zenith of the city; in the two seasons of the year in which he passes by it, on the days which are pointed out by the stone; is shown with sufficient correctness, and consequently the fixed time of celebrating their principal festivals; as we shall see hereafter. The triangles which are one each side of the said house [box] T, serve also as indexes which equally make known the year of 13 Reed; which is the middle of the cycle, or the 26th; in which almost six days and a half were already omitted; and the beginning if that year retarded as much.

67. The remainder of the zone, of both parts, represents the Milky Way, or that assemblage of small stars which forms a white belt in the heavens, which is vulgarly called the Camino de Santiago, and which the Indians know by the name of Citlalinycue; a celestial sign, to which they gave dominion in the 16th *trecena* of the *tonalamatl;* accompanied by Ollin Tonatiuh; where they are seen drawn nearly alike. The two heads with their ornaments alike, which are on the inferior part of the circle designated by the letter O, and which divide it at that part; represent the Lord of the Night, named Yohautecuhtli; whom they imagined divided the nocturnal government, and distributed it among the *acompañados* [patron deities] of the days, giving to each one, what belonged to him, from midnight (for this division which the two faces form, signifies). He was the god whom sorcerers, thieves, and other malefactors, who covered themselves with the black veil of night whilst committing their enormities, frequently invoked. The judicial astrologers supposed it had particular pre-eminence of the other signs which they used for their heathen prognostics. They kept a festival to him very splendid, with sacrifice of human blood, on the night of the day, which they celebrated in honor of the sun, namely Nahui Ollin; as is related by Dr. Hernández;[57] and on the evening of every day they saluted him, and the priests of the temple of the sun, burnt incense.

68. I am ignorant of what the hieroglyphics are, which are seen all round the circumference between the rays and nubeculae (*ráfagas*)[58] of the sun; which are distinguished by the letter V. Although they appear to me to be symbols of the clouds, which I have never seen drawn in the ancient paintings of the Indians; but I know that they worshipped them also, as some of their gods, calling them Ahuaque; and supposed them inseparable companions of Tlaloc. D. Pedro Ponze, who was curate at Tezompahuacan, in a small manuscript treatise on the heathen customs, says, that they remained among the Indians even to his time:[59] "They worshipped the clouds, and called them Ahuaque, and named the god who governed them Tlaloc; and of the mountains where the clouds are begotten, they say Tlalloque-Tlamacazque.... They also attribute the diseases of children to the winds and clouds, and they say *qualani in ehecame, qualani in ahuaque,* 'and they blow on the winds, conjuring them.'" From whence it also appears, that the uniform figures marked with the letter e, which are seen below the foregoing, are the mountains where the clouds are found, or begotten; being almost like those with which they symbolized them. This is conformable to what Father Torquemada says:[60] "They also believed that all the eminent mountains and high chains of hills partook in this condition or state of divinity; on which account, they imagined that in each of those places there was a lesser god than Tlaloc, and subject to him, by whose command he made clouds to be formed, which dissolved in water on those provinces that were protected by that place and mountain." They also worshipped fog as a god, and considered it as a celestial constellation which governed in one of the *trecenas* of the *tonalamatl,* by the name of Ahuilteotl. I am equally ignorant of what the two figures marked ff mean, which are close by Yohautecuhtli, on both sides.[61]

69. On sides of the triangle I, two figures are seen designated by the letters G and K; that of the letter G, which has the number 1 close to it, is a flint, like to the one at No. 18 of the circle of the days; and signifies the day Tecpatl; the beginning of the tenth *trecena* of the *tonalamatl;* in which they celebrated one of their principal festivals in honor of this same flint; to whom they attributed divinity under the name Teotecpatl, and held it to be a celestial sign, which governed in company with Tetzauhteotl Huitzilopochtli, in the twentieth and last *trecena* of the *tonalamatl.* To this festival, the one they kept to fire was joined; whose symbol was the *acompañado* of this day; and is that figure which is marked with the letter K, and as may be seen, has no numerical character. From this day (which corresponds to the 6th of our May, in the beginning of the cycle of the Mexicans; and to the 30th of April, in a year of 13 Reed); which is that represented on the stone, marked T, they prepared themselves with fasts and other mortifications, to celebrate the great festival of Toxcatl, which was kept on the beginning of the month called by his name, in honor of Huitzilopochtli, which the Mexicans, as well as the Spaniards had good reason to remember. On the 14th day of this month Toxcatl, the symbol Nahui Ocelotl occurred; and on it they kept a great festival to the sun; as he passed that day the zenith of the city, and darted his beams vertically upon it.

70. The figure below, denoted by the letter N, is the day Ce Quiahuitl, as is demonstrated by the symbol which is like to that depicted at 19 of the circle of the days of the month, and by the number one which accompanied it; and this day would concur with the penultimate of the month Tlacaxipehualiztli, in which they made so many festivals and sacrifices, and amongst others, that of Nahui Atl, which coincided with the ninth day, on which also they kept a festival to Tlaloc. The fourth day of the *trecena,* which began with the before mentioned day Ce Quiahuitl, was of the character Nahui Ehecatl, which corresponds to the 2nd of the following month named Tozoztontli. And in this month, and in the one following, which was Hueytozoztli, they kept fasts to the sun, which lasted forty days, as Torquemada says; and they terminated on the day Ce Tecpatl. On the right side of Ce Quiahuitl, is seen the symbol Ome Ozomatli, pointed out by the letter M, which represents the head of a monkey, with its numerical characters; and both symbols, Ce Quiahuitl and Ome Ozomatli, are immediately below the sun, and show in these days, two of his principal movements, as we shall see.

71. Over the symbol Malinalli, which is found in the house [box] 12 of the days of the month; five small circles, or numerical points are seen; which point out the day Macuilmalinalli; a name which they gave to one of their gods; and they kept a festival in his own temple to him, and to another who accompanied him, called Topantlacaqui; but not on this day, which concurs with the 12th of the month Ochpaniztli; but in another, of the month Xochilhuitl; as Torquemada has it:[62] or three days after, according to Dr. Hernández; that is, on the day Nahui Calli, which agrees with the 3rd of the month Quecholli, the three hundred and third of the year. This festival was also kept in honor of the sign Xochilhuitl.[63] On this account the number five, is not put within the house [box], as it should be, but over it: and also not to interrupt the order, since no other [box] contains a number. It would be to confound the progressive series of the days of the month, which the portion of the circle that contains the 20 symbols, represents, if the number 5 had been placed within the house [box]; the 12 corresponding to it, according to the place in which it is found; beginning to count from the first symbol, which is Cipactli. This number and symbol, in the form that they are seen in the stone; signify, that from this day, on which the sun was approaching, in his return from the equinoctial line, the festivals which they kept to him, began; and continued ten days; amongst which, the day 10 Ollin occurred, and is represented by the ten numerical characters in two divisions of five each; which are found in the principal figure, above the letter

H. With those festivals, the twentieth and ultimate *trecena* of the *tonalamatl* terminated; and the account of the year continued, beginning to count again by Ce Cipactli, the day on which the sun was at the equinox; as will be said hereafter.

72. All the festivals which are contained in this stone, the special ones, which were kept in the space of nine Mexican months, or 180 days; preparing themselves for them, some little time before; when the sun was already near to the equinox, and to the places in the heavens which served them as a rule for their celebration. Amongst their chief festivals, were those of Macuilcalli, Macuilcipactli, Macuilquiahuitl, and others of the symbols which carried with them the number 5; and which were kept in honor of the gods, known by the same names: with the others which concurred from the beginning of the vernal equinox, until the autumnal; or in the nine Mexican months; or six of ours. They, for the other festivals of the nine remaining months of the year, making use of the other stone, which as has been said, must have been joined to this one on the left side; on which the festivals, or ceremonies corresponding to the time in which the sun traversed the other half of the ecliptic; from the period at which he left the equinoctial line, for the Tropic of Capricorn, until his return to it; must have been found. In both intervals of time, they also celebrated the common festivals of each month, which were kept every twenty days.

73. All the mechanism of this stone, by which the movements of the sun were known, and by them, the precise time of keeping their festivals; consists in eight holes, or perforations, which are yet visible, near to the projection of the circle, in the plane inferior to it, and which in figure 3 are marked with the letters XZ, PP, CC, and SY, in which holes they fixed as many indexes, or gnomons; by which means, the shade [i.e., shadow] which the sun made, pointed out the respective times with sufficient precision. No historian, either Indian or Spanish, makes mention of this stone; neither of the mode in which they measured time; although all agree that they divided it exactly. But seeing it, and combining it with another document, which I shall give; the method which they made use of to know the different times, will be evident to the least reflecting mind. Supposed, then, the position of the stone, as has been said, seated upon a horizontal plane, erected vertically upon a line, which should have the direction from east to west, with the face to the south; two equal gnomons of a certain length, fixed in the perforation XZ; and two other larger (whose difference should be respectively equal to what there is from our zenith to the Tropic of Cancer; which they were well acquainted with, from repeated observations; as they were accustomed to make them in all their works) in the holes SY; and cords drawn from each one to its correspondent; the shade made by the upper cord on the day Ce Quiahuitl, in the year of the character 13 Acatl, ought to concur exactly with the line, where the plane of the stone cut the horizontal plane; or with another parallel to it, on the same stone; according to the length of the gnomons; the shade of the cord forming with the vertical plane of the stone on the day of the equinox, an angle equal to the latitude of the city.

74. The same shade of the upper cord, ought to concur with that of the one below (the above said difference of the size of the gnomons supposed) on the day Ome Ozomatli, in the same year of the character 13 Reed; in which the sun arrives at the Tropic of Cancer. The reason of this is, because the day Ce Quiahuitl of the Mexican calendar, concurring with the 28th day of our March, at the beginning of the cycle; at the middle of it, or at the 26th year, which is that of the character 13 Acatl; in which they had omitted 6 bisextiles, and some hours over; the beginning of their civil year had retrograded something more than 6 days in respect to their solar tropical year. … And for this reason the day Ce Quiahuitl, which ought to concur with the 28th day of March,

at the beginning of the cycle; in this year concurs with the 22nd day, or rather with the 21st day and a half. Thus between this period, and the coming 22nd the sun arrived at the first point of Aries, or the beginning of the vernal equinox. The same happens with the summer solstice, which the day Ome Ozomatli points out. This symbol at the beginning of the Mexican cycle, coincides with the 28th day of June; but retarding six days and a half in this year of 13 Reed, the summer comes to begin the 21st and 22nd days of June; at which time the sun certainly arrives at the Tropic of Cancer.

75. The remaining four holes equally distant from each other, marked with the letters PP and QQ, served to fix four other gnomons, all of equal length, from which they stretched two cords parallel with each other, and with the horizon; and by means of them, they knew the two days of the year in which the sun arrived at our zenith, on his journey from the equinoctial line, to the Tropic of Cancer; and on his return from thence, to the equinoctial. For on these two days, the shade formed by the upper cord, ought exactly to cover that of the lower, precisely at noon. This took place on the day Nahui Ocelotl, or on that immediately following; which concurred with the 22nd and 23rd day of May, in our calendar. But in the year 13 Reed (for the reasons which have been given) they coincided with the 16th and 17th of May; between which days the sun passes exactly by [through] our zenith, the first time, having then $19°$ and twenty-six and a half minutes north declination, which is equal to the latitude, or height of the Pole, of this city [Mexico City]. The second time, on its return from the tropic, that it has the same declination is the 26th of July; and although the symbol Nahui Quiahuitl concurs with the latter date, at the beginning of the cycle, and consequently it ought in the year 13 Reed, to retrograde to the 20th of July; and the day 10 Cohuatl to be counted in the place which corresponds to the 26th. But as all this *trecena,* which was the 16th, was subject, as it appears in the *tonalamatl,* and as related by Cristóbal del Castillo, to the sign Nahui Tonatiuh, accompanied by Tlaloc Quiahuitl, and Citlalinycue, or Citlalcueye; it was all dedicated to the sun, as the principal planet which reigned in it, and governed it; and in whatever day of it, the shade of the superior cord fell upon the inferior; they were able to celebrate the festival of the fifth movement, or second vertical transit of the sun over the city. And in this manner, in whatever year of the Mexican cycle, the passage of the sun by the zenith, was correctly verified (or, nearly ascertained), within the same *trecena;* since it was not easy for those four movements to concur always in symbols, which should have in [with] them the number four. It was enough for them, that these [symbols] were near to the day, in which, each one of the four movements happened. And by means of the shade formed by the upper cord PP, they knew perfectly well the day of the said *trecena,* on which they should celebrate their respective festivals: and the charge of this was committed to the care of the principal minister or priest, named Epcoaquacuiltzin, who was, according to Dr. Hernández,[64] the master of ceremonies. Besides it was sufficient for them, that at the beginning of the cycle, or in any year of it, each one of the aforesaid symbols should concur with the precise day, in which the sun had the movement they ought to observe, for the accomplishment of their rites: since they knew very well, that at the end of the cycle, the beginning of their civil year had retrograded thirteen days; which days, they intercalated, to equalize it with the solar year. It was easy for them to know, in any year, the days which they ought to compute in their account, to verify in them, the precise time of the equinoxes, and solstices, and of the transit of the sun by the vertex of the city.

76. I ingenuously confess, that until I had seen the stone, I did not comprehend what the sign Nahui Ollin signified; nor had I imagined how it could relate to the fable of the four suns. For,

although I had seen its figure represented in the *tonalamatl,* and in other paintings of the Indians, as these were small, they did not contain the symbols and numbers in their squares, which those of the stone contain: and I was persuaded that the four movements of the sun, which the words Nahui Ollin signify, had relation to the four periods in which he arrived at the equinoctial and solstitial points; without thinking that the two days, on which he passed by our zenith might also be included in this figure. I had no doubt that they were acquainted with the equinoctial and solstitial points, having previously found an ancient monument which proved it to me. This was another stone, which was discovered on the Hill of Chapultepec, when the rubbish which covered its summit was cleared away for the purpose of an excavation, which was made in it, by D. Juan Eugenio Santelizes, in the year 1775. This was one of those great rocks of which the hill is composed; and a horizontal plane was formed on it, which had three arrows sculptured on it, in relief, one upon another; which made equal angles at the middle. The points of the three looked to the east, where those of the sides pointed out the two solstitials; and that of the center, the equinoctial. At the junction of the three, a kind of ribbon was sculptured, which bound them up; and this formed a small line in its center, whose signification, or use, I did not immediately comprehend; until two other rocks which were at the sides of the plane, enabled me to discover it. One of these rocks was entire; the other broken in several places. The whole one, which looked south, had a hole sufficiently deep towards the superior extremity, whose diameter was smaller than that of a large bee.[65] The broken one looking north, had lost the hole; but on one side was seen a piece of furrow, or hollow of it. Having examined it, I found that it corresponded to that of the front rock, and that they were exactly north and south. From whence I inferred, that they fixed a cord in them, which served as a meridian, coming to be over the line of the center of the ribbon with which the arrows were tied; and that at the instant of noon, the shade of the cord ought to fall on the line exactly. So that in these rocks, the Mexicans had an instrument, by means of which, they knew the true points of east and west, at the time of the rising and setting of the sun, in the equinoxes and solstices; and consequently the four stations of the year: and at the same time, the true period of noon, throughout the twelve months. When I returned to visit these rocks, I found them all destroyed, with others which had been broken to pieces, for the construction of certain furnaces at the foot of the said hill. How many precious monuments of antiquity (for want of knowledge) have perished in this manner!

77. The stone we are speaking of, not only enabled them to know the equinoctials and solstices (since that of winter, or the arrival of the sun at the Tropic of Capricorn, might be shown by means of the shade of one of the cords, in a place, which, they should have determined on, in [on] the same stone; after repeated observations of succeeding years, without being necessitated to observe it in its fellow), and the passage of the sun by the zenith, but it also served them as a sun dial, which besides showing the midday by the vertical and parallel shades caused by the upper gnomons X and Z, also pointed out the hours of 9 A.M.; and 3 P.M., a time which was observed for their rites and ceremonies. The hour of nine was denoted by the shade of the gnomon Z when passing by the left side, z, of the square Nahui Ocelotl by the center of the little circle or ring, g, by the center of the sun, and by the right side, s, of the square Nahui Quiahuitl, it did coincide with the other gnomon, S, below. The same ought to happen at 3 o'clock P.M. The shade of the index, or gnomon X, passing by the side of the x, of the square Nahui Ehecatl, by the little circle, and by the center of the sun, and by the side, h, of the square Nahui Atl, until it meets with the other gnomon Y, of the inferior part. They needed only a knowledge of these hours; those being the four parts

of the day destined for worship of their gods; principally of the sun, to whom at these periods, they offered sacrifices, as also at the fourth parts of the night, or at 9 o'clock in the evening, and at 3 in the morning. Which hours the Mexicans knew by the ascension and culmination (meridian height) of the stars, according to the times of the year. Both are proved by what Father Torquemada,[66] and Dr. Hernández[67] relate, who expressly tell the hours in which they worshipped the sun every day, and offered sacrifices to him.

78. This stone and its companion were destined to other purposes than those related; which not being spoken of in the histories, cannot easily be known; and can only be inferred by a combination of reasonings, from the said histories. It is certain also that they kept festivals to the moon, and that by means of her they determined the diaries [*diarias,* "order"] of the *tonalamatl,* and distributed the days of the second calendar from 13 to 13 [in groups of thirteen], with respect to its appearances by night or by day, under the title of sleep and wakefulness: which they called each of these intervals; Metztli, the proper name of the moon; and to the whole period of 260 days, they gave the appellation Metzlapohualiztli, or account of the moon; as has already been said. Then it is likely they observed her movements as well as those of the sun; at least the hour of its transit by the meridian, at the time it was above our horizon by night: whose meridian, or culmination, should be denoted by the shade of the superior cord, in the same manner that the shade formed by the same cord, pointed out that of the sun at noon. The shades which the gnomons X and Z made, ought to have pointed out two equal times, one previous and one posterior to the culmination of the moon; these being at equal distances from the vertex of the circle of the stone; as they designated by day, the hours of nine in the morning and 3 in the afternoon. We do not know whether the observations they made of these and other lunar shades, besides being useful for their heathen rites, might not be employed beneficially in their astronomy, to obtain a knowledge of the movements of the moon; to whom they paid the same veneration and worship, as to the sun, and had a beautiful temple dedicated to her, called Tecuccizcalco, constructed with tortoise shell and conchs [*conchas y caracoles*], of which Torquemada[68] says, "It must have been dedicated to the moon, because the ancient Mexicans called it Tecucciztecatl. In this place they made many sacrifices at intermittent times of the year."

79. This little, is all I have been enabled to search out respecting this valuable monument of Indian antiquity. I have purposely omitted other significations applicable to their false religion, and no way conducive to a knowledge of their chronology and astronomy. These significations only having reference to their judicial astrology, and to their ridiculous and superstitious rites; not wishing to confound the clear knowledge which the Mexicans had of the principal planets; of the method of observing them to divide time, for their civil and religious distributions, with the darkness, which the Devil shed over them in their false predictions and heathen prognostics.

80. The size of this stone, and the address [*arte,* "skill"] with which they brought it from the quarry to the site of the Great Temple, where it was worked and placed, has filled many persons with admiration, and has furnished matter for dispute respecting the number of arrobas[69] it weighed. It was certainly astonishing to see the great labor employed to remove it from the place where it was discovered; to that to which it was taken; a distance of about a hundred yards; making use of rotary machines, and a great number of people, on an almost equal and horizontal plane; and to think of the many ravines and cliffs it had to pass over, in coming from the quarry, where the rock had its origin. The great number of leagues which it had to travel, over places not only unequal as to surface, but also in respect to the nature of the soils; some being marshy, and

others covered entirely with water. Such are the lakes, rivers, and drains, which on all sides surround the streets of the city, by which, it must necessarily have passed to arrive at the temple, and place where it was found. And finally the great difference of the bulk and weight which it had originally, when they brought it in its rough state to work it at the place of its destination; and what it now has, when it wants, not only all the matter which they took from it, in perfecting its figure; but also considerable pieces which belonged to it, which are pointed out by the letter W. The question of its actual weight, is not easy to decide, because of its present very irregular form. But that which the paralellepipedon, or quadrangular prism, of which it was formed, had; is easily solved by a geometrical problem, and by a hydrostatical one. Because its three dimensions being given, composed of the number 60, that is, four yards and a half long, as much in width (its sides being sensibly equal) and one yard in thickness. It results that whilst in its first shape of a paralellepipedon, it contained 603,260 cubic inches of the foot Royal of Paris; our Castilian yard (vara) containing 31 of these inches. By Mussembroek's most ample table of the specific gravities of various bodies, as well solid as fluid, compared with the weight of water; it is found that the specific gravity of a cubic inch of a stone less solid than the one in question, that is of the grindstone of Pennsylvania, is of 2,561, that is, two ounces, and five hundred and sixty-one thousandths of another. So that it results that 603,260 inches cubic, ought to weigh 1,544,948,860 ounces, which reduced, make 965 quintals, 2 arrobas, 9 pounds, and almost 5 ounces (43 tons, and 239 lbs.).[70] But suppose that it has lost the half of its weight, by the pieces which were taken off in fashioning it, as well as the large fragments which are now wanting to its perfect figure: its actual weight would be at least 482 quintals, 3 arrobas, 4 pounds, and 10 ounces.

81. The difference of the density of its substance, with that which it has been compared, will augment its weight. This stone being calcareous, hard, and compact, like to those of the species 107, no. 2, which Mr. Bomare describes in his mineralogy. Taking then a cubic inch of it (it being of one substance) and comparing the weight, with any metal whose specific gravity is known, or with an equal volume of water, its total weight might be known with more certainty. The Lt. Col. of Engineers, D. Miguel Costanzo, whose information, and practice in the mathematical sciences are well known; made use of a method like this second; weighing in open air, a piece of the said stone; repeating the operation in a vessel of water; and deducing from the difference of weight, how much a volume of water equal to the piece of stone, would weigh. He found by a rule of proportion, the total weight of the portion of cylinder which contains the sculptured figures; comparing according to its measures, with the weight of a cylindrical foot of the said water. But even thus the operation is defective, as the said colonel confesses; on account of the many cavities contained on its surface, caused by the works which have been sculptured on it. And either of these methods can only hold good, when applied to the whole bulk, which the stone had, before it was worked; supposing it to have been of a regular figure, as a paralellepipedon, which itself demonstrates.

82. I confess that I have not been able to learn how, or in what manner the Indians brought it from the place of its origin, to that where it was found. But I can assert, that in all their works, they sought the means the most simple, and easy to put into execution; making use of machines and tools so simple and light, that their use has been preserved until now. So that the size and resistance of the said machines, was no augmentation of weight; neither were operations rendered difficult to them by the necessity of employing various instruments, always accustoming themselves to perform a work with only one; for which other artificers would require many. It is

admirable to see them split a block of wood so equally and straight that the divisions are scarcely seen, and that with a single stone in form of a wedge, and another for a hammer; as is observed in the making of *taxamaniles* (shingles), which are thin plates of wood, as all know. The use of the lever, and of the hypomochlion,[71] or point of support, was very familiar to them; and they had in their language proper terms by which they were known. They supplied the want of carts and wheel carriages, by separate cylinders of wood, by means of which, they carried the heaviest and most voluminous bodies to considerable distances, only by changing the cylinders. I will give an account of the other natural and simple operations in the general history which I have begun, if I have time to conclude it, and the means of publishing it. Finis

Translated by William E. Hulings.

Query [from Hulings]. May not the mounds discovered in the western parts of our country, which bear the appearance of regular fortifications, have been the works of some of the nations since settled in Mexico; constructed during the frequent stops made by them in their journeys from their country Aztlan, which, in some places, were extended to a period of many years? This appears to me more than probable, as Aztlan is said to have been some where on the north west coast of America; and peopled perhaps originally from Asia, by way of Bering's Straits, or otherwise.

Notes

1. Alexander von Humboldt (1810) published a considerable amount of León y Gama's work, sometimes without credit. See Helena Maria Williams's English translation (1814) of Humboldt in the present volume.

2. Details of León y Gama's life drawn from Valdés 1802; Márquez 1832 (written in 1802); Moreno 1970, 1971, 1981; and Gutiérrez Haces 1995. Alzate noted that he and León y Gama were classmates (Alzate y Ramírez 1831, 4:411–12).

3. See Moreno 1970 for a comprehensive treatment of León y Gama's life and works.

4. Moreno (1970, 83) lists the other works as: (1) *De la existencia de los gigantes y tiempo en que habitaron la Nueva España,* (2) *Colección de notas sobre la aritmética de los antiguos mexicanos,* (3) *Colección de notas sobre una de las grandes piedras encontradas en la plaza de México 1790,* (4) *Método de dividir el tiempo que acostumbraban los mexicanos y otras provincias de la Nueva España,* (5) *Notas sobre la cronología de los antiguos mexicanos y descripción de su calendario con la concordancia al calendario europeo,* (6) *División del ciclo o siglo de los mexicanos en cuatro triadecateri-ades,* (7) *Descripción de la ciudad de México antes y después de la llegada de los conquistadores españoles,* and (8) *Descripción histórica y cronológica de las dos piedras que con occasion del Nuevo empedrado que se está formando en la plaza principal de México, se hallaron en ella el año de 1790.* Gama's papers are primarily in the Bibliothèque nationale de France, Paris, whence they came after J. M. A. Aubin purchased them in Mexico in 1830, thence to the collector Eugene Goupil (Boban 1891). Others can be found in the Deutsche Nationalbibliothek in Berlin; the Bancroft Library of the University of California at Berkeley; the Huntington Library in San Marino, California; and in Mexico in the Archivo General de la Nación and the Biblioteca Nacional de Antropología e Historia.

5. See León y Gama 1804; Márquez 1804; and López Luján 2008b.

6. See Río 1822; Navarrete 2000; Griffin 1974; and Stuart 1992.

7. For more on these writers and their approaches to history writing, see Keen 1971; Cañizares-Esguerra 2001; and Alexander von Humboldt, this volume.

8. In another work, Moreno (1970, 46) underscores the contrast between Alzate and León y Gama, the one a bureaucrat and the other the inheritor of sufficient resources to publish his works. Alzate enjoyed much official support, and Gama very little.

9. León y Gama 1792, 113. See Gutiérrez Haces 1995 for a detailed discussion of León y Gama's strategies for dealing with the *Coatlicue,* which to everyone's eyes was obviously an idol.

10. See León y Gama 1792, 8; and Moreno 1970, 59.

11. See *Gacetas de literatura de México* (12 June 1792, 13 July 1792).

12. See *Gazeta de México,* 26 June 1792.

13. As Margain (1964) notes, Alzate's criticisms are largely irrelevant to León y Gama's discussion of either the *Calendar Stone* or the *Coatlicue* sculpture and focus on such points as whether Cristóbal del Castillo was a native Mexican or of mixed heritage and whether astronomical phenomena such as the zenith passage of the Pleiades and eclipses happened as León y Gama imagines. Alzate also repeatedly asks León y Gama for a "key" to deciphering the Mexican hieroglyphs. The dispute between the men began years earlier in 1789 with a disagreement over León y Gama's explanation of a rare occurrence of the northern lights in Mexico. See León y Gama 1789; and Moreno 1970, 54.

14. See Margain 1964 for a discussion of how the edition of 1832 omits some plates, which José F. Ramírez discovered and had lithographed in Paris in the 1860s but which were unpublished until 1886 (Sánchez 1886a).

15. His source for the legend of the suns was the manuscript of Fernando de Alva Ixtlilxóchitl's "Sumaria relación de todas las cosas que han sucedido en la Nueva España," first published in vol. 9 of Kingsborough's *Antiquities of Mexico* (Kingsborough 1831–48). See also Alva Ixtlilxóchitl (1891–92).

16. See Moreno 1971, 260–70, for the full inventory of León y Gama sources.

17. Moreno (1971, 266) notes that he had a section of book 4 of Sahagún's *Florentine Codex,* which he misattributes to Cristóbal del Castillo.

18. León y Gama, letter to Andrés Cavo, 30 August 1795, fol. 1, Archivo religioso de la Sociedad de Jesus, Roma, vitae, 100s. Cited in Gutiérrez Haces 1995, 124.

19. Gama drew the plate published in 1832, with his description of further stones, and also those images published by Sánchez 1886a and Gutiérrez Haces 1995. Each image shows many smaller numbered images.

20. Figure 1 (*Coatlicue*) in León y Gama 1792 is signed by Agüera as draughtsman and engraver; the *Calendar Stone* images (figs. 2, 3) are unsigned.

21. See Lozano 1794 (with an illustration of Saint Ignatius of Loyola); Pinzón y Baeza 1797 (with a full-page engraving of the Virgin Mary by Francisco de Agüera); Valdés 1808 (with an image of Felipe de Jesus by Francisco de Agüera); Campo y Rivas 1803 (with an engraving of the Virgin of Guadalupe by Francisco de Agüera); and *La visita más feliz y compañía misteriosa* 1811 (with an engraving of the Virgin of Guadalupe by Francisco de Agüera).

22. Teixidor (1931, xxix) lists the main ex libris artists in eighteenth-century Mexico as Francisco Agüera y Bustamante, Gordillo, José de Nava, and Manuel de Villavicencio y Benito de Orduña. He singled out a bookplate made by Agüera in 1797 for Pedro García Valencia y Vasco, canon of the cathedral of Mexico City. See also Tablada 1939; and Sala 1925.

23. See also Bolaños 1992; *Twenty Centuries of Mexican Art* 1940, 174, no. 138; and López Casillas 2008. José Guadalupe Posada clearly appreciated Agüera's skeletons.

24. Leonardo López Luján illustrates an Agüera drawing of an Aztec sculpture from a group of renderings of ca. 1794 in the León y Gama papers at the Bibliothèque nationale de France, Paris (López Luján 2005, 99).

25. See http://www.amphilsoc.org/library/mole/l/leon.pdf (26 May 2009). Life dates drawn from the description of miniature portraits of William and Mrs. Hulings by James Peale Sr., dated 1789, in Bolton 1921, 125; for the same works, see Louisiana Historical Society 1917, 113; Wehle and Bolton 1927; and Sotheby Parke Bernet sale catalog, no. 2622, 1967, lot 121. The American Philosophical Society also has a map by Hulings, of the Mississippi River up to Natchez, dated 1807.

26. *Diplomatic and Consular Instructions* 1969, 10. See also Hulings's letter to the governor of Georgia, James Jackson, 4 May 1799: http://neptune3.galib.uga.edu/ssp/cgi-bin/tei-natamer-idx.pl?sessionid=7f000001&type=doc&tei2id=tcc377 (26 May 2009).

27. Hulings 1803; James Madison to Hulings, 18 October 1802, in Madison 1998, 4:30. There is also a letter from Madison to Hulings at the Center for American History, University of Texas at Austin. See also Lewis 2003, 43.

28. In the Third Treaty of San Ildefonso of 1800, Spain secretly ceded Louisiana to Napoleon. Spanish intendants remained in New Orleans until March 1803, when Napoleon's representatives arrived. At the end of the year, with Jefferson's Louisiana Purchase, the United States assumed control. See Kastor 2004.

29. Biographical details drawn from: http://www.amphilsoc.org/library/mole/b/barton.htm (1 May 2009). See also Ewan et al. 2007.

30. See the finding aid to the Barton papers at the American Philosophical Society: http://www.amphilsoc.org/library/mole/b/barton.htm (1 May 2009).

31. See Boorstin 1993, chap. 2.

32. Hulings: or Festivals.

33. Hulings: Unknown to the Spaniards who supposed every thing of the kind pertained to the worship of false Gods.

34. [Apart from the discussion in the *Descripción,* León y Gama never published a work on Indian chronology. This may be one of the manuscripts listed by Moreno (see n. 4 above), housed at the Bibliothèque nationale, Paris. In 1875, Pérez Hernández published an article, "Calendario Azteca," that may be this lost work. See León y Gama 1875. This article does not appear in any account of León y Gama and his writings.]

35. [León y Gama here refers to the matter of how the ancient Mexicans corrected their calendar to match the true length of the solar year, an obsession of writers during this period. Most students of ancient Mexico today agree that no Pre-Columbian people corrected their calendars of 365 days to account for the true length of the solar year.]

36. Those who were best acquainted with the customs and rites of the Indians were the historiographer Francisco López de Gómara, Dr. Francisco Hernández, and Father Fr. Juan de Torquemada. D. Fernando de Alva Ixtlilxochitl says of the history of the first of these authors, in the place cited, that it is the one, which is something conformable to the Indian original. Dr. Hernández, besides his learned writings relative to the natural history of plants, animals, and minerals of New Spain; on which he formed an ample work, preserved in the royal library in the Escorial; from which work, Dr. Nardo Antonio Reccho, extracted a small part, which was lately published, illustrated with various notes and additions by the academicians Linceo. He sought and obtained a knowledge of many particular, and true facts relative to the rites and ceremonies of the Mexicans; with circumstances not met with in any other author. He gave an exact description of them, and of the 78 parts, of which the great Temple of Mexico was composed. This was published by Father Juan Eusebio Nieremberg in his work entitled: *Historia Naturae maxime peregrinae,* printed in Antwerp in 1635. But this work is very rare, and difficult to be met with. We are promised by the learned Dr. D. Casimiro Gomez de Ortega, who by authority published three volumes of the said Hernández, which only contain what belongs to the vegetable kingdom; that he will give us the remainder of his writings in two more volumes; which we anxiously look for, as the fifth volume will contain his writings on the Mexican rites. The Father Friar Juan de Torquemada, although in many places of his *Monarquia Indiana,* errors are found, together with anachronisms, which we have been under the necessary of confuting; yet in others, and principally in those which he has copied from the writings of Fathers Olmos, Sahagun, Venavente, and other of the first ministers who preached the Holy Gospel, and who were well acquainted with all the idolatries that should be done away from amongst Indians, entire credit ought to be given. [The work by Francisco Hernández, cited above, extracted by Reccho and published with notes by Linceo and others is: *Rerum medicarum Novae Hispaniae thesaurus. Nova plantarvm, animalivm et mineralivm Mexicanorvm historia a Francisco Hernandez…primum compilata, dein a Nardo Antonio Reccho in volvmen digesta, a Io. Terentio, Io. Fabre, et Fabio, Colvmna Lynceis notis, & additionibus longe doctissimis illustrata. Cui demum accessere, aliqvot ex principis Federici Caesii frontispiciis Theatri naturalis phytosophicae tabulae vna cum quamplurimis iconibus ad octingentas, quibus singula contemplanda graphice exhibentur.* Romae, sumptibus B. Deuersini & Z. Masotti, typis V. Mascardi, 1651. There were at least two editions published in Rome in 1651. The Juan Eusebio Nieremberg work is: *Historia naturae, maxime peregrinae, libris XVI. distincta: in quibus rarissimae natura arcana, etiam astronomica, & ignota Indiarum animalia…enodantur; accedunt de miris & miraculosis naturis in Europa libri duo, item de iisdem in terra Hebraeis promissa liber vnus.* Ioannis Eusebii Nierembergii. Antverpiae, ex officina Plantiniana Balthasaris Moreti, 1635.]

37. The most exact are those of D. Cristóbal del Castillo, of D. Fernando de Alvarado Tezozómoc, of D. Domingo Chimalpain, and others; who, although their books do not contain the names of their authors (concealed through modesty), yet from the circumstances of the relations themselves, and times in which they wrote them; they are well known.

38. [A *trecena* is a term, coined in the Spanish-language literature of the colonial era, that refers to a period of thirteen days in the Tonalpohualli, or 260-day ritual calendar, erroneously called the *tonalamatl* by León y Gama and other early writers. The 260-day calendar is composed of twenty days that are numbered one through thirteen. There are 260 possible combinations of numbers and days, twenty *trecenas* of thirteen days each.]

39. Hulings: Tezontli: a stone of a darkened color, pretty hard, porous, and light. United most firmly with lime and sand, and is therefore more in demand than any other for building at the capital, where it is marshy. [Hulings attributes this to Clavigero.]

40. There was another chapel Tetlanman, where they worshipped a god named Chantico (Wolf's Head); who had no fixed day for his sacrifices. But they were performed when ordained by their chiefs, and lords, according to their devotion. This took place when the character or sign called Ce Xochitl, reigned. *Monarq. Indian.,* vol. 2, bk. 8, chap. 13, p. 151. [This work is *Primera (segunda, tercera) parte de los veinte i vn libros rituales i monarchia indiana, con el origen y guerras, de los Indios Occidentales, de sus poblaciones descubrimiento, conquista, conuersion, y otras cosas marauillosas de la mesma tierra.… Compuesto por F. Juan de Torquemada…*3 vols. Madrid, N. Rodriquez Franco, 1723. There was an earlier edition, in 1615, but this is the preferred version. See Torquemada 1723, 1969, and 1975.]

41. On the tenth day of the month Tecuilhuitl (which was the last of the Mexican year) captives who represented the figures of the gods Chantico and Cohuaxolotl, were put to death (Torquemada 1723, 1:177).

42. Vigesima nona Tetlanman vocata, aedes erat dicata deae Quaxolotl Chantico, ubi captivos sponte mactabant, dominante signo Ce Xochitl…Vigesima septima Tetlanman Calmecac nuncupata, Coenobium Sacerdotibus habitatum, dicatumque deae Chantico, ubi noctu, diuque ministrabatur ei (Nieremberg 1635, 144).

43. Hoc fiebat…coram solis imagine…quae erat in templo Quauhxicalco aut picta, aut insculpta humana facie, et hodie a nostris exprimi solet, adjectis radijs in rotae speciem undequaque prodeuntibus (Nieremberg 1635, 149–50).

44. Dr. Hernández says Quauhxilco, but it is without doubt, an error of the press; as is caoalo, for cualo, or qualo, which is the proper word. This fault is frequently seen in almost all the Mexican words contained in the description he gives us of the 78 parts, which composed the great Temple of Mexico; and in the chapters where he treats of the rites, ceremonies, and ministers of the Mexican gods. That those who have knowledge of the idiom of this nation may understand the native words used in future quotations, shall be written with their proper letters. The edifice which Torquemada says was magnificent, this author says was small. It is certain that this building was the work of the magnificence (or at least the finishing of it) of the great Moontezuma II; in whose entrance [dedication] they sacrificed 12,210 persons taken prisoners in the wars against the province Tlachquiauhco, were sacrificed. But this is nothing to the purpose, since much majesty and grandeur may be contained in a small edifice, from the beauty of its construction, and from the ornaments and riches belonging to it; like the one called Teccizizcalli, built entirely of shells, where also the king lodged, to so like penance in other festivals. The words of Hernández are literally as follows: Octava pars Quauhxilco nuncupata, aedicula erat, in quam rex poenitentia ductus sese recipiebat, celebraturus jejunium vocatum *Netonatiuh qualo,* cuator dierum intervallo in honorem solis, quod jejunium ducensis quibusque, trecentenisve diebus transactis consueverant exercere. Mactabantur etaim ibi quatuor captivi, quorum duos Chachame nuncupabant, duos vero alios solis, ac lunae simulacra, cum multis alijs, quos deinde in ejusdem solis honorem interficiebant. Nieremberg 1635, chap. 22, p. 143.

45. Torquemada 1723, 2:283.

46. Torquemada 1723, 2:151.

47. [The "four movements" refers to the annual progress of the sun through the two equinoxes to the two solstices.]

48. [A *casilla* is a square, box, or compartment. León y Gama is referring to the ring of boxes with quincunx signs within.]

49. [These are the four dots that compose the "4" of Nahui Ollin.]

50. "One of these temples which accompanied this great one; was dedicated to the god of Air.… The entrance of this temple had the form and make of the mouth of a great and ferocious serpent; and painted in the manner, in which our painters express the mouth of Hell; with its eyes, teeth, and fangs, horrid and frightful" (Torquemada 1723, 2:145).

51. The Spanish historians, and some of the Indian, amongst them, D. Fernando de Alva Ixtlilxochitl, confound the fables of the sun, one with another; and they mistakenly attribute this [that] of the four movements to the four ages, which they say the Indians computed. The first, from the creation of the world, until the destruction of the giants; the second, from that epoch to the great hurricanes which carried off the men. Those of them, who had hidden themselves in the caves of the mountains, being converted into monkeys. The third, from that period to the deluge. And the fourth was that in which they lived, and which they had an idea was to be destroyed with fire. Notwithstanding the Father Torquemada notes, although cursorily, what they said about there having been five suns, in Torquemada 1723, 2:79. And at greater length (although also mistakenly), López de Gómara 1554, 208, 231. But because that in the aforesaid manuscript in the Mexican tongue, they are expressed with the circumstances related, and in the order of time in which they suppose the destruction of the four suns to have taken place. In condescension to intelligent persons of that tongue, who are learned in the history of the Indians (to save them the chagrin that the omission of the Father Florencia caused Boturini, in not having put at the end of his work the song or cantata, which he promised, of Our Lady of Guadalupe; composed in the Mexican tongue by D. Francisco Placido, lord of Atzcapotzalco; of which he complains, in Section 35, no. 7, of the Catalog of his Museum [Boturini 1746, pt. 2:87]). I will give here literally some clauses of those which conduce to prove what has been said, as to the reason which they had of describing the sun in this manner. He says then thus: "Iniquac in iz ceppa nonoca Oceloqualoque ipan Nahui Ocelotl in Tonatiuh, auh in quiquaya chicome malinalli initonacayouh catca, auh inic nenque centzon xihuitl ipan matlacpohual xihuitl ipan yepohual xihuitl ipan yenocaxtolxihuitl occe, auh inic tequanqualoque matlac xihuitl, ipan ye xihuitl, inic popoliuhque inic tlamito, auh iquac poliuh in Tonatiuh auh inin xiuhcatca ce Acatl: auh inic peuhque in qualoque in cemilhuitonali Nahui Ocelotl, zan no ye inic tlamito inic popoliuhque…Inin Tonatiuh nahui Ehecatl itoca iniquehi inic oppa onoca yecatocoque ipan nahui Ehecatl in Tonatiuh catca, auh inic poliuhque yecatocoque Ozomatin macuepque inincal no in quauh moch ecatococ, auh inin Tonatiuh zan no yecatocoque, auh quiquaya matlactlomome cohuatl inin tonacayouh catca; auh inic nenca caxtolpohual xihuitl ipan yepohual xihuitl ye no ipan nahui xihuitl inic popoliuhque zan cemilhuitl in ecatocoque nauh Ecatl ipan cemilhui tonali inic poliuhque, auh inin xiuhcatca ce Tecpatl. = Inin Tonatiuh Nahui Quiahuitl iniquehi inic etlamanti nenca nahui quiahuitl in Tonatiuhipan, auh inic poliuhque tlequiahuiloque totlme mocuepque, auh no tlatlac in Tonatiuh, moch tlatlac inincal, auh inic nenca caxtolpohual xihuitl ipan matlac xihuitl omome…auh inin xiuh ce Tecpatl, auh icemilhui tonali Nahui Quiahuitl inic poliuhque…Inin Tenatiuh Atl itoca, auh inic manca atl ompohual xihuitl on matlactli omome iniquehi inic nauhtlamantinenca, ipan nahui Atl in Tonatiuh catca…auh inic popoliuhque, apachiuhque, mocuepque mimichtin hualpachiuh in ilhuicatl…auh inin xiuhcatca ce Calli, auh icemilhuitonali Nahui Atl inic poliuhque, etc." Afterwards, he introduces the fable of the Syphilitic One, of which, Torquemada, Boturini, and Clavigero make mention; joining it to the production of the fifth sun, which they named with the number and title, which correspond to the fourth day of the second *trecena,* that is, to Nahui Ollin itself. So that from the absurdities of their fables themselves; the great antiquity of their chronology may be known. Since they had, from the existence of the first sun, formed their calendars; enumerated and marked the days of them, with the names of the signs, or stars, to which they dedicated them.

52. This stone evidently demonstrates the falsity of the systems of Dr. Gemelli, of the Chevalier Boturini, and D. Mariano Veytia, and of the Abbe Clavigero; since it is seen in it, that the symbol Cipactli was indifferently, the beginning of any year whatever. For, the character of the year above exhibited being 13 Reed, as we shall see hereafter. Notwithstanding, the symbol Cipactli is under it, and not that of Reed, as Boturini and Veytia pretend. Neither that of Death, according to Gemelli and Clavigero; and much less with the numbers they invented.

53. This figure, and the 15th and 16th, were already half effaced when the stone was first taken up. Others that are now damaged, received their injury afterwards.

54. [These are the four groups of ten quincunx turquoise symbols in the ring adjacent to the ring with the twenty day signs.]

55. This same year of 13 Reed corresponds also to our present year 1791, which coincides with the half [middle] of the fourteenth cycle, counting from the first that the Mexicans began at Acahualtzinco, on the 26th year of their epoch, or departure from Aztlan, their country.

56. [An indiction is one group of thirteen years; four groups make a cycle of fifty-two years.]

57. Cum thus offerebant inchoante jam nocte, eam salutabant, dicentes: Jam progressus est noctis dominus vocatus Yohualteuhtli, nescimus quo pacto cursum suum peraget. Festum hujus Yohualteuhtli celebrabatur in signo nuncapato Nahui Ollin, ducentesimotercio die rationis Tnalamatl: jejunabant quatuor dies ante illus (Nieremberg 1635, 149).

58. [These *ráfagas* are the eight rectangular protuberances (two partly covered by the heads at the outer ring), each with a dot above, marked on the plan with the letter L.]

59. This manuscript is the one Boturini speaks of, in Section 8, no. 13, of his Museum (1746, pt. 2:17–18); which is found at the end of the history written in the Mexican language by Ixtlilxochitl; which it appears he copied about the year 1556 or 1558; from whence it is inferred, that the curate Pedro Ponce [sic.] wrote this treatise in the preceding years.

60. Torquemada 1723, 2:46.

61. [These are the front feet of the dragon.]

62. Torquemada 1723, 2:53.

63. Quinquagesimum septimum aedificium vocatum Macuilmalinalyteopan, templum erat, ubi simulacra duorum deorum colebantur, nempe illus Macuilmalinal, alterum vero Topantlacaqui, in quo signo solemnia hic peragebantur cujusvis anni tercentesima ternaque luce; necnon in honorem signi Xichilhuitl (Nieremberg 1635, 145).

64. Epcoaquacuiltzin curae erant festa Catalogi, caerimoniaeque exercendae in eis, ut in nihil negligenter perageretur; erat enim veluti caerimoniarum Magister (Nieremberg 1635, 148).

65. Hulings: Humble, or Bumble Bee. [But the word is *arbejon,* which is a pod vegetable, a large pea. There is no bee.]

66. Torquemada 1723, vol. 2, bk. 9, chap. 34, and bk. 10, chaps. 33, 36.

67. Quotidie offerebatur sanguis, ac thus Soli, cum primum summo mane oriebatur, sanguis nempe detractus auriculis, aut e coturnicibus confossis destillans, quas vulsis captibus, ac fluente sanguine versus Solem attollebant, velut hunc sanguinem illi offerentes, atque dicentes ortum jam esse Solem nuncupatum Tonametl xiuhpiltontli, quauhteoamitl…Mox vero ipsum Solem adorabant dicentes: Domine nostre perage feliciter munus tuum. Quod fiebat quotidie juxta Solis exortum. Quater quotidie thus illi offerebant, quinquies vero noctu. In die semel ipso oriente, rursus ad nonam horam vocaram diei, tertio meridie, quarto occidente jam Sole: noctu vero, primo cum jam tenebrae terras obscurabant, secundo, cum jam omnes cubitum se recipiebant, tertio, cum canebant cochleis ij quibus curae erat ceteros ad laudes dijs concinendas excitare; quarto, non multo post noctem intempestam; quinto vero, paulo ante diluculum. Nieremberg 1635, chap. 26, p. 149.

68. Torquemada 1723, 2:150.

69. Hulings: A Spanish measure, about 26 lbs. English.

70. This stone has been chosen, as being friable, less compact than any other of the common ones; and consequently lighter than that we are treating of; which circumstance must rather augment, than diminish the weight resulting from the operation. Although the error in the calculation cannot amount to one hundred weight at most. The specific gravity differing so little in the common stones contained in this table, that it is composed only of the thousandths parts of ounces.

71. [The fulcrum, or roller.]

ALEXANDER VON HUMBOLDT

Researches Concerning the Institutions and Monuments of the Ancient Inhabitants of America, with Descriptions and Views of Some of the Most Striking Scenes in the Cordilleras! (1810)

Editor's Commentary

Alexander von Humboldt (1769–1859) was a key figure in the historiography of the Calendar Stone because his writings were widely read in Europe, the United States, and Latin America. With official permission from King Charles IV, he traveled to Spanish America with the botanist Aimé Bonpland in 1799–1804 and collected data on all aspects of the New World, from botany to archaeology and from natural resources to economic and population statistics.[1] Humboldt passed a year in Mexico, beginning in March 1803 (Minguet 2003, 172), and visited the principal archaeological sites in and around central Mexico. He arrived in Mexico City seven months after Antonio de León y Gama's death and purchased some of his manuscripts at a sale and from José Pichardo at the church of San Felipe de Neri. Pichardo, who inherited León y Gama's library, had the greatest collection of Mexican materials in New Spain at the beginning of the nineteenth century (Humboldt 1814, 136, 190).

Humboldt and Bonpland published thirty folio and quarto volumes on all aspects of the New World (Stuart 1992, 8).[2] Humboldt's comments on ancient Mexican culture and objects appear in several of his published works, most notably in his folio-sized atlas Vues des cordillères et monumens des peuples indigènes de l'Amérique *(1810), which was intended to supplement the* Voyage aux régions équinoxiales du nouveau continent *(Humboldt and Bonpland 1814–25; Stuart 1992, 6–7). The* Vues *presents sixty-nine plates accompanied by long explanatory essays; the treatise on the* Calendar Stone *alone runs to 133 pages in the English edition of 1814. Although the atlas covers the entire journey of Humboldt and Bonpland, the majority of the images are ancient Mexican objects, architecture, and manuscripts. There are chapters on and illustrations of the* Calendar Stone, *the* Stone of Tizoc, *and the* Coatlicue *sculpture, which Humboldt caused to be exhumed from the corner of the university patio. He also illustrated and expounded upon many manuscripts he either acquired in Mexico or consulted in Europe, including the* Mapa Sigüenza *and the codices* Borgia, Dresden, Mendoza, Rios (Vaticanus A), Telleriano Remensis, Vaticanus B, *and* Vienna. *Several of these works were unknown to León y Gama.*

Humboldt's ideas were influential as soon as they were published, and they played a key role in what Marie Louise Pratt terms "the discursive and ideological reinvention of Spanish America during the early nineteenth century" (1992a, 584). For Humboldt, the Calendar Stone *was significant because it demonstrated that the Aztecs—a term used widely for the first time in his works—developed calendars that required a sophisticated grasp of astronomy and mathematics. Possessing such*

Excerpted from Alexander von Humboldt, *Researches Concerning the Institutions and Monuments of the Ancient Inhabitants of America, with Descriptions and Views of Some of the Most Striking Scenes in the Cordilleras!* translated by Helen Maria Williams, 2 vols. in 1 (London: Longman, Hurst, Rees, Orme & Brown, J. Murray & H. Colburn, 1814), 1:276–81, 1:397–409. Introductory text by Khristaan D. Villela.

advanced knowledge, they could not possibly be uncivilized savages, as they had been characterized by Georges-Louis Leclerc de Buffon (1749–67), Cornelius de Pauw (1768–69), Guillaume-Thomas Raynal (1774), and William Robertson (1777).[3]

Since the sixteenth century, writers had explained and valorized ancient Mexican civilization by comparing it to that of the Greeks and Romans. Humboldt took a different approach, arguing that the ancient Mexicans descended from the same ancestral cultures that produced China, Tibet, and Japan.[4] Asiatic connections were manifest in the many similarities between Mexican and Asian calendars, languages, astronomy, astrology, and mythology. Humboldt pursued these connections for a hundred pages in his chapter on the Calendar Stone, and the discussion as a whole leaves the impression that he is advancing a diffusionist explanation of ancient Mexican culture. But, as Benjamin F. Keen noted (1971, 329–36), Humboldt was really arguing for the parallel development of Asiatic and Mexican civilizations.

Humboldt reprinted long sections of León y Gama nearly verbatim, especially those dealing with the sequence of the Aztec months, commenting that the pamphlet of 1792 was very difficult to acquire and virtually unknown in Europe (1814, 289). Like León y Gama before him, Humboldt was fascinated by the question of how the ancient Mexicans corrected their calendar to account for the difference between the true length of the year and the 365-day calendar they used. He discusses the Calendar Stone as such very little. The stone is lost in seemingly endless comparisons to other ancient calendar and zodiacal systems, including those used by the Greeks, Persians, Hindus, Tibetans, and Chinese. Data from the Inca, the Maya, and the Muiscas are also adduced to explain the Aztec calendar.[5]

Humboldt accepts León y Gama's erroneous translation of Nahui Ollin as the four movements of the sun—the solstices and equinoxes (Humboldt 1814, 352)—and also accepts the notion that the Calendar Stone tracked only the annual festivals from the spring equinox to the autumnal equinox; another identical object mapped the festivals for the remainder of the year (1814, 406). He further notes that, when they emigrated from Aztlan, the Aztecs had no divinity other than the sun (1814, 283). Significantly for later Calendar Stone studies, he also mentions that when the Aztecs left Aztlan they did not practice human sacrifice, adopting this rite in 1317 only after the war with Xochimilco (1814, 216). Alfredo Chavero later used the same sources as Humboldt to draw a distinction between the peaceful Mexicas who left Aztlan and the bloodthirsty Aztecs who built an empire and were conquered by Hernan Cortés.[6]

Most Europeans learned of the Calendar Stone's appearance from the engraving Humboldt published in the various editions of the Vues (fig. 1). Although Humboldt may have sketched the Calendar Stone, his image clearly derives from that published in 1792 by León y Gama, as can be observed by the extra space in the box with the date 4 Jaguar, to the upper right of the central face.

*   *   *

Researches Concerning the Institutions and Monuments of the Ancient Inhabitants of America, with Descriptions and Views of Some of the Most Striking Scenes in the Cordilleras!

RELIEF IN BASALT, REPRESENTING THE MEXICAN CALENDAR

[1]

Among the number of monuments which seem to prove, that the people of Mexico, at the time of their conquest by the Spaniards, had attained a certain degree of civilization, we may assign the first rank to the calendars, or different divisions of time, adopted by the Toltecks and the Aztecks; either for the use of society in general, or to regulate the order of sacrifices, or to facilitate the calculations of astrology. This kind of monument is so much the more worthy of fixing our attention, as it is a proof of knowledge, which we have some difficulty in considering as the result of observations made by a nation of mountaineers, in the uncultivated regions of the New Continent. We might be tempted to compare the circumstance of the Azteck calendar, with that of those languages rich in words, and in grammatical forms, which we find among nations, whose actual mass of ideas is not correspondent to the multiplicity of signs adapted to explain them. Those languages so rich and flexible, those modes of intercalation which suppose an accurate knowledge of the duration of the astronomical year, are perhaps only the remains of an inheritance, transmitted to them by nations heretofore civilized, but since relapsed into barbarism.

The monks and other Spanish writers, who visited Mexico a short time after the conquest, gave but vague and often contradictory notions of the different calendars in use among the nations of the Tolteck and Azteck race. We find these notions in the works of Gomara, Valades, Acosta, and Torquemada. This last writer, notwithstanding his superstition, has transmitted to us in his *Monarquía Indiana,* a collection of important facts, which discovers an accurate knowledge of local circumstances. He lived fifty years among the Mexicans: he arrived at the city of Tenochtitlan at a period, when the natives were yet in possession of a great number of historical paintings; and when, before the house of the Marquis del Valle,[7] in the Plaza Mayor, were seen the remains of the great teocalli[8] dedicated to the god Huitzilopochtli. Torquemada made use of the manuscripts of three Franciscan monks, Bernardino de Sahagun, Andrea de Olmos, and Toribio de Benavente, who were very intimately acquainted with the American languages, and who went to New-Spain in the time of Cortez, before the year 1528. Notwithstanding these advantages, the historian of Mexico has not furnished us with all the information respecting the chronology and calendars of the Mexicans, that we might have expected from his zeal and his instruction. He expresses himself with so little precision, that we read in his work, that the year of the Aztecks finished at the month of December, and began at the month of February.[9]

Materials more instructive than the narratives of the first Spanish historians, had long existed at Mexico, in the convents and public libraries. Some Indian authors, Christoval del Castillo, a native of Tezcuco, who died in 1606, at the age of eighty years, Fernando de Alvarado Tezozomoc, and Domingo Chimalpain, have left manuscripts composed in the Azteck language on the history and chronology of their ancestors. These manuscripts, which contain a great number of dates, reckoning at the same time according to the Christian era, and according to the civil and ritual calendar of the natives, have been studied with advantage by the learned Carlos de Siguenza, professor of mathematics at the university of Mexico: by the Milanese traveler, Boturini Benaducci; by the Abbé Clavigero; and latterly by Mr. Gama, whose astronomical labors I have had occasion to mention in another work.[10] Finally, in 1790, a stone of enormous bulk, covered with characters evidently relative to the Mexican calendar, the religious festivals, and the days in which the sun passes the zenith of the city of Mexico, was discovered in the foundations of the ancient teocalli.[11] This served at the same time to clear up some doubtful points, and call the attention of some enlightened natives to the Mexican calendar.

I endeavored, not only during my stay in America, but after my return to Europe, to study carefully every thing that has been published on the division of time, and the mode of intercalation among the Aztecks. I examined on the spot the celebrated stone found in the Plaza

Mayor, and represented in the twenty-third plate: I have drawn some not uninteresting notions from the hieroglyphic paintings preserved in the convent of San Felipe Neri at Mexico: and I perused at Rome the manuscript commentary, which P. Fabrega composed on the Codex Mexicanus of Veletri [*Codex Borgia*]: but I greatly regret, that I am not sufficiently versed in the Mexican language, to read the works written by the natives in their own tongue, and in the Roman alphabet, immediately after the taking of Tenochtitlan. Consequently I have not been able to verify the whole of the assertions of Siguenza, Boturini, Clavigero, and Gama, on the Mexican intercalation, by comparing them with the manuscripts of Chimalpain and of Tezozomoc, whence those authors assure us they derived the notions which they have published. Whatever be the doubts which remain on several points in the minds of the learned, habituated to scrutinize every fact, and adopt only what is rigorously proved, I am happy to have excited attention to a curious monument of Mexican sculpture, and to have given some new particulars respecting a calendar, which neither Robertson nor the illustrious author of the History of Astronomy appears to have treated with all the consideration it deserves. This calendar will be rendered still more interesting by the ideas we shall furnish relative to the Mexican tradition of the *four ages,* or four Suns, which exhibit remarkable analogies with the *yougs* and the *calpas* of the Hindoos: and on the ingenious method employed by the Muysca Indians, a nation of mountaineers of New Grenada, to correct their lunar years by the intercalation of a thirty-seventh moon, called *deaf* or *cuhupqua.* It is by collecting and comparing the different systems of American chronology, that we can judge of the communications, which appear to have existed, in very remote times, between the nations of India and Tartary, and those of the New Continent.

[2]

The valuable monument represented in figure 1, which had been already engraved at Mexico twenty years ago, confirms a part of the ideas we have just unfolded respecting the Mexican calendar. This immense stone was found in the month of December, 1790, in the foundations of the great temple of Mexitli, in the great square of Mexico, nearly seventy metres to the west of the second gate of the Viceroy's palace, and thirty metres north of the flower market, called *Portal de las flores,* at the small depth of five decimetres. It was so placed, that the sculptured part could be seen only by putting it in a vertical position. When Cortez destroyed the temples, he broke the idols, and every thing that belonged to the ancient rites. Those masses of stone, which were too large to be destroyed, were buried, in order to conceal them from the eyes of a vanquished people. Though the circle, which contains the hieroglyphs of the days, is only three metres four decimetres in diameter, we found, that the whole stone formed a rectangled parallelopipedon of four metres length, as many metres broad, and one metre thick.

The nature of this stone is not calcareous, as Mr. Gama asserts; it is blackish gray trappean porphyry, with basis of basaltic *wakke.* On carefully examining some detached fragments, I perceived hornblende, several very slender crystals of vitreous feldspar, and, what is very remarkable, sprinklings of mica. This rock, cracked and full of small cavities, is destitute of quartz, like almost all rocks of trappean formation. As its actual weight is more than twenty-four tuns, and no mountain within eight or ten leagues could furnish a porphyry of this grain and color, we may easily imagine the difficulties, which the Mexicans must have found in transporting so enormous a mass to the foot of the Teocalli. The sculpture in relievo is as well polished as any other to be found in Mexican works; the concentric circles, the numerous divisions and subdivisions, are

Fig. 1.
Aztec Calendar Stone, engraving by
Jean Baptiste Antoine Cloquet (French,
d. 1828), 1810

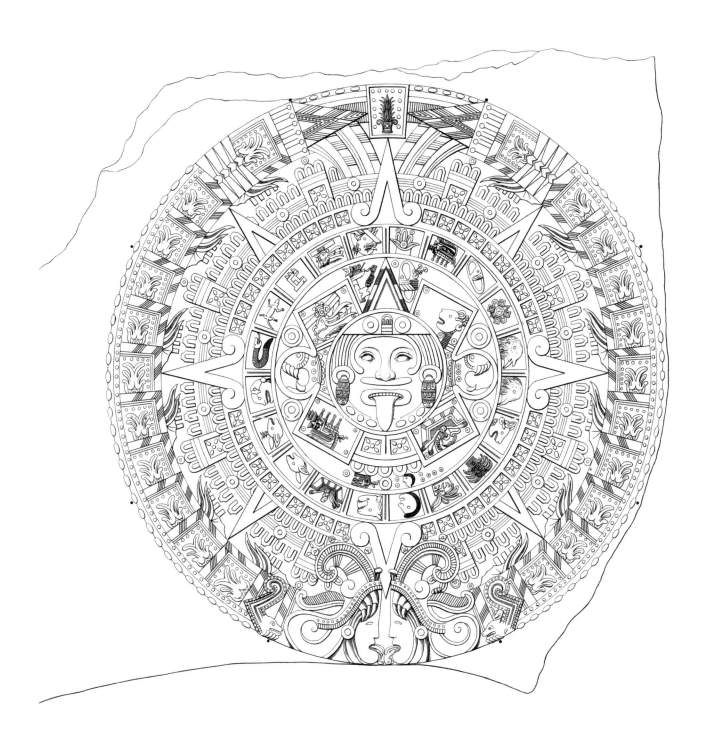

traced with mathematical precision; the more minutely the detail of this sculpture is examined, the greater taste we find in the repetition of the same forms, that attention to order and feeling of symmetry, which among half civilized nations is a substitute for the feeling of the beautiful.

In the centre of the stone is sculptured the celebrated sign *nahui ollin Tonatiuh* (the Sun in his four motions), of which we have already spoken. The Sun is surrounded by eight triangular radii; which are also found in the ritual calendar *tonalamatl,* in historical paintings, and wherever there is a representation of the Sun, *Tonatiuh.*[12] The number eight alludes to the division of the day and the night into eight parts.[13] The god Tonatiuh is figured opening his large mouth, armed with teeth; this yawning mouth, and protruded tongue, remind us of the figure of a divinity of Hindostan, the image of *Kala, Time.* According to a passage of the Bhagvat-Gheeta, Cala "swallows the worlds, opening a fiery mouth, exhibiting a row of dreadful teeth, and protruding an enormous tongue" (*The Bhagvat-Gheeta* 1785).[14] Tonatiuh, placed among the signs of the days, measuring the year by the *four movements* of the solstices and the equinoxes, is in fact the real symbol of time; it is *Krishna* assuming the form of *Kâla,* it is Chronos devouring his children, whom we imagine we find under the name of Moloch among the Phoenicians.

The inner circle contains the twenty signs of the days; recollecting that *cipactli* is the first, and *xochitl* the last of these asterisms, we here, as elsewhere, perceive, that the Mexicans arranged the hieroglyphics from right to left. The heads of the animals are placed in an opposite direction, no doubt because the animal, which turns his back to another, is supposed to precede it. Mr. Zoega observed this peculiarity among the Egyptians.[15] The death's head, *miquiztli,* placed near the serpent, and accompanying it as a sign of the night in the third periodical series, is an exception to the general rule; this alone is directed toward the last sign, while the animals have their faces turned toward the first. This arrangement is not the same in the manuscripts at Veletri, Rome, and Vienna.

It is probable, that the sculptured stone, which Mr. Gama has endeavoured to explain, was anciently placed in the enclosure of the teocalli, in a *sacellum* dedicated to the sign *ollin Tonatiuh.* We know by a fragment of Hernandez, preserved by the Jesuit Nieremberg in the eighth book of his Natural History that the great teocalli contained within its walls six times thirteen or seventy-eight chapels, several of which were dedicated to the Sun, the Moon, the planet Venus, called *Ilcuicatitlan* or *Tlazolteotl,* and to the signs of the zodiac.[16] The Moon, considered by all nations as the planet that attracts humidity, had a small temple (*teccizcalli*) built in shell work. The great festivals of the Sun (*Tonatiuh*) were celebrated at the winter solstice, and in the sixteenth period of thirteen days, over which presided both the sign nahui ollin Tonatiuh, and the milky way, known under the name of *Citlalinycue,* or *Citlalcueye.* During one of these festivals of the Sun, the kings were wont to withdraw into an edifice, built in the midst of the enclosure of the teocalli, and called *Hueyquauhxicalco.* They passed four days in fasting and penitence; a blood sacrifice was afterward offered in honor of the eclipses (*Netonatiuhqualo,* the *unfortun-ate Sun devoured*). In this sacrifice one of two masked victims represented the Sun, Tonatiuh, the other, the Moon, Meztli, as emblems to show, that the Moon is the real cause of the eclipse of the Sun.

Beside the asterisms of the Mexican zodiac, and the figures of the sign *nahui ollin,* the stone gives also the dates of ten great festivals, which were celebrated from the spring to the autumnal equinox. As several of these festivals were correspondent with celestial phenomena, as the Mexican year is vague during the space of a cycle, and as the intercalation takes place only every fifty-two years, the same dates do not denote four years successively the same days. The winter solstice, which, the first year of the cycle, took place on the day 10 *tochtli,* retrograded two signs eight years later, and fell on the day 8 miquiztli. Hence it follows, that, in order to indicate the dates by the signs of the days, we must add the year of the cycle with which these dates correspond. In fact the sign 13 canes, or *matlactly omey acatl,* placed above the figure of the Sun, toward the upper edge of the stone, shows, that this monument contains the *fasti* of the twenty-sixth year of the cycle, from the month of March to the month of September.

In order to give a clearer view of the signs, which indicate the festivals of the Mexican religion, I must again observe, that the rounds placed near the hieroglyphics of the days are terms of the first of the three periodical series, of which we have already explained the use. Reckoning from right to left, and beginning at the right of the triangle resting on the forehead of the god, *Ollin* Tonatiuh, with the point toward *cipactli,* we find the eight following hieroglyphics: 4 *tiger;* 1 *silex; tletl,* fire, without marking the number; 4 *wind;* 4 *rain;* 4 *ram;* 2 *ape;* and 4 *water.* We now come to the explanation of the Mexican festivals, according to the calendar of Mr. Gama, and the order of the festivals indicated in the works of the historians of the sixteenth century.

In the year 13 *acatl,* which is the last year of the second indiction of the cycle, the beginning of the year retrograded six days and a half, because the intercalation had not taken place for twenty-six years. The first day of the month *tititl,* which bears the sign 1 *cipactli tletl,* consequently corresponds not to the 9th but the 3d of January; and the sign, which presides over the seventh period of thirteen days, 1 *quiahuitl,* or 1 *rain,* coincides with the 22d of March, or with the vernal equinox. It is at this period, that the festivals of *Tlaloc,* or the god of water, were celebrated; which indeed had already begun ten days before the equinox, on the day 4 atl, or 4 water; without doubt, because on the 12th of March, or the 3d of the month *Tlacaxipehualiztli,* the hieroglyphic of water, *atl,* was the sign both of the day and of the night.[17] Three days after the vernal equinox, the day 4 *ehecatl,* or 4 wind, began a solemn fast of forty days, in honor of the Sun. This fast finished on the 30th of April, which corresponds to 1 *tecpatl,* or 1 flint. As the sign of this day is accompanied by the Lord of the Night *tletl,* fire, we find the hieroglyphic *tletl,* placed near the 1 *tecpatl,* on the left of the triangle, the point of which is directed toward the beginning of the zodiac. At the right of the sign 1 *tecpatl* is 4 *ocelotl,* or 4 tiger, this day is remarkable from the passage of the Sun through the zenith of the city of Mexico. The whole of the small period of thirteen days, in which this passage takes place, and which is the eleventh of the ritual year, was dedicated to the Sun. The sign 2 *ozomatli,* or 2 ape, corresponds to the epocha of the summer solstice, it is placed immediately near 1 *quiahuitl,* or 1 rain, the day of the equinox.

We might be puzzled to explain 4 *quiahuitl,* or 4 *rain.* In the first year of the cycle, this day corresponded exactly to the second passage of the Sun through the zenith of the city of Mexico; but in the year 13 *acatl,* the fasti of which are found in this monument, the day 4 *rain* preceded this passage six days. As the whole period of thirteen days, in which the Sun reaches the zenith, is dedicated to the sign *ollin Tonatiuh,* and the milky way, *citlalcueye;* and as the day 4 rain constantly belongs to this same period; it seems probable, that the Mexicans indicated this last day in preference, in order that the figure of the Sun should be surrounded by four signs, which had all the same number four; and particularly to form an allusion to the four destructions of the Sun, which tradition places in the days 4 tiger, 4 wind, 4 water, and 4 rain. The five small rounds, which are found on the left of the day 2 ape, immediately above the sign *malinalli,* seem to allude to the festival of the god *Macuil-Malinalli,* who had particular altars; this festival was celebrated about the 12th of September, called *Macuilli Malinalli.* The point of the triangle, which separates the sign of the day, 1 silex, from the sign of the night *tletl,* or fire, is directed toward the first of the twenty asterisms of the signs of the zodiac, because, in the year 13 canes, the day 1 *cipactli* corresponds to the day of the autumnal equinox: about this time was celebrated a festival of ten days, the most solemn of which was the day 10 *Ollin,* or 10 Sun, which corresponds to our 16th of September. It is believed at Mexico, that the two compartments placed under the tongue of the god Ollin Tonatiuh present twice the number five; but this explanation appears to me as doubtful, as that which has been attempted to be given of the forty compartments surrounding the zodiac, and of the numbers 6, 10, and 18, which are repeated toward the edge of the stone. We shall not examine whether the holes made in this enormous stone were made, as Mr. Gama thought, to place wires to serve as gnomons. What is more certain, and highly important to Mexican chronology, is, that this monument proves, in opposition to the opinion of Gemelli and Boturini, that the first day, whatever be the sign of the year, is constantly presided by *cipactli,* a sign which corresponds to the capricorn of the Greek sphere. We may suppose, that near this stone another was placed, which contained the fasti from the autumnal equinox to that of the spring.

We have now collected under the same point of view all that is hitherto known of the division of time among the Mexican nations, carefully distinguishing what is certain from what is merely probable. We see from what has been explained respecting the form of the year, how imaginary are those hypotheses, by which sometimes the lunar years, sometimes years of two hundred and eighty-six days divided into twenty-two months, have been attributed to the Toltecks and the Aztecks.[18] The knowledge of the system of the calendar followed by the most northerly nations of America and Asia would be highly interesting. Among the inhabitants of Nootka, we still find the Mexican months of twenty days; but their year has only fourteen months, to which they add, by very complex methods, a great number of intercalary days.[19] When a nation does not regulate the subdivisions of the year after the same lunations, the number of months becomes very arbitrary, and its choice seems to depend only on a particular predilection for certain numbers. The Mexican nations preferred the double decads, because they had simple signs only for the units, for twenty, and for the powers of twenty.

The use of periodical series, and the hieroglyphics of the day, have exhibited striking analogies between the nations of Asia and those of America. Some of these examples have not escaped the penetration of Mr. Dupuis (Dupuis 1806, 99), though he has confounded the signs of the months with those of the days, and had but a very imperfect knowledge of the Mexican chronology. It would be contrary to the end we have proposed to ourselves in this work, to dwell on theories respecting the ancient civilization of the inhabitants of the north, and of the centre of Asia. Thibet and Mexico offer analogies sufficiently remarkable in their ecclesiastical hierarchy, in the number of religious assemblies, in the severe austerity of their penitentiary rites, and in the order of their processions. It is impossible not to be struck with this resemblance, in reading with attention the recital, which Cortez made the Emperor Charles V, of his solemn entrance into Cholula, which he calls the holy city of the Mexicans.

A people who regulated its festivals according to the motion of the stars, and who engraved its *fasti* on a public monument, had no doubt reached a degree of civilization superior to that which has been allowed by Pauw, Raynal, and even Robertson, the most judicious of the historians of America. These writers consider every state of society as barbarous, that did not bear the type of civilization, which they, according to their systematic ideas, had formed. We cannot admit these abrupt distinctions into barbarous and civilized nations. After having examined in this work with scrupulous impartiality whatever we ourselves have been able to discover respecting the ancient state of the nations of the New Continent, we have endeavoured to combine the features by which they are immediately characterized, and those by which they seem to be connected with different groups of Asiatics. The state of nations and of individuals is the same: as, in the latter, the whole faculties of the mind unfold themselves but gradually, so, in the former, the progress of civilization does not manifest itself at once in the melioration of public and private manners, in a taste for the arts, and in the form of general institutions. Before we class nations, we should study them according to their specific characters, since external circumstances may give an infinite variety to the shades of civilization, which distinguish tribes of a different race; especially when, fixed in regions far remote from each other, they have long lived under the influence of governments and religious rites hostile to the progress of the mind, and to the preservation of individual liberty.

Notes

1. Humboldt's contribution to studies of Mexico ancient and modern has been the subject of many studies. See Bernal 1962; Cañizares-Esguerra 2001; Keen 1971; Kirchhoff 1962; Kubler 1991; León-Portilla 1962; Matos Moctezuma 1969; Miranda 1962; Ortega y Medina 1960; Pagden 1993; Pratt 1992a, 1992b; Quiñones Keber 1992, 1996; Stuart 1992; and Zea and Magallón Anaya 1999.

2. And these were only the editions he published between 1805 and 1834 (Stuart 1992, 8).

3. For extensive discussions of eighteenth-century European views of the New World, see esp. Keen 1971; Cañizares-Esguerra 2001; and Gerbi 1982.

4. See Cañizares-Esguerra 2001, 55–59, 125–29, for a discussion of Humboldt's reorientation of the debate from Greece and Rome to Asia and also for an account of how his work contributed to the genre of philosophical history.

5. Although Humboldt published the first accurate reproduction of several pages of the *Dresden Codex,* his discussion of the Maya calendar is vague and derives from Francisco Núñez de la Vega's work on Chiapas (1702), as filtered through Lorenzo Boturini Benaduci, Mariano Fernández de Echeverría y Veytia, and Francisco Saverio Clavigero.

6. See Stacie Graham Widdifield, this volume.

7. See Humboldt 1810 (folio edition), 7, pl. 3d.

8. The year 1577. Torquemada 1723, 2:157.

9. Torquemada 1723, 2:33, 34, 36.

10. Humboldt 1811–12, 2:24.

11. [The exact location of the Aztec Templo Mayor was not known until the early twentieth century. In Humboldt's time, the Zócalo of Mexico City seemed a likely site for the Templo Mayor. See Boone 1987.]

12. *Codex Borgia* 1900, fol. 49, pl. 15, no. 4 [not reproduced here].

13. See Humboldt 1810, 282.

14. See also Moor 1810.

15. Zoega 1797, 464; where, by an error of the press, the words *dextrorsum* and *sinistrorsum* are confounded with each other.

16. Nieremberg 1635, bk. 8, chap. 22, 142–56. Parts of the temple, nos. 3, 8, 9, 20, 25.

17. Nahui atl, atl, atl. . . .

18. Waddilove, in Robertson's *The History of America* (1803, 3:403).

19. Don Joze Mozinno, "Viage a Noutka," MS; see Humboldt 1811–12, 1:335.

The "Aztec Calendar Stone" (1876)

Editor's Commentary

Alfredo Chavero (1841–1906) was one of the most prominent late nineteenth-century writers on ancient Mexico in a group that included Leopoldo Batres, Nicolas León, Gumesindo Mendoza, Manuel Orozco y Berra, Francisco del Paso y Troncoso, and Jesús Sánchez. He was an attorney, a congressman in Mexico for more than twenty years, and a close associate of the Mexican statesman and hero Benito Juárez. Chavero's reputation rests upon his efforts as an editor of the Durán Codex *and* Codex Aubin *(Durán et al. 1867–80), the works of Fernando Alvarado Tezozómoc (1878), writings by Fernando de Alva Ixtlilxóchitl (1891–92), the* Historia de Tlaxcala *(Muñoz Camargo 1892), the* Lienzo de Tlaxcalla *(1892), and the* Codex Borgia *(1900). He was also a successful playwright and writer of popular works, such as* Xóchitl *(1878b),* Quetzalcóatl *(1877b), and* Los amores de Alarcón *(1879).*

Many writers between Antonio León y Gama and Chavero published descriptions of the Calendar Stone.[1] But Chavero's interpretations, beginning in 1875 and continuing in the Anales del Museo Nacional de México *(1877a, 1882, 1886, 1903) and a long treatment in the first volume of* México a través de los siglos *(1888), dominated the discourse about the monument in Mexico during the Porfiriato. He repeated and reprinted his arguments often, and other writers, such as Philipp J. J. Valentini, Adolph Bandelier (1879), Orozco y Berra (1880), Dionisio Abadiano (1889), and Eduard Seler (this volume), must be read as responding to Chavero. His earliest study, "Calendario Azteca" (Chavero 1875), reprinted nearly verbatim in 1876, was a reply to a previously unpublished essay on the Mexican calendar by León y Gama in the* Diccionario geográfico, estadístico, histórico, biográfico, de industria e comercio de la República Mexicana *(León y Gama 1875; Pérez Hernández 1874–75).*

Chavero's essay of 1875 was printed at the end of the same volume as the León y Gama contribution, and an editor's note states that he was prompted to write to refute the idea that the Calendar Stone actually depicts the Aztec calendar; *instead he argues that its solar associations would be better acknowledged by calling it* La Piedra del Sol, *the Sun Stone, the name by which it is still known in Mexico and the Spanish-speaking world.[2] Chavero also demolishes León y Gama's proposal that there were actually two* Calendar Stones, *one horizontal and one vertical, and that a series of gnomons and strings between the two tracked the equinoxes, solstices, zenith passages, and various anniversaries. He asserts that there was but one stone, installed horizontally, and it was*

Excerpted and translated by Khristaan D. Villela from Alfredo Chavero, *"Calendario Azteca": Ensayo arqueológico,* 2nd ed. (Mexico City: Jens & Zapiain, 1876). The same text also appears in Chavero's collected works (1904, 1:231–85). Introductory text by Khristaan D. Villela.

a cuauhxicalli, *a kind of sacrificial vessel described by Diego Durán, a source unknown to León y Gama. Chavero purchased José F. Ramírez's library and papers after the latter's death in 1871, and some comments in* Calendario Azteca *(Chavero 1876) suggest that he had access to an unpublished, and now lost, Ramírez manuscript on the monument. Again based on Durán, Chavero attributes the* Calendar Stone *to the Aztec ruler Axayacatl. He also expands León y Gama's discussion of the previous world creations, or suns, by linking references on the* Calendar Stone *to an image from the* Codex Vaticanus A, *published by Alexander von Humboldt in 1810.*

Although other writers in the 1870s and 1880s commented on the Calendar Stone,[3] *Chavero's only peer was the German Valentini (1824–99), who was trying to publish a study on the monument in 1875, seemingly* before *Chavero's first study appeared in November of the same year.[4] Valentini presented a summary of his research in German in New York in April 1878, and the lecture was later published in German, English, and Spanish (1878b, 1878a, 1877). Between Valentini's lecture and its publication by the American Antiquarian Society in October 1878, the editors of the* Nation *accused him of plagiarizing Chavero's work, noting that it was "singular and striking to what extent the* cuaderno *of the learned Mexican scholar agrees, if not verbatim, at least substantially with Mr. Valentini's essay." They also objected to Valentini's statement that he was the first writer on the* Calendar Stone *since León y Gama. Valentini responded in the* Nation *in a letter to the editor on 10 September that he and Chavero had arrived independently at many of the same conclusions and that whereas he used the works of Alvarado Tezozómoc, his Mexican colleague based his conclusions on Durán.[5]*

Unfortunately, in addition to attacking Valentini, the editors at the Nation *also drew from the work of both authors to state that the* Calendar Stone *was nothing more than a gigantic "slaughter block" and not proof that the Aztecs practiced advanced science and astronomy. We can better understand why they fixed upon this detail by recalling that Lewis Henry Morgan's influential essay "Montezuma's Dinner," published in July 1876 in the* North American Review, *presents a negative image of ancient Mexican civilization. Morgan and Bandelier argue that the Aztec cities, temples, and kings described by the superstitious (read Catholic) and credulous Spanish were actually pueblos, longhouses, and sachems, or chiefs, like those found among native North Americans.[6]*

Chavero discusses his relationship with Valentini in his article (1877a) in the Anales del Museo Nacional de México. *But many details lead us to conclude that Chavero's article and the first volume of the* Anales *were not published until 1878, and more likely 1879; he makes reference to Valentini's New York lecture (April 1878) and the exchange in the* Nation *(August and September 1878). Chavero, writing in a cautious manner, notes that the Mexican consul in New York gave Valentini a copy of his pamphlet and that they corresponded about the* Calendar Stone. *In a later essay, Chavero addresses the plagiarism charge again, and although he adopts a conciliatory tone, it seems clear he felt aggrieved (1886, 1n1). Valentini's published interpretations of the* Calendar Stone *are remarkably similar to Chavero's, but he departs from the latter by arguing that the monument contained historical references, in addition to mythological and astronomical ones.[7] Today we remember Valentini mostly for arguing that Diego de Landa's Maya hieroglyphic alphabet was a forgery (1880). But during his lifetime, Valentini was well respected, and his death was recorded in the* American Anthropologist *and the* New York Times.[8]

Chavero was partly responsible for the persistent idea that the Calendar Stone *presented a complete cosmology, an Aztec cosmogram in which every element should be counted and multiplied to arrive at significant calendrical or astronomical figures. At times he seems unable to parse the imagery into meaningful units, splitting iconographic elements that should have been left whole, and vice versa. This approach only exacerbates his tendency to interpret symbols by counting them, a method of iconographic analysis also observed in nineteenth-century studies of Maya hieroglyphic writing. The long-term impact of his ideas was also blunted by imaginative and fabulous passages that begin (in 1875) as minor digressions and gradually become extended discussions of the ice ages and mammoths depicted in Aztec manuscripts and remembered in mythology.*

Chavero's study includes just one illustration of the Calendar Stone, *which seems to be redrawn and slightly corrected from Carl Nebel (1836). There are no illustrations of the various sculptures and codices he draws on to support his arguments. Although Chavero's study was the first that made use of Durán, we have cut most of the sections referring to this key source, since they either are reproduced in the Durán chapter in the present volume, are discussed in Emily Umberger's essay excerpted herein, or are less relevant because they refer to stones commissioned by Axayacatl.*

∗   ∗   ∗

The "Aztec Calendar Stone"

CALENDARIO AZTECA

I.

The large stone that is mounted vertically on the west side of the base of one of the towers of the cathedral of Mexico is known by this name. It was discovered during the paving of the Plaza Mayor in 1790 and moved to the site it still occupies. D. Antonio de León y Gama described and interpreted it in 1792 and, believing it was a calendar, gave it the name by which it is generally known.[9]

The description and explanation of our monument given by a man as learned as Gama is well known. His ideas have acquired the authority of law, and European and American authors, without exception, have accepted this classification of this stone, which is illustrated in countless works, always called the *Calendario Azteca.* Although learned men like Humboldt and Prescott did not doubt this, long study has convinced me that the monument is no calendar. We will see my reasons because, in their way, they prove a most interesting point about our ancient history; they address first the history of the stone, up to today unknown, which will be most important in dispelling doubts and contradictions.

Father Durán says, in his *Historia de las Indias de Nueva España:*

> He (the king Axayacatl) was also occupied in carving the famous and great stone, carved in great detail with the signs of the months, years, days, and weeks, with such care that it was a thing to see. Many of us saw and encountered this stone in the large square, next to the acequia. It was ordered buried by the Most Honorable and Reverend Sr. D. fray Alonso de Montúfar, most honorable Archbishop of Mexico, who is remembered fondly, because of the great offenses of murders committed on it.[10]

Sr. D. Fernando Ramírez adds to this paragraph the following note: "This would seem to describe [the monument] known as the Calendario mexicano located today at the foot of the base of one of the cathedral towers. It was discovered on 17 December 1790." There is no doubt it refers to this stone, because today, with the aid of the chronicles of Durán, Tezozómoc, and the anonymous manuscript called the *Codex Ramírez,* all the great sacrificial stones are known, and the one that concerns us was dedicated to the sun, constructed by order of Axayacatl. This agrees with the location of its discovery. We have already seen that Durán says that he and many others saw it in the great plaza, next to the acequia, and that it was buried by order of Archbishop Montúfar. Given its great weight, one would imagine it was buried in the same spot, next to the acequia. And so, in explaining the site where it was discovered, Gama says, "during the new paving, while they were lowering the old ground level of the Plaza, on 17 December of the same year, 1790, the second stone was discovered, only a half-vara deep,[11] and at a distance of 80 varas to the west of the second doorway of the Real Palacio, and 37 north of the Portal de las Flores, on its rear surface, etc." (1792, 11). By the distances given here, the stone ought to have been found near the southeast corner of the garden of the plaza, and thus on the banks of the acequia that passed in front of the Diputación and the Portal de las Flores. It was at first uncovered, and when Sr. Montúfar ordered it buried, it was turned over, so that one could not see the carving, and they placed earth on top of it, leaving it only a half-vara beneath the pavement, since this was all its great weight permitted.

. . . The monument that today we call the Calendario Azteca is the same one discovered in 1790 in the Plaza Mayor, that is, the same that was ordered buried by Archbishop Montúfar, who held the miter of Mexico between 1551 and 1569; and this monument is the sun stone that Axayacatl ordered carved. And since there are no more facts about the history of this stone, we will now concern ourselves with it.

II.

. . . Durán does not say in which year the stone was completed, but the stone itself shows us because it was customary to record on monuments the date of notable events, and in this way its completion is recorded in the upper rectangle marked T (fig. 1), in which one can see the symbols . . . of the year 13 Acatl, or 1479, two years before the death of the king Axayacatl.

Gama thought this date referred to the halfway point or middle of the Mexican cycle, since the year comprised 365 days, and they made the correction at the end of the cycle; in this middle year they would verify with fair accuracy the arrival of the sun at the equinox, at the solstices, and at the zenith in the city. But this entire system is false, as we shall see. But for the time being we will simply assert that the *matlactli omey acatl* [13 Acatl, or 13 Reed] is the date of the construction of the monument. . . .

Gama's system is based on two assumptions: that there was not just one stone, but there was another similar one, which was associated with it, and that it was mounted on a horizontal base, erected vertically on an east-west line, and with its face to the south: in this way, with the gnomons fixed and the strings placed, which he refers to in his explanation, the two stones would successively mark the different movements of the sun during the year and serve as clocks during the day. Although it was an ingenious idea born in the brilliant imagination of Gama, it has no support.

In contrast, we will see that two stones are never mentioned; there is only one on the cathedral, only one discovered in 1790, only one ordered buried by Archbishop Montúfar, and only one that King Axayacatl ordered built. And so, the main support of [Gama's] system is entirely lacking.

The second fact is also false: the stone was lying horizontally. Much can be deduced from [Durán's] description of the construction that was ordered to house it, which we have seen was *twenty fathoms around,* to put the stone in the center—a construction and position that would not be understandable if it were placed vertically. One can infer with more certainty that sacrifices were made on it, which would demand horizontal placement, similar to the object that one can

Fig. 1.
Drawing of the *Aztec Calendar Stone,*
lettered for explanation by the author

see in [see pl. 20], in the second part of the Durán atlas; and for this reason it was ordered buried, because of the great offenses of murders committed on it. In describing the ceremonies of its consecration, we see that there is no doubt on this point.

Durán continues: "Once the stone was placed, all the lords present decided to discuss the way the sun stone should be celebrated and inaugurated, and from where the people should be brought for that sacrifice, and ordering them to wait for another day, the king and Tlacaelel decided to propose to the lords the Michoacán war, and with this decision they left it for another day."

The war in Michoacán was unfortunate, during which the Mexicans sought captives to sacrifice to the sun: beaten and routed, they returned to the city to bury their dead:

> After these funeral rites (Durán says),[12] Tlacaelel and the king decided to finish the ceremony
> of the sun image, and agreeing among themselves on who should be invited, they decided to call
> the lords of Huejotzingo and Cholula, and the lord of Metztitlan…the lords of those two cities
> prepared and readied themselves to come, and once prepared they went to the messengers and
> said to them: we are now ready, let us see what our nephew orders, and so they left, almost as
> one, from their cities, and arriving in Mexico they entered the city at night, without being seen,
> and were very well received by the king and well lodged. The lord of Metztitlan arrived later,
> who was called Cozcatotli.…These three lords having arrived, along with the lord of Tlaxcala,
> according to the account related in this chapter, the stone was ordered prepared and readied, and
> also those they had to sacrifice, for which the king prepared, who was the principal figure in this
> ritual, and then his assistant Tlacaelel; and then those who represented all the gods, which were
> Quetzalcoatl and Tlaloc, Opochtli, Itzpapalotl, Youalana, Apantecutli, Vitzilopochtli, and Toci,
> Ciuacoatl, Izquitecatl, Yenopilli, Mixcoatl, and Tepuztecatl, all these deities dressed to sacrifice
> ON TOP OF THE STONE, ALL OF THEM ON IT. Having prepared, before the dawn the king appeared
> very well dressed, and with him Tlacaelel, dressed in the same way, and with their flint knives
> in their hands THEY CLIMBED ATOP THE STONE: then they brought out the captives, all painted
> white and their head decorated with feathers and some large bunches of feathers in their lip-
> plugs,[13] and they placed them in a line at the place of the skulls, and before they began sacrificing
> them a censer came out of the temple with a large ax of incense, shaped like a snake, that they
> called *xiuhcoatl,* which was lit, and he made four circuits around this stone, smoking it with
> incense, and finally he threw it still on fire on top of the stone and there it ceased burning: once
> this was done the sacrifices began, with the king sacrificing, until he became tired, those captive
> men, and then Tlacaelel continued until he tired, and then those who represented the gods, in
> succession, until they finished with those seven hundred men that had been brought from the
> Tliliuhquitepec war. Once they were finished, leaving all of them stretched out next to the place
> of the skulls, and the whole temple and patio covered with blood, which was a fearful thing, and
> something that nature itself abhors, the king went and offered his guests very rich mantles, and
> jewels and rich feathers. Having fed them very well, he sent them back to their lands, and they
> returned to their lands frightened and astonished by such a horrendous thing.…

Now we have the history of our stone from its construction in 1479 until its dedication in 1481. It was an unlucky stone for the king Axayacatl. To honor it with sacrifices he undertook the disastrous Michoacán campaign. Two years passed before he could consecrate it, and the sacrifices he performed upon it led to his death.

The account above confirms our ideas and is contrary to those of Gama. They would climb atop it because it was placed horizontally, and it was for the same reason a true *cuauhxicalli.* Therefore, the gnomons set in it, and the cords whose shadows ought to have marked the seasons and the hours never existed; this stone was never a calendar, it was the *Piedra del Sol* [*Stone of the Sun*], as it is called in the chronicle, and on its surface they did not seek to track the passage of time, but rather to tear out the hearts of victims.

This *cuauhxicalli* was in the Templo Mayor [district], in a place called Quauhxicalco. In the list of the seventy-eight parts of the great *teocalli* that Nieremberg gives us,[14] we find various locations with the same name; but being that this stone is principally a manifestation of the four movements of the sun, it was found without a doubt, on account of its connection to the symbolic [number] four, in the eighth house, that, according to Nieremberg, was called the Quauhxilco, in which the king would give penance and celebrate the fast called the Netonatiuh Caoalo, which lasted four days, and was undertaken in honor of the sun. There they would kill four captives, two in the image of the sun and moon, and another two called Chachame....

III.

The real calendar of the Mexicans was the *tonalamatl:* it gave them each day with its *acompañado,* or respective patron god,[15] the *trecenas,* or religious weeks of thirteen days, during which certain deities ruled, the sacred year of 260 days, and finally, repeating the series of days, the solar year of 365 days; it also gave them for each day the auguries and superstitions that played such a principal role among the Mexicans. All of this constituted and had to be part of the Aztec calendar. Does the stone that occupies our attention have this? We see the image of the sun, in its symbol *nahui ollin,* or four movements—A, B, C, D—surrounded by the symbols of the days 1 through 20, but I see no more. How would a Mexican come to recognize the different *trecenas* on the stone, if they are distinguished by their respective gods, and there are none here? How would one recognize even one day of the year, if each is distinguished by its successive Lord of the Night [*acompañado*] and number, since there are only twenty day signs, their repetition by themselves eighteen times per year would cause confusion? How would they be distinguished, if on our stone the Lords of the Night are absent? Would they be able to tell the years when one can see the symbol for only one of them, *acatl,* with *tochtli, calli,* and *tecpatl* entirely missing? If the festivals were determined by the combination of their gods and their signs, and here we lack the gods and the signs are not combined, what practical use could this stone possibly have? Did it tell the season and the hours of the day by means of the gnomons that, according to Gama, were fixed at points X, Z, P, P, Q, Q, S, and Y? Hardly, because that combination required two stones, and we have seen that there was never more than one; it also required a vertical position, and our stone was placed horizontally. In addition, the said eight points, or holes in which the gnomons would be fixed, do not exist. And so, what kind of calendar is this stone that does not give us the years, the months, the *trecenas,* the days, the hours, or the religious festivals? We must, then, acknowledge that this was no calendar. Then what was it? The chronicle tells us: it was the stone of the sun, a monument raised to the father of the light, which they consecrated with sacrifices on it. We will examine this most interesting stone in this light, which is the correct one, and we will lose nothing if we abandon the fantastic combinations of Gama, because I believe that in no other monument from antiquity can such science and such wonder be found as in this one....

And so, among the Tlapaltecans and later among the Toltecs there were three earlier suns, and they lived in the fourth sun. Among the Mexica, the number was increased; there were four earlier suns, and they lived in the fifth. In not keeping the epochs [of the sources] apart, our writers have found contradictions where there are none. It is true that sometimes the chroniclers tell us of four suns and other times of five, but everything agrees if one is careful to distinguish the different ages of the sources. The Toltecs had four suns and the Mexica five; clearly the change from the fourth to the fifth sun ought to have happened in the time between the Toltec and Mexican empires. Sr. Orozco y Berra thinks that the event that served as the start of the fifth sun was the dedication of the pyramids of Teotihuacan. Gama had already advanced the same idea (León y Gama 1792, 97). "The Mexicans," this author says, "believed that the sun had died four times, or that there had been four suns, that had ended in other times or ages.... After these fictions they made up the myth of the gods that met for the creation of the fifth sun and the moon, with the ridiculous accounts of Torquemada, Boturini, Clavigero, and others that tell the fable of the syphilitic god [Buboso], who threw himself into the fire to become the sun."

If one connects this legend with that of the death of the gods,[16] one can of course see that the theme is a change of religion, not a cataclysm. Every sun ended with a cataclysm, and the death of the gods, in contrast, was the passage to a new and more advanced religious era. The tradition relates another end to the fourth sun. The interpreter of the *Codex Vaticanus*[17] gives us the key to this difficulty. "The fourth age, according to what the legend says, was that in which the province of Tula was founded, that was said to have been destroyed because of vices, and for this reason the people are shown dancing. On account of these vices great famines ensued, and thus the province was destroyed." Thus the fourth sun ended with the Toltec nation, and that was the source of the idea the Mexica had that the fifth sun would end with them.

IV.

Returning to our stone, we have already seen that it represents the sun as a heavenly body, within the form that encircles everything and ends with the rays L and R. In this form the sun is the heavenly body, the god, and thus in the hieroglyphic composition it is called by the name *teotl,* god, and with the phonetic value of *teo,* as it can be seen repeatedly in the *Codex Mendoza.*[18] But in the central form, in the four rectangles or arms A, B, C, and D, is the Nahui Ollin, which literally means four movements, and represents [the movements] of the sun at the two solstices and two equinoxes. But here, inside its rectangles, we have the representations of the four suns, or ages about which we have spoken; so that in addition to its four movements in the year, the sun shows us its four cosmogonic epochs previous to the Aztecs.

However, it bears mentioning that on this stone, an authentic record of the religious and cosmogonic beliefs of the Mexicans, that the order of the cataclysms is different. The reading order of the signs is left to right [or counterclockwise], as can be seen in the order of the twenty day signs, from Cipactli 1 to Xochitl 20. Also, rectangle B would be the first, and represents Ehecatonatiuh, the wind sun; C, the second, which is Tlequiahuilli, or the rain of fire; D, the third, which is Atonatiuh, and lastly Tlaltonatiuh, A, the sun of the earth. In the same way, one can observe that among the writers there are some that, setting aside the Toltec tradition, follow the order on this stone. Leaving this study for a more extensive work, it should of course be mentioned that, just as the historical or calamitous event of the destruction of Tollan was the origin of the fourth sun and changed the Tlapalteca tradition, the order of the Mexican tradition should also have been changed by something. The combination of these four cataclysms with the four movements of the sun on our stone gives us the simple explanation. And so the four arms A, B, C, and D give us: (1) the four movements of the sun, (2) the four suns or calamities, (3) the four elements, air, fire, water, and earth, (4) the four seasons.

This last fact produced the change of order. The Mexican year began, at least at the time when this stone was carved, in our month of January: in Mexico, this month and also February and March are notable for strong winds that we call Carnestolendas, and for this reason in this first season and first arm of the Nahui Ollin, Ehecatl or wind, was placed, and the Ehecatonatiuh calamity was placed first. The warmest months follow, April, May, and June, and this is the reason that Tlequiahuilli, the rain of fire, is found in the second arm. The rainy season follows in July, August, and September, and for this reason the third arm is occupied by the symbols for Atl, water, and by the Atonatiuh, or flood. Finally, in the last three months the winter dries the land, and with reason the calamity of the earth, Tlaltonatiuh, occupies the last arm....

VI.

Sr. Don Fernando Ramirez, in his manuscript notes, says that the circles [E and F] enclose some teeth that refer to the god Tlaloc. Although the symbolic teeth of this god resemble the signs inside the circles, I believe that Sr. Ramirez was misled, since examining the image carefully, one can see that these are no teeth, but two claws perfectly depicted.

Gama more closely approaches the truth. "The circular forms, that is, of the letters E and F, that unite the four images, contain within them some kind of claws that denote or are related to the aforementioned creators of the *tonalamatl,* Cipactonal, and Oxomoco, who are shown in it in some hideous images in the form of Eagles or Owls."[19] A little further on,[20] completely in error, he adds: "The two heads, with their adornments, similar in every way, which are at the lower part of the circle, shown by the letter O, and that interrupt the circle at that part, represent the Lord of the Night, named Yohautecuhtli, who they imagined to divide the rule of the night, and divided it among the Lords of the Night, giving to every one that which was assigned to it, from midnight (which is signified by the division formed by the two faces)." This, as we will see below, was one of the errors of Gama. The claws of Nahui Ollin, and the two faces mentioned refer to the same myth, to the duality of Oxomoco Cipactli.

What do these two personages signify? The popular tradition relates, according to Gama:[21] "The inventors of the *tonalamatl,* who were Cipactonal and his wife Oxomoco, great sorcerers and judicial astrologers." This story did not satisfy me, from the moment that I understood that the mythical personages of the Nahuas always symbolized some astronomical idea. Considering the idea of dualism in the gods, this marriage attracted my attention, which is not however, represented in the calendar, but rather in the person of Cipactli, the first day of the religious year. I then suspected that both myths conveyed the same idea, expressed in duality: one idea and two persons....

...Cipactonal had as his wife Oxomoco or Xomico, who represented the night, the one that, as we have seen, is depicted as an owl. Being one and two, both myths are mixed up, and the same is true for Cipactonal and Oxomoco. In the same way on our stone the central form A, B, C, and D, with the circles of claws E and F, is the owl, Cipactonal and Oxomoco, the duality that created the calendar and representation of the annual course of the sun. The man and woman in the *Codex Borgia* (1900, 9), who are wrapped up in the same mantle, seemingly procreating, are the same Cipactonal and Oxomoco, and the ray that comes out between them is not a symbol of ruin [*perdición*], as Fabregat thought, but rather it is the arrow H and I on our stone, that represents the line of the meridian, on the sides of which the sun makes its four movements, on account of which one always sees it in the center of the Nahui Ollin. The double figure R, that serves as the base [outer ring] of the stone, and that has the two heads O in its teeth, is the Cipactli, the light, the foundation of all of this sublime combination. The snakes S and Y are its forelegs. The light also surrounds the entire image of the sun, like an aureole, and the fantastic signs V, that Gama thought were clouds are not, but rather they are the Cipactli, the atmosphere of light that surrounds the sun Tonatiuh.

To conclude with this point, more than interesting, sublime, of the light and its creation, I will observe that one of the large sacrificial stones, which is still buried in front of the Palacio Nacional, and that in its painted reliefs was thought to show the gladiatorial contest, shows at its center the duality Ometecuhtli creating Cipactli. The god has his distinctive headdress and raises his head to the sky, where the first light appears. A copy in colors, taken directly from the stone, can be found in the museum, and one can see a lithograph that was published in the translation of the *Conquest of Mexico* by Prescott, published by Sr. Garcia Torres.[22]

VII.

…Now we will examine what new ideas we can offer for Oxomoco. Guided by the idea of duality and the fact that she was the wife of Cipactli in the establishment of the calendar and in the story of the ages, it is easy to presume that if Cipactli is the light, Oxomoco ought to be the darkness; that if the first, as Tonatiuh, is the sun, the second, as Metztli, is the moon; and finally, that if Tonacatecuhtli is the day, Tonacacihuatl ought to be the night.

In the *Codex Borgia,* two images after the one previously cited, [p. 11] Oxomoco is represented in the form of Tonacacihuatl and with a cloud full of stars in her hand, that is, the Milky Way, and from this comes the name Mixcoatl, "cloud shaped like a serpent," a perfect conception of our nebula. Her symbol above is an owl, a nocturnal animal that has in its claws an arc of the dark circle of night. Its companion is the symbol of the moon, a kind of *comitl* made of stars, with a white rabbit inside.

…The two forelegs S and Y are also representations of the Mixcoatl, and their bodies appear studded with stars.…

To conclude this point, I will observe that on the forelock of Cipactli are thirteen stars, which are in my view some constellation of the Nahuas.

Finally, the Nahui Ollin symbol, accompanied by the twenty characters of the days, as one can see in the center of our stone, can also be found on page 14 of the *Codex Borgia.*

VIII.

…It is not a calendar, as Gama believed, and with him many wise men, but it is a stone that keeps the greatest mysteries of Nahua science: longer studies will uncover more about this hieroglyph that is the light and from which the brilliant rays will come one day to illuminate the secrets of Aztec theology.

Notes

1. See, for example, Alexander von Humboldt, this volume; Bullock 1824b; Poinsett 1825; Ward 1828; Nebel 1836; Calderon de la Barca 1843; Mayer 1847, 1853; Tylor 1861; and Bullock 1866.

2. In his last works on the *Calendar Stone,* for the Museo Nacional de México, Chavero decided that the *Calendar Stone* should actually be called the *Cyclographic Stone.*

3. See, for example, Bandelier 1879, 1884.

4. On 1 October 1875, the American Philosophical Society voted to ask Daniel Brinton to write Valentini for more information on his *Calendar Stone* manuscript, which was proposed for publication. Valentini's response to Brinton two months later was apparently unsatisfactory, since the latter soon criticized the German's work for using doubtful codices and outdated sources. See *Proceedings of the American Philosophical Society* 14 (1875): 642; and Philipp J. J. Valentini to D. G. Brinton, 29 December 1875, American Indian Manuscripts item no. 2195, and Daniel G. Brinton to J. P. Lesley, 20 January 1876, American Indian Manuscripts item 2170, American Philosophical Society, Philadelphia.

5. See *Nation* 27 (684): 84, 8 August 1878, and 27 (690): 176–77, 10 September 1878.

6. See Villela 2001; and Keen 1971.

7. Valentini thought the *Calendar Stone* was both a complete exposition of the 365-day calendar (according to him, composed of 260- and 105-day counts) and also referred to the year A.D. 231, arrived at by subtracting 1248 years (twenty-four symbols on the stone, erroneously interpreted as each representing fifty-two years) from 1479, the supposed dedication date of the monument.

8. See Gatschet 1899; and *New York Times,* 19 March 1899.

9. See León y Gama 1792, 1804, 1832.

10. Durán et al. 1867–80, 1:272.

11. [A vara is .84 m.]

12. Durán et al. 1867–80, 1:300, 301, 302.

13. [Heyden (Durán 1994, 289) has "nose-plug," but Durán wrote *bezotes,* "lip plug" or "labret."]

14. Nieremberg 1635, bk. 8, chap. 22.

15. [The *acompañados* were the Lords of the Night.]

16. Mendieta 1870, bk. 2, chap. 1.

17. Kingsborough 1831–48, vol. 5, pl. 10.

18. Kingsborough 1831–48, vol. 1.

19. León y Gama 1792, 99.

20. León y Gama 1792, 103.

21. León y Gama 1792, 98.

22. See Prescott 1844, vol. 1, facing p. 85, the now-lost *Stone of the Gladiators.* There never was such a stone. The work is actually a manuscript leaf of an Aztec-related pictorial codex that is now in the Bibliothèque nationale de France, Paris. The work was purchased by J. M. A. Aubin in 1830 and taken from Mexico, which is perhaps why writers for the rest of the century throught it was a stone sculpture. It was reproduced as early as the 1770s, in William Robertson's *The History of America.*

GUMESINDO MENDOZA AND JESÚS SÁNCHEZ

Catalog of the Historical and Archaeological Collections of the Museo Nacional de México (1882)

Editor's Commentary

Although the first true catalog of the national archaeological collections of Mexico was not published until 1882—it is excerpted below—many colonial-era and early nineteenth-century writers collected materials about Pre-Columbian Mexico, including Juan de Torquemada, Carlos Sigüenza y Góngora, Antonio de León y Gama, Mariano Veytia, and Carlos María de Bustamante. Although there were colonial-era collections of Mexican antiquities, especially during the eighteenth century, much activity focused on amassing documents, both the famous pictorial codices and lienzos *and prose descriptions of native Mexican languages, culture, religion, and the calendar.[1] Perhaps the most famous collector among this group was the Milanese Lorenzo Boturini Benaduci (ca. 1698–1750), who gathered about 350 documents in Mexico during a seven-year visit that began in 1736. Boturini ran afoul of the Spanish colonial authorities in 1743, and his collection was seized and gradually dispersed; some of the most important works are now found in Europe (Codex Azcatitlan, Aubin Tonalamatl), the United States (Fernando Alvarado Tezozómoc's* Crónica mexicana, *Fernando de Alva Ixtlilxóchitl's* Relaciones*), and Mexico (Boturini Codex [La tira de la peregrinación], Matrícula de tributos).[2] The history of Boturini's collection is intimately related to that of the* Calendar Stone, *because León y Gama's interpretations, and those of the writers who followed him, were shaped and even limited by which remnants of the Boturini collection they knew of or had access to.*

The Museo Nacional de Antropología was founded in 1825, within the walls of the old Real y Pontificia Universidad de México, which was located on the south side of the Palacio Nacional and to the east of the Plaza del Volador (where the Suprema Corte de Justicia de la Nación has stood since 1935). Various antiquities (like the Coatlicue*), documents (including some Boturini items), historical objects, and natural history specimens had been housed at the university since colonial times.[3] Others were scattered across Mexico City, kept at the art school Academia de San Carlos, and even incorporated into buildings, such as the snake-head sculpture that is still visible as a cornerstone of the Palacio de los Condes de Santiago de Calimaya, now the Museo de la Ciudad de México. Guillermo Dupaix compiled an unpublished inventory of Mexican antiquities in as early as 1794, and León y Gama's treatise (1792, 1832) attempted to describe key works of ancient Mexican manufacture.[4] After Independence from Spain in 1821, Isidro Ignacio de Icaza and Isidro Rafael Gondra attempted to write a catalog of the archaeological holdings of the Museo Nacional (with lithographs by J. F. Waldeck), but only a few works were described in the edition of 1827 (Icaza and*

Excerpted and translated by Khristaan D. Villela from Gumesindo Mendoza and Jesús Sánchez, *Catálogo de las colecciones histórica y arqueológica del Museo Nacional de México* (Mexico City: Impr. de I. Escalante, 1882). Introductory text by Khristaan D. Villela.

101

Gondra 1827, 1927). Between these early efforts and the beginning of the French Intervention in 1862, José F. Ramírez served as museum director several times and published three brief descriptions of Pre-Columbian objects stored in the university (1844, 1855–56, 1857), but Mexico's political instability precluded more formal efforts to catalog and publish the national collections. With the exception of León y Gama's work, the Calendar Stone *is not part of the several short descriptions of Mexican antiquities written and published by Mexican authors until 1882. Perhaps it was not described because it was not on site in the Museo Nacional. But in contrast, the* Calendar Stone *is invariably present in the accounts of Mexican antiquities published by foreign travelers and writers, such as Alexander von Humboldt (1810, 1814), Carl Nebel (1836), and Brantz Mayer (1844). One visitor, the English showman William Henry Bullock (1824a), assembled a museum-like exhibit with casts of the* Calendar Stone, *the* Coatlicue, *and the* Stone of Tizoc *that would have been impossible in Mexico because the monuments were not gathered together, and indeed the* Calendar Stone *could not be moved from its place on the cathedral (see p. 7, fig. 1; p. 22, fig. 9).*

Emperor Maximilian moved the museum from the university to the old mint on Calle de la Moneda in 1864 and refounded it as the Museo Público de Historia Natural, Arqueología e Historia, with the Austrian Dominik Bilimek (1813–84) as its curator (Jurok 1991). Although Bilimek is best known for his research on plants and insects, he collected approximately eight hundred Mexican archaeological objects, including the eponymous Bilimek Pulque Vessel *(see p. 284, fig. 9).[5] With the execution of Maximilian and the restoration of the Benito Juárez government in 1867, a younger generation entered Mexico's archaeological arena, and within a decade the Porfirio Díaz regime placed new emphasis on professional historical and archaeological research at the institution rechristened the Museo Nacional de México.*

Gumesindo Mendoza (1829–86) was a medical doctor who was a professor of pharmacy and chemistry at the Escuela Nacional de Medicina. After his appointment as director of the Museo Nacional de México in 1877, he founded the Anales *of the museum, an important publication for the history of the* Calendar Stone *and Mexican archaeology in general. Mendoza served as director until 1885 and oversaw (with Leopoldo Batres) the relocation of the Aztec* Calendar Stone.[6] *Like Mendoza, Jesús Sánchez (1842–1911) was a medical doctor by training. He succeeded Mendoza as director of the Museo Nacional de México in 1885, a position he held until 1889. During Sánchez's tenure, President Díaz inaugurated the Salón de Monolítos on 16 September 1887, with the* Calendar Stone *prominently displayed opposite the main doorway, and Mexico also planned its participation in the* Exposition universelle, *held in Paris in 1889.*

The Mendoza and Sánchez catalog of 1882 was the first attempt to publish a complete catalog, and it was followed by several other versions, both official and unofficial, with the most important written by Jesús Galindo y Villa (1895), republished in at least three editions into the early twentieth century.[7] The Calendar Stone *appears twice in the Mendoza and Sánchez catalog, in the form of Dionisio Abadiano's cast and the real monument, which is listed as object no. 1, almost as if the authors willed the work to be part of a museum from which it was removed by several hundred yards.[8] Three years later, in 1885, the* Calendar Stone *was moved to the patio of the museum on Calle de la Moneda, where it is listed in the catalog entry below.[9]*

✻   ✻   ✻

Catalog of the Historical and Archaeological Collections of the Museo Nacional de México

PATIO OF THE MUSEUM[10]

No. 1.

Calendario Azteca.– La Piedra del Sol.[11] Diameter, 3m 35.

On 17 December 1790, while lowering the ground of the Plaza Mayor in order to level it, this notable Aztec monument was discovered, buried a half-vara deep, at thirty-seven varas north of the Portal de las Flores and eighty from the second doorway of the Palacio Nacional. The commissaries of the building of the cathedral, D. José Uribe and D. Juan J. Gamboa, asked the viceroy for it, and by a verbal order it was delivered to them on the condition that they look after it and exhibit it in a public place.[12]

Baron Humboldt calculated its weight at 482 quintals, or 24,400 kilograms: he said it is a blackish-gray trappean porphyry, with a basis of basaltic wacke. On carefully examining some fragments, he recognized hornblende, numerous crystals of vitreous feldspar, and, notably, small grains of mica. The famous scholar observed that none of the mountains that surround the capital, to a distance of eight or ten leagues, could have furnished porphyry of this grain and color, which shows the great difficulty that the Aztecs had in transporting it to the Templo Mayor.

Our celebrated archaeologist León y Gama published an instructive historical and archaeological description of this and other Indian monuments. According to him, it is an Aztec calendar that marked the religious festivals and a sundial used by the priests for their sacrifices and ceremonies. Sr. Lic. A. Chavero argues that it could not be this kind of calendar since it lacks elements indispensable to timekeeping; it is rather a monument dedicated to the sun, upon which were performed sacrifices, and he calls it the *Piedra del Sol* (Chavero 1877a, 353).

Notes

1. A *lienzo* is a large cotton cloth painted by native Mexican artists with mythical, historical, genealogical, and geographic content.
2. See Boturini's *Catálogo del Museo Histórico Indiano,* an appendix of ninety-six pages to his work of 1746. Among the many sources on Boturini are Graham 1993; Martínez Hernández 1995; and Ramírez 1903. Glass (1975) reviews the various inventories made since 1743 and lists the current locations of the works, if known.
3. On the history of museums in Mexico, see Fernández 1987; Graham 1993; and Morales Moreno 1994.
4. Perhaps León y Gama intended to use Dupaix's drawings for the second half of his treatise, also begun in 1794, but published posthumously in 1832.
5. These works were shipped to Miramar, Maximilian's castle in Trieste, Italy, when the empire collapsed in 1867, and were given to the old Kaiserlich-Königliches naturhistorisches Hofmuseum in 1878. See Bahnson 1889, 88.
6. Biographical details on Mendoza from *Proceedings of the American Antiquarian Society* 1888, 172–74.
7. See *Álbum de antigüedades* 1902; Galindo y Villa 1895; and Blake 1891. Galindo y Villa's catalog features a lithograph of the *Calendar Stone* by the Swiss artist Jonas Engberg. We wonder why Galindo y Villa did not use either José María Velasco's drawing, published in Antonio Peñafiel's *Monumentos del arte mexicano antiguo* (1890) or that by Hesequio Iriarte, published in Batres's *IV Tlalpilli* (1888). Did every new interpretation require a new drawing?
8. The Abadiano cast appears in a section listing objects not on view, and Mendoza and Sánchez note that it was well regarded for its accuracy. Some copies of Dionisio Abadiano's treatise of 1889 on the *Calendar Stone,* including the one at the Research Library of the Getty Research Institute, have an albumen photograph of the cast; other examples have Francisco Abadiano's drawing of the monument.
9. As was the case with Alfredo Chavero's *Calendar Stone* article in the first volume of the *Anales del Museo Nacional de México,* dated 1877 but likely actually released up to two years later, the Mendoza and Sánchez catalog, in the same *Anales* series, must have been published after the date of 1882 on the title page, since it mentions the *Calendar Stone* on the cathedral but also lists it as in the patio of the museum, whence it was moved in 1885. Perhaps it was a case of wishful thinking.
10. The monuments located in the patio of the museum should be moved to the gallery on the ground floor, which is being prepared for this purpose.
11. This monument is mounted on the side of one of the towers of the cathedral and should be moved to the museum.
12. León y Gama 1832, pt. 1:10.

Collected Works in Mesoamerican Linguistics and Archaeology (1888, 1899, 1901, 1915)

Editor's Commentary

Eduard Seler (1849–1922) discussed the Calendar Stone *in several works published near the end of the nineteenth century and introduced both the iconographic methodology and most of the interpretations that have dominated modern studies of the monument. He argued that the* Calendar Stone *was both a* temalacatl, *a ring-shaped sacrificial stone, and a* cuauhxicalli *sacrificial basin, a ceremonial vessel described in the prose sources and illustrated in the pictorial manuscripts (1899). He later reversed himself in 1901 and argued that the* Calendar Stone *could only be a* cuauhxicalli, *since* temalacatls, *although similar in function, were drilled through the center to allow for the ropes that held captives in the gladiatorial sacrifice. Writers down to the present day, beginning with Hermann Beyer, have followed Seler's earlier theory in arguing that the* Calendar Stone *was both a* temalacatl *and a* cuauhxicalli.

For Seler, the Calendar Stone *simply depicts the sun, the sun god, and the dates of the previous creations enclosed in the Nahui Ollin sign, the name of the fifth, or present creation. He recognizes that the claws flanking the central face properly belonged to the earth god but does not suggest that it was a depiction of either that deity or a hybrid entity, like the night sun. He thinks that the stone's visual content would have been obvious to any ancient Mexican viewer and disagreed with writers who thought that its imagery encoded secret knowledge. Seler's iconographic analyses proceed from the imagery on the* Calendar Stone *to similar motifs on other objects and to interpretations grounded in prose and pictorial manuscript sources. His methodology demonstrates a conservative approach to interpretation; he advances judgments only when they seem reasonably secure and carefully avoids the kind of speculation and counting of iconographic elements that have characterized much* Calendar Stone *research. Only his reading of the four glyphs carved near the center of the relief as directional symbols has not proven productive.*

The first of the four works excerpted below, originally published in 1888, discusses the origin of the day sign Ollin. Several earlier writers argue that the Ollin glyph, and the imagery of the Calendar Stone *as a whole, is a graphic representation of the annual course of the sun, from the equinoxes to the solstices, represented as the bow shapes to the left (north = summer solstice) and right (south = winter solstice) of the arrow that pierces the sign from bottom to top in some examples.[1] Instead,*

The four excerpts presented here are from Eduard Seler, (1) "The Day Signs of the Aztec and Maya Manuscripts and Their Divinities," (2) *Quauhxicalli,* the Mexican Vessel for Sacrificial Blood," (3) "Excavations at the Site of the Principal Temple in Mexico," and (4) "The Creation of the World and of Humans, and the Birth of the Sun and Moon," in Eduard Seler, *Collected Works in Mesoamerican Linguistics and Archaeology, by Eduard Seler,* ed. Frank E. Comparato, 7 vols. (Lancaster, Calif.: Labyrinthos, 1990–2002), 1:119–65, 3:79–83, 3:114–93, 5:24–38. Originally edited 1939 by J. Eric Thompson and Francis B. Richardson. Courtesy Tozzer Library of Harvard College Library. Introductory text by Khristaan D. Villela.

Seler argues that the two "halves" of the Ollin refer to the day sky and the night sky, through which the sun travels every day.

Like Alexander von Humboldt a century earlier, Seler knew many more sculptures and was more conversant in the imagery of the codices than his American peers. He edited new editions of the Aubin Tonalamatl *(1900), the* Codex Fejérváry-Mayer *(1901), the* Codex Vaticanus B *(1902a), and the* Codex Borgia *(1904–1909, 1963) and published monograph-length studies of many ancient Mexican objects, such as that reproduced below, on the Ethnologisches Museum, Berlin,* cuauhxicalli. *He accepted Alfredo Chavero's attribution of the* Calendar Stone *to the reign of Axayacatl and thinks that it must have been placed in the Temple of the Sun, variously called the Cuauhcuauhtinchan, Cuauhcalli, Cuauhxicalco, or Cuauhxilco, southwest of the Templo Mayor itself.*

The present translations from Seler's Gesammelte Abhandlungen (1902–23, 1960c) were prepared under the supervision of Charles Bowditch (1842–1921) at Harvard University, who also oversaw an earlier volume of Mesoamerican articles translated from the German (Bowditch 1904). J. Eric S. Thompson and Francis Richardson edited and published the first two articles excerpted below in 1939; the last work was unpublished in English until 1996.

✳   ✳   ✳

Collected Works in Mesoamerican Linguistics and Archaeology
"THE DAY SIGNS OF THE AZTEC AND MAYA MANUSCRIPTS AND THEIR DIVINITIES"

…17. *olin.* Durán explains *olin* as "cosa que se anda ó se menea," and says that the sign was applied to the sun. We have indeed the verb *olini, oolin,* or *olinia, oninolini,* "menearse ó moverse," which, however, implies the above word as root. On the other hand we find *olli, ulli,* "caoutchouc," and "ball of rubber," with which the national game, *tlachtli,* was played. We know that the sun's course in the firmament was illustrated by the picture of the ball game.

The two antagonists, Quetzalcoatl and Tezcatlipoca, who seem to represent the contrast of summer and winter, of day and night, play ball together (according to Mendieta 1870, 2:82). The two bright heroes of the Qui'ché, Hunahpuh and Xbalanqué, who are explained in one place of the Popol Vuh as "sun" and "moon," are the noted ball players with whose playing the earth rings, who, at the call of the princes of the underworld, descend into the kingdom of the dead, Xibalba, and after vanquishing the underworld powers ascend victoriously again to the surface of the earth.

In Codex Borgia, on plate 35 (= 4 of Kingsborough's numbering) we find the familiar figure of the ball ground, *tlachco,* bordered by star-eyes. Above this lies a *cipactli* holding in its gaping jaws the face of the sky god Tonacatecutli. On the ground itself two black divinities are playing ball. The ball of one is dark (blue) and looks like a death's head; the other represents a yellow radiating disk with an eye in the middle. I am quite positive that these two balls symbolize the day and night planets, sun and moon, traveling the sky.

The pictorial representation of the day sign *olin* exhibits two differently colored fields, one blue, as a rule, and the other red. There is a round place in the center and two slanting ends either lie close together, divided only by a yellow line, or the ends diverge. In the representations of Codices Telleriano Remensis and Vaticanus A, as well as on sculptures, there is also a kind of arrow that forms a middle line between the two diverging fields. The small circle, in which the two diverging fields touch, appears in these more elaborate pictures as an eye. A small circle is

marked here and there on the rounding sides (e.g., Kingsborough 1831–48, vol. 1, *Codex Mendoza,* s.v. *Olinalan*).

Finally, the large picture of the *olin* sign occupying the center of the top of the so-called calendar stone, the large sun stone made under King Axayacatl, has in the middle, in place of an eye, the face of the sun god, and in the curves of the sides, the paws, armed with claws, of a jaguar. As a special variant I mention…Codex Borgia 10 (= Kingsborough 29). Here the diverging fields meeting in the middle are replaced by two bow-shaped, curved pieces, likewise of different colors (blue and red), which are interlaced.

An attempt has recently been made (Paso y Troncoso 1882) to ascribe to this sign a definite astronomical meaning, and it is explained as the graphic representation of the apparent course of the sun during a year. According to this view, the arrow that is seen on some representations of the *olin* sign would denote the direction from east to west, and the lines of the diverging fields would designate the directions which, from the standpoint of the observer, proceed from the extreme northern to the extreme southern point of the rising or setting of the sun.

To me the two fields of different colors seem to denote simply the bright and dark vault, the day sky and the night sky, on which the day and night planets roll along, like the rubber ball flying over the ballground. Thus I compare the day sign *olin* to the pair of fields that in the Maya manuscripts hang from the rectangular shields and bear on their surface the picture of the sun or of the day and the moon or night (fig. 1).

The astrological significance of the sign is doubtful. According to Sahagún those born under it are, with good training, fortunate, and with bad breeding, unfortunate. According to Durán it guarantees fortune to men—they are children of the sun and shine like the sun, and they will be fortunate and powerful, for the sun is queen of the stars. On the other hand, women born under this sign will be rich and powerful, to be sure, but will be stupid.

"QUAUHXICALLI, THE MEXICAN VESSEL FOR SACRIFICIAL BLOOD"

…In Sahagún's description of the eighteen annual feasts of the Mexicans, at the passage where the bloody sacrificial rite is first mentioned, the name of the vessel is also given that was intended to receive the hearts of the victims and in which, therefore, the food of the gods was set before them.

According to this account the heart of the victim is called *quauhnochtli,* "eagle-cactus fig," the cactus fruit which the eagle devours. The priest elevates it, as an act of dedication, toward the sun, the turquoise prince, the soaring eagle, and thus gratifies and nourishes the sun with it. After the heart has been offered in this manner it is laid in the *quauhxicalli.* The body of the victim, however, which is called the *quauhtecatl,* "the one from eagle land," is thrown down the steps of the pyramid, where it is afterwards taken up by the priests to be cut into pieces and to be eaten at a cannibalistic sacrificial feast.

In a subsequent passage there is a similar description of the way in which the priest cuts open the breast of the captive, tears out his heart, raises it as an act of dedication to the sun, and then lays it in the *quauhxicalli.* At the same place it is also stated that afterwards another priest comes, who places a reed in the wide opening where the heart has been torn out, fills the reed with blood, and likewise elevates this toward the sun as an act of dedication.

The priests collect the blood of the victim in a blue vessel with feathers on the rim, and this is the portion of the "lord of the captive," i.e. of the warrior who captured the victim in war and presented him for sacrifice. In this vessel there is a suction pipe that is also decorated with

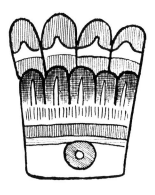

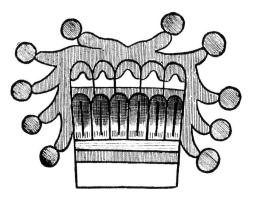

Fig. 2.
Dish for sacrificial blood, drawing by the author after *Codex Borbonicus,* fol. 8

Fig. 3.
Dish for sacrificial blood, drawing by the author after *Codex Borbonicus,* fol. 18

feathers. The "lord of the captive" goes with this to all the sacred places and moistens the lips of the idols with the blood.

The *quauhxicalli,* the vessel for the sacrificial blood, was perhaps originally nothing more than a *quauhxicalli,* a vessel (*xicalli*) of *quauh,* i.e. *quauitl,* "wood."[2] Subsequently, for reasons that are readily understood, this was transformed into "eagle vessel"; for *quauh,* or, with the article, *quauhtli,* is also the name of the eagle. Not only are the other expressions explained above, *quauhnochtli* and *quauhtecatl,* a strong argument that the *quauhxicalli* was actually interpreted as "eagle dish," but we likewise find proof in the pictures of such vessels and in the ornamentation of the vessels themselves.

Recently, thanks to the assistance rendered by the great promoter of Americanist studies, the Duke of Loubat, and by the Mexican government, the magnificent picture manuscript in the Library of the Corps Législatif at Paris has been published. It has been named the Codex Borbonicus by its editors, i.e. the picture codex of the Palais Bourbon. In the Tonalamatl, which forms the first part of this picture writing, we find the figures of the deities presiding over the calendar sections, accompanied by a goodly number of symbols.

The vessels for the sacrificed blood occur frequently among these and are of exactly the same character. I reproduce two of the pictures in figures 2 and 3, in the first the vessel is empty and in the second it is filled with blood. Figure 2 is the more distinct. The bottom of the vessel is brown, corresponding to the material, which originally was probably wood. A small green disk indicates an overlay or inlay of some kind of beautifully colored stone, which may have been of the class called *chalchiuitl* by the Mexicans. A blue and red stripe above this may denote painting.

Above, however, there is a wreath of eagle feathers, drawn and colored in the same fashion as that in which the eagle's tail and wing feathers are usually represented in the Mexican picture writings. We have seen that the vessel, in which the "lord of the captive" carried the sacrificial blood to the idols, was adorned on the rim with feathers. Now, if they wished to use especially precious material—or thought it should be used—for this feather decoration, they took *quauhtlachcayotl,* "eagle down"; hence it might readily be supposed that this feather decoration was intended to be expressed by the wreath of eagle feathers.

This supposition is weak, however, for the wreath of eagle feathers does not form the rim of the vessel, and, moreover, the wreath is not of eagle down but of the tail or wing feathers of the eagle. I think there is no doubt that this wreath of eagle feathers expresses, hieroglyphically, as it were, the name of the vessel, *quauhxicalli.* And, as I have already stated, the fact that the word *quauhxicalli* was interpreted as "eagle vessel" is a distinct proof of this.

Fig. 4.

Torn-out hearts, drawing by the author
a, b: after *Codex Borgia,* fols. 22, 23; c:
neck ornament of Coatlicue; d, e: after
Codex Magliabechiano, fols. 54r, 3v

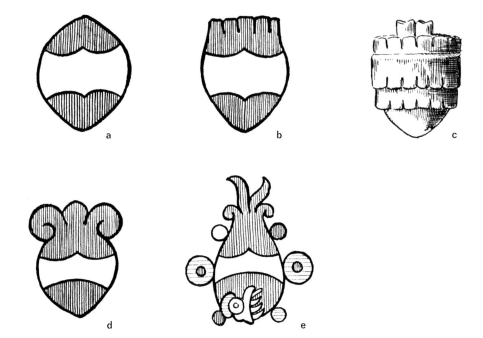

In figures 2 and 3, above the wreath of eagle feathers, there is a wreath of hearts that forms the rim proper of the vessel. That these figures are actually intended for hearts, which are placed with the aorta end downward around the rim of the vessel, is proved by comparison with other ancient Mexican representations of torn-out hearts, some types of which I have reproduced in figure 4a–e, and by painted forms, which are red with the center yellow.

Just as the wreath of eagle feathers expresses the name, so the wreath of torn-out hearts expresses the significance of the vessel. The whole picture, as is so frequently the case in ancient Mexican representations, is not a mere illustration, but also and chiefly a hieroglyph. The decoration of the utensil is not arbitrary—employed to serve some aesthetic purpose—but is closely connected with the vessel's existence and use.

The illustrations of the Codex Borbonicus, which are explained in the foregoing, were of interest to me not alone in themselves, but also because they explain one of the most conspicuous specimens of the ancient Mexican collection of the Royal Museum of Ethnology, Berlin. Since the year 1844 the Royal Museum has possessed an ancient Mexican stone vessel, the side view of which is reproduced from a photograph in figure 5. For various reasons it has always been clear to me that this stone vessel had served as a sacrificial vessel, or was intended to serve as such.

In figures 5 and 6 we have again the elements of the ornamentation of the outer wall of this stone vessel. A glance shows us that its exterior has exactly the same decorations as figures 2 and 3 from the Codex Borbonicus, viz.: the wreath of eagle feathers and the wreath of torn-out hearts placed reversed about the rim, and this decoration clearly shows that the vessels are to be regarded as filled with blood. Thus we have strong proof that our vessel, figure 5, was also a *quauhxicalli,* a sacrificial vessel.

But the ornamentation of the stone vessel of the Royal Museum displays much more than is to be seen in the simple illustrations of the Codex Borbonicus, which are apparently drawn merely as hieroglyphs. On the inside . . . (see p. 121, fig. 8) we see the picture of the sun and the ring of rays on the bottom; the sign *naui olin,* "four motion," the day of the symbol of the present day

Fig. 5.
Exterior of stone vessel for
sacrificial blood
Central Mexico, greenstone,
14.5 × 23.8 cm (5¾ × 9⅜ in.)
Berlin, Museum für Völkerkunde

Fig. 6.
Section of fig. 5, drawing by the author

[i.e., the present sun, or creation], the historical sun surrounds the picture of the sun and takes up the rest of the bottom of the bowl.

On the outside, at the bottom (see p. 205, fig. 5), there is the picture of the earth, the toad, which with gaping jaws swallows the stone knife, i.e. the light, and which is clad as a goddess with the *citlalcueitl,* "female skirt of stars," with the rattling belt pendants of snail shells dangling from a plaited strap, and also provided with various death symbols.

The wild things which in front, rear, and above the eyes form a wreath represent the wild, pitch-black hair of the god of death (who in the codices is generally surrounded with eyes, i.e. stars). A death symbol is also the belt consisting of the body of a snake, on which a death head is established as a belt closure (*tezcacuitlapilli*). Furthermore, the death heads that are arrayed on pieces of serpent body parts decorate the bracelets (*matemecatl*) of hand and foot joints. Finally, the hands and feet are formed like paws of jaguars or claws of eagles, even though an eye is placed above them—probably because the claws might have looked like teeth—so that the whole looks like a face.

The picture of the toad, the earth, is evidently intended only as a counterpart, or foil, for that of the first, the sun, in the interior of the vessel. The picture of the sun, however, must be closely connected with the meaning of the vessel. But what kind of connection have we here?

I mentioned in the beginning that the heart and blood of the victim were offered to the sun; the soul of the victim also went to the sun, to the house of the sun, to the eastern sky, as his servant, *quauhtecatl.* And correctly, for the sun as the heavenly body that dispenses warmth and life, that banishes the specters of night, is considered everywhere among these races as the first and most primitive worship.

There was, however, an established notion among the ancient Mexicans that the man who was offered, or was intended as a sacrifice to a god, was his image—the representative of the god. Hence the heart and blood of the victim, which were offered to the sun, or at least the vessels in which they were offered, must be representatives of the sun.

In fact, this idea was so firmly established that, vice versa, the sun was identified directly with this dish for the blood. When the Chichimecs departed from Chicomoztoc—as narrated in the "Historia Tolteca Chichimeca" of the Aubin-Goupil manuscript collection—*in tota totepeuh,* "our father, our lord" (i.e., the sun), remained at a standstill on earth four days and four nights. Then the children of the Chichimecs spoke as follows:

> *Ma yecuellê, ma tiquizcaltican, ma ticnenequiltican, ma tictzinanacan in quauhxicalli in tonacapiaztli,*
> Come, let us feed, appease, assist the eagle vessel, the sustenance reed (the suction reed of the lord of food), i.e. let us with sacrificial blood give strength to the sun.

Hence, as a matter of course the vessel for the sacrificial blood, the *quauhxicalli,* bears the picture of the sun on its surface. Besides the small specimen in the Royal Museum of Ethnology, this picture also appears on the larger stone vessels that were set up for the same purpose in the large temples of Mexico.

With these belongs the beautiful stone vessel of the Museo Nacional de México, which is 0.47 m. high and 1.06 m. in diameter, and is described by Jesús Sánchez (1886b). This vessel, like that in the Berlin Museum, is ornamented on the bottom with the picture of the earth toad swallowing a stone knife, i.e. the light.

If, however, the ornamentation of the stone vessel in the Berlin Museum of Ethnology still more distinctly expresses the hieroglyph *quauhxicalli,* this more graphic ornamentation has been dispensed with in the larger specimens of this kind. The specimen pictured by Jesús Sánchez has on its cylinder walls the design of the starry sky, and below what are assumed to be pictures of stars;[3] they form an interesting variant of the starry eyes or eyes of rays whose core forms an eye that is, so to speak, changed into a face (with mouth and teeth).

The same elements, eyes on sticks and eyes of rays, meant to illustrate a starry sky, are shown on the great Tiçoc stone above the triumphant warrior groups; below them, however, are four earth jaws that are elongated, since they form a decoration of the edges.

In addition to the great Tiçoc stone, the same class of monuments also includes the great Calendar stone, so called, which has in its center the sign *naui olin,* the symbol of the sun, surrounded by various chronological symbols. And the *temalacatl,* "stonewhirl," on which the *sacrificio gladiatorio* took place, and the surface of which was likewise ornamented with the picture of the sun, as is seen from different illustrations, may also be only a monument of the same cult, which here served a special purpose and may never have been permanently and exclusively devoted to the sun. Thus the ancient contention, whether the Tiçoc stone was a *temalacatl* or a *quauhxicalli,* is, after all, null, for the *quauhxicalli* and the *temalacatl* both belonged to the same class of monuments.

Furthermore, the Tiçoc stone and the Calendar stone were not the only monuments of their kind. Examination of the various structures that were within the limits of the Great Temple of Mexico reveals six different *quauhxicalli* and this probably by no means exhausts the list, for the examiner will find it troublesome to keep in mind smaller chance specimens of this type.

"EXCAVATIONS AT THE SITE OF THE PRINCIPAL TEMPLE IN MEXICO"

…On December 17, 1790, a second large stone sculpture was discovered as a result of further pavement work in the middle of the main square; thirty-seven yards north of the Portal de las Flores, in line with the second portal of the Palacio Real, but eighty yards west of it. This was the discoidal stone subsequently known in the literature as the "Calendario azteca" (León y Gama 1832, 1:10, 11).

Durán identified this sculpture with the *temalacatl,* "spindle whorl-like stone," to which captives were tied during the *sacrificio gladiatorio,* when they had to defend themselves against their attackers. Everything we know about the *temalacatl* from depictions and descriptions contradicts this explanation. It is true that the *temalacatl* was decorated on its surface with a rendering of the sun, just like the Calendario azteca and the various *quauhxicalli;* but as the name *temalacatl* indicates, it had a hole in its center for the rope that was used to tie the captive; such a hole is missing in the other sculptures.

In a former paper about these monuments I have stated the possibility that the peculiar groove cutting across the representation of the sun on the surface of the stone of Tiçoc, and running on the under side, opposite the relief of the king, could be conceptualized as a guide for the rope; in other words, the possibility exists that the stone sculpture usually—and also above—called a *quauhxicalli* could in fact have been the oft-mentioned *temalacatl.* I have, however, changed my mind and now believe that the *temalacatl* of the Great Temple of Mexico no longer exists or in any case has not yet been found. I now interpret the Calendario azteca differently, and presently agree in essence with Orozco y Berra.

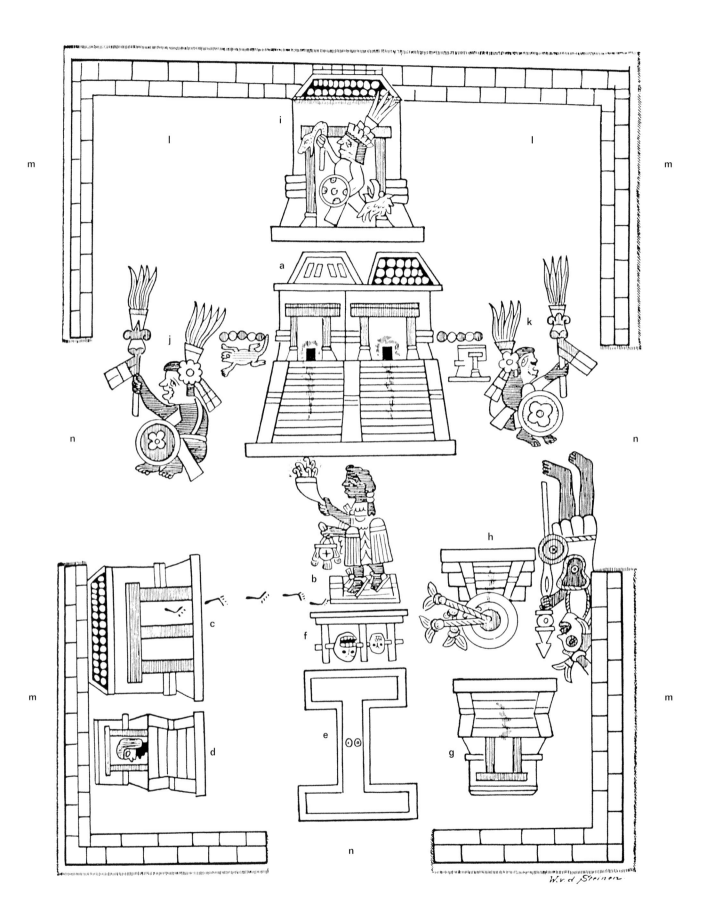

The temple of the sun was located in the southwestern corner of the compound. Durán[4] called it Quaquauhtinchan (fig. 7d); it is called a *quauhcalli* in the text. Durán tells us that a sacrifice was made on the day *naui olin,* "four movement," i.e. the day dedicated to the current sun. A specially selected captive was supplied with a staff and knapsack, delegated as a messenger to the sun, after being taught his message. It is said that he climbed the forty stairs to the shrine that was decorated with the image of the sun.

The captive climbed those stairs slowly, resting on each step, just as the sun slowly climbs into the sky. Upon arriving at the top, he is supposed to have climbed atop the *quauhxicalli* stone, whose surface was carved with the relief of the sun. There he proclaimed his message, partly to the painted mural of the sun and in part to the actual sun; he was then caught by the priests, who sacrificed him after taking off his clothes and travel accoutrements.

Durán identified this *quauhxicalli* with the large *quauhxicalli,* the stone of Tiçoc, that stood in front of the staircase of the large temple pyramid of Uitzilopochtli. His entire description indicates that this sacrifice took place at the height of the temple of the sun, immediately in front of the room with the painting of the sun; this *quauhxicalli* must therefore have been at the height of the temple of the sun and not in front of the staircase of the pyramid of Uitzilopochtli. Durán's illustration of his *quauhxicalli,* where the sun's victims were sacrificed, also shows a different design than that of Tiçoc's *quauhxicalli.*

In Durán's representation of the *quauhxicalli* at the top of the sun's temple we see in the center the sign *naui olin,* "four movement," the symbol of the current sun, apparently surrounded by a circle that contains the twenty day signs. None of that appears on the stone of Tiçoc. However that is exactly what we see on the large Aztec calendar disk. It is therefore certain that the Calendario azteca found in December 1790 was the *quauhxicalli* that stood at the height of the Temple of the Sun on the southwest corner of the temple compound.

Much has been written of the details of this Calendario azteca.…My friend the late Philip J. J. Valentini[5] wrote an entire article about it, published in English translation in the *Transactions* of the American Antiquarian Society. But he has definitely gone too far in his explanations. One cannot interpret an entire calendar out of those beautiful and sharply delineated designs covering the entire surface of this stone. This "Aztec Calendar" is only an image of the sun, no more and no less, and an expression of the conceptions of the Mexicans connected with the sun.…

The sequence in which these prehistoric ages are listed varies in different accounts. They all agree that the present historical sun came into being only after the four previous suns and their worlds had been destroyed. This last sun was born in the year *matlactli omei acatl,* i.e. the year "thirteen reed."

The year that follows "thirteen reed" is the year *ce tecpatl,* "one flint," the first year in which all historical annals of the Mexican Nahua peoples begin. The Aztecs believed that the present sun is destined to be destroyed by an earthquake (*tlalolin*); for that reason it is called earthquake sun (*olintonatiuh*) and its symbol is the day *naui olin.* This is the day they gave the number four, meaning all the cardinal directions, or "all" in general, and the sign "movement," which to them meant "all is moving" or "everything shakes."

On this day, which recurred every 260 days, Mexicans feared that the sun and the world would collapse, and they tried to prevent this by a solemn four-day fast of the entire population.

These beliefs are the subject of the reliefs carved in the center of the Calendar stone, forming its core. The principal space on the stone is occupied by a large ring, peculiarly decorated

Fig. 7.
Plan of the main temple of Mexico and its buildings, drawing by Wilhelm von den Steinen (German, act. 1895–1908) after Bernardino de Sahagún, *Codex Matritense* (*Primeros memoriales*), fol. 269r; 1901
a: temple (*teucalli*), b: eagle bowl (*quauhxicalli*), c: priests' living quarters (*calmecatl*), d: eagle house, warrior house (*quauhcalli*), e: ballcourt of the gods (*teutlachtli*), f: skull rack (*tzumpantli*), g: Yopico temple, the temple of Xipe (*yopico teucalli*), h: round temple (*temalacat*), i: temple of Colhuacan (*colhuacan teucalli*), j: the god Five Lizard (*macuil cuetzpalli*), k: the god Five House (*macuil calli*), l: place to dance or temple court (*ytvalli*), m: serpent wall (*coatenamitl*), n: door of the temple through which one enters from three sides (*teuquiyaoatl yc excan callacovaya*)

Fig. 8.
Hieroglyph of the soul of dead warriors
(*tonatiuh ilhuicac yauh*), drawing by
the author

as if by precious stones and feathers; rays emanate from it to the four main directions and to the four directions between them. The eight spaces between these rays are decorated similarly, with designs ending in double circles or eyes; these can be taken as an abbreviation of the hieroglyph *chalchiuitl,* if one compares it with the designs and colors of the manuscripts. It is the customary manner in which the Mexicans usually represented the solar disk.

The inner space of the ring has another ring; between these two rings, the hieroglyphs of the twenty days are shown, as they follow each other according to the vigesimal system. In the center of the inner ring we find the large and beautifully elaborated sign *naui olin,* "four movement," the day or symbol of the present, historical earthquake sun, with the face of the sun on its nadir [in original text, *mitte,* or "middle"] (the place where the eye usually appears as the abbreviation of the movement insignia in simpler designs).

On the four spokes of the sign "movement" one can see the signs of the days *naui ocelotl,* "four jaguar," *naui eecatl,* "four wind," *naui quiauitl,* "four rain," *naui atl,* "four water," the symbols of the above-named four cosmic suns.

One can observe dates and a special sign in the interval of the spokes of the *olin* sign and the arrow that complements the sun-eye of the *olin* sign and makes a complete sun-face of it. It seems as though a relationship is established here between the spokes of the *olin* sign and the indicated prehistoric suns or world periods, on the one hand, and the four cardinal directions, on the other. Indeed, the large stone knife with the numeral one alongside, standing to the left of the spoke with the jaguar head, indicates the date *ce tecpatl,* "one flint." This is the first day of the Tonalamatl group dominated by Mictlantecutli, the lord of the land of the dead, Mictlan, also the Aztec name of the north.

At the right of the spoke with the wind god (the date "four wind," the second sun, the wind sun), we see the figure 8 sign. For a long time, this was quite mysterious to me. It shows the royal headband (*xiuhuitzolli*) turned into a death symbol, since the triangular part on the forehead is shown as the stone knife; it also contains the indented breast plate of the fire god as well as the *yacaxiuitl,* the nose decoration of a mummy bundle, which was given to a dead warrior.

This hieroglyph has the appearance of the one of King Motecuhçoma. I formerly considered it to be the one of the fire god, on account of the breast plate. But my studies of the stone boxes have led me to the conclusion that this is the hieroglyph of *tonatiuh ilhuicac yauh,* "soul of the dead warrior," indicating the eastern sky where such souls reside, or merely "the east."

The date *ce quiauitl,* "one rain," is located a little below and to the right of the lower left spoke with the head of the rain god (the date "four rain," the symbol of the fire-rain sun); "one rain" is the first day of the seventh Tonalamatl section, presided over by the rain god who represents [a, or the] fire-rainstorm. This sign signified "the south."

Finally, the date *chicome oçomàtli,* "seven monkey," is alongside the spoke with the head of the goddess of water—the date "four water" represents the water sun; this sign (Sahagún 1950–82, bk. 4, chap. 20, 73–74) is the symbol of happy people, jesters, and of women, which naturally indicates Ciuatlampa, "Region of women," i.e. "the west"....

Thus these dates and signs give the identical information that the magicians furnished Motecuhçoma, upon his request, when they said to him:[6]

> *ca vmmati in mictaln, yoan tonatiuh ichan, yvan tlalocan, yoon cincalco,*
> there exists a region of the dead (the north) and the house of the sun (the eastern sky, the

residence of the sacrificed warriors, the east), and the region of the rain god (the south) and the house of maize (the west.)

Fig. 9.
Ballcourt (*tlachtli*), the basic form of the Ollin sign (?), drawing by the author

This relief is additional proof how firm and stereotyped the mythical and symbolical belief system was within the same narrow region.

Two peculiar stylized serpent- or dragon-bodies are depicted outside the circle of the sun, up to the edge of the Aztec Calendar sculpture; they are the kind the Mexicans called *xiuhcoatl,* "turquoise snake" or "blue snake." For them this serpent was the representation of the disguise of the fire or war god, because the concepts of sun and war were interconnected. The blood and hearts of victims were dedicated to the sun; it was nourished by them to become strong enough for the performance of its daily task. Only war supplied those victims. Mexican histories always stress that war had to be created before the sun was born, because it provided the victims so necessary for its nourishment.

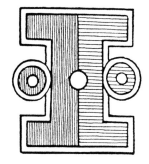

The open fangs of these snakes are at the lower end of the disk, opposite from each other, with a human face looking out of each of them. The tails of the serpents, at the upper end, do not touch each other; in the small space between them we find the symbol of the day *matlactli omei acatl,* "thirteen reed," as indicated above, the year of the birth of the present historical sun.

Pictured here then is the present sun, surrounded by the four prehistoric suns, its birth year, the twenty day signs, the symbols of fire and war, all on this so-called Calendar stone…which came from the old Great Temple. It was almost an idol of the sun, as it was conceived by the Mexicans and no doubt was so understood in all its details by the average person. We do not agree with the assumption of some authors that a kind of secret wisdom is recorded here.

This monument with its association of sun and war is a true symbol of that warrior tribe that established its home in the middle of a saltwater lagoon, "in the middle of rushes, in the middle of reeds, in the murmuring blue water"—a second Venice.…

"**THE CREATION OF THE WORLD AND OF HUMANS,**

AND THE BIRTH OF THE SUN AND MOON"

… [The] fifth sun of the present world has found its classical expression on the so-called "Calendar stone of the Aztecs," a stone in the form of a disk whose upper side is covered by rich sculpture; it was found at the end of the eighteenth century under the pavement of Mexico City and unquestionably at one time belonged to one of the sacred places that were within the walls of the main temples of Mexico.

The center of the sculpture is formed by the day *nahui olin,* "four movement," the sign or the embodiment of the fifth sun of the present world period. The sign *olin* consists of a dark (blue) and a light (red) field which appear to pull apart but touch in the middle, at which point they surround an eye (at least in the fully executed designs). The sign itself originated perhaps from the picture of a ball ground, whose ends widen out in T-form and whose two stone rings (*tlachtemalácatl*) in the long side walls were drawn outside (see fig. 9).

The eye in the middle of the sign is evidently the symbol of a body of light that moves from the light field to the dark, from the heaven to earth, or vice versa. In certain forms of the *olin* sign this eye is increased to a picture of the sun by adding to it one of the elements which, organized in four-fold and cruciform, make up the Mexican picture of the sun; included is a ray and a part of the object between rays that in the form and color of the green precious-stone picture

Fig. 10.

Four sides of the *Stone of the Suns* (*Altar of the Suns*), found near the principal square of Mexico City, ca. 1500,
60 × 63 × 59 cm (23⅝ × 24¾ × 23¼ in.)
Mexico City, Museo Nacional de Antropología
a: the day 4 Jaguar, sign of the first or Jaguar Sun (Ocelotonatiuh), b: the day 4 Wind, sign of the second, or Wind Sun (Ehecatonatiuh), c: the day 4 Rain, sign of the third, the (Fire) Rain Sun (Quiautonatiuh), d: the day 4 Water, sign of the fourth, the Water Sun (Atonatiuh)

a

b

c

d

is almost like a section of the hieroglyph *chalchiuitl.* The *olin* sign in the middle of the Calendar stone has this form.

Instead of the eye, the sculpture has the picture of the god of the sun. And on the four spokes of the *olin* sign the four historical suns are depicted in exactly the same form as on the simple sculpture of figure 10. The lateral outward extensions, corresponding to the stone rings of the ball ground (see fig. 9), are enclosed by paws with large claws, similar to those depicted on the earth goddess (Tlaltecutli) (see p. 205, fig. 5; p. 189, fig. 7). The *olin* sign, just like the ball ground, is a symbol of the earth. For this reason it is translated in the Maya lists of day signs simply as "earth" (*caban*) and depicted by characteristic elements of the face of the earth goddess....

Notes

1. See Paso y Troncoso 1882; and Nuttall 1886, 1901.
2. In the texts we finds words having this significance, as, for example, *cen quauhxicalli,* "a wooden dishful," an expression for a measure of capacity; also *cen quauhacalli,* "a wooden canoefull," an expression that the vocabulary of Molina translates "media fanega, medida."
3. Jesús Sánchez explains the elongated eyes as fire drills! and considers the vessel one devoted to the worship of the fire god.
4. Durán et al. 1867–80, vol. 2, chap. 10.
5. Note by Brian D. Dillon: Philip J. J. Valentini (1828–1899), a colleague, lived in Germany and wrote on various New World subjects.
6. Sahagún 1950–82, vol. 12, fol. 14.

HERMANN BEYER

The So-Called "Calendario Azteca": Description and Interpretation of the Cuauhxicalli of the "House of the Eagles" (1921)

Editor's Commentary

A native German who lived and taught archaeology in Mexico from 1908 to 1927, Hermann Beyer (1880–1942) wrote widely about the iconography of ancient Mexican deities, monuments, and codices. After joining Tulane University's Middle American Research Institute in 1927, he became active in Maya hieroglyphic studies, deciphering the variable element in the Initial Series Introductory Glyph, writing works on dating by style, and authoring one of the first treatments of the texts at Chichén Itzá.[1]

The study of 1921 translated here for the first time was the most important of several Calendar Stone *studies Beyer published in El México antiguo, a journal he founded.[2] It showcases Beyer's skill at recognizing significant iconographic units, which he later developed into the substitution pattern methodology for deciphering Maya hieroglyphs. Beyer never lost himself in counting the individual elements in the* Calendar Stone. *He also apologized in advance to those who might object that his methodology and results strip the monument of its mystery.*

Beyer wrote in response to the studies that Enrique Juan Palacios began publishing in 1918, and his meticulous description of every iconographic element, with identifications based on comparative objects and images from the codices, derives from the approach pioneered by Eduard Seler and was the most art historical effort up until this point. Beyer deserves credit for introducing many of his compatriot's ideas into Calendar Stone *studies. Like Chavero, Beyer thought the stone was commissioned by Axayacatl and contributed evidence in support of identifying the central face as Tonatiuh. He argued that the* Calendar Stone *was intended to be a disk, like the* Stone of Tizoc, *stating that it broke during the carving process and was never completed. Whether or not one agrees that the central face represents the sun god, Beyer's study does not seem outdated. His interpretations of the* Calendar Stone *essentially went unchallenged until the 1970s and were reinforced whenever new theories were advanced. For example, Alfonso Caso defended his former professor's ideas in the* American Anthropologist *in the early 1930s.[3]*

In his preface (not reproduced below), Beyer notes that he was urged to write his study of the Calendar Stone *both to commemorate the centennial of Mexico's independence from Spain and to honor the contributions of the German community to the nation; he lists more than one hundred Teutonic students of Mexico. His nationalism is perhaps what led to his internment during World War II in a camp for alien nationals in Stringtown, Oklahoma, where he died in 1942.*

Excerpted and translated by Khristaan D. Villela, with assistance from Mary Ellen Miller and Richard Kristin, from Hermann Beyer, *El llamado "Calendario Azteca": Descripción y interpretación del cuauhxicalli de la "Casa de la Águilas"* (Mexico City: Verband Deutscher Reichsangehöriger, 1921). Introductory text by Khristaan D. Villela.

The So-Called "Calendario Azteca": Description and Interpretation
of the Cuauhxicalli of the "House of the Eagles"

I. CLASSIFICATION OF THE MONUMENT

Fig. 1.
The sun god accepting a human sacrifice, drawing by the author after *Codex Selden A,* fol. 12 (detail)

The fact that the "*Calendario Azteca*" has always been taken as a unique artifact, a monument *sui generis,* is the principal reason that it has been the focus of such diverse and extravagant opinions. This erroneous idea has resulted in a series of fantastic interpretations that reached their extreme in works such as that of Abadiano (1889) and have had the effect that, for many people, the "*Calendario*" represents the ultimate summation of all of the knowledge and philosophy of the ancient Mexicans, a kind of repository of a vanished civilization, a profound mystery never to be decoded.

In reality, the stone in the Museo is neither a unique monument, nor does it guard secrets. It is an object dedicated to the solar cult and all—absolutely all—of its decorative motifs refer to the sun. This is the subject matter of this study in a nutshell.

Although there might be differences of opinion on some insignificant detail, all of the most important figures carved on this stone can be identified and interpreted with absolute certainty.

The monolith belongs to a class of monument called a *cuauhxicalli,* "eagle vessel." This term refers to a concept found among many peoples of this land: the sun symbolized by an eagle

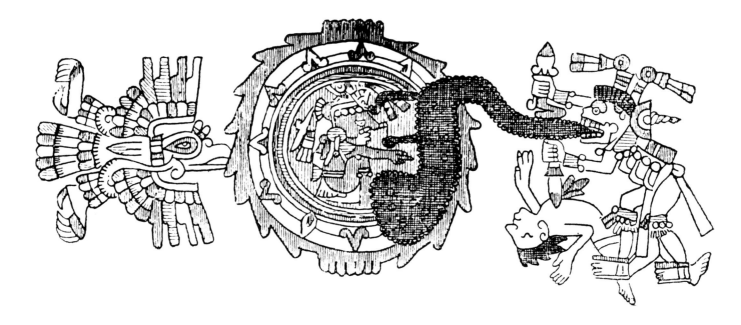

Fig. 2.
Human sacrifice before the sun god,
drawing by the author after *Codex Laud,*
fol. 1 (detail)

Fig. 3.
Eagle devouring a heart and blood,
drawing by the author after *Codex Cospi,*
fol. 7 (detail)

(Siecke 1915, 55–60). In this sense, we see in figure 1 an eagle as an animal or a solar symbol. In the lower part of the scene reproduced from one of the illustrated manuscripts in the Oxford University library, one can see a victim stretched over a *techcatl,* sacrificial stone, resting upon a band with stepped designs [*almenas*] below. The sacrificial priest plunges the blade into the victim's chest, opening a wound from which blood flows. Both personages have calendrical names: the ritually killed man is named 13 Deer and the priest 9 House. Two mythological beings—one in a turtle carapace and the other an eagle with a human hand—carry the heart and blood to the solar god who watches from the sky and sucks the blood.[4]

Figure 2 also shows a human sacrifice before the sun god. The sacrificer is the death god himself, from whose mouth a black cloud flows to the sun disk. The disk is completely surrounded by blood and the mythological eagle appears on the other side.

In figure 3, the same eagle devours a heart and blood....

Various expressions surviving from pagan times convey the idea that the eagle was taken to represent the sun. For example, *cuauhtlehuanitl,* "ascending eagle," was a name for the sun; *cuauhnochtli,* "the eagle's tuna" (prickly pear cactus fruit) was a way of referring to the heart of the sacrificed person offered to the sun; and the term *cuauhxicalli* is found translated as the "vessel of the sun."

Some images of *cuauhxicallis* are literally "eagle vessels." In figure 4, an eagle head issues from the base of a kind of bowl, and its feathers circle the rim. Atop the vessel, blood pours from two hearts pierced with reeds.... Figure 5 shows the wings and rows of feathers. Figure 6 also shows bleeding hearts pierced with reeds, but the decoration is reduced to eagle feathers and is similar in form to actual objects. Our figure 7 is a drawing of this kind of *cuauhxicalli,* in the collection of the Naturhistorische Museum in Vienna. Inside it has a relief of the sun disk (fig. 8).

Another class of *cuauhxicalli* frequently found in central Mexico has this solar image on its upper face (fig. 9). In this case the receptacle exhibits minimal or no concavity. Celestial emblems are then carved on the upper surface of the cylinder. The example in figure 9 is one of the simplest of this group and the "*Calendario*" the most elaborate of all; they represent two

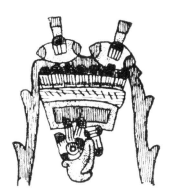

Fig. 4.
Cuauhxicalli, drawing by the author
after *Codex Borgia,* fol. 49 (detail)

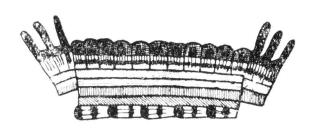

Fig. 5.
Cuauhxicalli, drawing by the author after
Codex Borgia, fol. 42 (detail)

Fig. 6.
Cuauhxicalli, drawing by the author
after *Codex Borgia,* fol. 59 (detail)

Fig. 7.
Exterior of a *cuauhxicalli*
Mexico (Tenochtitlan), 1450s–1520s,
greenstone, 6.4 × 15.5 cm
(2½ × 6⅛ in.)
Vienna, Museum für Völkerkunde;
drawing by the author

Fig. 8.
Interior of a *cuauhxicalli*
Mexico (Tenochtitlan), 1450s–1520s,
greenstone, 6.4 × 15.5 cm
(2½ × 6⅛ in.)
Vienna, Museum für Völkerkunde

Fig. 9.
Cuauhxicalli of Cuernavaca; Mexico
City, Museo Nacional de Antropología;
drawing by José María Velasco
(Mexican, 1840–1912), ca. 1889

extremes of scale and decoration. However, both variants share two essential features: the sun disk and the sky band. Although the "*Calendario*" is covered with a multitude of secondary details, the sun disk is the principal theme of the upper surface. In contrast, the well-carved designs on the sides of the figure 9 example are so compressed on the larger monument [i.e., the *Calendar Stone*] that they become insignificant.

The reason for such intricate decoration on the upper surface of the "*Calendario*" is simply its scale. What on a small- or medium-sized object are narrow lines or bands become, with the enormous increase in size of the "*Calendario*" monotonously plain fields that call for ornamentation. If, for example, we were to draw the arms [*aspas*] of the Ollin sign (fig. 10) without decoration, we would have great blank rectangles that would completely destroy the harmony of the upper surface.

If it was not difficult to discover the *raison d'etre* for the elaboration of the gigantic monument, however, the motive for the extraordinary compression of the cylindrical part cannot be explained without resorting to conjecture, and on this point I can only offer a more or less plausible hypothesis. Viewing the monument in profile (see pl. 3), it is surprising that the Aztecs brought such an enormous block of stone to the capital city and carved hardly a quarter of its thickness, leaving most of the rock uncarved. As the transport of this heavy stone must have constituted a supreme effort for primitive engineering, it is not probable that from the beginning they planned a *cuauhxicalli* as flat as the "*Calendario.*" I believe instead that the original idea was to make a cylinder like the monument of Tizoc.... They had already carved the circular upper surface when a large piece of the left side broke, making the original plan impossible to execute. There was no other solution but to extend the carvings on the sides only to the edge of the break.

Naturally, I have no proof that the proposed breakage was not the result of postconquest mutilation. But it is possible that the stone had a crack in this area that led to the breakage and that was noted by the ancient sculptors. Whatever the explanation, the disproportionate relation between the carved and uncarved sections is for me a problem that must be explained.

Given the identification of the monument as a *cuauhxicalli,* its original display position naturally would have been like that of figure 9, with the sun disk facing upward and not vertically, as it is now displayed.... The Aztecs and the other tribes of the large Nahua linguistic and ethnic group believed that humans lived in the world to serve the gods, procuring their food and drink: hearts and blood. The sun especially needed constant bloody offerings to complete its mission to benefit humanity. An ancient source relates that at the beginning of the present creation, before the sun could appear, humans had to be created so that it could be fed. In the speeches recited before the king-elect, he was exhorted to see to the sacrifices to the gods. According to the Mexicans, war was instituted so that the gods would never lack sustenance, and this was accomplished either by capturing enemies for sacrifice or by dying on the *techcatl,* giving their own blood to the god. If humans depended on the gods, they, for their part, also depended on humans, since they constantly needed to fortify themselves with the vital liquid.

The least cruel form of blood sacrifice was that when the penitent offered his own. With stone blades, bone awls, or maguey spines the fervent servant of the gods let blood from the ear, the tongue, the breast, or the calf. In figure 11 we see a small human figure plunging the blade into his ear, with the stream of blood flowing to the mouth of the sun god before him. During the fes-

Fig. 10.
The date 4 Movement on the *Aztec Calendar Stone,* drawing by the author

Fig. 11.
Autosacrifice before Tonatiuh,
drawing by the author after
Codex Borgia, fol. 75 (detail)

Fig. 12.
Sun disk, Tonatiuh, and stream of
blood, drawing by the author after
Codex Vaticanus B, fol. 7 (detail)

BEYER

tival of the sun, which was celebrated every "4 Ollin" date, everyone, even children in the crib, had to offer blood tribute, resulting in lacerated tongues and ears....

[Discussion of quail sacrifice omitted here.]

But the most valuable offering, the preferred diet of the sun god, was human hearts and blood. In figures 1 and 2 we have already seen two indisputable [*auténticos*] images of Tonatiuh accepting human sacrifices. The *cuauhxicalli* was the receptacle in which the hearts were deposited after being consecrated to the sun by raising them skyward. The cylindrical variety of *cuauhxicalli*, to which the "*Calendario*" belongs, had the advantage that the offering was visible to those believers gathered at a distance. On cold days one would have been able to see the steam rising from the hot organ, confirming by its appearance that the vital spirits, the principle of life, ascended to the sky....

II. THE FACE OF THE SUN GOD

The central circle of the *Calendar Stone* is occupied by a rather damaged face that, in spite of its disfiguration, can be securely identified as the sun god Tonatiuh. The partial destruction of this face, and of the two gods that appear in the jaws of the dragons that encircle the disk, was without doubt carried out intentionally at the time of the conquest....

Almost every writer on this monument agrees that the central image is the face of the sun god, this being one of the few details about which there is such unanimity of opinion. The obvious reasoning has been that in the center of the sun disk one should find the face of the sun god. The conclusion is logical and is, in effect, a well-founded assertion. But there are also direct proofs of this identification.

Tonatiuh, the personification of the sun, often appears simply, with a red body and face

Fig. 14.
Tonatiuh's face, drawing by the author
after *Codex Cospi,* fol. 12 (detail)

Fig. 15.
Tonatiuh's face, drawing by the author
after *Codex Borgia,* fol. 66 (detail)

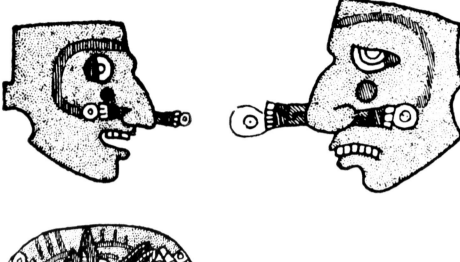

Fig. 16.
Tonatiuh, drawing by the author after
Aubin Tonalamatl, 9 (detail)

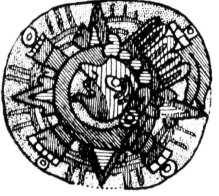

paint, as in figures 2 and 11 through 13. But in other examples the color is yellow or pink, and in this case there is one (figs. 14, 15) or various (fig. 16) curved lines that begin on the forehead and encircle the eyes. Two of these lines or narrow bands are clear on the "*Calendario*" relief, with the inside line somewhat thicker than the outside. Only where they end over the cheeks are these lines somewhat effaced. It is also impossible to say whether there was originally a small disk [under the eye], as can be seen in figures 14 and 15. In any case, the remaining lines are enough to securely identify the face in question as the sun god.

Some authors have interpreted this symbolic feature as the wrinkles of old age.[5] That a double band of a certain width and prominence indicates wrinkles would be at least odd, and the red color in which these features are painted in the codices also fails to support this hypothesis. On the other hand, representations of old people show wrinkles depicted in a very different way. The sun deity, in contrast, is a young god, the prototype of warriors.

The Abadiano brothers, who have made various casts of our monument, found in their molds traces of color that attracted their attention. A drawing in color based on the observations of these men was published on the title page of a magazine dedicated "to the defense and attainment of the highest ideals of humanity."[6] Although this engraving clearly has many errors in the details, it at least establishes the fact that the "*Calendario*" was originally a polychrome sculpture. The errors of the Abadianos cannot be easily explained by the fact that remains of pigments are best conserved in the deepest parts of the relief, in cracks of the stone, in lines carved between two forms, etc. Naturally, with adjoining forms, it is impossible to always decide securely to which to

Fig. 17.
Face of the sun on the *Aztec Calendar Stone,* schematic drawing by the author

assign a vestige of color. And if two distinct colors mix in a crack, a third color could easily result; for example, blue and yellow, mixed or superimposed, yield green.

And so, in my reconstruction of the deity face (fig. 17), I have not taken into consideration the Abadiano image, but rather have indicated the colors by means of different lines, according to the colors of these details in Precolumbian paintings. As the images in the various codices are always painted in identical or very similar colors, my approach is both secure and practical....

The nose and its ornament have disappeared completely. However, there is no doubt that the sun god should have had in the septum of the nose a tubular bead of *chalchihuite,* since this is how he appears in his most common representations (fig. 18; see figs. 11, 13–15)....

III. THE CLAWS OF THE SUN GOD

On each side of the face of Tonatiuh can be found an outward-facing claw, the right claw being illustrated in figure 19. Various writers have interpreted these as eagle talons,[7] but basic zoological knowledge is sufficient to refute this hypothesis. More serious is Seler's hypothesis that they are jaguar claws (1902–23, 1:439). This author bases his identification on the fact that the gods of the earth and of death appear with extremities that are, in effect, tiger paws. If that were always the case, the archaeologist from Berlin would have a compelling case, but figure 20 is an example that

Fig. 20.
Mictlantecuhtli, drawing by the author after *Codex Magliabechiano,* fol. 79 (detail)

Fig. 21.
Tonatiuh in the *xiuhcoatl,* drawing by the author after *Codex Zouche-Nuttall,* fol. 69 (detail)

shows that other animals must be taken into consideration. The claws in the illustration are unde-niably avian. This being true, most probably the claws flanking the face are from the same fantas-tic animal that has in its jaws another sun god face and that encloses the disk of our "*Calendario,*" that is, a *xiuhcoatl.* And since in figure 21 we have a second example of a sun god with the claws of this mythical serpent, I feel very certain of my identification....

In summary, I believe I have demonstrated that the two claws that flank the central face on the "*Calendario*" are those of the *xiuhcoatl* serpent, which grasps a human heart and [whose claws] are embellished with a *chalchihuite* bracelet....

IV. THE "4 OLLIN" HIEROGLYPH

The face of the sun, the claws, and four other signs enclosed in rectangles fill the inside of a con-ventional sign, the contours of which are reproduced in figure 10. This hieroglyph is one of the twenty symbols of the days and is named Ollin, "movement."

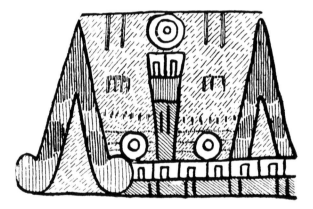

… In the pictorial codices of the Valley of Mexico and nearby regions, this hieroglyph is even more elaborate: the central disk is transformed into an eye and between the arms two more details are inserted: above a solar ray and below a *chalchihuite* pendant (figs. 22, 23). These items are a ray and a pendant, not an "arrow" as Chavero (1882, 110, 117–19) and Palacios (1918, 11) believe.

The "*Calendario Azteca*" presents this exact variant of Ollin. Some details can be explained by technical or aesthetic reasons. The hieroglyph is so broad because it must fill a circular space. The relatively large size of the central circle was necessary so that Tonatiuh's face could be carved with all its diagnostic features. In this case, the pointed ray has an interior line or band lacking in the rays that surround the solar disk. These parallel lines can be observed in the example in figure 23. The transverse bands in the figure 10 ray likely indicate different colors, and figure 24 shows how it was: two shades of red, one pale and one intense....

The profuse elaboration of the Ollin sign on the "*Calendario,*" although without precedent, can perhaps be traced to the image in figure 23. In this case the arms are filled with a design that repeats elements on the edge of the solar disk. An elegantly curved eyebrow sits atop the central eye, and the ray is somewhat varied by parallel and transverse lines....

V. THE FOUR PREHISTORIC SUNS

Like the peoples of classical antiquity, the Aztecs believed that the present age was preceded by distinct earlier epochs, more or less imperfect creations that were always destroyed by cataclysms. The ancient Mexicans based their cosmology on the doctrine of four or five distinct and successive "suns." They also believed that the last sun would be destroyed. Since the cosmic ages had each lasted a number of complete cycles, they feared the destruction of the world at the end of every cycle, or period of fifty-two years. On the last night of a cycle, they awaited with trepidation the transit of the Pleiades through the zenith, the moment that would decide the fate of everyone alive. When the priests saw that the stars continued on their course, everyone rejoiced that the gods had given humanity another fifty-two years.

The basis of this belief in distinct prehistoric periods derived from certain discoveries of a geological nature that did not escape an attentive people, including giant bones belonging to no living creature,[8] shells, and other remains of marine life both deep inland and also at considerable altitudes, and probably also by artifacts and other evidence of humans in layers beneath lava flows. Using very primitive methods, they could have cut stone from the Pedregal area and thus would have easily and inevitably encountered cultural material, vestiges of cultures destroyed by vulcanism, beneath the lava.

These observations were combined with certain mathematical speculations from the hieratic science of the calendar along with the supposed influence of the cardinal directions, resulting in the fusion of ideas that is the curious system of ages and cataclysms preserved in several variants from pagan times.

This theme is, of course, very interesting, but here we must limit discussion to those points that are directly related to the forms that affect the symbols of the ages on the so-called "*Calendario Azteca.*" As for the rest of the matter, the general topic has been treated in detail by other writers (Chavero 1882, 10–46, 107–26; Fernández del Castillo 1913, 5–10)....

[Discussion of the four suns as depicted on three monuments omitted here.]

The names of the world epochs on the three archaeological objects we have just discussed (the "*Calendario Azteca,*" the New Haven *cuauhxicalli* [in the collection of the Peabody Museum of Natural History at Yale University], and the *Stone of the Suns*) should be the same as appear in the "Leyenda de los soles" (Paso y Troncoso 1903),[9] since the figurative signs correspond to the names used in that document. According to this account, the four suns were:

1. Ocelotonatiuh, "Tiger Sun"

2. Ehecatonatiuh, "Wind Sun"

3. Quiatoniatiuh, "Rain Sun"

4. Atonatiuh, "Water Sun"

The "Historia de los Mexicanos por sus pinturas" also presents this sequence of ages. However, the *Anales de Cuauhtitlan,*[10] the "Histoyre du Mechique" (de Jonghe 1905, 1–41), Fray Pedro de los Rios (*Codex Vaticanus A* 1900), and other sources place the suns in a different order....

Fig. 25.
Section of the edge of the sun disk,
drawing by the author

[Extended discussion of the iconography of the four suns on the *Calendar Stone* omitted here.]

VI. THE SIGNS OF THE FOUR REGIONS

Between the ring that encloses the 4 Ollin sign and the sign itself are some empty places above and below that are filled in one case with a group of symbols and in the others with dates. I generally accept Professor Seler's interpretation of these symbols, who takes them to be emblems of the four cardinal points (1902–23, 2:799), although I offer differing interpretations of some details....

[Extended discussion of the directional symbolism of the date and other hieroglyphs around the center of the monument omitted here.]

VII. THE TWENTY SIGNS OF THE DAYS

All of the details of the "*Calendario*" studied up to now—that is, the face of Tonatiuh, the 4 Ollin sign, the ages, and the directions—have also been found on other *cuauhxicallis* and related monuments, although usually in simpler forms. The ring with signs that surrounds the images just listed, however, cannot be found on other representations of the solar disk and is unique to the great monolith of the Museo. But in this case the theory of the solar nature of the new material still holds true. The Aztec term for the day sign was *tonalli,* which still means "day" in Nahuatl today. The word *tonaltzintli* was given to me as a name for the sun not long ago in Xochimilco, this being *tonalli* with the reverential ending. So it is not unusual to find the hieroglyphs of the days on an altar dedicated to the sun.

This zone of the twenty day signs at first seems to lend credence to the idea that the monument was a pagan calendar. But if we were to discover, to give a simple example, a stone

that was carved with a list of the seven days of our week, we would not call it a *"Calendario."* Thus the circular band with the twenty signs is nothing more than a new example of elaboration with symbols related to the sun....

[Discussion of the iconography of the day signs omitted here.]

VIII. THE EDGE OF THE SOLAR DISK

Between the ring of the days and the backs of the serpents that encircle the solar disk is a wide band with variable decoration. We will discuss in detail the different elements that comprise this zone, which forms the edge of the solar disk.

Also, this part of the *"Calendario"* is more elaborate than the other known examples. Figure 25 reproduces a segment of the edge that includes all of the elements that repeat. We can easily see the difference by comparing the solar disks of the *cuauhxicallis* of figures 26 and 27.

Just beyond the zone of the day signs is a band composed of rectangles with a central point and four elements [*barritas*] in the corners. These quincunxes have been the fodder for many fantastic explanations. It is true that in Gama's time it was impossible to offer a satisfactory explanation of this sign, owing to the paucity of comparable material. We now have, however, sufficient examples of this symbol to attempt its interpretation and to arrive at correct conclusions. We must treat the series of quincunxes with the adjacent and smaller band of feathered objects and with the *chalchihuite* pendant.

This last detail, of which I have made special drawing, presents the elements in their most complete form and allows us to understand their significance. The upper part of our figure— that is, the part that encloses the quincunx—corresponds to a detail colored green in [images of *chalchihuites* in the codices. The quincunx is a variant, a hieroglyph, of the *chalchihuite*]....

The concept that the ancient Mexicans wished to convey by means of this symbolism was probably simply that the sun was precious, highly valued, and sublime. They employed in a

Fig. 26.
Sun disk on the upper surface of the *Stone of Tizoc*; Mexico City, Museo Nacional de Antropología; drawing by José María Velasco (Mexican, 1840–1912) (Peñafiel 1910, pl. 76)

Fig. 27.
Drawing of the sun disk on the upper surface of the *cuauhxicalli* of Cuernavaca; Mexico City, Museo Nacional de Antropología; drawing by José María Velasco (Mexican, 1840–1912) (Peñafiel 1890, pl. 299)

similar way the feathers of the *Pharomacrus mocinno* [the so-called Resplendent Quetzal] in representations of the "feathered serpent," Quetzalcoatl.

But this relationship of *chalchihuites* and the sun resulted in the quincunx being considered a solar emblem....

And so the mysterious quincunx that León y Gama and his followers considered a sign for a period of five days, and that they also saw under the solar rays (1832, pt. 1:99), is a variant of *chalchihuitl* with the symbolic meaning of "day," "solar," or other related concept.... A proof that the sun disk of the "*Calendario*" really extends to the backs of the serpents can be seen in the small open section of the background between the heads of the deities that appear face to face.

The three parallel and curved lines above the feathered forms (see fig. 28 for this detail) are also found in some illustrations from the codices, although in those cases there are generally just one or two (figs. 12, 16). Figure 24, however, has three lines, as on the "*Calendario.*"

The last details are those small forms that appear as pointed arches between the two features just discussed (see fig. 28). These constitute another sign that has greatly exercised the imagination of the interpreters of the monument. For León y Gama, they were "the mountains where clouds are born" (1832, pt. 1:101). Enrique Juan Palacios writes at length on their significance, opining that "the monolith has no other more interesting glyphs." He compares them to the pectoral ornament of Quetzalcoatl and believes that they signify the value of five Venus cycles, or 2,920 days (Palacios 1918, 73). But the most preposterous theory is surely that advanced by Professor Valentini in a lecture on the *Aztec Calendar Stone* delivered in 1878 in New York and translated into various languages. Following León y Gama, Valentini took the flames to be clouds that discharged rain, "raining four drops falling on a bed of earth, represented by three furrows in which there lies a seed-corn" (1879, 24).

Fig. 29.
Blood spatters, drawing by the author after
Codex Fejérváry-Mayer, fol. 41 (detail)

Fig. 30.
Xipe sacrificed, drawing by the author
after *Codex Zouche-Nuttall,* fol. 84 (detail)

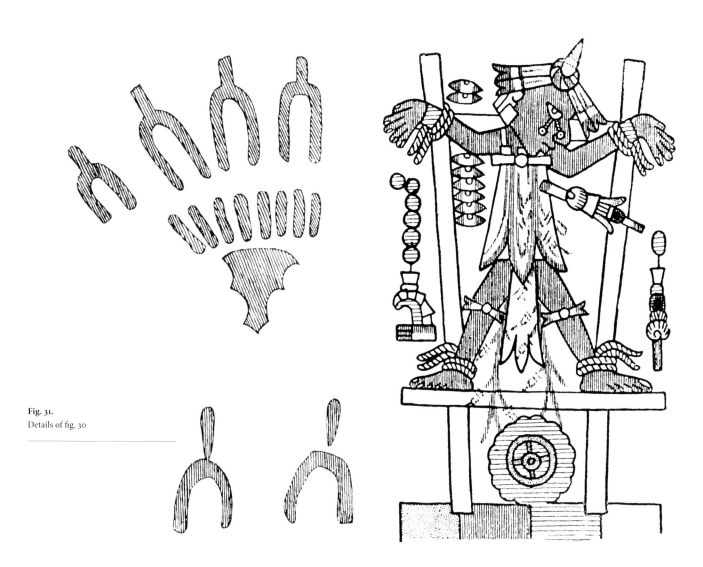

Fig. 31.
Details of fig. 30

The small arches rather resemble four details in figure 29, and these without a doubt represent blood spatters. The same kinds of blood drops can be seen in figure 30, which shows the god Xipe Totec wounded by a dart. And this case clearly reveals the genesis of the enigmatic detail. Figure 31 reproduces two of the signs, one exactly as in figure 29 and the other divided into a line and a hook. Our pointed arch form evidently originated from the combination of the hook or yoke and the line, forms always used to represent blood spatters. In figure 24, a sign composed of three or four vertical lines connected by a horizontal line seems to be analogous.

The similarity of the arched form and images of blood is probably not coincidental, but rather has a more profound significance. Given the relation so often demonstrated between the sun and blood, all of these bars, lines, and arches (fig. 28) may well be stylized representations of the traces of blood that ought to have marked the images of the sun disk after sacrifices.

Fig. 32.
Xiuhcoatl, drawing by the author after
Codex Borgia, fol. 46 (detail)

Fig. 33.
Drawing of a relief on a stone box, ca.
1500; Mexico City, Museo Nacional de
Antropología

IX. THE FIRE SERPENTS

Two fantastic beings, with serpentine heads and bodies but also with prominent horns and front legs, encircle the image of the sun on the *"Calendario."* These mythic serpents, of which there are many images both painted and carved (figs. 32–38), were called by the name *xiuhcoatl,* "turquoise serpent." However, they generally do not appear colored blue, but instead they are usually red and yellow, the colors of fire. The creature's fiery nature is accentuated in some cases by flames that emit from the fabulous animal's back (see fig. 32). In figure 33, the flames assume the form of a stylized butterfly, and in figure 34 the flame is found in front of the head. In figures 32 and 35, flames exit the mouths of the dragons, and they have them at the foot in figure 36....

Fig. 34.
Xiuhcoatl from the *Bilimek Pulque
Vessel;* Vienna, Museum für
Völkerkunde; drawing by the author
after Eduard Seler (German, born
Prussian, 1849–1922)

Fig. 35.
Xiuhcoatl, drawing by the author after
Codex Borgia, fol. 49 (detail)

Fig. 36.
Sacred burner, drawing by the author
after *Codex Zouche-Nuttall,* fol. 18
(detail)

To facilitate the comparison of the "*Calendario*" serpents with the rest of the fire serpents, I have drawn one of them, straightening its body (fig. 39). I think that figure 32 clearly shows that the details in figures 25 and 28 that are partially covered by the four bars belong to the *xiuhcoatl* and represent the flames that emit from its back.

The fiery character of the "*Calendario*" dragons is also expressed by another detail. Each of the segments that compose the body of the fantastic reptile has on its surface the form of a flame, stylized in a different manner than those on the back....

The fact that the *xiuhcoatl* appears so many times as a fiery animal has a parallel in the figure of the god Xiuhtecuhtli. The word "turquoise" (*xihuitl*) is also found in his name and, he is precisely the god of fire. Only rarely is he painted blue.... He is generally painted the colors of fire—red and yellow (see fig. 37; figs. 40, 41). In another essay (Beyer 1908b, 394–97), I explained this phenomenon: Xiuhtecuhtli personifies the blue firmament, which is at the same time the diurnal sky, with the sun that emits light and heat, or rather the celestial fire. In the same way, the *xiuhcoatl* represents the blue arc along which the sun turns, thus forming a "pendant" to the zodiac, to *quetzalcoatl*. This hypothesis was also published some time ago (Beyer 1908a, 157–58; 1910, 92). Logically, *quetzalcoatl* ought to have been conceived first, and the *xiuhcoatl* later, as it represents a band of the blue sky that corresponds to the area occupied by the zodiac at night.

Fig. 37.
Xiuhtecuhtli with a *xiuhcoatl,* drawing
by the author after *Codex Borbonicus,*
fol. 20 (detail)

Fig. 38.
Xiuhcoatl with sun disk, drawing by
the author after *Codex Vindobonensis
Mexicanus,* fol. 30

Fig. 39.
Xiuhcoatl on the *Aztec Calendar Stone,*
schematic drawing by the author

In reality, only in this way can we properly explain a detail that we see on many fire dragons, including the examples on the great monolith: the "horn." We saw this strange attribute earlier, in figures 33 through 35, and figure 42 shows how it appears on the "*Calendario Azteca.*" The horn that rises over the nose is decorated on its outer edge with round eyes. Each of these eyes represents a star, and this curious appendage, therefore, is nothing less than a group of stars, or rather a constellation. As a matter of fact, a constellation in the form of a curve of seven stars occurs in the materials of Father Sahagún (fig. 43), along with its name, *xonecuilli.* A constellation as a symbolic adornment of a fire serpent is, of course, inexplicable, but it is quite natural for a zodiacal serpent that would necessarily represent stellar bodies. A snake that represents this band of constellations in which the moon and planets move, on the other hand, is an easily understood concept. Consequently, the *quetzalcoatl* with a horn of stars was the primordial creation, and in the *xiuhcoatl* this horn was automatically copied as the emblem of a mythic serpent. . . .

. . . Just as the *quetzalcoatl* carries the moon, the *xiuhcoatl* in figure 38 carries the sun. This image is incorrectly rendered in Kingsborough's work, and so I made my own more exact version while I was in Vienna. This representation of a variant of the *xiuhcoatl* carrying the solar disk suggested to me that perhaps the "*Calendario*" dragons were conceived as the bearers of the sun [*astro rey*]. The fact that two serpents are carved on the monument can be explained by artistic reasons: my understanding is that they wanted to preserve the bilateral symmetry that would have been lost by carving just one snake, and that in this case they would have sought out the most unusual forms of the animal's head and tail. . . .

X. THE PROFILE OF THE FIRE GOD

Each of the two serpents that occupy the edge of the monument has in its jaws the face of a deity. These faces are similar in two details: they extend their tongues and have a symbol in front of their noses. Other details distinguish them: one has a simple disk with a circle as an ear ornament, the other a disk with a hanging *chalchihuite;* there is also a small curved piece of this precious stone in front of his forehead. We will first treat the face that appears in the mouth of the dragon on the right side.

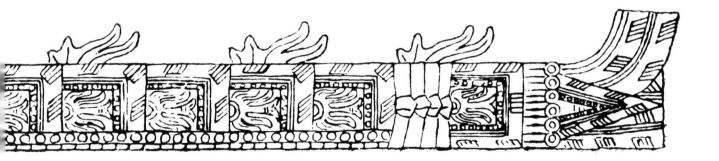

… What is most important for identifying the divine face is the evidence of facial paint. It consists in a type of mesh or net that covers the entire lower part of the face. One can see its limit perfectly clearly in a line that extends from the side of the nostril to the upper edge of the ear ornament. The teeth of the lower jaw of the dragon substantially cover this symbolic decoration. This is undoubtedly the face of the god Xiuhtecuhtli, the "lord of turquoise," and figure 37 presents precisely the same face paint. He generally also has a horizontal band in the eye area (see fig. 40), but this is lacking for some reason and is not present in figure 37 either.

Xiuhtecuhtli, the fire god, appears often with the *xiuhcoatl,* the fire serpent. Figures 37 and 40 offer two examples [from a corpus] that could be easily expanded. In reality, the *xiuhcoatl* is the animal that always accompanies the god of the fiery element.

The Xiuhtecuhtli of the "*Calendario,*" and the other face in front of him, share the detail of the extended tongue, which, just like the face of the central solar deity, is decorated with the face of a supernatural in an inverted position. The three curved and pointed teeth can be distinguished without difficulty, but the eye and eyebrow below are rather erased.

The teeth are quite visible in the open mouth of the god, in both upper and lower jaws. The nose and eye of Xiuhtecuhtli are deteriorated. The hair is carved to fall over the forehead and the temple and reaches the ear ornament. There is no indication of the ear itself.

As a last detail, I have left the form, unfortunately much mutilated, that one can see in front of the upper lip and nose of the god. However, I think that its position allows us to securely identify it as the same sign that we see in figures 37, 40, and 41 in the same place. This is a scroll that was left white in figures 37 and 40, but in figure 41 it is colored blue. As a conjecture, I offer the explanation that this may be the remains of the *yacaxihuitl,* one of the scrolls that are often connected to this emblem (figs. 44–46).

XI. THE PROFILE OF THE SUN GOD

The face of the deity that appears in the jaws of the other mythic serpent has been correctly identified by Palacios as that of the sun god (1918, 21, 79). Some time ago, I took this god to be a representation of Huitzilopochtli, since he had the *yacaxihuitl* and appeared in the mouth of the *xiuhcoatl,* features this god has in some cases (Beyer 1912, 368). However, the symbol in front of the nose in plate 10 is probably not the *yacaxihuitl,* but rather another object, and with this my previous hypothesis fails. After a more thorough examination of the detail in question, I have arrived at the conclusion that it is a variant of the speech scroll that is so often found in front of the face of personages. It would be, therefore, a sign composed of or ended with two slightly curved forms and with a longitudinal groove. The lower part of the sign is too damaged to be able to comment on its carving; one can only note that its outer edge is round, as if it were coming from the mouth of Tonatiuh. The two parts that we have mentioned are divided by a transverse bar, a detail that actually belongs to the nose ornament of the god and thus has nothing to do with the speech scroll....

The *chalchihuitl* ornament that the god has in front of his forehead is much damaged in its lower section. However, there could be no doubt that it is a curved jewel like that worn, for example, by Tonatiuh in figure 13 and like the central face of our monument must have also had.

Between this detail and the large teeth of the dragon's upper jaw, there is an indication of hair; that also appears between the third tooth and the ear ornament. This ear ornament is composed of two concentric disks and a hanging *chalchihuite* and is the same as its counterpart on the central face.

From the mouth extends, just as in the case of Xiuhtecuhtli, a sizable tongue with the eye and teeth of a monstrous face. The rows of teeth are also visible and one can easily see the lower jaw.

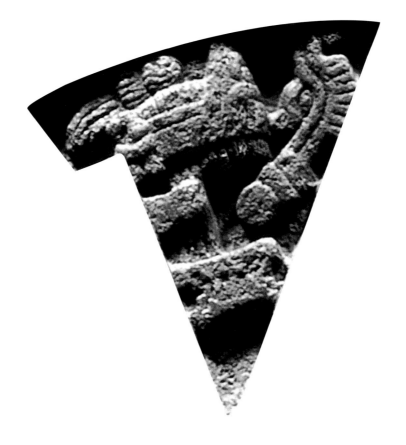

Fig. 45.
Priest, drawing by Eduard Seler (German, born Prussian, 1849–1922) after Bernardino de Sahagún, *Codex Matritense* (*Primeros memoriales*), fol. 253r (detail)

Fig. 46.
Fire god, drawing by the author after *Codex Borgia,* fol. 46 (detail)

I have already spoken about the small bar that pierces the cartilage of the nose. This piece of jewelry is quite destroyed and one can only see its outline, but with the aid of figures 13, 14, 15, and 18 it is not difficult to find its trace on the monument.

I find no evidence of the facial paint that, on figure 17, consists of two lines in the middle of the face. Instead, one can make out on the cheek, near the end of the nose ornament, half of the circle that one can see in complete form in figures 14 and 15.

Tonatiuh does not appear with the *xiuhcoatl* as frequently as we saw in the case of Xiuhtecuhtli. However, in figure 21 we have one example. Another can be observed in figure 47, where Kinich Ahau, the solar god of the ancient Mayas, appears in the jaws of a fantastic serpent. I have extracted the essential parts of the representation of the serpent from a drawing of the extremely intricate decoration on a precious ceramic vase published by Saville (1919; 1921, 66–67) [carved vessel from San Augustín Acasaguastlan; Washington, D.C., National Museum of the American Indian].

XII. THE DATE 13 REED

In the upper part of the monument, between the two points of the dragon tails, can be found a rectangle that contains thirteen small disks and the sign Acatl, "reed."... Although slightly deteriorated, the date was correctly read, from its earliest interpretation, as *matlactli omei acatl,* 13 Reed (Léon y Gama 1832, pt. 1:99–100).

The number is divided in two columns of five units, and is completed with three small circles above....

Like everything else having to do with the "*Calendario,*" there are a variety of opinions about the significance of the date. The correct one, in my view, is that of Dr. Seler, who asserts that it refers to the sun's birth year (1903b, 247). Not only do the *Anales de Cuauhtitlan* (*Historia de los reinos de Colhuacan y de Mexico*), cited by this author, refer to the creation of the present sun in the year 13 Reed but also the *Historia de los mexicanos por sus pinturas* relates that "the sun began to shine" on this date (García Icazbalceta 1886–92, 3:236)....

[Brief discussion of the associations of reeds, fire making, and fire in general omitted here.]

The use of reeds to light fires evidently was the source of the association with the sun, the fiery globe.

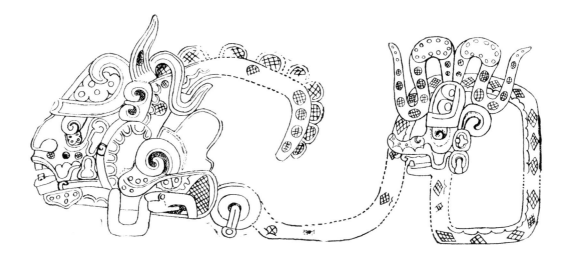

XIII. THE SKY BAND

The edge of the monument, the low cylindrical section, is decorated with a design that I have reproduced in figure 48. The examples of this emblem that can be seen from below [i.e., on sections of the monument visible in its present installation] are all somewhat erased, and the drawing was possible only by combining details from various figures.

The principal motive can be seen in a large and well-carved variant in the Museo Nacional that shows all of the diagnostic traits clearly executed (fig. 49). Above we have an eye with its brow of two scrolls below, and so it is an upside down eye. From this eye, stone knives and more eyes extend on all sides, arranged in a form that makes a tripartite figure. The crossed bands that can clearly be seen inside the form can hardly be distinguished on the "*Calendario*" examples. The stone knives in figure 49 have a simple interior design: three skeletal teeth. In the corresponding area of figure 48, they can be seen only indistinctly. In contrast, they can be easily seen in the two isolated and larger knives....

The group of symbols in figure 48 occurs in many variants. Figures 50 and 51 reproduce two examples. Its meaning is known from its use in the hieroglyph of Motecuhzoma Ilhuicamina; there they represent *ilhuicatl,* the sky. The sun and sky are two natural phenomena so closely related that there is no difficulty understanding that they appear together on *cuauhxicallis.*

That is the general meaning of the sign. Now we will address its diagnostic elements, although summarily.

The upper band that we see in figure 48 has a row of small disks that correspond to two rows in figure 51 and three in figure 50. In figure 51, which is colored, the meaning of these white disks on a black ground is not difficult to interpret: they are stars. Consequently, the night sky is indicated by the first band of the decoration on the cylindrical side of the "*Calendario.*"

The two narrower bands underneath are colored yellow and red, respectively, in figure 51.

The complicated central emblem of figure 48—and the rest—represents the planet Venus, because the god of the dawn and of the dusk wears this along with another sign, the stellar eye, as a pectoral ornament (fig. 52). The morning star, the brightest star, was not represented simply by a white disk or by a round eye like the other stars (see fig. 51), but rather by hanging stemmed eyes and flint knives that express the rays it emitted. Earlier we saw that the knife indicated the solar ray. In the same way, evidently, the rays in figures 48 and 49 are expressed by large

Fig. 49.
Stone disk with the sign of
the planet Venus
Mexico (Tenochtitlan), 1325–1521,
stone, diam.: 33.5 cm (13⅛ in.),
depth: 12 cm (4¾ in.)
Mexico City, Museo Nacional
de Antropología

Fig. 50.
Image of the heavens on a *cuauhxicalli*
Central Mexico (probably Tenochtitlan),
ca. 1500, stone, basalt, 54.6 × 45.7 × 25.6
cm (21½ × 18 × 10 in.)
New Haven, Yale Peabody Museum

Fig. 51.
The heavens, drawing by the author after
Codex Borbonicus, fol. 16 (detail)

Fig. 52.
Tlahuizcalpantecuhtli, drawing by the
author after *Codex Vaticanus B,* fol. 80
(detail)

Fig. 53.
Detail of the daytime sky on the
Stone of Tizoc
Mexico (Tenochtitlan), 1481–86,
stone, basalt; height: 90 cm (35½ in.),
diam.: 270 cm (106¼ in.)
Mexico City, Museo Nacional
de Antropología

Fig. 54.
Daytime sky, drawing by the author after
Codex Borgia, fol. 33 (detail)

stone blades. In figures 51 and 53 hanging eyes substitute, and in figure 54 both signs appear. The eye that indicates a particle of light, a beam, is an easily understood concept. But it is more difficult to grasp that a sacrificial knife might play the same role; probably its form led to its use as a symbol of a sun ray....

XIV. THE FUNCTION OF THE "CALENDARIO AZTECA"

In the first chapter I wrote that the monolith in the Museo Nacional, commonly known as the "*Calendario Azteca,*" is a *cuauhxicalli* and that all of the themes of its symbolic decoration refer to the sun. I believe I have proven this thesis for each of the many details with sufficient comparative material. However, I cannot accept the name *Stone of the Sun* that the Lic. Chavero (1877a) gave the monument and that other writers have repeated,[11] because I deem it too vague and ambiguous. It is certain that the "*Calendario*" and the other *cuauhxicallis* are "sun stones," but so are the ballgame rings (fig. 55) and the perforated disks employed in the "gladiatorial sacrifice."[12] For this reason it seemed better to me to keep the ancient word *cuauhxicalli* as a technical term that clearly denotes those monuments that functioned as altars on which hearts were deposited. Additionally, the expression "stone of the sun," given on page 272 of the first volume of the *Historia de las Indias de Nueve España,* of Father Durán, refers undoubtedly to the Tizoc *cuauhxicalli,* not the "*Calendario*" (Durán et al. 1867–80, 272–73).

Fig. 55.
The Tlachtemalacatl from Tepeaca

Chavero was justified in connecting the following paragraph in Durán with the "*Calendario Azteca*," and also in determining that the monument was a *cuauhxicalli* (1904, 231–85). Unfortunately, in later works (Chavero 1877a, 1882, 1886), the well-known writer diverged so much from his original concept that it became lost in the multitude of new ideas that his fecund imagination produced in the interim.

According to the cited chapter 35 of the work of Father Durán, the two monoliths, the "*Calendario*" and the monument that we know as the *cuauhxicalli* of Tizoc, were carved in the reign of Axayacatl. In chapter 88, Durán relates the ceremonies they performed for the Nauholin [i.e., Nahui Ollin] festival in great detail, during which a war prisoner was sacrificed and his soul sent as a messenger to the sun. The stone the victim had to climb atop is described as if it were like the *cuauhxicalli* of Tizoc; the drawing that accompanies the text, however, more resembles the "*Calendario*" (see pl. 21). In this case, one must decide whether to follow the text *or* the illustration. As this is undoubtedly based on an indigenous painting, I prefer to give more credence to the image, and in this sense, I believe, with Seler (1902–23, 2:796–97), that the "*Calendario Azteca*" is the *cuauhxicalli* that was placed in front of a building in the Templo Mayor district, called the Cuauhcuauhtinchan, the "Abode of the Eagles," or the Cuauhcalli, the "House of the Eagle."

On account of its broad and flat form, the "*Calendario*" could have served in the ceremonies discussed above, and its principal function was to be used in the 4 Ollin festival. Two unique aspects of the monument can be explained by the fact that this religious festival occurred only once or twice in the year. One of these is the painted surface that the monument undoubtedly originally had and that for a *cuauhxicalli* in constant use would have been impractical. The other is the fact that it has eight hollow cavities around the cylinder. I offer a hypothesis for this second detail that at first must seem very brash and arbitrary: I believe that these holes served to receive the bases of shafts that were the armature for a covering that protected the painted surface of the monument and that only during the festival of 4 Ollin was it removed, when the victim delivered his message to the sun. Although I cannot directly prove this theory, I can, at least, cite a parallel. In figure 36 we see a ritual object, a burner, according to the correct identification of Seler (1904–9, 2:39), with the head and claw of the *xiuhcoatl*....

These same cavities convinced León y Gama to interpret the monument as a kind of solar clock, believing that they originally contained gnomons. Although this author erred in his interpretation, we should not completely deny the existence of these indentations, as Chavero did, arguing, "Additionally, the eight points or holes in which the gnomons would be fixed do not exist" (1904, 245). Every visitor to the Museo Nacional can confirm with the greatest ease that the monument has on its carved edge and on its socle readily visible holes.

With this I end my interpretation of the controversial Indian monument. I thought to write another chapter on the history of the decipherment of the "*Calendario Azteca*," from León y Gama to the present, but I was unable to finish in the brief space of time at my disposal. If one day a second edition of this study is necessary, I will take care that it contains this historical review. The description and explication of the monument itself, however, is complete in the form that it now appears....

Notes

1. See Beyer 1931, 1932, 1937, and 1941.

2. See Beyer 1921, 1922, and 1923. These works were reprinted as Beyer 1965d, 1965e, and 1965a, respectively.

3. See Dellenbaugh 1933, 1935; and Caso 1934.

4. This drawing is mentioned briefly by Clark (1913, pt. 1:135–36).

5. For example, Palacios 1918, 23ff.

6. *Acción mundial* (29 January 1916).

7. See León y Gama 1832, pt. 1:97.

8. "traxeron vn hueso, o çancarrón de vno dellos y era muy grueso. El altor tamaño, Como vn hombre de rrazonable Estatura y aql çancarrón era desde la rrodilla hasta la cadera. yo me medi con El y tenia tan gran altor Como yo, puesto que soy de razonable cuerpo, y truxeron otros pedaços de huesos como El primero, mas Estavan ya comidos y deshechos de la trra, y todos nos Espantamos de ver Aqllos çancarrones y tuvimos por çierto, aver abido gigantes en Esta tierra"; Díaz del Castillo 1904–5, 1:227.

9. According to Dr. W. Lehmann (1906, 752–60), this fragment is the second part of the *Historia de los reinos de Colhuacan y de Mexico,* and thus, it represents Aztec traditions.

10. The *Anales de Cuauhtitlan* would be the first part of the manuscript cited in the previous note.

11. For example, Palacios 1918.

12. The only authentic example of this curious object, dedicated to this cult, I was able to identify in Beyer 1920.

Pl. 1.
Aztec Calendar Stone
Mexico (Tenochtitlan), ca. 1502–19,
basalt, disk diam.: 348 cm (137 in.)
Mexico City, Museo Nacional
de Antropología

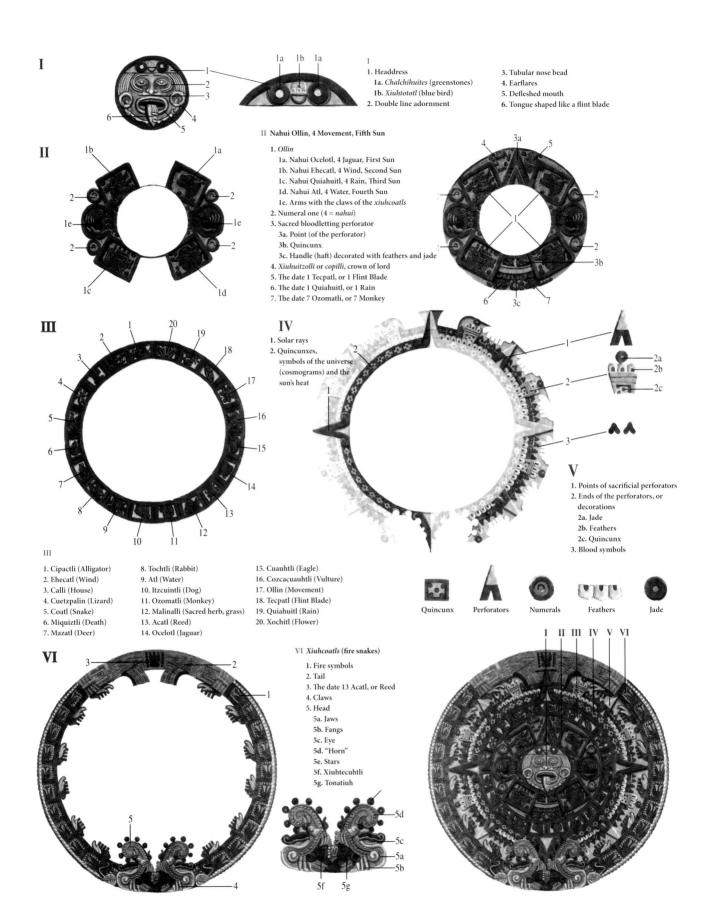

I
1. Headdress
   1a. *Chalchihuites* (greenstones)
   1b. *Xiuhtototl* (blue bird)
2. Double line adornment
3. Tubular nose bead
4. Earflares
5. Defleshed mouth
6. Tongue shaped like a flint blade

II Nahui Ollin, 4 Movement, Fifth Sun
1. *Ollin*
   1a. Nahui Ocelotl, 4 Jaguar, First Sun
   1b. Nahui Ehecatl, 4 Wind, Second Sun
   1c. Nahui Quiahuitl, 4 Rain, Third Sun
   1d. Nahui Atl, 4 Water, Fourth Sun
   1e. Arms with the claws of the *xiuhcoatls*
2. Numeral one (4 = *nahui*)
3. Sacred bloodletting perforator
   3a. Point (of the perforator)
   3b. Quincunx
   3c. Handle (haft) decorated with feathers and jade
4. *Xiuhuitzolli* or *copilli*, crown of lord
5. The date 1 Tecpatl, or 1 Flint Blade
6. The date 1 Quiahuitl, or 1 Rain
7. The date 7 Ozomatli, or 7 Monkey

IV
1. Solar rays
2. Quincunxes, symbols of the universe (cosmograms) and the sun's heat

2a.
2b.
2c.

V
1. Points of sacrificial perforators
2. Ends of the perforators, or decorations
   2a. Jade
   2b. Feathers
   2c. Quincunx
3. Blood symbols

III
1. Cipactli (Alligator)
2. Ehecatl (Wind)
3. Calli (House)
4. Cuetzpalin (Lizard)
5. Coatl (Snake)
6. Miquiztli (Death)
7. Mazatl (Deer)
8. Tochtli (Rabbit)
9. Atl (Water)
10. Itzcuintli (Dog)
11. Ozomatli (Monkey)
12. Malinalli (Sacred herb, grass)
13. Acatl (Reed)
14. Ocelotl (Jaguar)
15. Cuauhtli (Eagle)
16. Cozcacuauhtli (Vulture)
17. Ollin (Movement)
18. Tecpatl (Flint Blade)
19. Quiahuitl (Rain)
20. Xochitl (Flower)

Quincunx Perforators Numerals Feathers Jade

VI *Xiuhcoatls* (fire snakes)
1. Fire symbols
2. Tail
3. The date 13 Acatl, or Reed
4. Claws
5. Head
   5a. Jaws
   5b. Fangs
   5c. Eye
   5d. "Horn"
   5e. Stars
   5f. Xiuhtecuhtli
   5g. Tonatiuh

I II III IV V VI

Pl. 2.
Diagram of *Aztec Calendar Stone* iconography based on the interpretations of Felipe Solís, R. van Zantwijk, and Michel Graulich; drawing assembled by Fernando Montes de Oca from drawing by Víctor Manuel Maldonado, ca. 2000 (see p. 157, pl. 11)

Pl. 3.
Profile showing sacrificial knives and designs that symbolize Venus

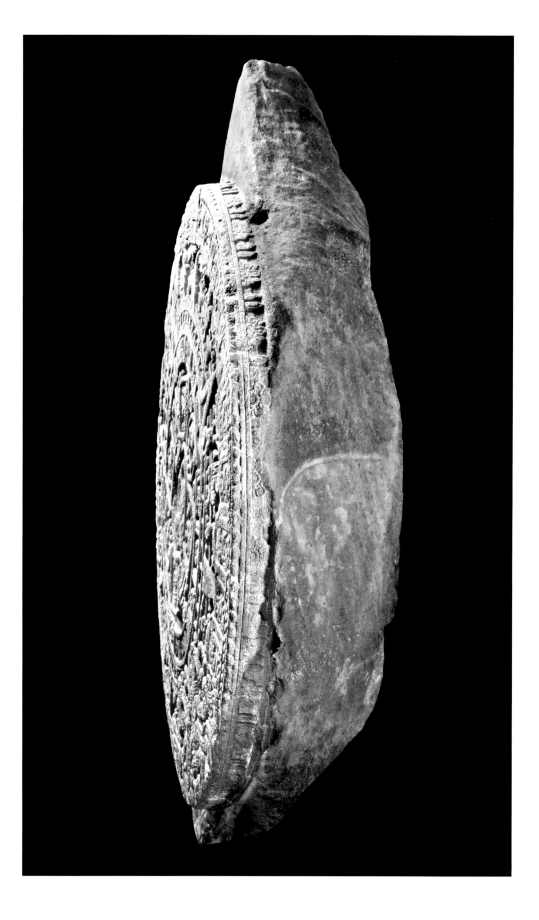

Pl. 4.
The glyph enclosed in the large square corresponding to Nahui Ehécatl, or 4 Wind, the Second Sun

Pl. 5.
The glyph enclosed in the large square corresponding to Nahui Quiáhuitl, or 4 Rain (of fire), the Third Sun

Pl. 6.
The central deity of the *Aztec Calendar Stone*

Pl. 7.
The glyph enclosed in the large square corresponding to Nahui Océlotl, or 4 Jaguar, the First Sun

Pl. 8.
The glyph enclosed in the large square corresponding to Nahui Atl, or 4 Water, the Fourth Sun

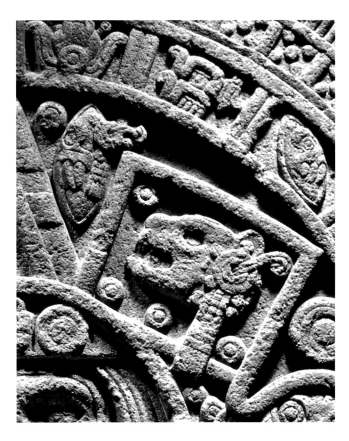

Pl. 9. *top*
The date 13 Reed, enclosed in a square, between the tails of the *xiuhcoatls,* or fire serpents

Pl. 10. *bottom*
The faces of Tonatiuh, the sun god (left), and Xiuhtecuhtli, the fire god (right), emerging from the jaws of the *xiuhcoatls,* or fire serpents

Pl. 11.
Reconstruction of the original coloring
of the *Aztec Calendar Stone,* drawing by
Victor Manuel Maldonado, ca. 2000

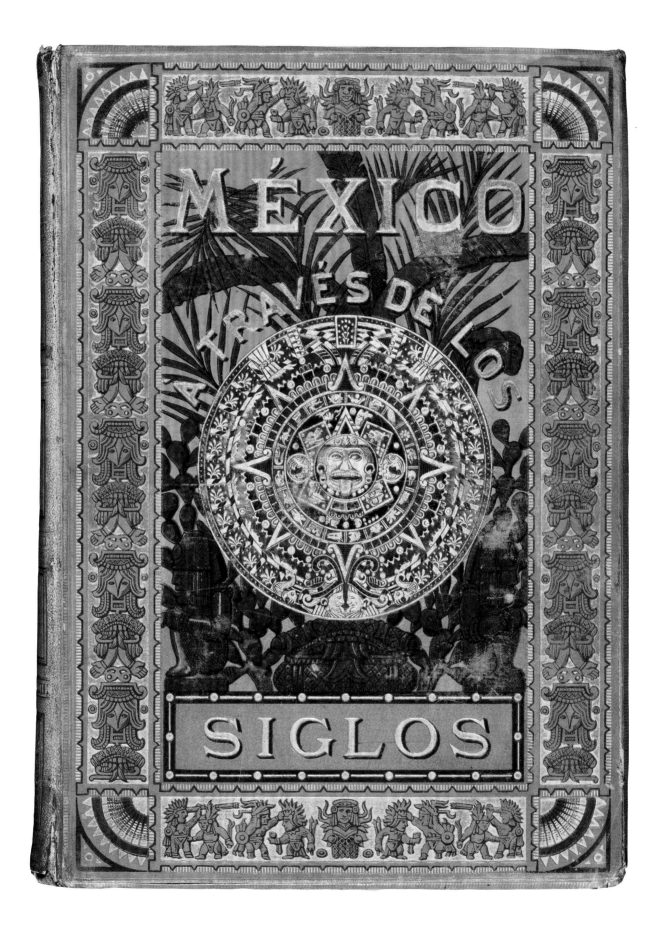

Pl. 14.
Title page of Alfredo Chavero, *Historia antigua y de la conquista,* 1888, vol. 1 of the series *México a través de los siglos*

Pl. 15.
Reconstruction of the original coloring of the *Aztec Calendar Stone,* drawing by Roberto Sieck Flandes, 1939

Pl. 16.
Reconstruction of the original coloring
of the *Aztec Calendar Stone,* drawing
by Miguel Covarrubias (Mexican,
1904–57), 1953

Pl. 18.
Humberto Limón (Mexican, b. 1931)
Magnificent Sculptors, 1975, oil on
canvas, 100 × 80 cm (39⅓ × 31½ in.)
Mexico City, Museo Soumaya

Pl. 19.
José Bribiesca Casillas
(Mexican, 1891–1946)
Untitled, ca. 1946, chromolithograph,
57.2 × 44.1 cm (22½ × 17⅜ in.)
Mexico City, Museo Soumaya

Pl. 20.
Prisoner from Coaixtlahuaca being sacrificed on a *cuauhxicalli* or *temalacatl, Durán Codex,* fol. 70r
Mexico, ca. 1581, watercolor on European paper
Madrid, Biblioteca Nacional de España

Pl. 21.
Prisoner of war carrying a message to the sun before he is sacrificed on top of a sun stone, *Durán Codex,* fol. 271r
Mexico, ca. 1581, watercolor on European paper
Madrid, Biblioteca Nacional de España

ENRIQUE JUAN PALACIOS

"The *Stone of the Sun* and the First Chapter of the History of Mexico" (1921)

Editor's Commentary

Enrique Juan Palacios (1881–1953) was a Mexican archaeologist of the generation after Alfredo Chavero. He was active primarily from the 1920s through the 1940s, and his peers included Manuel Gamio, Alfonso Caso, Miguel Angel Fernández, Sylvanus G. Morley, and J. Eric S. Thompson. Palacios taught Spanish literature at the Escuela Nacional Preparatoria in Mexico City beginning in 1906 and was a member of the Ateneo de la Juventud Mexicana, a group of young artists, writers, and educators who organized lectures and debates critical of the intellectual climate of the late Porfiriato. In addition to his work on the Aztec Calendar Stone, published in several versions (1918, 1922, 1924, 1937), he wrote a lengthy history of the city of Puebla (1917) and important early works on the ruins of El Tajín (Palacios and Meyer 1932), the sculpture of the Teocalli de la Guerra Sagrada (1929), and the symbolism of stone ballgame yokes (1943) and the Chacmool figures (1940). In the Maya area, he discovered the ruins of Santa Elena Poco Uinic in Chiapas (1928), made a reconnaissance of Calakmul and Edzna, and published guides to Chichén Itzá (1935a) and the Puuc cities (1945). As one of the few Mexicans active in Maya hieroglyphic studies before 1950, he published the first account of the Tablet of the 96 Glyphs from Palenque (1936), deciphered the glyph for the number 2 (1935b), and completed works on chronology and the correlation between the Maya and European calendars (1932, 1933).[1]

Palacios published his study of the Calendar Stone just two years before that of Hermann Beyer, and the German author clearly undertook his study in response. Both are early examples of the kind of iconographic analysis pioneered by Eduard Seler a generation before. A major difference, however, is that Palacios, following both Antonio de León y Gama and Chavero, attempts to make the events recorded in native histories agree with the monument by counting elements carved on the stone; Beyer places far more emphasis on iconographic traits common to the Calendar Stone, the codices, and other Aztec stone monuments. Palacios argues below that the Calendar Stone was of Toltec origin and was made either at Tula or at Teotihuacan, which many archaeologists in the early twentieth century believed to be a Toltec city. For Palacios, its imagery and the numbers that can be gleaned by counting iconographic elements make it an allegory that records mythical and historical events, especially the previous creations, the Venus cycle, and what he believed to have been a congress of Toltec savants who gathered to correct the calendar in the year A.D. 700.[2] He praised the lithographs of the Calendar Stone made for Leopoldo Batres in 1888 by Hesiquio Iriarte (ca. 1820–97)

Excerpted from Enrique Juan Palacios, "The *Stone of the Sun* and the First Chapter of the History of Mexico," translated from the Spanish by Frederick Starr, University of Chicago, Department of Anthropology, *Bulletin* 6 (Chicago: University of Chicago, 1921). Introductory text by Khristaan D. Villela.

EX LIBRIS · MEXICANIS

FREDERICK STARR

J.W.Spenceley·Boston·1905
Copyright Frederick Starr, 1905

(see p. 11, fig. 4) and by José María Velasco (see p. 10, fig. 3) and adds that it was accurate enough to count elements such as the number of quincunxes, the "pentagons," the bars on the serpent bodies, and so forth. Although Palacios makes the important point that there are no signs in the relief that are simply decorative, his approach makes us question where meaning lies in Aztec iconography. Does counting the minute elements of larger iconographic programs lead to expanded knowledge? Or is it an ultimately fruitless exercise?

The present translation was made in 1921 by anthropologist and bibliophile Frederick Starr (1858–1933), whose bookplate featured the Aztec Calendar Stone *(fig. 1). Starr made some minor edits, and we have further reduced the length of the essay by cutting sections that repeat material covered in other chapters of this book.*

Fig. 1.
J. Winfred Spenceley
(American, 1865–1908)
Bookplate for Frederick Starr, 1905,
copper engraving, 12 × 9.2 cm
(4¾ × 3⅝ in.)
Collection of Khristaan D. Villela,
Santa Fe, New Mexico

*   *   *

"The **Stone of the Sun** *and the First Chapter of the History of Mexico"*

INTRODUCTION

In a course upon Mexico, which has been given repeatedly to my students at the University of Chicago during the last twenty-five years, we have always devoted some time to the study of the "Aztec Calendar Stone." As a specimen of native American art it is of extraordinary interest; as a mass of symbols, in which the astronomical and chronometric knowledge of the ancient Mexicans is, in a sense, summarized, it is of the highest importance.

It has long been my intention to print a sort of study guide regarding the stone for the use of my students. My plan was to prepare a careful summary of the argument of each and every worker who had seriously attempted to interpret the stone; to arrange these summaries in chronological order; to subject them to critical investigation in order to extract from them what appear to be final conclusions; to add some original suggestions as to significance; and, finally, to point out what further study was necessary in order to [arrive at] a full understanding of the monument.

While I delayed, another worker has done a task so nearly like the one I proposed that mine seems no longer necessary. Mr. Enrique Juan Palacios, of the City of Mexico, has presented a paper, entitled *La Piedra del Sol y el primer capítulo de la historia de México,* before the *Sociedad Científica "Antonio Alzate,"* which has been printed in its *Memorias.* It is an admirable piece of work. I have felt that it would be better for me to translate it into English than to write a new work. …His long-continued and capable study deserves and earns serious consideration of his views. Faithful examination of his work will show students what may be accepted as settled; it will also indicate what problems remain to be solved.

—Frederick Starr. Chicago. June 21, 1921.

————

…Rare must be the traveler who does not admire the architecture of the metropolitan cathedral, whose towers, crowned by bell-shaped terminations, majestically distinguish it among all the basilicas of the world. It was precisely the author of a considerable part of this façade, and in particular of the towers, Don José Damián Ortiz de Castro, who made the discovery of the stone, under the pavement of the Plaza Principal, on the seventeenth of December of the year 1790.

They were about to bury it anew, imitating an archbishop who two centuries before had been guilty of so strange a blunder; fortunately the viceroy of the colony at the time was a man of the character of the second Count of Revillagigedo, Don Juan Vicente de Güemes Pacheco de

Padilla. This able and progressive governor opposed the execution of their plan, ordering that educated individuals should take charge of the stone, that they should measure and study it, and that it should be transported to the Royal University and placed in a public place "where it should be forever preserved as a notable monument of Indian antiquity."... William Bullock relates that by 1823 the people of Mexico called the monument *reloj de Moctezuma* ("Montezuma's watch"), a statement which Brantz Mayer repeats in his work *Mexico as It Was and Is* (1844).... The expert and notable artist, Don José María Velasco, drew it with his customary fidelity and precision (see p. 10, fig. 3). Finally in the year 1885, the monument was transported to the place which it now occupies in the grand salon of the Museum of Archaeology.

[Lengthy and detailed description following Chavero omitted here.]

The fourth zone or circle contains two hundred dots distributed in groups of five (each group in a little frame) which are commonly designated with the term *quintiduos* ("quincunxes"). In the asps already mentioned [see p. 94, fig. 1, where they are marked *L*] (six of which are entirely visible and two concealed in such a manner as induces us to assign the same elements to them) are eight *more quincunxes,* giving a total of forty dots. We ought yet to add the ten circumscribed in the arrow of the *naolin* and the ten placed between the face and the claws of the Tonatiuh. These last are dots like the others; but the necessities of distribution of the relief do not permit their being arranged in an actually identical form. Altogether they sum up to two hundred and sixty numerals of equal kind, a reading already made by archaeologists.

Until now it has been assumed that the elements in question represent the *tonalámatl* or *cecempohualli,* [a] fundamental computation of native chronology. Nevertheless, this is an error.... The distribution of the 260 numerals in groups of five, and not of thirteen, dots demonstrates by itself alone that we are not here dealing with the sacred book composed fundamentally of thirteens. The dots in question denote years, not days as has been supposed; and if they appear distributed in fives it is because they allude to years of the planet Venus, that is to say, the synodical movements of that planet, five of which form a cycle in the calendar of the aborigines for reasons which we shall explain later.

The dots of the fourth circle, joined with the other elements of the same kind represent then a period of 260 Venus years. Taking the synodical revolution of the planet as very close to 584 days, the total amounts to 151,840 days, or 416 solar years, [a] great cycle of the aboriginal chronology, repeatedly figured in the monolith, as we shall see. It is inferred that the Indians carried on simultaneously two calendars, that of the sun and that of Venus, and by their combination they computed the course of time; in this method, with purely astronomical elements, they formed their system of chronology.

Interrupted in its turn by the great and small rays, the fifth circle is formed of eight zones or glyphs which archaeologists have agreed in considering solar. Six of these zones contain ten glyphs, and each of the other two contain five: in all there are seventy glyphs of the same kind, to which are added the three which border each of the eight asps before mentioned, and the ten, a little smaller but of identical form, placed between the face and the talons of Tonatiuh. In total, they sum 104 solar glyphs, indicative of so many years.... The circle expresses the Indian century, or *huehuetiliztli....*

Nothing concrete has been said until now about the following circle. Some call the figures that compose it temples; others have seen them to resemble leaves or mountains; some simply call them little arches; but no one has penetrated their exact significance [see p. 94, fig. 1, where they are marked *J,* between every *L* and *R*]. In the most authorized descriptions they have generally been designated with the descriptive term "pentagons" (Chavero 1875) or "trapezoidal figures," symbolism of the most general kind having been attributed to them....

The monolith has no glyphs more interesting than these.... They appear in four groups, separated by the great solar rays. The two upper groups present thirteen signs; and each one of the lower, twelve, with presumably the missing one hidden by the plumes [upturned snouts] of the serpents which adorn this part of the stone. In total they sum up four groups of thirteen glyphs of the same form, the significance of which is somewhat of the most important which the relief contains. It explains the tenacity with which the glyphs guard their secret.

The archaeologists have said that the characters of which we treat are a kind of pentagons. They may be considered as made up of five somewhat irregular sides; there is, at the same time, the concavity of the inferior side. This is the figure of the jewel of Quetzalcóatl, as may be seen in many representations: on pages 42 and 59 of the *Codex Borgia,* which depict the double morning and evening star; in the beautiful statue belonging to the Trocadero Museum; on page 16 of the *Codex Borbonicus;* on page 17 of *Codex Vaticanus A;* and in others of the *Codex Telleriano-Remense,* etc. The jewel shows an elegant outline with five indentations or sides.... In converting itself into a chronographic glyph, it received many conventionalizations—Hamy has described them minutely in his *The Jewel of the Wind* (Hamy 1903)—which we may see in the monuments; but all are alike in the important details.

Ah well, was it a result of fancy or was it due to deliberate intention that this form attaches to the jewel of the deity? The more important pictographs (e.g., the *Dresden Codex*) reveal this practice of the *tonalpouhque:* to take as a unity the five years of Venus, which coincide with eight solar years. Such was the origin of the festival *atamalqualiztli,* celebrated at the end of this term. The unity thus formed was repeated thirteen times, as we see in the *Dresden Codex* itself (Kingsborough 1831–48, 1:24), in the Cospi, in the Borgia, in Vaticanus B, and in other documents. The conjunct equals 65 years of the planet, exactly equal to 104 solar, by virtue of the well-known equations:

$$584 \times 5 = 365 \times 8 = 2{,}920 \text{ days}$$
$$584 \times 65 = 365 \times 104 = 37{,}960 \text{ days}$$

The form of the jewel is allegorical of the five movements of Venus; for corroboration, see the eight dots at the bottom of the representation of the double star on page 59 of the *Codex Borgia;* see eight solar glyphs under the face of the stone figure of Tepezintla corresponding to the five circles which the same beautiful figure has upon the forehead. That this stone represents Quetzalcóatl (the star Venus) in his descent of eight days into hell is without doubt.

But there was another motive for dividing the jewel of the deity into five parts or distributing it into five points. In developing the calendar of the star, the periods of 584 days are begun with the symbols *Cipactli, Cóatl, Atl, Acatl,* and *Ollin,* and, continuing the series of Venus years, the same characters are repeated in identical order, giving the result that of the twenty day signs of the native month; only five preside over the revolutions of the star, a fact discovered by the learned Seler....

We have then a little cycle of five revolutions of Venus equal to eight solar years, which are 2,920 days. Each of the frames enclosing five dots, each of the little pentagons, expresses this chronological value. Supposing the planet at the beginning of its matutinal apparition or its heliacal rising, it will have recovered the identical position, with respect to the star of the day, at the termination of the cycle. The fact is a phenomenon of astronomical observation which could not pass unobserved to scrutinizers of the heavens like the Indians. . . . But we have seen that this unity is repeated thirteen times. There are two reasons for this: one, to equal with Venus years the great period of 104 solar years, a cycle equivalent to 65 synodical movements of the planet; the other, to equalize the two calendars, because when five Venus years have passed, the sixth commences anew with *Cipactli,* but this character goes this second time not accompanied by the numeral 1, but by 9, necessitating that the five years shall be repeated thirteen times, in order that *Cipactli* should return to be accompanied by 1, as at the beginning of the period.

The cause of this phenomenon is known. The *tonalámatl,* that is to say, the series of twenty periods of thirteen days, runs through the book of the planet the same as through that of the sun, calendars, one and the other, which are made up by the combination of thirteen numbers in order with the twenty day characters, so that these may not be confounded on being repeated. As the number 584 does not contain an exact number of thirteens, there are twelve units over in the first Venus year, eleven in the next, ten in the next, and so on successively, so that *Cipactli* comes to be accompanied by different numerals, the thirteen times that it begins the year, until the 65 counts of the planet's calendar are complete. . . .

Day names and numbers which accompany the initial signs of the Venus year, in a series of 65 years:

Cipactli	1-9-4-12-7-2-10-5-13-8-3-11-6
Cóatl	13-8-3-11-6-1-9-4-12-7-2-10-5
Atl	12-7-2-10-5-13-8-3-11-6-1-9-4
Acatl	11-6-1-9-4-12-7-2-10-5-13-8-3
Ollin	10-5-13-8-3-11-6-1-9-4-12-7-2

With the beginning of the 66th year of the series, *Cipactli,* with the numeral 1, returns to begin the count like that of the 37,960 days passed, and on this same day the sign with the same number gives beginning to the 105th year of the solar calendar; one and the other count are thus adjusted to each other:

$$584 \times 65 = 365 \times 104 = 260 \times 146$$

Now we may understand the thirteen pentagons in each one of the four parts of the circle of the monument. They denote the number of times that the five characters enter as initials of the Venus year in one *huehuetiliztli.* . . . And that the intention of the astronomer-director of the engraving of the relief was to inscribe this number of glyphs is plainly seen in the upper groups of the sixth circle; without aesthetic prejudice and almost compelled by the demand of symmetry, other pentagons might very well have been located in the space covered by the bands which issue from the serpents' tails. The artist might, with the greatest good taste, have placed six glyphs in this double empty space, but he deliberately prolonged the bands instead. The purpose was the engraving of a number, not of an ornament. This suffices to show us that there are no simply decorative signs in the relief: it is an incomparable synthesis of art and science.

But there are four groups of Venus cycles, four zones of thirteen pentagons. To what necessity of the system can this repetition correspond? Given the synodical movement of Venus of 584 days, there result 37,960 for each group, or 151,840 for the total of 52 pentagons of the circle. This period represents exactly 416 solar years. In other terms, if each group signifies 65 Venus years, equivalent, as we know, to a *huehuetiliztli,* the four correspond to as many sacred cycles, which is what is indicated by the great numerals that surround the head of Tonatiuh, conforming to the interpretation which we have already given. Two circles, the second and the sixth, say exactly the same thing: 416 solar years. The fourth zone expresses an equal thing: 260 Venus years, which number is considered sacred. Everything in the monolith concurs in declaring one single and well-considered thought; we shall speak of its origin and admire its profundity and transcendence. Meantime we say, as proof that we are not dealing merely with arbitrary theories or purely speculative systems, that the numbers 37,960 and 151,840 appear in the *Dresden Codex.* Förstemann, its able interpreter, has read them in that admirable astronomical book.

Let us pass to the seventh zone.... Two magnificent serpents encircle the relief and at the lower part of the stone join heads, from whose opened throats peer out human faces confronting each other.... Let us commence by observing that the heads which appear in the throats are distinct beings or deities, differentiated by characters which permit their identification. From both heads protrude tongues, joining or touching them together in the clearest fashion; here is symbolized the idea of the relief.... In a similar manner, the face of Tonatiuh, central to the relief, has the tongue out, signifying the irradiation of light through the universe.... These tongues indicate the lights of special celestial bodies....

Now let us undertake to identify the deities; if known, it will be easy to recognize the cycle. The figure of the left is undoubtedly the sun himself.... The head of the solar snake has before the nose the sign of the double cane, a character closely related with Tonatiuh and with Xiuhtecuhtli, as is seen in the codices.... Others have recognized in the glyph a handful of herbs, giving us, anyway, the name of Xiuhtecuhtli (lord of the herb and the year).[3]

On the other hand, the figure on the right [*sic*] shows a netting clearly defined, peculiar to Quetzalcóatl in his multiple representations.... But that which in a special mode distinguishes the two beings is the ear ornament (*nacochtli*), which is lacking in the figure to the right [*sic*] and identical with that which adorns the central Tonatiuh in the figure to the left [*sic*]. The ear ornament possesses distinctive value in representations of deities. More is not necessary for our purpose; it suffices to affirm that the sun is the star represented in this figure.

What star can it be that [this serpent on the right] symbolizes?... The sign before the nose appears as if it were 1-cane, unlike the double one of the sun, which gives us one of the names best known of the personage, *Ce ácatl* (1-cane), the day of his birth. Together, in the reunion of the tongues, the two serpents indicate the *huehuetiliztli,* the sacred cycle of 104 years, indicated in the wrinkled face of the central Tonatiuh....

Let us continue the analysis of the seventh zone. If the heads which face each other, joining tongues, yield the *huehuetiliztli,* then in the body of the serpents is directly indicated the number 416 which we have found in other parts of the relief. The reading is made from the groups of four rays, interpreted until now as symbols of fire and in various other fashions, all arbitrary or at least vaguely symbolic, as emblems of the highest indefiniteness. Nevertheless, their meaning is most clear: each group says *ácatl, técpatl, calli, tochtli,* names of the four successive years in the ordinary chronology. Very well, the serpent that symbolizes the sun presents 52 groups of four rays equivalent to 208 years; added to the 208 corresponding to the other serpent, we have a total of 416 solar years, a most interesting fact which we are the first to indicate. Here there is no necessity of resorting to allegorical conceptions. And so deliberate was the intention of inscribing in each one of the serpents precisely 52 groups of rays that the artist, not having sufficient space, was compelled to add those bands which issue from the points of the tails, the only element of the relief which might appear somewhat arbitrary.... If up to the present none of the draughtsmen and lithographers who have reproduced the stone—except the most skillful Iriarte, who devoted four months to the work in order to illustrate a study of Señor Leopoldo Batres (1888)—copied this and some of the other elements with exactness, it is because, the meaning of the glyphs being unknown, their number and complicated distribution easily caused them to make errors. Further on we shall say in what the principal errors have consisted and shall speak of one very curious artificial anomaly of the stone.

We have still to explain the signs which form the scales or divisions or the body of the serpents and to count the numeral dots placed at the border of the stone and around the said divisions. Beyer and other archaeologists maintain that they symbolize fire. We have no reason to deny it; but our own opinion is that together they indicate the number of cycles or meetings of Venus and the sun.... With respect to the dots, Señor Chavero counted them and interpreted them well, finding in them the number of days in the native year. Nothing more logical: the cyclical coincidence of the 104 solar years and 65 Venus years is effected by the aggregation, one after the other, of series of 365 days. It was natural to place these dots where we find them. And they do not find themselves duplicated in the two serpents because it is the common element of both reckonings; it was sufficient to inscribe them once.

We, however, differ somewhat from Señor Chavero in our way of counting them. There are ten dots each in as many scales; there are eighteen in the single scale which follows the tyings or ligatures; twelve more are within the triangle which forms the tail. In sum there are 130 dots in each side, or 260 in going all around, which gives us the fundamental basis of the chronology: the *tonalámatl.* If, on the other hand, we count the 63 large points of the border of the stone, added to the hundred of the first ten scales, we have 163 numerals, and with the 18 which follow the tyings, they add up to 181 on each side, or 362 in the entire circumference; almost hidden within the claws of the first scale (the first on each side, of course) are two other points, that is, four altogether. In sum there are 366. This is the result which we obtain, and thus we shall state it, even if in this case it appears a little defective; but we do not attempt, as some interpreters, to fit the facts to our theories, but from the facts themselves to infer the true decipherment. It might be admitted that this last dot signifies the intercalated day: the native bissextile.

As for the four tyings located on the tail of each serpent, archaeologists have been in accord in attributing to them the value of so many *tlalpilli* of 13 years, four of which, as everyone knows, formed the classical *xiuhtlalpilli, xipoualli,* or *xiuhmolpilli* of the chronological reckonings: 52 years. Each serpent has four ligatures; that is to say, 104 solar years are symbolized in the total of the representation....

Dates

We arrive at the important matter of the dates inscribed upon the famous monolith. Only one has until today been definitely fixed by archaeologists: the *13-ácatl* carved within a frame between the tails of the serpents. It is the prominent date of the stone, the one engraved with the most deliberate purpose; its position emphasizes it.

No one is ignorant that the capital defect of the chronological system of the Indians is that the names of the years repeat themselves every 52 years. The *13-ácatl* of the tablet may be the year 1479, which is the one generally admitted, but that same year took place in 1427 and 1375 and

1323 and 1271 and 1167 and 1115 and 1063 and 699, etc., etc. It is certain that the minute account of Durán, invoked by Don Alfredo Chavero, gives much force to the presumption that the date expresses the year in which the monolith was completed, during Axayacatl's reign, in 1479. More than that, the stone was in the great temple of Tenochtitlan; it was found in those precincts; there they buried it again between 1551 and 1569, and there later on it was rediscovered….There are reasons, then, for believing that it is the stone described by the friar, the consecration of which was the object of so great ceremonies and to which alludes the statement of the natives, therein cited, that it bore "the figure of the sun." Tezozomoc gives a similar account.

Withal, this does not go beyond supposition, and there might be reason for doubt amid the multiplicity of conflicting opinions: that the stone was completed in the time of Chimalpopoca, as Don Antonio Peñafiel believed; in 1352, as Abadiano asserted; in 103 or 231, dates which some have claimed to read in the relief; and in 699, and that it was made by the Toltecs, as there are very strong reasons for believing. What we may indeed affirm is that we have here not the date with which the last sun or the historic sun began, as Joyce says and Spinden repeats, because the statements are in agreement, not only in the Aztec traditions but in the Toltec, in assigning the sign *Ce técpatl* (1-knife) to this event: the codices prove it without any manner of doubt….

Near the face of the sun, in the next following great circle, it will be remembered that we meet with a flint knife with one dot, that is *Ce técpatl.* Together with the *técpatl* is seen the *mamalhuaztli,* sign of the new fire….

[Discussion of how Palacios believes certain symbols can be read as dates omitted here.]

Let us repeat in order, for greater clearness:

Direct, that is to say, by summation of elements:

Year 4992 (twice)

Year 5096

Year 5720

Year 5876

Native reading, for us indirect:

13 ácatl

1-tecpatl

Two other dates, *Ce quiáhuitl* (1-rain) and *Chicome ozomatl* (7-monkey), are below the great central arrow.

Interpretation

The historian Ixtlilxóchitl, great-grandson of the last king of Texcoco, is held to be the most faithful and informed conservator of the traditions, history, and cosmogony of the Toltecs. There reigns, however, the most extraordinary confusion and an incredible disorder in many of the dates which he gives, which is due to the fact that he did not know how to harmonize the native with the Christian chronology; but the basis of his narrative, submitted to a *cabildo* of Indian savants, very nearly approaches historical truth. Men of no less merit than Clavijero, Prescott, Count Cortina, Fernando Ramírez, and Manuel Orozco y Berra, have rendered justice to this man, unduly unesteemed by some.

According to the data of his *Relaciones,* the human species from the creation of the world on had been three times destroyed: the first time by inundations (*Atonatiuh* or the sun of water); the second by hurricanes (*Ehecatonatiuh* or the sun of the air), after a lapse of time equal to that which passed before. The third age concluded in the year 4992, which is just 12 complete cycles of 416 years, and ended by terrestrial calamities (wars, eruptions, earthquakes, etc.), "... those of this earth had another destruction, who were the giants; and thus also many of the Tultecs died in the year *Ce técpatl* (4993); and this age they called *Tlacchitonatiuh* (sun of earth)." In it Ixtlilxóchitl places the Ulmecas and the Xicalancas, gives data regarding Quetzalcóatl, and speaks of the first pyramid of Cholula. The destruction of the giants (*quinamétzin*) marked the end of the era in 4993.

It should be noticed that 4993 is equal to three exact periods of 1,664 years, which is in turn made up of 4 cycles of 416: the Indians distributed the evolution of their history in fixed periods of equal duration. Thus is explained the allegory carved in the center of the relief which represents the four ages of the world, the duration of each one of which appears determined by 4 dots, the chronological value of which has not been discovered until now. It is easy for us to suppose that the Toltecs, always obedient to the quadrupartite conception which permeated diverse phases of their social organization, their philosophy, and their religio-cosmogonic beliefs, would assign to each period, even if it had scarcely begun, 1,664 years, [a] number formed by four great cycles of 416 years, made up in turn of four *huehuetiliztli....*

The above might seem to be speculative; but it is a fact that the Texcocan chronicler fixes the date 4992 and that this is read twice in the relief. When 4,992 years had run their course, three ages only had been completed; 104 years later, Ixtlilxóchitl affirms that the Toltecs initiated a new chronology, "they added the bissextile, in order to adjust the solar year to the equinox," and in fine, they perfected their calendar, determining the rules relative "to the months, the weeks, and the signs and planets": the event occurred in *Ce técpatl* (1-knife) 5097, counting from the creation of the world in the Indian cosmology.

The important *Anales de Cuauhtitlan* (which surpasses all those known in the antiquity and precision of its chronology, which embraces eight great cycles) confirm the data of Ixtlilxóchitl. They locate the arrival of the mysterious nation of the Ulmecas, in the beginnings of the third age, very nearly a thousand years before Christ, and categorically fix the beginning of the second Toltec monarchy in the year 674 of our era. Twenty-six years later, the year 700 was *Ce técpatl;* and all the traditions affirm that the Toltecs initiated a new epoch in *Ce técpatl....*

Very well, if the third age began 1,664 years before that event, its commencement dates from the year 964 B.C. Ordóñez de Aguiar has discovered in the traditions of Chiapas, that "almost a thousand years" before our era, took place the apparition and began the migrations of the Quiches. Brasseur de Bourbourg, with data from the codices, indicates the coming of the Ulmecas in the Plateau in the year 955 B.C., a date admitted by Chavero in relation to the Vixtoti, who were fundamentally the same people; then is "when the sun began to divide the lands between men." There is but nine years difference from 964.

We shall infer that the Ulmecas and the Quiches were the same people, which explains to us the arrival of the first from the east. Some circumstance set them in movement about a thousand years before our era, and about the year 964 or 955 they began to show themselves in the high table-land of Anahuac, coming from the direction of the Gulf, as all traditions assert. It is necessary to admit the probability that they constructed the first pyramids and other monuments, as legend persistently claims. Sahagún, Torquemada, and various chroniclers collected the story from the lips of the Indians....

Somewhere about the year 596 of the vulgar era, [a] date suggested by Clavijero, there appeared on the Plateau, or at least began their movement, the advance guards of the Toltec migration. The best documents, the *Anales de Cuauhtitlan* among them, agree that the land was then occupied by the Ulmecas. Some grave event permitted the newcomers to witness the last ruins of the catastrophe in the regions which had been occupied by their predecessors; the vestiges of human work found under the lavas of Xictli and of Cerro Pelado in the Pedregal of San Angel and on both slopes of Ajusco strongly corroborate this hypothesis. It was then the year 4992 in the chronology of the aborigines. After the cataclysm the Toltecs employed another 104 years, a *huehuetiliztli,* in establishing themselves in the district, and, in the year 700 of our era, founded their final seat, initiated a new period in the fourth age of the world, arranging the chronology, consolidating their monarchical institutions, and electing their first king.

Chavero agrees with these data, although he believes that six years earlier, in 694, some very important event occurred, which some, like Orozco y Berra, connect with the dedication of the pyramids to the astronomic cult; but he accepts the mentioned date anyway. Torquemada had gathered from the traditions which came within his reach the same date 700, adding that the Toltecs had "wandered" for 104 years before, a statement which accords with others that we have. Clavijero and other authors vary slightly as to the founding of Tula, assigning the dates 661, 667, 674—the *Anales de Cuauhtitlan* gives this—and even 694, given by Motolinía as the year of the beginning of the epoch; but the date mentioned (A.D. 700; *Ce técpatl* in the native calendar), whether we relate it to that event or to the exaltation of the first monarch, best resists analysis for which reason the erudite author of the first volume of *México a través de los siglos* (Chavero 1888), after a thorough investigation, decides in favor of it. The *Anales,* although they declare that Tula was founded in 674, add that the nation existed for twenty-seven years without a monarch, that is to say, they arrived at the notable date 700. It cannot be denied that the date floats with singular persistency upon the tumultuous waves of tradition. Buelna, whose talent and breadth of documentation no one denies, also encounters it in his investigations, although the learned author of the *Peregrinación de los Aztecas* refers it to one of the principal stations in the journey of the tribe of Tenoch—the arrival at Mexcala or Coatlicamac—an assertion with which we do not agree, because it conflicts with the statements of the *Codex Ramírez,* or Durán, and of Chimalpahin, who unanimously assign a much less ancient date to that event. But even if it is not related to the race of the Mexi, the suggestive thing is that this date appears in all the studies, so that surely it does allude to some event of capital importance in the history of the aborigines; all the circumstances suggest that it treats of the Toltecs. The relatively few discrepancies which we mention in themselves manifest the precision of the chronology in question. There are those who (Seler 1902–23, 2:19; Joyce 1914, 365) in place of the year 700 prefer to assign the initial references of the document of Cuauhtitlan, relative to the Toltecs, to the year 752.[4]…Ixtlilxóchitl and the *Anales de Cuauhtitlan* result then on the whole in agreement: the year 700 of the vulgar era is 5097 of the chronology of the Indians.

Here follows a most important passage from Ixtlilxóchitl, which one might almost say was directly deduced from the data of the relief:

> …In the year 5097 of the creation of the world, which was *Ce técpatl,* and 104 from the total destruction of the *quinamétzin* (giants), there being peace throughout this New World, all the Toltec savants came together, the astrologers as well as the other arts in Huehuetlapallan, head city of their kingdom, where they treated of many things such as the events and calamities that had happened and the movements of the heavens since the creation of the world.

This was the famous meeting of Toltec astronomers, a meeting in which was made the reorganization of the calendar. This important reunion took place in the year 5097 from the creation of the world (native chronology), a year that was *Ce técpatl* in its series (commenced with the same name and number).

We have seen that some event of the greatest importance occurred in the year 700 of the Christian Era, and the synchronological tables (see those of Veytia) (1907) tell us without room for error that the year 700 was *Ce técpatl.* At the same time, the paragraph of Ixtlilxóchitl states that the third age of the world ended in 4992, since 104 years before 5097 the *quinamétzin* perished; this was the *Tlacchitonatiuh,* or the sun of the earth (*Tlaltonatiuh*). So the Indians considered their third epoch finished in the year 596, and it is to be noticed that three historians, Torquemada, Clavijero, and Veytia, are in harmony regarding this date; but as they delayed a century (104 years) in consolidating and regulating the calendar, they adopted the year 700 for the chronological beginning.

Ah well, the monument of the museum shows the two dates clearly: in the glyphs in the backs of the serpents, which added to the 104 years of the meeting of the heads give the number 5,096, and in the glyphs at the margin of the stone, which express the number 4,992. In order to confirm it, the character *Ce técpatl* joins to the face of Tonatiuh in a prominent part of the relief; here also are the four cosmogonic ages; here at the edge of the stone the hieroglyphs alluding to the three ages completed. The reference could not be more explicit. The monolith appears worked expressly to record the facts discussed at the memorable assembly of the astronomers, that "movement of the heavens and the calamities that have occurred since the creation of the world." Already we know what these were: Chavero has read them to perfection in the rectangles which surround the *naolin: Ehecatonatiuh, Tletonatiuh, Atonatiuh,* and *Tlaltonatiuh,* which was the present, initiated by *Ce técpatl:* the ages, suns, and catastrophes of the air, fire, water, and earth....

And what is the native year 5097 in our chronology? The synchronological tables, Ixtlilxóchitl, and the *Anales,* all tell us: this *Ce técpatl,* commencement of the Toltec epoch within the fourth age of the world, corresponds to 700 of the vulgar era, when the compatriots of Huemántzin declared their new history begun and founded the second Tula, or, what is more probable, elected their monarch Mixcoamazátzin, as Chavero says. Torquemada gives the same year, but changes the king's name to Totepeuh; Motolinía varies only by six years, since he says that the present age commenced in 694, while the tables prove that the *Ce técpatl* mentioned by Ixtlilxóchitl could only be 700.[5] So many testimonies drive us to think that the stone of the museum was made a little after the year A.D. 700, by the hands of a people who, on account of their knowledge in the arts and sciences, have left fame in the traditions as learned and artistic.

[Extended discussion omitted here of elaborate calculations that support Palacios's belief that the monument dates back to the Toltec era, which was thought at the time of his writing to be in the first millennium A.D. and centered at the great city of Teotihuacan. We join Palacios as he describes the fourth circle of the Calendar Stone.]

The year 699 was a *13-ácatl,* the date indicated by the tails of the serpents in whose heads and bodies we have read so simply the number 5,096.... [We claim] that the monument dates from 1,200 years ago and that it was sculptured to record the most famous assembly of Toltec astronomers, of which this relief seems the imperishable official record.

There is another circumstance suggesting the Toltec origin of the stone, at least as concerns the ideas represented: the importance which the planet Venus has in the relief. Quetzalcóatl was the symbol of Venus; Quetzalcóatl changed himself into Vesper, states the fragment attributed to Olmos, *Histoyre du Mechique;* Quetzalcóatl was the evening star, declares the commentators of *Codex Vaticanus A.*...Son of Ixtacmixcóatl, "the serpent of the white clouds" (the Milky Way), tradition says that this personage was one of the brothers engendered by the divine creator, that is to say, one of the original races, called Olmecas, Xicalancas, etc....Quetzalcóatl is the representative of the Toltecs, their symbol and metaphorical incarnation, and the Toltec priests and kings were accustomed to adopt his name....From his movements combined with those of the star of the day they made the basis of their chronological system, the basis of their calendar....The worshipers of the star are the inventors of the system, the true inventors of the *tonalámatl.*...

To summarize: always the same data will be found: the four ages of the world, the number 4,992 twice placed (in one of which the numbers 1,664 figures), the number 5,096, the *13-ácatl* correspondent to the same year, the *Ce técpatl,* the following year (5097), and the cycles of 104 and 416 solar years indicated in different modes, the dates mentioned being the result of the addition of these same cycles. What a simple and highly logical conception!

Translating this into our language and relating it to modern chronology...we may say: The date 5096 corresponds to the year 699 of the Christian Era; this year was a *13-ácatl,* and 1,664 years had passed since 964 B.C. when, in their legends, with discrepancies of about nine years, the natives declared the third era of the world had begun, assigning to it a duration of four cycles of 416 years. The 32 *itzpapalotl* (obsidian butterflies) of the edge of the relief each symbolize a new fire. One hundred and four years before the year 4992 of their chronology it is declared that the *quinamétzin* were destroyed....The Toltec savants met together then and discussed the creation of the world, the calamities that had occurred, and the movement of the heavens: this means that they proceeded to the regulation of the calendar, basing it upon the observations of the heavenly bodies. Sahagún says that "the Toltecs knew the movement of the heavens and this by the stars." Clavijero discovered data that suggested that the astronomer Huemántzin, governing Ixtlilcuecháhuac, made the sacred book, the *Teoamoxtli,* wherein was explained the movement of the heavens, and he assigned to the event the date that Boturini fixes for the beginning of what he calls the third age. Both authorities agree in fundamental fact, but the rigorous and most minute chronology of the *Anales,* recording the dates 674 and 700, is irreproachable; to it we ought to attach ourselves, supported by the double authority of Torquemada and Chavero: that the year 700 was *Ce técpatl* is certain....No more fitting means existed than to sculpt the auguries and predictions of a race which lived ever scrutinizing the secret of the firmament in indestructible material, which should preserve the marvelous secret for following ages.

If the relief of the museum is that commemorative monument, we must admit that its glyphs, so long mysterious, were the work of a master-workman and the conception of a mind which in genius does not yield before Hipparchus, nor Kepler, nor Newton, nor Arago. Thus Bullock was impelled to declare: "...The stone is a conspicuous proof of the perfection to which these races had attained in certain sciences: even in the most enlightened cities of the present day, there are few persons who would be capable of executing such a work" (1824a, 333–34).

Slow has been our analysis....But to the eyes of the Mexicans of Tenochtitlan, who placed the relief in a prominent part of their temples, whether they worked it themselves or received it already made, the reading was easy and significant in the extreme. Translating it, so far as is possible, its form would be more or less as follows:

In the year 4992 the third age of the world came to an end; with four more great rounds, four ages. At its termination Tonatiuh and Quetzalcóatl met in the heavens, and in the *tonalámatl* it was *Ce cipactli,* the first of the count. It was the end of the year *13-ácatl.* One hundred and four years later the Toltec savants founded their city and elected a king, and the old men, the astronomers, and the principal diviners having assembled said: We are about to commence again the count of time. And they did so with the commencement of the following year, *Ce técpatl,* which was the 5,097th year from the creation. And they added that this age would have to end through terrestrial calamities, after 4 × 416 years, since the preceding ages had come to end through the force of water, of air, and of fire, because so the two lords of heaven, who come together every 8 and 104 years, will it. And they decided to record it in a monument, strong and eternal as time, that it should be preserved in the history of the world.

…There arises one question then: if the constructor were the Toltecs, how did its monument come to be in the *teocalli* of a *Mexican* city?

…The question of transportation involves little difficulty, supposing that it was transported from the [Teotihuacan] or from Tula. Modern archaeologists recognize that the rock mass itself must have been transported, at least from the mountains of Aculco, the nearest locality where this kind of basalt is to be found. If the Aztecs could transport a monolith of 30 tons weight from there, they could have done so from a greater distance, for example, from Teotihuacan, sacred city concerning which more and more reasons accumulate for maintaining that it was the Toltec metropolis.

Notes

1. Biographical details after Thompson 1953; and López Hernández 2006.

2. Fernando de Alva Ixtlilxóchitl (1891–92) is the main source for this event. Palacios wrote at the same time that many students of the Maya thought that Altar Q at Copan recorded a similar congress of astronomer priests.

3. [In Nahuatl, the word *xihuitl* means herb, leaf, plant, and year.]

4. And Seler himself (1902–23, 2:30), so learned and well documented generally, studying similar problems affirms (*Über den Ursprung der mittelamerikanischen Kulturen*) that the beginning of the Toltec culture and of the system of the *tonalámatl,* or "the historic sun" for the Indians, dates from an epoch around the year A.D. 700.

5. Further, the narratives of the history of the Aztecs and their predecessors, the Culhuas (who were Toltecs), which were ordered to be written down by the daughter of Motecuhzoma, Doña Isabel, and which were published by Señor Icazbalceta, coincide in assigning to the first king a year of the eighth century, which is notably near to the year 700. Certainly the princess utilized the services of some truly learned native priest (García Icazbalceta 1891, 3:264–65).

"How Was the Stone Called the *Aztec Calendar Stone* Painted?" (1942)

Editor's Commentary

Roberto Sieck Flandes presented the first reconstruction of the colors of the Aztec Calendar Stone *in 1939 at the International Congress of Americanists, which met in Mexico City (see pl. 15). Although his drawing suffers from errors where he "corrected" what he perceived to be the faults of the Aztec artists, his colored version has become the canonical image of the* Calendar Stone *and has been reproduced many times in forms as diverse as postcards, apparel, and liquor bottles. Sieck Flandes developed his reconstruction from traces of pigment on the stone and from the coloring of similar motifs in the codices and on other stone sculptures in the Museo Nacional de Arqueología in Mexico City. In the late 1990s, Felipe Solís directed new studies of the remaining color on the sculpture and, although those results were published in 2000 (see pl. 11), the Sieck Flandes version, memorable for its bright colors, has not been supplanted.*[1]

✻   ✻   ✻

"How Was the Stone Called the Aztec Calendar Stone *Painted?"*

Concerning the monolith in the Museo Nacional de Arqueología in Mexico City called the *Piedra del Sol,* or the *Aztec Calendar Stone,* I have completed this study of its colors, forms, and details, reconstructed from all of the sources of information we have at the present time, with the desire that through my humble work one can admire all the beauty of this monument, as in the days of splendid grandeur reached by the Aztec race.

 For the aid that has been afforded me, the documents placed at my disposal, and the facts and opinions about my work given by Don Alfonso Caso, Don Luis Castillo Ledón, Don Mateo A. Saldaña, and the directors and staff of the Museo Nacional de Arqueología and of the Biblioteca Nacional de México, I am most grateful for their impartial cooperation.

 I began this study by consulting the most authoritative works on this aspect of the monolith, namely "El llamado *Calendario Azteca,*" by H. Beyer (1921); "*La Piedra del Sol,*" by A. Chavero (1886; 1903); "Estudio Arq. Jeroglífico del *Calendario,*" by D. Abadiano (1889); "*La Piedra del Calendario* y la Historia de México," by E. J. Palacios (1918); "Las medidas del *Calendario Azteca,*" by Alfonso Caso, in vol. 2 of the *Revista Mexicana de Estudios Históricos* (Caso 1928); *La Acción Mundial,* by Dr. Atl; "México a Través de los Siglos" (Chavero 1888); the

Translated by Khristaan D. Villela from Roberto Sieck Flandes, "Como estuvo pintada la piedra conocida con el nombre de 'El Calendario Azteca'?" in *Vigesimoséptimo Congreso Internacional de Americanistas, actas de la primera sesión celebrada en la ciudad de México en 1939* (Mexico City: Instituto Nacional de Antropología & Historia, 1942), 1:550–56. Published with permission. Introductory text by Khristaan D. Villela.

codices *Borbonicus, Telleriano Remensis, Magliabechiano, Borgia, Zouche-Nuttall,* and *Laud;* and the *Matrícula de Tributos.*

After reviewing what they had said on this theme, and the sources I have enumerated, I was able to make a line drawing of the front and of the edge with all the details reconstructed, which I colored, studying the balance of the whole and especially its tone, taking this from similar forms on monoliths that still conserve stucco, from frescoes or wall paintings, and from ceramics, which can be found, some in the Museo Nacional and others in the archaeological zone of Teotihuacan, Mexico, and at the ruins found at the corner of Seminario and Guatemala streets in this city. In the stucco remains extant on the stone itself, the red of the "Light Rays" can still be seen, and when I was allowed to clean and moisten the stone, particles of stucco in some nooks and crannies reacted, enabling me to detect the other colors. This information and that taken from the codices are contained in my detailed report on each motif. I have emphasized those details that still show vestiges of color.

Next I will list the reasons that led me to color each of the different motifs of the stone, beginning with the center and addressing each of the distinct rings on its upper surface from the right to the left (counterclockwise).

SOURCES FOR RECONSTRUCTING THE COLOR

The face of Tonatiuh: according to the "Jarrón de Tonatiuh," which can be found in the Salón de Cerámica Azteca in the Museo Nacional, and according to page 10 of the *Codex Borbonicus.*

The sign 4 Ocelotonatiuh: according to page 3 of the *Codex Borbonicus* and folio 9v of the *Codex Telleriano Remensis.*

The sign 4 Ehecatonatiuh: according to the date 4 Wind on page 7 of the *Codex Borbonicus.*

The sign 4 Quiatoniatiuh: according to the date 4 Rain and the upper left figure on folio 19v of the *Codex Telleriano Rememsis.*

The sign 4 Atonatiuh: according to page 5 of the *Codex Borbonicus.*

The claws of the solar deity: according to page 69 of the *Codex Nuttall,* page 20 of the *Codex Borbonicus,* and folio 12v of the *Codex Telleriano Remensis.*

The frame around the figures above, which forms the Ollin sign: according to page 14 of the *Codex Borbonicus* and the date 1 Movement on folio 16v of the *Codex Telleriano Remensis.*

The four points that are the numbers of the sign 4 Ollin: according to traces of blue stucco that I found on the upper left number, according to page 14 of the *Codex Borbonicus,* and pages 58 and 71 of the *Codex Borgia.*

The rays of light: according to the ceramic vessel with solar disks in the Museo Nacional, page 14 of the *Codex Borbonicus,* and the traces of color that can still be seen on the stone itself.

The ornaments and groups [*colgajos y adornos*] of forms decorated as *chalchihuitls,* feathers, and pearls [*perla*]: according to remains of green stucco that I found in the background of the third square with the *chalchihuitl* symbol on the upper left side; according to remains of white stucco on the feathers and pearl [or jewel; *perla*] of the adornment [*colgajo*] next to the aforementioned square; according to polychrome vases found in the Museo Nacional; pages 3, 7, 11, and 14 of the *Codex Borbonicus;* the date 4 Ollin on folio 8v of the *Codex Telleriano Remensis;* folio 53 of the *Codex Magliabechiano;* and plate 11 on page 19 of the *Matrícula de Tributos.*

The date 1 Tecpatl: according to page 19 of the *Codex Borbonicus* and the *tecpatls* in the *Codex Laud.*

The *xiuhuitzolli* with a *tecpatl* at its upper front point, *aztaxelli,* hair, terraced plates, and the *yacaxihuitl* with a flourish [*vírgulas*], the eyebrow, and eye: according to pages 9 and 10 of the *Codex Borbonicus.*

The date 1 Quiahuitl: same as for the sign 4 Quiatoniatiuh.

The date 7 Ozomatli: according to the date 3 Monkey on page 7, the date Monkey on page 9, the date 8 Monkey on page 12, the date 10 Monkey on page 18, and the date 4 Monkey on page 20 of *Codex Borbonicus.* Although the color is not very appropriate for a monkey's face, it is the one that best harmonizes with the grouping of signs and is most often used in the Aztec codices.

The day Cipactli: according to the date 9 Crocodile on page 5 of the *Codex Borbonicus* and the date 2 Crocodile on folio 10v of the *Codex Telleriano Remensis.*

The day Ehecatl: same as for the sign 4 Ehecatonatiuh.

The day Calli: according to the date 5 House on page 7 of the *Codex Borbonicus,* the date 13 House on page 47, and the date 11 House, on page 5 of the *Codex Nuttall.*

The day Cuetzpallin: according to the date 10 Lizard on folio 23 of the *Codex Telleriano Remensis.*

The day Coatl: according to the day 3 Snake on page 15 and pages 9 and 19 of the *Codex Borbonicus.*

The day Miquiztli: according to the date 7 Death on page 4 of the *Codex Borbonicus.*

The day Mazatl: according to the date 11 Deer on page 14 of the *Codex Borbonicus* and the date 2 Deer on folio 12v of the *Codex Telleriano Remensis.*

The day Tochtli: according to page 19 of the *Codex Borbonicus* and the date 3 Rabbit on folio 12v of the *Codex Telleriano Remensis.*

The day Atl: according to page 10 of the *Codex Borbonicus* and the date 2 Water on folio 23v of the *Codex Telleriano Remensis.*

The day Itzcuintli: according to page 14 of the *Codex Borbonicus.*

The day Ozomatli: same as the date 7 Ozomatli.

The day Malinalli: according to the date 13 Grass on page 4 of the *Codex Borbonicus* and the date 12 Grass on folio 8 of the *Codex Telleriano Remensis.*

The day Acatl: according to the date 2 Reed, on page 8 and the date 2 Reed on page 34 of the *Codex Borbonicus* and the date 3 Reed on folio 15 of the *Codex Telleriano Remensis.*

The day Ocelotl: same as the sign 4 Ocelotonatiuh.

The day Cuauhtli: according to the date 3 Eagle on pages 5 and 14 of the *Codex Borbonicus.*

The day Cozcacuauhtli: according to the date 10 Vulture on folio 3 and folio 20v of the *Codex Telleriano Remensis.*

The day Ollin: according to page 14 of the *Codex Borbonicus* and the date 1 Movement on folio 16v of the *Codex Telleriano Remensis.*

The day Tecpatl: same as for the date 1 Tecpatl.

The day Quiahuitl: same as for the date 1 Quiahuitl.

The day Xochitl: according to page 25 of the *Codex Borbonicus* and the date 13 Flower on folio 24 of the *Codex Telleriano Remensis.*

The solar disk: according to remains of yellow stucco in the background of the square with the sign 4 Ehecatonatiuh, the polychrome vases with solar disks, page 11 of the *Codex Borbonicus,* and folio 12v of the *Codex Telleriano Remensis.*

The droplets of blood: according to the polychrome vases in the Salon de Cerámica Azteca in the Museo Nacional, pages 83 and 84 of the *Codex Nuttall,* and page 23 of the *Codex Vindobonensis.*

The *xiuhcoatls:* according to the *xiuhcoatl* heads in the Salón de Monolítos in the Museo Nacional, and the one in the ruins at the corner of Seminario and Guatemala streets in this city, which has in one eye white stucco divided by a black line; according to the incense burners with handles in the form of *xiuhcoatls* (Museo Nacional), pages 9 and 20 of the *Codex Borbonicus,* pages 46 and 49 of the *Codex Borgia,* page 76 of the *Codex Nuttall,* page 30 of the *Codex Vindobonensis,* and the *xiuhcoatls* of the *Codex Laud.*

The date 13 Acatl (between the tails of the *xiuhcoatls*): same as for the day Acatl.

The sign *tlachinolli* (the main form in the body segments of the *xiuhcoatls,* and in profile on their backs): according to pages 12, 17, and 20 of the *Codex Borbonicus* and page 14 of the *Codex Mendoza* (Kingsborough).

The face of Xiuhtecuhtli: according to page 20 of the *Codex Borbonicus;* in the facial markings [*maya facial*] I found traces of black stucco.

The face of Tonatiuh: same for the central figure.

On the edge of the Piedra del Sol, Ilhuicatl: according to pages 11 and 16 of the *Codex Borbonicus* and page 33 of the *Codex Borgia.*

*

The Piedra del Sol has slight defects, perhaps owing to flaws in execution on the part of its makers or the porosity or seams in the stone. I found the following defects:

The grouping of four small bars (at the end of the left *xiuhcoatl,* next to the date 13 Acatl), which do not follow the angle of its group and which have instead the inclination of the opposite group.

The small squares with *chalchihuitl* symbols—just to the left and right of the middle left light ray—are rectangular rather than square, as the majority are, and so their frames are not precisely aligned beneath the light ray.

The upper labial volute (of the date 1 Quiahuitl) lacks in its posterior part the same elaboration as can be found in the lower volute or on the similar forms in the sign 4 Quiatoniatiuh and on the day Quiahuitl. (On the *Stone of the Suns,* which is in the Museo Nacional, the sign 4 Quiatoniatiuh has the upper labial volute rendered in the same way.)

The scrolls [*apertura interna*] at the [lower] extremities of the upper and middle right rays are placed higher than those of the other similar and opposite rays.

The heads of the *xiuhcoatls* do not meet exactly at the lower center (it is noticeable along the entire edge of the space between). The head in whose jaws Xiuhtecuhtli's face appears is more at the center and even crosses the middle line. The opposite head, with the face of Tonatiuh in its jaws, is farther from the center and slightly compressed. This does not seem the result of an error but was more likely on account of some mythological or astronomical order or ranking.

Note

1. See Felipe Solís, this volume.

CARLOS NAVARRETE AND DORIS HEYDEN

"The Central Face of the *Stone of the Sun:* A Hypothesis" (1974)

Editors' Commentary

Carlos Navarrete and Doris Heyden's essay is the first of a series of articles published in the 1970s, including works by Cecelia Klein (1976a, 1976b) and Richard F. Townsend (1979), to demonstrate that many specialists were no longer satisfied with some of the standard interpretations of the Aztec sculptural corpus. What prompted these reevaluations is not immediately clear; they may have been a result of the number of objects found during Mexico City's Metro subway excavations of the late 1960s and early 1970s that required identification and interpretation. They may also have shared in the revisionist spirit of contemporary Maya studies, where breakthrough decipherments of hieroglyphic writing were similarly overturning long-held ideas. The two authors brought wide-ranging expertise in Mesoamerican studies to this central problem of Aztec sculpture. Born in Guatemala in 1931, Navarrete trained as an anthropologist in Mexico and carried out projects as diverse as an early reconnaissance of the ruins of Dos Pilas, Guatemala (1963); a work on the carved bricks at Comalcalco, Tabasco (1992); and several essays on Aztec sculpture, including a short work on the Aztec Calendar Stone (1968) translated by Heyden. An American expatriate in Mexico, Heyden (1905–2005) wrote many works on Pre-Columbian architecture and the iconography of ancient Mexican deities, plants, and animals, as well as an influential article on the cave tunnel discovered under the Pyramid of the Sun at Teotihuacan (1975); her efforts as a translator helped introduce the works of Diego Durán to English-speaking audiences.[1] Heyden's articles on the Aztec sculptures recovered in the Metro excavations likely led her to Calendar Stone studies (1970, 1971), a connection made explicit in the latter work.

* * *

"The Central Face of the Stone of the Sun: *A Hypothesis"*

This article is the result of observations that each of the authors made independently, and based on different sources, of the so-called *Sun Stone* or *Aztec Calendar Stone.* The fact that we both used similar archaeological and historical sources, and came to similar general conclusions, convinced us to join forces, since our hypothesis was the same, namely that the face carved at the center of the monument was not Tonatiuh, as many well-known writers have suggested,[2] but rather Tlaltecuhtli, Lord—or Lady—of the Earth.

Excerpted and translated by Khristaan D. Villela from Carlos Navarrete and Doris Heyden, "La cara central de la *Piedra del Sol:* Una hipótesis," *Estudios de cultura náhuatl* 11 (1974): 355–76. Published with permission. Introductory text by Khristaan D. Villela and Matthew H. Robb.

Fig. 1.
Tlaltecuhtli, drawing by Eduard Seler
(German, born Prussian, 1849–1922)
after *Codex Borbonicus,* fol. 16

TLALTECUHTLI—THE EARTH

This character is the earth deity par excellence, although there were many gods associated with the earth: Coatlicue, the mother goddess; Tlaloc, god of rain and the earth; the Tepictoton and the Tlaloque, the assistants of Tlaloc, the mountains, and the guardians of the sustenance and food within the mountains; Tepeyólotl, the Heart of the Mountain.

According to Mendieta (1971, 81), the earth "was a goddess, and they depicted her as a fierce frog, with mouths at all of the joints, filled with blood, and they said that she ate and drank everything." One of her most well-known representations, formally similar to Mendieta's description, is on page 16 of the *Codex Borbonicus* and shows how "they depicted her as a fierce frog" (fig. 1). Figures 2 and 3, and especially the sculpture fragment in figure 4, show the "mouths at all of the joints."

Some Mexica sculptures show Tlaltecuhtli depicted in two forms: as a monstrous mouth with teeth and fangs and adorned with feathers and other elements (figs. 5, 6), and as a being covered with skulls—since people are not only born from the earth, but it is also their tomb—with arms and legs in the form of claws (see figs. 2–4, fig. 7). Below we will refer to the face depicted in figures 3 and 7, with its skeletal mouth with exposed teeth and tongue carved as a flint blade with an eye and fangs.[3]

TONATIUH, THE SUN

Among the names of the sun, we find Tonatiuh, "the shining one" or "he that warms"; Temoctzin, "he that descends"; and Tepan Temoctzin, "he that descends in our favor"—these last two referring to the descent of the sun from zenith—Chimalpopoca, "smoking shield"; and Nanahuatzin, the syphilitic or pustulant deity who became the Fifth Sun (González Torres 1975).

The sun, patron of warriors and one of the aspects or avatars [*advocaciones*] of Ometeotl,[4] the creator couple, appears in the codices as a young god, with yellow hair, with a tubular nose

Fig. 2.
Tlaltecuhtli on the underside
of a feathered serpent sculpture
Mexico (Tenochtitlan), 1450s–1520s,
stone, 28 × 45 × 45 cm
(11 × 17¾ × 17¾ in.)
Mexico City, Museo Nacional
de Antropología

Fig. 3.
Tlaltecuhtli with flint-blade tongue
and skulls and claws on the body
Panel from base of a column from the
Catedral Metropolitana de la Asunción
de María, Mexico City, image ca. 1500,
column carved ca. 1650, stone, panel
height: 61 cm (24 in.)
Mexico City, Museo Nacional
de Antropología

Fig. 4.
Tlaltecuhtli with claws and with
eyes and eyebrows on the joints and
extremities on the underside of a
fragmentary feathered serpent sculpture
Mexico (Tenochtitlan), 1450s–1520s,
stone, radius approx. 70 cm (27½ in.)
Mexico City, Museo Nacional
de Antropología

Fig. 5.
Tlaltecuhtli depicted inside stone
offering box
Mexico (Tenochtitlan), 1450s–1520s,
stone, box: 21 × 32 × 32 cm
(8¼ × 12⅝ × 12⅝ in.)
Mexico City, Museo Nacional
de Antropología

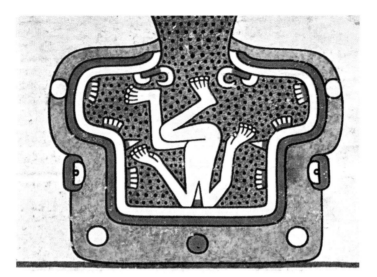

Fig. 6.
The great Earth maw, *Codex Laud,*
fol. 21 (detail)
Mexico (Tenochtitlan), early sixteenth
century, watercolor on deerhide
Oxford, Bodleian Library

Fig. 7.
Tlaltecuhtli, with a flint-blade tongue
and skulls on the body, carved on
underside of a *cuauhxicalli*
Mexico City, ca. 1500, stone,
45 × 105 × 28 cm (17¾ × 41⅜ × 11 in.),
diam. of underside: 105 cm (41⅜ in.)
Mexico City, Museo Nacional
de Antropología

Fig. 8.
Tlaltecuhtli-Sun, *Codex Borgia,*
fol. 43 (detail)
Mexico (Tenochtitlan), sixteenth
century, perhaps before 1519, watercolor
on deerhide
Rome, Biblioteca Apostolica Vaticana

bead passing through his septum. Tonatiuh also carried the image of the sun on his back, or he appears coming out of the center of that heavenly body, as can be seen on page 23 of the *Codex Borgia,* and with the sun disk forming part of his body on page 43, with the face and the extremities in the same position as found on the aforementioned sculptures (fig. 8).

It is important to emphasize the fact that none of the pictorial codices show the sun with the same face as that of the earth in figures 3 and 7.

In an earlier work (Heyden 1971, 153–70), one of us made a study of the so-called *Coatlicue of the Metro,* later identified by Nicholson (1971b, 428) as a sculpture in the round [*escultura de bulto*] of Tlaltecuhtli (fig. 9). In that work, we pointed out the fact that the face on the *Sun Stone* is the same as in images of Tlaltecuhtli. At that time we did not go into more detail, since our object was to show that this sculpture was not the goddess Coatlicue, but a male figure related to the earth.

THE SUN-EARTH COMPLEX

Comparing the faces of figures 3 and 7 with the central face of the *Sun Stone,* we can see that they are identical. Although in general the example on the *Sun Stone* is drawn with the nose plug passing through the nose—a trait of Tonatiuh—the monument's state of deterioration makes it difficult to absolutely confirm the existence of this ornament.

We believe that on the *Sun Stone* we are presented with the face of the earth, set within a complex of solar and cosmic symbols. The claws with eyes, fangs, and the bracelet of beads on each side of the face are the same as those that we find on the sculptures of Tlaltecuhtli (fig. 10). The fact that he has a band around the eyes and circles on the cheeks does not concern us, since

Fig. 9.
Tlaltecuhtli in the round, the
so-called *Coatlicue of the Metro*
Mexico (Tenochtitlan), ca. 1500, stone,
93 × 57 × 34 cm (36⅝ × 22½ × 13⅜ in.)
Mexico City, Museo Nacional
de Antropología

THE CENTRAL FACE OF THE STONE OF THE SUN

Fig. 10.
The face of Tlaltecuhtli, detail of fig. 9

Fig. 11.
Tlalchitonatiuh, drawing by the authors
after *Codex Borbonicus,* fol. 14

many ancient Mexican deities had bisexual characteristics. The circles on the cheeks are a typical characteristic of the mother goddess, especially in her avatar [*advocación*] as Xochiquetzal. The "Leyenda de los soles" refers to the sun as "Our mother is Tlalchitonatiuh" (1945, 122). Alva Ixtlilxóchitl speaks of the Chichimecs, who "called the sun father and the earth mother" (1965, 76).

The idea of the sky as father and the earth as mother is nearly universal (Hastings 1912–27, 5:128; Williams 1960, 454). In Mexico, the great earth maw—seen in many pictorial codices—consumes the sun at dusk and thus begins its nocturnal journey through the earth, to be born again in the east at dawn. Tlalchitonatiuh, the sun at sunset, is shown as a monstrous figure (Xolotl?) on top of a sun, which is devoured by the earth (fig. 11).

We see this daily union not solely as a marriage of masculine and feminine elements, but rather as evidence of the existence of a supreme being with dual characteristics. Since the sun enters the earth and forms part of her during the night, they are at that time inseparable. Garibay comments that Tloque Nahuaque, a name given to the supreme god, is a "*difrasismo* that refers to the divine being…the lord of the near and the nigh…it refers to the sun, to the earth" (1953–54, 2:408).[5]

In Nahuatl literature we find frequent mention of *in Tonan, in Tota*—"our mother, our father"—used to refer to the gods that give life, as for example Xiuhtecuhtli, the fire, or Chalchiuhtlicue, the water, and often *in Tonan, in tota, tonatiuh tlaltecuhtli:* "our mother, our father, the sun, the earth" (Sahagún 1969, 74). The references to the sun associated with the earth are so frequent, that here we will cite only from book 6 of Bernardino de Sahagún's *Florentine Codex…* [to show] that they considered, on certain occasions, the sun and the earth as a single entity, as the mother and father of warriors who they had to feed—both the sun and the earth—with blood spilled in battle or sacrifice.[6]

Now we will return to the *Sun Stone.* If the central face is the earth, why does it occupy the central position? It is well known that this face, together with the claws and the signs of the four suns, are all enclosed within the *ollin* sign, or rather a stylized X, with a circle enclosing the central face at the crossing of the X. This *ollin* is the symbol of the sun "in butterfly form" with its wings extended (Durán 1967, 1:105). The festival of the sun was celebrated on the day 4 Ollin, which was also the name of the Fifth Sun, created at Teotihuacan, the sun, or epoch in which we live. *Ollin* is not only the symbol of the heavenly body but also means "motion" or "earthquake," or "motion of the earth." Also, the Fifth Sun was to end on the day 4 Ollin. The fact that it symbolizes the sun as well as the motion of the earth is another link in the chain of the earth-sun complex.

THE POSITION OF THE SUN STONE

A related problem is the monument's original position, or the position planned for it by those who directed its fabrication, since it is obvious that the stone broke before it was completed, which motivated the abandonment of the piece. With respect to this issue, Beyer notes:

> They had already carved the circular upper surface when a large piece of the left side broke, making the original plan impossible to execute. There was no other solution but to extend the carvings on the sides only to the edge of the break. Naturally, I have no proof that the proposed breakage was not the result of postconquest mutilation. But it is possible and probable that the stone had a crack in this area that led to the breakage and that was noted by the ancient sculptors. Whatever the explanation, the disproportionate relation between the carved and uncarved sections is for me a problem that must be explained. (1965d, 137–48)

Independent of the fact that we also do not have the explanation, one must again quote the studious German, who classified the monument in the series of carved altars, or sculptural receptacles that are called *cuauhxicalli:* "Accepting the classification of the monument as a *cuauhxicalli,* its original position would naturally have been as in (see p. 122, fig. 9), that is, with the sun disk facing up, and not positioned vertically, as it is now situated." The author refers, in this figure, to the *cuauhxicalli* of Cuernavaca, which is decorated with a sun disk facing upward and encircling it a sky band with star signs.

As a monumental work, the closest in conception to the *Sun Stone* is the so-called *Stone of Tizoc,* which also shows the same disposition of its images: the sun on the top face, as the source of life and the motive and justification of Mexica wars of conquest, and on the side, a celestial band above, on the upper rim, and the earth below, where the scenes of warfare take place.

Against this idea, one could present the fact that on the sculpture known as the *Teocalli de la Guerra Sagrada,* the sun is shown vertically, on the front of the second level of the monument. Only in this case the sun presides over a whole series of symbols assembled to express the concept of sacred war and the sacrifice implied by the same (Caso 1927). This is a very special and particular aspect of the solar cult.

On the other hand, there is in all Mexica sculpture an invariable logic: the designs and the elements of the world are always represented as they really are; they are never inverted. The sky is never placed in the position occupied by the earth, for example. Therefore, the fact that the *Sun Stone* is encircled by a celestial band (see p. 144, fig. 48)—where the signs for the stars, the planet Venus, and the stone rays are obvious—is indicating the correct position of the monument, just as Beyer thought and as we can see illustrated by similar objects in Beyer (see p. 122, fig. 9; p. 145, fig. 50).

Why, then, is Tlaltecuhtli represented on the upper portion, when in all other sculptures he is always hidden, in direct contact with the ground? It is essentially for the reasons that we have advanced in treating the earth-sky relationship and also because it commemorates the beginning of the earth-sun, or rather the Fifth Sun, whose position corresponds to *the center,* in the center of Nahui Ollin, which encloses the four worlds previous to the one in which we live....

The relationship between the four suns and the face of Tlaltecuhtli is also affected by the vertical position in which the stone is now found: the Rain Sun and the Water Sun are inverted and lose their sense of converging on the center where the earth is.

CONCLUSION

In conclusion, it seems to us that the face carved in the center of the *Aztec Calendar Stone* or the *Sun Stone,* is not of Tonatiuh, but rather of Tlaltecuhtli, which bursts out, facing upward and looking at the sky, in accordance with the true position of the monument, carved and dedicated to the Fifth Sun, the sun of Earth Motion, Nahui Ollin, or 4 Motion.

Notes

1. See Diego Durán, this volume.

2. Among them, Beyer (1965d, 149–58) and Caso (1953, 47).

3. For other examples of Tlaltecuhtli iconography, see Nicholson 1967a.

4. Nicholson (1971b, 423–24) made the connection between these deities.

5. A *difrasismo* is a Mesoamerican grammatical construction referring to two words used in combination to form a single metaphor.

6. [See the original article by Navarrete and Heyden for this list of references from book 6 of the *Florentine Codex.*]

ANDRZEJ WIERCIŃSKI

"The Dark and Light Sides of the Aztec Stone Calendar and Their Symbolical Significance" (1976)

Editors' Commentary

Andrzej Wierciński (1930–2003), a professor of anthropology at the Uniwersytet Warszawski, was best known as a cultural diffusionist. He wrote on magic, shamanism, kabbalah, and physical anthropology, especially as used to determine an individual's race. In one essay, he argues for the African racial origin of skulls found at the central Mexican site of Tlatilco (1972). Although his Calendar Stone *article appeared at the same time as those by Carlos Navarrete and Doris Heyden (1974), Cecelia Klein (1976a, 1976b), and Richard Townsend (1979), Wierciński wrote in dialogue with earlier writers, such as Eduard Seler and Hermann Beyer, who thought that the imagery on the monument is arranged according to the cardinal directions. Wierciński asserted that we should instead interpret the iconography with reference to left-right opposition and the concepts of light and darkness.*

*   *   *

"The Dark and Light Sides of the Aztec Stone Calendar and Their Symbolical Significance"

The *Aztec Calendar Stone* represents a structural model of world processes expressed as a concentrically organized system of the iconic-numerical signs. It corresponds to the Mandala Concept, which constitutes the basis of astrobiological ideologies flourishing in all the ancient centers of urbanized civilizations. Its essence consists of the dynamic and informational principle of a transformation of the Absolute One into the pairs of polarized opposites that, in turn, create the universal and organizing system of cardinal points of the time-spatial order of rhythmic repetitions of the cosmic, biological, and social processes, mutually synchronized. Its typical and simplified symbol is the quincunx, which frequently appears in the *Calendar Stone*....

…Our aim is to show that this division may reflect, among others, the principle of polarization into opposites. If so, it should manifest itself in the meaning of symbolic elements that are asymmetrical in relation to themselves in both halves of the *Calendar Stone*.

Let us consider the following elements:

a) four signs on both sides of the central arrow;

b) four signs of the previous Cosmic Eras;

c) two-by-ten signs of Tonalpohualli days; and

d) the physiognomies of two deities appearing in the mouths of *xiuhcoatls*.

Excerpted and slightly revised from Andrzej Wierciński, "The Dark and Light Side of the Aztec Stone Calendar and Their Symbolical Significance," in *Actas del XLI Congreso Internacional de Americanistas, México, 2 al 7 de septiembre de 1974* (Mexico City: Comisión de Publicación de las Actas & Memorias, 1976), 2:275–78. © The Estate of Andrzej Wierciński, 1976, and the Instituto Nacional de Antropología e Historia, Mexico City, 1976. Introductory text by Khristaan D. Villela and Matthew H. Robb.

The decipherment of the four first symbols connected with the central arrow, i.e., the complex of attributes of the warrior and Xiuhtecuhtli (*xiuhuitzolli, aztaxelli,* pectoral adornment, and *yacaxihuitl*) without numeral, 1 Quiahuitl, 7 Ozomatli, and 1 Tecpatl, is a most difficult task owing to a greater number of various possible meanings. The interpretation suggested by Beyer (1921)—that is, that they represent simply the signs of four cardinal points—is not very convincing since the latter ones have been so distinctly marked out by the four main arrowheads located at the prolongation of the central arrow and both rings of Tlachtli of the sign 4 Ollin.

First of all, it should be emphasized that 1 Quiahuitl and 7 Ozomatli may denote only the dates of the days, and so 1 Tecpatl might not be the date of the year but of the day too. Second, since the complex of adornment attributes has been ascribed to Xiuhtecuhtli, it is possible that the remaining signs may denote the individual deities through their calendric names. If so, 1 Quiahuitl does not signify Tlaloc (as Beyer suggested) but Ilamatecuhtli, and 1 Tecpatl may be the name of Huitzilopochtli or Camaxtle and not that of the Black Tezcatlipoca.[1]

Unfortunately, there is a lack of information for the mythological meaning of 7 Ozomatli. However, we may follow Beyer that 7 Ozomatli should be rather connected with Xochipilli since it appears together with his temple in the codices *Fejérváry-Mayer* and *Vaticanus B* and because Xochipilli has been invariably associated with odd numerals. Also, 1 Tecpatl here seems to be bound with Huitzilopochtli rather than with Camaxtle because this date is more richly and intimately related with this principal tribal god and is more important, in such connections, in the mythical history of the Aztecs.

Consequently, we arrive at a first opposition: Xiuhtecuhtli and Ilamatecuhtli versus Huitzilopochtli and Xochipilli, the latter both solar deities, which might correspond to the opposition of the terrestrial (left) and heavenly (right) regions.

Given the actual state of our knowledge, a more detailed analysis of symbolic significances of all the above-mentioned signs as mythical dates would be premature, as would their associations with the cardinal points. In reference to the latter question, only Huitzilopochtli has been securely connected with the South while a creative and omnipresent god like Xochipilli appears not merely in the West but also (and more frequently) in the East, South, and North or in the Upper Center. Xiuhtecuhtli, inhabiting the "Navel of the Earth," may appear in the East, South, or West.[2] The cardinal position of Ilamatecuhtli is difficult to define.

Next we face the question of the possible left-right opposition between the signs of four Cosmic Eras, which seem to be reversed in reference to the previously described symbols.... Accordingly, a proper reading of the sequence of the suns will be: 1. Atonatiuh (East-Acatl), 2. Yohualtonatiuh (North-Tecpatl), 3. Ehecatonatiuh (Calli-West) and 4. Tlaltonatiuh (South-Tochtli), which fully agrees with the *Anales de Cuauhtitlan* and differs from the "Historia de los mexicanos por sus pinturas" (1965) and "Histoyre du Mechique" (1965). However, in the latter case, the eras start also with the sun of Chalchiuhtlicue, or Atonatiuh.

Interesting conclusions may be drawn from the comparison of symbolic meanings of the two left and right sequences of Tonalpohualli signs of days and the patron deities hidden behind them. The possibility that they are treated as polarized entities is clearly demonstrated by two images from the *Codex Borgia,* where Mictlantecuhtli and Quetzalcoatl as Lords of Death and Life preside over various divisions of Tonalpohualli days into two equal sequences. One of them refers to the terrestrial region and the other one to the heavenly region.

On the *Calendar Stone,* the lefthand sequence of ten day signs, starting from Cipactli and ending on Itzcuintli, can be opposed to the righthand sequence, from Ozomatli to Xochitl.... Cipactli denotes fruitful earth floating in the primeval ocean, with creative and providential Tonacatecuhtli and Tonacacihuatl. Polyvalent meanings also identify Ehecatl with Quetzalcoatl; Calli is a temple house of the setting Tonatiuh and, logically, its patron is Tepeyólotl, the underground god of caves and earthquakes. In the Maya Tzolkin, the sign Akbal (night) corresponds to Calli, the third day name in both sequences. Cuetzpallin is an earthly animal and appears in one of the underworld's zones according to Sahagún. Its patron deity is Huehuecoyotl, who governs dark and orgiastic forces, both creative and destructive and, in the *Codex Borgia,* he is accompanied by a mysterious, infernal bird. Also, Coatl is here an animal of the underworld, whose placement is strengthened by its connection with Chalchiuhtlicue, night sacrifice, and a similar, demoniacal bird.

The undoubtedly dark and lunar meanings bring Miquiztli together with Tecciztecatl. Mazatl, beyond its rich symbolism as a feminine celestial fire, is also a numen of earth without water, and Tlaloc as its patron deity may be regarded here rather as the Lord of the Night, since he is associated with the lunar water of conch shells that stems from a burning temple. Also, terrestrial, dark, or lunar meanings should be ascribed to Tochtli with Mayahuel, Atl and Itzcuintli with Mictlantecuhtli. In a considerable majority of the days in the sequence on the left, we find the symbols of earth, moon, and underworld.

On the contrary, the right-hand sequence of days shows a concentration of the light, creative, or solar meanings, though not devoid of their opposites. Ozomatli invokes Xochipilli; Cuauhtli and Cozcacuauhtli are both solar birds. Ollin is a sign of Tonatiuh; Xochitl links to the diurnal and creative Xochiquetzal. Nevertheless, dark or destructive meanings may be attributed to Acatl (Tezcatlipoca-Ixquimilli or Itztlacoliuhqui), Malinalli with its mysterious though creative link to Patecatl, Ocelotl with Tlazolteotl and Itzpapalotl, and Tecpatl with Chalchiuhtotolin....

... Finally we turn to the faces of the two gods appearing in the mouth of both the left and right *xiuhcoatls* at the base of the *Calendar Stone.* Beyer (1921) has established their most probable identifications. Accordingly, the right face represents Tonatiuh since he possesses all the characteristic attributes of the face from the center of the *Calendar Stone.* The left face may be ascribed to Xiuhtecuhtli owing to a lack of Tonatiuh attributes at the forehead and in the ears, combined with the typical dark coloration of the lower half of the face and, presumably, his nose adornment.

These identifications solve the question of the polarization of both *xiuhcoatls.* The right one, with the head of Tonatiuh, is the Snake of the Day and Light, while the left one should be its opposite. And this is the case for the left head, especially if Xiuhtecuhtli is considered here in his more specific form as the Lord of the Polar Star and the Central Fire as the Navel of the Earth. Also, it is noteworthy that all Xiuhtecuhtli's known calendric names (4 Cipactli, 1 Tochtli and 1 Itzcuintli) belong exclusively to the left sequence of Tonalpohualli days.

However, another alternative may be considered for the head in the left serpent, namely, Tlaltecuhtli. Her face is also adorned by a lower facial paint and, what is more important, a flint blade (*tecpatl*) emerges from her mouth. In any case, it will not change the essential meaning of the left *xiuhcoatl,* but it will be still more specified into the earthly significance.

At the same time, the calendric names of Tonatiuh (4 Ollin and 13 Acatl) are derived from the right sequence, since he presides over the day Quiahuitl (interchangeable with Chantico) and, less specifically, the days Malinalli and Acatl from the same right side, as mentioned above. The left-right opposition of both Snakes of Fire and Time was also fully assessed by Caso (1958).

There is, then, a clear polarization (though not in the sense of bilateral symmetry) discernible in the same center of the *Calendar Stone,* i.e., in the main components of the sign 4 Ollin: Ollin invokes a *tlachtli,* or ballgame: within that symbol is the face of Tonatiuh, who represents and governs the sun.

In conclusion, these very abbreviated considerations seem to demonstrate that the Aztec Calendar in its left-right division, as well as in its center, is strongly organized by the principle of polarization into opposites.

Notes
1. See Caso 1967.
2. See, for example, the comments of Seler on the *Codex Borgia* (Seler 1963).

"The Identity of the Central Deity on the *Aztec Calendar Stone*" (1976)

Editors' Commentary

A professor of art history at the University of California at Los Angeles, Cecelia Klein has written widely on the iconography of ancient central Mexico, including works on death imagery (1975), the god Tlaloc (1980), sin and punishment (1990/1991), and divine excrement (1993b) and a group of important contributions on gender role, gender construction, and female deities (1988, 1993a, 1994, 2008). Klein's article of 1976 on the Aztec Calendar Stone *was the first to address a Pre-Columbian object in art history's flagship journal, and it constituted a major voice in the chorus of new interpretations of the monument that emerged during the 1970s. Derived in part from her dissertation of 1972, which establishes frontality as a primary organizing principle of Postclassic visual culture (1976b), the article forcefully rejects Tonatiuh as the identity of the central face in favor of Yohautecuhtli, a "hybrid deity" combining the nighttime sun and the planet Venus. Rather than rely on the iconographic vagaries of the then rapidly expanding corpus of Aztec sculpture, Klein weaves together an array of codices and early colonial sources to make her case.*

＊   ＊   ＊

"The Identity of the Central Deity on the Aztec Calendar Stone*"*

Of the extant artistic monuments created by the Aztecs of Pre-Columbian Mexico, the Aztec Calendar Stone is undoubtedly the most important (see pl. 1).[1] The thirteen-and-a-half-foot circular polychromed basalt relief has been used to illustrate Postclassic Mexican cosmological concepts and the nature of their manifestation in Postclassic visual art more often than any other single image of the period.[2] Discovered in 1790 lying face down in the Plaza Mayor of Mexico City (formerly the Aztec capital Tenochtitlán), and seen today in the Museo Nacional de Antropología in Mexico City, the Calendar Stone has, further, come to symbolize for the Mexican people the beauty and complexity of their Pre-Columbian heritage. Given its dual role as a national symbol and a key to scholarly understanding of Postclassic art and cosmology, it is critically important that the iconography of the Calendar Stone be fully comprehended.

The fundamental meaning of the Aztec Calendar Stone has been understood for some time. Scholars have typically accepted the interpretations offered by Eduard Seler and Hermann Beyer who are in essential agreement on the matter (Seler 1903a, 6:1–2; 1960–61, 2:796–99; Beyer 1921).[3] According to them, the Calendar Stone functioned as a graphic symbol of the Postclassic concept of cyclical time and space.[4] This theory is based on the form of the carving itself, which depicts a giant disk with pointed projections that in standard Postclassic iconography invariably represents the sun. The rim of the stone takes the form of two serpents meeting at tails and heads; they are typically identified as Xiuhcoátls, or Fire Serpents, mythological creatures who symbolize the twenty-four-hour course of the sun through the daytime sky and the earth at night. An inner ring contains all twenty day-signs of the Aztec calendar.[5] In the center of the reliefs there appear the frontal, or *en face,* face and the hands of what is certainly a deity; these are enframed by the six-lobed Postclassic graphic symbol for the word Ollin, which means "earth," "movement," or "earthquake." The Ollin sign is accompanied by four small circles that convert it into the date *naui ollin,* 4 Ollin, or "4 Earthquake." In each of the four angles of the Ollin sign there is an image that similarly refers to a specific date in the Aztec calendar.

In connection with this imagery Seler and Beyer point out that the Aztecs believed that the universe had passed through four cyclical epochs, each of which had had its own sun. Each of these epochs or "suns" had been violently destroyed at the end of a fifty-two-year cycle, or Aztec "century." The Aztecs themselves, on the eve of the Spanish Conquest in the early sixteenth century, were living in the fifth and last epoch or "sun" and believed that it too would be destroyed, thereby obliterating both man and his universe for all time. This present sun, whose name was *naui ollin,* 4 Ollin, was expected to be destroyed by earthquakes again at the end of an unspecified Aztec "century" of fifty-two years.[6] Since the date 4 Ollin appears on the Calendar Stone relief, and since the four dates located in the four angles of the Ollin sign are the exact dates of the destruction of the four previous "suns," Seler and Beyer safely conclude that the monument is a graphic symbol of the Aztec concept of the five mythological solar epochs and the end of the world.[7]

We know, however, that fear of the cataclysmic destruction of the fifth and final sun, *naui ollin,* led the Aztecs to hold elaborate vigils and rituals at the end of every fifty-two-year cycle, proceedings designed to stave off the disaster. These vigils took place around midnight when the appearance of a particular constellation and star at the center of the night sky guaranteed that the sun would rise as usual at the eastern horizon at dawn and that life would continue for at least another fifty-two years. The anticipated destruction of the sun was therefore apparently expected to take place at night, at which time it was believed to be dead and hidden in the underworld at the navel of the female earth goddess Tlaltecuhtli who systematically "devoured" it each day at sunset. Only proper ritual and sacrifice could ensure that the sun would be "reborn" in the east in the morning to pursue its important travels across the sky.

The navel of the earth, moreover, was located at the center of the universe. The Aztecs divided both space and time into segments corresponding to the five world directions and arranged them in a cyclic sequence that ran east, north, west, south, and center. The east and north were associated with sunrise and noon, and thus the sky by day; the west, south, and center were associated with sunset and midnight, the night sky, the earth, and death. The south and center in particular were associated with the precise moment of midnight and the underworld; it was at this time and in these regions that all Postclassic cosmic cycles came to an end.[8] Accordingly, since each of the five mythological solar epochs referred to on the Aztec Calendar Stone were similarly assigned to a particular direction in the traditional sequence, the fifth and final sun, *naui ollin,* fell to the center. It is clear, therefore, that, in referring to the anticipated destruction of the fifth sun at the end of the entire Aztec spatio-temporal cycle, the Aztec Calendar Stone specifically alludes to midnight, the earth, death, and the center of the world.

In view of these additional implications, the identity of the deity represented *en face* at the very center of the Calendar Stone relief becomes increasingly problematic. Scholars have traditionally identified this deity as Tonatiuh, an Aztec sun god, an identification that on first analysis would seem appropriate within the context of the solar disk and references to the five mythological solar epochs. Tonatiuh, however, like all Aztec deities, had specific functions and connotations, and these functions and connotations are in fact incompatible with the cosmological context of the stone. Tonatiuh was a god of the day sky, not of the night sky and the earth, and he was invariably associated with the world direction of the east in the Postclassic calendar and codices. Since death and destruction, like the earth and darkness, were associated with the world directions of west, south, and center in Postclassic cosmology, Tonatiuh's affiliation with the east dissociates him from these concepts as well. To identify the central deity of the Aztec Calendar Stone as Tonatiuh is therefore to locate a god of the east, and thus of the beginning of cosmic cycles, of daylight, of the sky and life itself, within a context of cosmic destruction and completion at midnight at the dark center of the earth. In short, to accept this identification is to cast the consistency of the Postclassic mind into disrepute.

The deity represented at the center of the Aztec Calendar Stone is not, however, Tonatiuh. It is not a deity of light or the day sky of the east, nor is it a god of life and the beginning of cosmic cycles as opposed to one of death and cyclic completion. Evidence for this is both linguistic and literary as well as visual. According to Miguel Covarrubias's reconstruction drawing of the badly damaged and faded face and hands at the center of the monument (see pl. 16), the deity represented there within the solar disk originally had yellow hair, a jewel-tipped nose plug, circular dangling earrings, large teeth in an open mouth, and a long protruding tongue, which takes the standard graphic form of the flint knife used by Aztec priests to remove the hearts of their sacrificial victims. The deity wore a red fillet decorated with two jade rings separated by an abstract jewelled ornament at its center. The facial painting was divided into two horizontal zones, the lower half of which was red, the upper half of which was a lighter red or pink.[9] Two contiguous red bands, which may have read as either a single or double band, surrounded the outer edges of the eyes. The hands, which are still clearly clawed and which clutch human hearts, take the profile form of devouring monster heads. The absence of a body suggests that the god is viewed from above, his head upturned and hands upraised, thus hiding from view the body beneath them.

In the Postclassic codices, the sun god Tonatiuh also wears circular dangling earrings, a jewel-tipped nose bar, and a blond wig; his fillet is decorated with jade rings (fig. 1). In the literature of the period, moreover, Tonatiuh was associated with the eagle, a bird sometimes depicted in the codices in conjunction with Tonatiuh in the act of grasping human hearts with its claws. The god frequently appears—both in the form of a full-length figure and as a disembodied head—in company with the solar disk; occasionally his head, unlike that of any other deity, is set directly in the center of that disk. At times his eyes are framed on three sides by a single red band (fig. 2).

Tonatiuh never, however, appears with the monster-faced hands seen on the deity of the Aztec Calendar Stone, nor does he ever appear with a protruding tongue of any kind. His fillet is typically yellow rather than red and is typically decorated with at least three jade rings on each side and a central ornament that takes the form of the head of a bird. As a rule his eyes are not banded; when they are, a contiguous double band is never used. The god does appear frequently in the Aubin Tonalámatl in his role of fourth of the thirteen Postclassic Mexican Lords of the Day, as a disembodied head set in the center of the solar disk and wearing not only a double (sometimes triple) eye band, but a pink and red bi-zoned face painting as well (fig. 3). Since the Aubin Tonalámatl image was one of the major bases for Beyer's original identification of the Calendar Stone deity as Tonatiuh, however, it is instructive that the identical markings appear in the same codex on the faces of the night sun gods Xochipilli and Piltzintecuhtli (fig. 4) (Beyer 1921, 15). Both double eye-bands and a bi-colored face painting are in fact occasionally found elsewhere on both Xochipilli and Piltzintecuhtli, while, with the single exception of the Mixteca-Pueblan Codex Borgia, 55 (see fig. 2), where Tonatiuh's face is painted in two shades of red, the day sun god's face is elsewhere either solid red or solid yellow. In other words, only single eye-bands, not double eye-bands, or a bi-zoned face painting, are characteristic of Tonatiuh.

Tonatiuh, moreover, never appears in the rare frontal, or *en face,* two-dimensional form adopted by the Calendar Stone deity. Even in the seemingly comparable Aubin Tonalá-matl images the sun god is seen in profile view. Frontality, in fact, is always reserved in Post-classic two-dimensional imagery for those deities who are related to the female earth goddess Tlaltecuhtli who herself invariably appears two-dimensionally in *en face* form and who connotes earth, darkness, agricultural fertility, death, and the world directions of west, south, and center (fig. 5).[10] Tlaltecuhtli is characterized visually by her dorsal "displayed" posture in which both arms and legs are bent and outspread in the traditional pose assumed by native Mexican women during childbirth (Seler 1900–1901, 103). Her head is typically upturned, as is better seen in a three-dimensional Aztec statue which represents her or her "sister" aspect Coatlicue (see p. 190, fig. 8). Her monstrous face bears round, ringed, or banded eyes, an open mouth with sharp teeth, and a protruding tongue that often takes the form of a sacrificial flint knife. Her joints and extremities take the profile form of monstrous faces that frequently clutch human hearts. When she appears in two-dimensional form as Coatlicue, her frontal face, with its differentiated lower portion, its exposed teeth, its flint-knife tongue and its circular dangling earrings bears a striking resemblance to that of the deity of the Aztec Calendar Stone (see p. 189, fig. 7).

Since only deities who shared Tlaltecuhtli's connotations of earth, death, darkness, and cyclic completion could adopt her frontal form and unique insignia, and since this form and many of these insignia appear in the Calendar Stone deity, but never on Tonatiuh, there can be little doubt that the former refers, not to Tonatiuh, but to a solar deity of the earth, night, fertility, death, and the western, southern, and/or central world directions. This assumption is supported by the fact that throughout Postclassic Mexico, round, ringed, and banded eyes, long tongues, flint knives, and human hearts—all encountered on the Calendar Stone image—symbolize death (Thompson 1960, 45, 173; Seler 1904b, 323).[11] It is further supported by the fact that the Aztec land of the dead, Mictlán, was originally located in the south or center of the world, at the navel of the female earth monster herself where it was associated in the calendar with the hour of midnight (Thompson 1934, 222–25).[12] Since the sun, like all celestial bodies, was believed to die and descend to the land of the dead each time it disappeared at the western horizon, it follows that a solar deity bearing the form and attributes of the female earth monster would represent the dead sun at night housed within her. We know, in fact, that the Aztecs believed that Tonatiuh, at the moment at which the sun disappears at the western horizon, was converted into another deity, a solar god of earth, death, and darkness, who passed through the underworld each night. This deity, who represented the dead sun at night in the body of the female earth monster, was variously known as Xochipilli, "Prince of Flowers," Piltzintecuhtli, "Lord of Princes," Yoaltonatiuh, "Night Sun," Tlalchitonatiuh or Ollintonatiuh, "Earth Sun," and Yohualtecuhtli, the "Lord of the Night."

KLEIN

Fig. 1.
Tonatiuh, *Codex Borgia,* fol. 55 (detail)
Mexico (Tenochtitlan), sixteenth
century, perhaps before 1519, watercolor
on deerhide
Rome, Biblioteca Apostolica Vaticana

Fig. 2.
Tonatiuh, *Codex Borgia,* fol. 23 (detail)
Mexico (Tenochtitlan), sixteenth
century, perhaps before 1519, watercolor
on deerhide
Rome, Biblioteca Apostolica Vaticana

Fig. 3.
Tonatiuh, *Aubin Tonalamatl*, fol. 9
(detail)
Central Mexico, sixteenth century,
ca. 1521, watercolor on deerhide
Paris, Bibliothèque nationale

Fig. 4.
Xochipilli, *Aubin Tonalamatl*, fol. 9
(detail)
Central Mexico, sixteenth century,
ca. 1521, watercolor on deerhide
Paris, Bibliothèque nationale

Xochipilli, the "Prince of Flowers," was a southern deity who was incorporated into the Aztec pantheon in the course of military conquest (fig. 6). He was the patron of music, dance, songs, and games and was affiliated with sexual pleasure, lust, fertility, and the sun. In an Aztec hymn addressed to him, the god refers to himself as "I, the maize"; he is linked here, as elsewhere, with the maize god Cinteotl (Sahagún 1950–82, 3:213). Seler titles Xochipilli the "Lord of the South" and designates him as chief representative of that world direction (Seler 1902–3, 1:139).[13] Together with the moon goddess Xochiquetzal he ruled the mythical land of Xochitlicacán, the "Land of Flowers," which was located in the south. Since the land of the dead and the hour of midnight were associated with the south as well as with the center of the world, it follows that Xochipilli was a god of earth, darkness, and death. In the Aztec hymn addressed to him, Xochipilli is indeed described as one who sings *yoaltica,* "in the night" (Sahagún 1950–82, 3:213).

In most literary accounts Xochipilli was the husband or lover of the moon and vegetation goddess Xochiquetzal, but he is replaced in this role by one Piltzintecuhtli in the *Historia de los mexicanos por sus pinturas* and in an Aztec hymn addressed to Xochiquetzal (Seler 1960–61, 2:1035). In the codices, as in the commentaries and legends, Xochipilli in turn occasionally substitutes for Piltzintecuhtli and frequently appears with that god's insignia. According to the *Histoire du Mechique,* Piltzintecuhtli was Xochipilli's father (Seler 1960–61, 4:60).[14]

Xochipilli was intimately related to and even interchangeable with Piltzintecuhtli because Piltzintecuhtli was also a solar deity. Piltzintecuhtli is often described as "the young sun god" and wears—like Xochipilli—a number of solar insignia (fig. 7). Although he appears as rattlebearer of the east in Codices Borgia 51, and Vaticanus B 21, and faces the flint-knife god Iztli in that section of the Codex Féjervary-Mayer world direction chart (page 1) which corresponds to the east, Piltzintecuhtli is normally affiliated with the west. He appears in the Féjervary-Mayer world direction chart in his capacity as third of the nine Lords of the Night in which he was actually regent of the third Mexican day-sign Calli (House), which Seler describes as the "dark house of the earth, the west" (Seler 1901–2, 67). Piltzintecuhtli was reported to have fathered the maize god Cinteotl in the mythical land of Tamoanchan which also was located in the west (Seler 1960–61, 2:1035). According to an Aztec hymn addressed to the moon goddess Xochiquetzal, Piltzintecuhtli descended into the underworld in pursuit of her, his beloved; here he was believed to have intercourse with the moon.[15] Since the moon was believed to be hostile to the day sun, or Tonatiuh, Piltzintecuhtli can only have represented the sun at night.[16] The Mayan counterpart of the third

Fig. 5.
Relief of Tlaltecuhtli on underside of a
cuauhxicalli (see p. 109, figs. 5, 6)
Mexico (Tenochtitlan), 1450s–1520s,
greenstone, 14 × 24 cm (5½ × 9½ in.)
Berlin, Museum für Völkerkunde

day-sign Calli (House) ruled by Piltzintecuhtli was in fact Akbal, "Night," which among the Maya was ruled by the Jaguar God who represented the sun at night. The Aztec hymn sung every eight years at the festival celebrating the completion of the Venus-solar cycle clearly identifies the young sun god with night:

> See if Piltzintecuhtli resteth in the house of darkness, the house of night.
> O Piltzintli, Piltzintli, with yellow feathers are thou pasted over. On the ball court thou placest thyself, in the house of the night. (Sahagún 1950–82, 3:212)

There can be little doubt, therefore, that Xochipilli-Piltzintecuhtli was a solar deity who specifically represented the dead sun at night at the navel of the female earth monster. He is associated, accordingly, with the phenomenon of frontality in two-dimensional art, which signifies a relation to that goddess. Both Piltzintecuhtli and his Mayan counterpart, the Jaguar God, were associated with the number seven, and in Maya hieroglyphic writing the number seven was actually interchangeable with a conventionalized frontal face (Thompson 1962, 224). The Jaguar God often appears two-dimensionally in frontal form. Xochipilli himself ruled the twentieth and final Mexican day-sign Xochitl (Flower) whose Mayan counterpart was the Ahau glyph which also took the form of a frontal face. J. Eric S. Thompson identifies the latter as the face of the sun and concludes that it is "almost certainly" that of the young sun god (Thompson 1960, 88). Moreover, since the Ahau glyph is always inverted when it appears in the Maya glyphs for east and sunrise, it would seem that its normal position refers to the sun in the underworld in the west, south, or center of the world. Its Mexican day-sign counterpart Xochitl always symbolized the south and, significantly, the hour of midnight as well.

Xochipilli-Piltzintecuhtli appears twice, moreover, in Codices Vaticanus B 96, and Borgia 53, in the full-length frontal displayed form of the female earth monster so closely related to the night sun (fig. 8). Here the god assumes the disguise of a deer, an act that surely refers to the Mexican legend that Piltzintecuhtli turned into a deer on the day 7 Xochitl (7 Flower), the day of the annual festival held in honor of his beloved, the moon goddess Xochiquetzal. Maya myths frequently tell how the young sun god dons a deer disguise in order to woo the moon (Thompson 1970, 364, 369–70). Again, since only the night sun—never the day sun—was on intimate terms with the moon, these *en face* images of Xochipilli-Piltzintecuhtli in deer disguise can only refer to the sun at night.

Xochipilli-Piltzintecuhtli, a god of the night sun in the underworld, therefore shares with the central deity of the Aztec Calendar Stone the ability to be represented in two dimensions in the frontal form characteristic of the female earth monster Tlaltecuhtli. He further shares with the Calendar Stone deity the bi-zoned face painting: in the Aubin Tonalámatl his face is painted in two shades of red, and elsewhere it is often painted red on the bottom and yellow on the top (see fig. 4). Xochipilli-Piltzintecuhtli appears, moreover, in Codex Borgia 14, 16, 28, and 57, as elsewhere, with double red bands surrounding the outer edges of his eyes (see fig. 6). The eye-bands reappear in Codex Borgia 39 on the disembodied face of an earth monster with upraised arms who has attributes of Xochipilli-Piltzintecuhtli. Xochipilli often appears in the codices wearing a red rather than yellow fillet decorated with only one or two jade rings on each side. During the Aztec Xochilhuitl, or "Flower Feast," held in honor of Xochipilli, that god's impersonator carried an impaled human heart. These rather remarkable correspondences between the young sun god of night and the deity of the Aztec Calendar Stone certainly support the contention that the latter represents the night sun and further suggest that it may in fact represent, at least in part, the god Xochipilli-Piltzintecuhtli himself.

Human hearts, however, like long tongues and clawed hands and feet, were also characteristic of the Tzitzimime, the stellar souls of dead warriors who descended to the center of the earth at midnight during certain critical periods in the Aztec calendar. At the end of the fifth and final "sun," when the world was to be destroyed by earthquakes on the day 4 Ollin at the end of a fifty-two-year cycle, the Tzitzimime were expected to descend; at this time, it was believed, the sun itself upon dying would be converted into a Tzitzimime. The commentator of Codex Telleriano-Remensis lists a certain "Yoalaotecotli" among the ranks of these stellar demons and Thompson equates him with the god Yohualtecuhtli, "Lord of the Night," whom Seler identifies as the night sun in the underworld (Thompson 1934, 228–29; Seler 1963, 2:28). Sahagún reports that incense was not only offered four times a day to the day sun Tonatiuh, but five times each night as well to the sun god *iovaltecutli,* or "Lord of the Night" (Sahagún 1950–82, 3:202). Sahagún further identifies as Yohualtecuhtli the star known to us as Castor, which formed part of a constellation called Mamalhuaztli, the "Fire Drill Sticks." Although Sahagún reports that it was the sight of the Pleiades at the zenith of the midnight sky that signaled the beginning of another fifty-two-year cycle, he notes that Mamalhuaztli was close to the Pleiades (Sahagún 1950–82, 60). The two constellations were in fact closely associated with each other at the moment of the drilling of New Fire; so close, apparently, was this relationship that Alfonso Caso contends that it was the appearance of the star Yohualtecuhtli in the center of the midnight sky at the end of every fifty-two-year solar cycle that signaled a temporary reprieve from the cosmic cataclysm that the Aztecs believed awaited them (Caso 1958, 20).[17]

A god known as Yohualtecuhtli who represented the sun at night and the Tzitzimime was therefore apparently associated with the end of the fifty-two-year cycle. Sahagún, moreover, further links Yohualtecuhtli directly to the date 4 Ollin. In the course of his discussion of the Aztecs' worship of the sun, Sahagún passes from a discussion of Tonatiuh to the night sun Yohualtecuhtli and reports that: "It was said: /'The Lord of the Night, he of the sharp nose, hath unfolded, and we know not how his office will end.'/ And his feast day came upon the day of the day-count called naui ollin, every two hundred and three days" (Sahagún 1950–82, 3:202).[18]

According to Beyer, the Ollin sign was itself a symbol of the constellation Mamalhuaztli, the "Fire Drill Sticks" (Beyer 1921, 34). In Codex Borbonicus 16, the date 4 Ollin is replaced by the "earth sun" deity Tlalchitonatiuh as co-patron of the sixteenth Aztec week. The dead sun at night at the center of the earth therefore shared his name and associations with the very stellar being who controlled the destiny of the Aztec nation.[19]

There are relatively few visual images of deities in Postclassic art that have been identified as Yohualtecuhtli, but it is significant that those that have been so identified share a number of features with the Aztec Calendar Stone deity. Seler identifies as "Yohualtecuhtli, the solar god of the underworld" a large full-length figure on page 40 of Codex Borgia whose body is frontal and displayed (fig. 9) (Seler 1963, 2:42). The god's profile head is upturned in the manner characteristic of the female earth monster and his eye is surrounded by a single red band on three sides. A giant sun disk forms the deity's torso; smaller sun disks, which take the form of anthropomorphic profile monster heads, adorn his joints and extremities. A comparable deity on page 43 of the same codex boasts the snout of a crocodile and a protruding tongue. On page 35 of Codex Borgia, two full-length figures, again wearing single red eye-bands and crocodile costumes, are specifically

Fig. 8.
Xochipilli in deer disguise, *Codex Borgia*, fol. 53 (detail)
Mexico (Tenochtitlan), sixteenth century, perhaps before 1519, watercolor on deerhide
Rome, Biblioteca Apostolica Vaticana

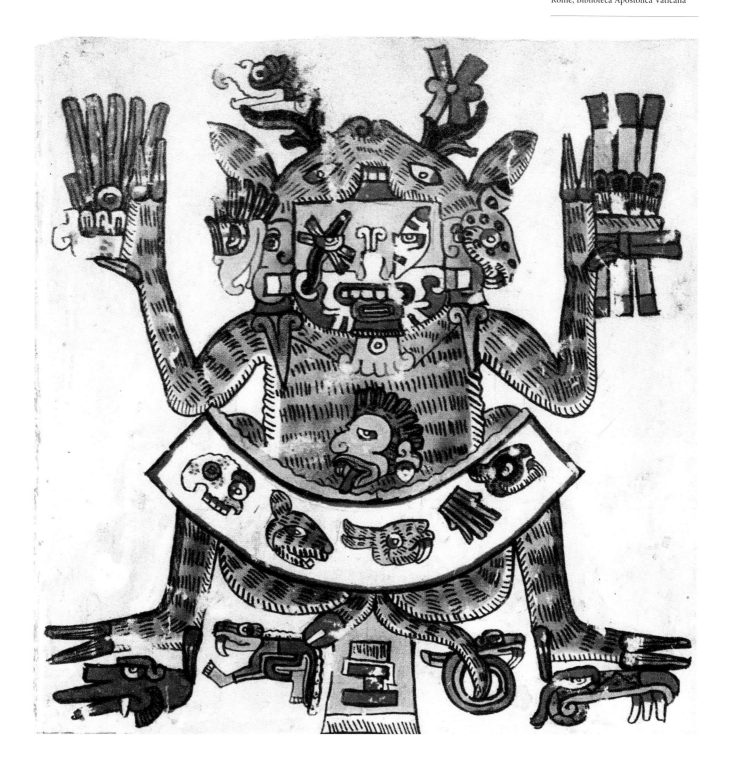

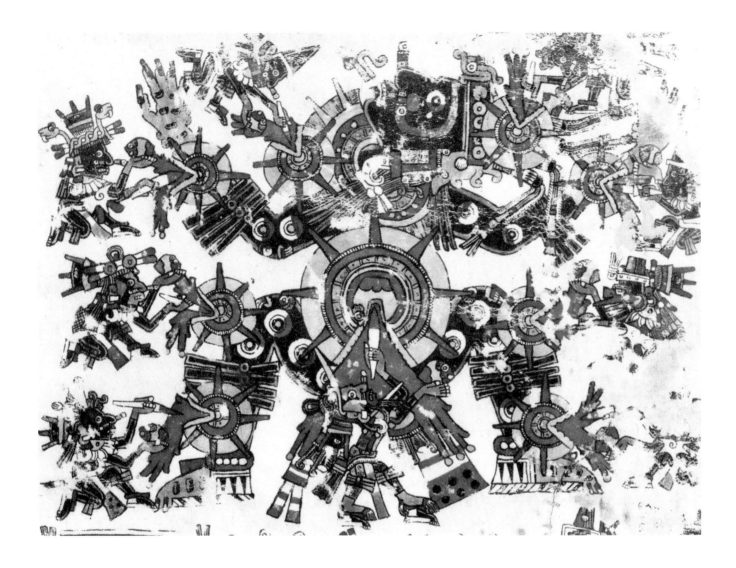

identified by Krickeberg as the dead sun who nightly passes through the underworld (Krickeberg 1948, 141, 164). The body of one is again frontal and displayed. Seler understandably identifies the Borgia 35 figures with Cipactli, the earth crocodile of the east, but simultaneously concludes that they, like the Borgia 43 figure, represent lunar deities (Seler 1963, 2:28). Since the moon was always affiliated with the female earth monster and the west, south, or center of the world—never with Cipactli or the east—the appearance here of crocodilian features must refer, like the frontal displayed form and anthropomorphic joints, not to Cipactli, but to Tlaltecuhtli and her association with darkness, death, and the earth.[20] Although Seler does not directly identify the Borgia 35 and 43 deities as Yohualtecuhtli, he does conclude that Yohualtecuhtli may have represented the moon in the underworld as well as the night sun.

Confirmation of the identification of the Aztec Calendar Stone deity as Yohualtecuhtli comes from the writings of Sahagún. In speaking of the feast held on the day *nahui ollin,* Sahagún reports: "And there was the image of that one [the sun] at a pyramid temple called Quauxicalli. There was erected his image, his image was designed as if it had the mask of a man [but] with [the sun's] rays streaming from it. His sun ornament was round, circled with feathers; surrounded with red spoonbill [feathers]" (Sahagún 1950–82, 3:203).

In the matching illustration provided by Sahagún's native artists, the deity is depicted as a frontal face set in the center of a large circular sun disk (see p. 270, fig. 8). Although the Aztec Calendar Stone lacks the red spoonbill feathers mentioned by Sahagún, Sahagún's illustration for obvious reasons has been frequently compared with that monument. Scholars have further assumed that Sahagún was specifically referring here to the day sun god Tonatiuh and have thus cited the accompanying illustration as proof that the Calendar Stone figure also represents that deity. Analysis of Sahagún's text reveals, however, that the passage referring to the frontal image of a solar deity immediately follows that discussing the Lord of the Night Yohualtecuhtli and his feast day *naui ollin*. The description of the solar image and the matching illustration therefore clearly refer to the sun in its nocturnal aspect.

In a number of Postclassic images, moreover, the Ollin sign, often in the context of the date 4 Ollin, is depicted with a single round half-closed eye at its center (see p. 130, fig. 23). According to Seler, this eye symbolized the Tzitzimime, the setting sun, and the night (Seler 1960–61, 2:723–24; 1900–1901, 108). The unique substitution in the Aztec Calendar Stone of a frontal face for the traditional eye within the Ollin symbol strongly suggests that the deity represented on the stone also represented the Tzitzimime, the setting sun, and the night. Throughout Meso-america the frontal face was and is conceptually equated with the eye; the Zinacantan Tzotzil word for "face" (*sat*), for example, is the same as that for "eyes," while the Zapotec *lao, loo* means "face," "eyes," and "frontside."[21]

Of the various Postclassic solar deities, only Yohualtecuhtli is listed as a Tzitzimime. Furthermore, since Seler concludes that the round eye at the center of the Ollin symbol functioned as a sign for the Nahuatl word for "night," *youalli,* it is probable that the substituted frontal face on the Aztec Calendar Stone served a related paralinguistic function. If this is the case, then the word for "night" may well even have appeared in the deity's name. Two solar deities include the Nahuatl word for "night" in their names—one is Yoaltonatiuh, the "Night Sun;" the second is his close relative Yohualtecuhtli, the great "Lord of the Night." The appearance on the Calendar Stone of attributes of Tonatiuh combined with attributes of the female earth monster and the nocturnal sun gods Xochipilli and Piltzinteculhtli in a solar context commonly reserved for the symbol for "night" therefore leaves little doubt that the deity represented there was a solar god of the night.

Yohualtecuhtli, however, represented not only the dead night sun in the underworld, but the "dead" planet Venus as well. Among the Mexicans, as among the Maya, the 584-day Venus cycle was divided into four phases, each of which corresponded to a specific world direction. The first phase was that of the Morning Star which appears at dawn in the east, the second was that of superior conjunction which was associated with the north, the third was that of the Evening Star which appears at dusk in the west, and the fourth was that of its disappearance in inferior conjunction in the south (or center) of the world. As was the case with all stars and planets, including the sun, Venus was believed to be "born" in the east as Morning Star and, as the god Xólotl, the Evening Star, to "die" upon its descent and disappearance at the western horizon. Upon entering the body of the female earth monster Tlaltecuhtli, Venus, like the sun, assumed that goddess's associations and insignia. Accordingly, the Evening Star of the west and the planet in inferior conjunction in the south or center of the world appear occasionally in Postclassic two-dimensional imagery in the frontal form of Tlaltecuhtli, with displayed limbs, upturned head, clawed hands and feet, round, ringed, or banded eyes, large teeth, and a protruding tongue (fig. 10). Moreover,

Fig. 9.
Yohualtecuhtli, *Codex Borgia,*
fol. 40 (detail)
Mexico (Tenochtitlan), sixteenth
century, perhaps before 1519,
watercolor on deerhide
Rome, Biblioteca Apostolica Vaticana

Fig. 10.

Xólotl on Huastec relief
Tepetzintla, Veracruz, ca. 900–1521,
stone, 165 × 110 cm (65 × 43¼ in.)
Mexico City, Museo Nacional
de Antropología

since the Venus cycle, like the solar cycles, began at dawn in the east and concluded at or around midnight in the south or center of the world, these *en face* images of the western and southern phases of the cycle must similarly refer to the conclusion of a cycle. The frontal so-called "Morning Star" reliefs seen on Mausoleum III at Chichén Itzá, which actually represent the Evening Star in inferior conjunction in the south or center of the world, are in fact accompanied by the date of the *completion* of a "Great Venus Cycle" consisting of 260 revolutions of that planet.[22]

The Great Venus Cycle, however, simultaneously ended on the same day as a cycle of eight fifty-two-year solar "centuries." The 584-day Venus cycle also terminated on the same day as a 365-day solar cycle every eight years and further coincided with the completion of every other fifty-two-year cycle; in other words, the rituals carried out at the end of every other fifty-two-year cycle marked not only the completion of the major Aztec solar cycle but the completion of a 104-year Venus cycle as well. At this time, as at any time in which the sun and Venus simultaneously completed a cycle, the two celestial bodies were believed to engage in mortal nocturnal combat and ultimately to fuse in the dark bowels of the female earth monster. The hymn sung during the Aztec Atamalqualiztli festival held at the conclusion of the eight-year Venus-solar cycle tells of such a nocturnal contest between the young sun god of night, Piltzintecuhtli, and Xólotl, the god of the planet Venus as the Evening Star. This hymn opens, significantly, with an address to "the lord of the night" (Sahagún 1950–82, 3:212–13).[23] One of the Maya names for Venus was *ah piz a'kab,* "Lord of the Night."

In pursuing his own interpretation of the Aztec Calendar Stone as a device for astronomical calculations, José Aviles Solares proposes that the date 4 Ollin, when it is pierced by an arrow-like device such as penetrates it on the Calendar Stone, refers to the conclusion of the eight-year Venus, solar cycle (Avilés Solares 1957, 36–37, 41–49). Seler demonstrates that the Ollin sign was associated with the fifth and final period (as opposed to phase) of the planet Venus as well as with the fifth and final sun; in Codex Borgia 25, as Seler points out, it appears in this context as a symbol of the central world direction (Seler 1963, 2:264).[24] As the seventeenth of the twenty Aztec day-signs, moreover, Ollin was ruled by Xólotl, the Evening Star, who was actually associated in the Postclassic mind with the dead sun as it sank beneath the western horizon. The commentator of Codex Vaticanus B states that the date 4 Ollin was merely another name for Xólotl and the commentator of Codex Vaticanus A designates the day 4 Ollin as the day of the disappearance into the Red Sea of Quetzalcóatl, a historical personage later associated with Venus who was believed to have died and to have been later reborn in the eastern sky as the Morning Star.[25] In Codices Borgia and Vaticanus B, the date 4 Ollin co-ruled the sixteenth week of the calendar with Xólotl. Both the end of the fifty-two-year solar cycle and the critical date 4 Ollin were therefore associated with the planet Venus in its final phase as the Evening Star in inferior conjunction in the south or center of the world. It would seem likely that the Aztecs, who envisioned a cataclysmic destruction of the universe at the end of a fifty-two-year solar cycle, expected that destruction to occur at the simultaneous completion of a Venus cycle as well.

A number of related Postclassic images confirm the possibility that the frontal face at the center of the Aztec Calendar Stone refers to the god Yohualtecuhtli at the end of a Venus as well as a solar cycle. In the center of page 28 of Codex Borgia, the rain god Tláloc appears in the guise of Xochipilli-Piltzintecuhtli, the night sun, as representative of the fifth and last of the Venus-solar periods. He wears the red and yellow zoned face painting and the double red eye-bands characteristic of that god and similar to the insignia of the Calendar Stone deity. According to Seler,

Tláloc as Xochipilli here represents the center of the world and the fusion of Venus with the sun (Seler 1963, 2:265). The Maya equivalent of Xochipilli's calendrical name 1 Xochitl (1 Flower) was 1 Ahau, or *hun ahpu,* the name of the Maya god of the dead planet Venus in the underworld. All of the Codex Borgia figures with frontal displayed bodies and red eye-bands are, moreover, located within that section of the codex that deals with the travels of Venus through the underworld. This includes the large figure on page 40 of that manuscript which Seler specifically identifies as Yohualtecuhtli (see fig. 9). This figure actually wears the conch-shell earrings of the Venus god Quetzalcóatl and the paper leg bows frequently worn by the Evening Star deity Xólotl. In Codex Borbonicus 16, Xólotl appears opposite the earth sun deity Tlalchitonatiuh, as co-patron of the sixteenth week of the Aztec calendar, with double-banded eyes, a flint-knife tongue, and clawed hands and feet.

The deity depicted at the center of the Aztec Calendar Stone can, therefore, no longer be identified as the sun god Tonatiuh who represented the day sky and the east. Neither the literary nor the graphic evidence supports this view. Even Durán's report that the human sacrifice performed in honor of the sun on the day 4 Ollin was theoretically carried out at midday when the sun was at the center of the day sky, rather than at midnight, does not negate this thesis (Durán 1964, 122). Since both the zenith and the nadir were regarded as part of the unifying central world direction, the two were often conceptually synonymous and, at times, even interchangeable.[26] In the version of the destruction of the second cosmogonic sun, 4-Ocelotl, "4 Tiger," presented in the Anales de Cuauhtitlan, the moment of death and darkness is actually reported to have occurred at noon rather than at midnight:

> Then it happened
> that the sky was crushed,
> the sun did not follow its course.
> When the sun arrived at midday,
> immediately it was night
> and when it became dark,
> tigers ate the people (León-Portilla 1969, 36)

Clearly, the spatial contiguity of zenith and nadir implied a temporal contiguity between noon and midnight as well. We know, in fact, that all beings temporarily located at the center of the sky were believed capable of descending directly to earth and to the crossroads at its center; among these were the stellar Tzitzimime alluded to on the Aztec Calendar Stone. That the same belief applied to the hour of noon and the sky by day is attested to by a contemporary Aztec story recorded by Madsen that tells of a man who hitched a ride with the sun at dawn; at noon the sun said to the man, "Here is where I leave you," and the man fell down into his own home below (Madsen 1960, 128).

The Aztec Calendar Stone image must therefore be regarded as a representation of the darkened sun and planet Venus at the center of the earth at the moment of cyclic destruction and completion in which they fused to create the hybrid deity Yohualtecuhtli, the great Aztec "Lord of the Night." Since Yohualtecuhtli was a god of the earth, darkness, death, and the south and center of the world, his appearance here in a context of the end of the world at the center of the earth in the middle of the night is far more logical than would be that of Tonatiuh. More understandable, too, are the appearance of traits of the female earth monster and the rare utilization of the frontal form that always indicates cyclic completion in Postclassic Mexico. Recognition of the Aztec Calendar Stone deity as Yohualtecuhtli thus avoids the logical and cosmological discrepancies involved in its identification as Tonatiuh [and] reveals a new level of beauty and profundity in the famous carving.

Notes

1. This article is a version of a paper presented to the Columbia University Seminar on Primitive and Pre-Columbian Art, 15 February 1974. It is based on a portion of my doctoral dissertation. I am particularly grateful to the Department of Art History and Archaeology, Columbia University for a 1968 Departmental Summer Travel Grant, which permitted me to pursue my dissertation research in Mexico, and to my dissertation adviser, Professor Douglas Fraser, for his direction, advice, and support.

2. Pre-Columbian Mexican history is traditionally divided into three major temporal periods: the Preclassic (or Formative), the Classic, and the Postclassic. The latter roughly covers the years between A.D. 900 and 1521, the year of the Spanish Conquest. At the time of the Conquest, most of central Mexico was under the control of the Aztecs, a Nahuatl-speaking people who rose to power in the 14th century during what is known as the Late Postclassic period. The Aztec Calendar Stone was carved by these people to sit atop their major ceremonial plaza where it presumably served in some way in the performance of Aztec rituals. The exact orientation and function of the monument have never been ascertained.

3. See also Caso 1958, 33, for a more recent presentation of the same interpretation.

4. Recent dissenting points of view are put forth by Avilés Solares (1957) and Noriega (1959).While the two authors disagree in their identification of the various astronomical cycles and symbols represented, both conclude that the Aztec Calendar Stone was an astronomical calculating device used to compute time. Curiously, neither dissents form the traditional identification of the central figure challenged in this article.

5. The Aztecs used two calendars that functioned independently but that ended on the same day every fifty-two years. The first, the *xíhuitl,* was an agricultural calendar based on the 365-day rotation of the earth around the sun. It was divided into eighteen months of twenty days each with an additional five days (*nemontemi*) at the end. The second, the *tonalpohualli,* was a divinatory calendar based on the meshing of an invariable series of twenty day-signs with a series of the numerals one through thirteen; each combination of day-sign and numeral could occur only once in 260 days. The 260-day cycle was divided into twenty periods, or "weeks," of thirteen days each. A larger cycle of fifty-two years, known as the *xiuhmolpilli,* always ended on a day that simultaneously concluded both a 365-day and a 260-day cycle. The *xiuhmolpilli* was itself divided into quarters and was of the greatest cosmic and ritual significance.

6. Owing to the nature of the Aztec calendar, the solar year, and thus the fifty-two-year cycle, could never have ended on the day 4 Ollin. It is therefore not clear how the Aztecs related their fear of the day 4 Ollin to the end of their fifty-two-year "century." The date 4 Ollin would have occurred at least once every solar year, however, and events of that day may have been interpreted as prophesies or determinants of the fate of the sun at the end of the current fifty-two-year cycle. The association of the day Ollin with the end of a fifty-two-year cycle may also derive from the earlier use in many parts of Mesoamerica of an Ehecatl-Mazatl-Malinalli-Ollin set of yearbearers. Such a system survived until the Conquest in parts of Oaxaca and Guerrero. If the names of the years, and hence the yearbearers themselves, were derived from the last day of the year, as Caso suggests, then the last day of the fifty-two-year cycle would have always fallen on a day Ollin (see Caso 1967, 128).

7. The dates of destruction and hence the names of the five mythological suns cited on the Aztec Calendar Stone are those mentioned in the *Leyenda de los soles* and the *Historia de los mexicanos por sus pinturas;* other accounts give different names and/or sequences. Those seen on the Calendar Stone are: (1) 4 Ocelotl, "4 Tiger"; (2) 4 Ehecatl, "4 Wind"; (3) 4 Quiahuitl, "4 Rain"; (4) 4 Atl, "4 Water"; and (5) 4 Ollin, "4 Earthquake" or "4 Movement." For a translation of, and commentary on, the relevant passages in the *Leyenda de los soles,* see León-Portilla (1963, 37–38). See also Nicholson 1971b, 398–99.

8. For a complete discussion and defense of this position, see Klein (1972). I presented a brief summary of the argument at the conference on "Death and the Afterlife in Pre-Columbian America" held by the Dumbarton Oaks Center for Pre-Columbian Studies on 27 October 1973, in a paper titled "Postclassic Mexican Death Imagery as a Sign of Cyclic Completion," published in the proceedings (Klein 1975).

The central world direction differed from the other four world directions in performing a transitional function. Since the Aztecs conceived of space, as well as time, in terms of recurring cycles, the end of one sequence automatically predicted, and even inaugurated, the beginning of the next. The central world direction, therefore, although typically associated with the end of a sequence, could also signify the beginning of a new one. For this reason it was often referred to as the "up and down" direction, a term based on the belief that the center of the universe extended vertically from the bottom of the earth to the top of the sky, thereby permitting easy access from one region to the other. In its temporal affiliations, as a result, it occasionally appears to have been more closely associated with the actual beginning of a cosmic cycle than with an ending. Such occurrences are rare, however; in the vast majority of instances, the center is clearly associated with the end of a cycle and hence with darkness, earth, and death. So strong was this association that the central world direction often appears to have been conceptually fused with the south and in many instances simply to have been left out of a sequence in favor of it.

9. Covarrubias does not give his reasons for reconstructing the coloration of the Calendar Stone figure as he does, but his reconstruction is confirmed by that of Robert F. Sieck who actually examined the pigments remaining on the stone (see Noriega 1959, opp. 64). Beyer (1921, 20) reconstructs the deity's face as solid red, but admits to doing so "because Tonatiuh was painted this way in the codices of the central region" (author's translation).

10. For a full defense of the thesis that frontality was reserved for deities associated with earth, death, darkness, and cyclic completion in two-dimensional Postclassic art, see my doctoral dissertation (Klein 1972).

11. The round, ringed, or banded eye was apparently roughly analogous to the closed eye, which also symbolized death. The closed eye is, however, relatively rare in Postclassic Mexican imagery and does not even appear on the major death deities Mictlantecuhtli and Micticacíhuatl, whose eyes are round and/or ringed, but always open. For evidence that the ringed or banded eye in Postclassic Mexico was symbolically synonymous with closed eyes in Postclassic Maya art, see Klein (1972, 206–17).

12. Thompson argues here that the reported assignment of Mictlán to the north at the time of the Conquest represented either a very late development or a mistake on the part of the chroniclers themselves.

13. See also Seler 1960–61, 2:1097.

14. See also Thompson 1934, 223.

15. See Soustelle 1940, 40.

16. There are a number of myths that reveal that the sun in the day sky was hostile to the moon; according to one, the sun's first act was to defend his mother, the earth, by cutting off the head of his sister, the moon, and putting his remaining siblings, the stars, to flight. According to Caso (1958, 13), the sun was believed to reenact this victory every morning upon rising. In contrast, many Mexican and Maya legends make it clear that the dead sun in the underworld at night was in love with the moon, who is repeatedly identified as his wife or consort. See Thompson 1939, 150.

17. See also Krickeberg 1964, 178–79. Caso, for reasons he does not cite, identifies the star Yohualtecuhtli with Aldebaran rather than Castor and states that it was observed in conjunction with either the Pleiades or Aries. Seler (1904a, 356–57) also repudiates Sahagún's identification of Mamalhuaztli with Gemini and concludes that it may have been part of Aries.

18. This statement includes an error on Sahagún's part since, owing to the nature of the *tonalpohualli,* the day 4 Ollin could recur only once every 260 days.

19. That a star in the center of the midnight sky should share the name and connotations of the dead sun simultaneously located at the center of the earth is understandable in view of the Postclassic belief that the underworld and its inhabitants nightly pass into, or are reflected in, the dark heavens. The stars were traditionally regarded as the "souls" of the dead in the underworld at the center of the earth and all nocturnal celestial bodies were affiliated with the earth, the underworld, and the western, southern, and central world directions. See Krickeberg (1964, 130) and Klein (1972, 33–34).

20. Although Tlaltecuhtli was reportedly a toad, she was the female counterpart of the earth crocodile Cipactli and as such was closely related to and occasionally even confused with him. While the directional and temporal associations of the two were in direct opposition, both deities represented the earth. In two-dimensional Postclassic imagery, Tlaltecuhtli's frontal face often appears to be formed of two profile heads of Cipactli conjoined at the back or front. Tlaltecuhtli thus typically shares with Cipactli a missing lower jaw, sharp pointed teeth, a curled nose and curled eyebrow, and a flint knife projecting from the nose.

21. The Yucatec Maya word for "face" (*ich*) similarly means both "eye" and "front." Sahagún's catalogue of his Aztec informants' descriptions of the parts of the human body includes the following: "Face; that is to say, eye…" (Sahagún 1950–82, 2:112).

22. See Seler 1960–61, 1:693–94, for an analysis of the Chichén Itzá reliefs. For a defense of the thesis that these reliefs, like all *en face* Postclassic two-dimensional images of Venus, refer to the planet in inferior conjunction in the south or center of the world at the end of a Venus cycle, see Klein (1972, 89–91).

23. Seler (1960–61, 2:1059) translates this as "he, the Lord of Midnight" (English translation mine). The passage equates this night lord with the word *xochitl* ("Flower") in two instances, thus providing further evidence that the god Xochipilli (Flower Prince), ruler of the day-sign Xochitl (Flower), was at least an aspect or element of the deity known as the Lord of the Night:

The flower of my heart lieth burst open,
  the lord of the night.
She hath come, she hath come, our
  mother, the goddess Tlazolteotl.
Cinteotl is born at Tamoanchan,
  the flowery place, on the day
Ce xochitl.

24. Seler also proposes here that the date 4 Ollin in Codex Borgia 28 represents the date of the disappearance of Venus as Morning Star into superior conjunction in the north. His arguments rest, however, on the faulty assumption that the Dresden Codex Venus tables begin with heliacal rising on the day 13 Kan, rather than on the day 1 Ahau, and on an erroneous assignment of the Acatl years to the north rather than to the east.

The five Venus periods were five consecutive Venus cycles of 584 days each which equaled exactly eight solar years. When the five Venus periods had recurred thirteen times, the final day coincided with both the end of the *tonalpohualli* and the fifty-two-year cycle. This could happen only once every 104 solar years.

25. See Caso (1967, 197) for a list of the various associations of the date 4 Ollin mentioned in the codices and chronicles.

26. This probably explains why Seler (1963, 1:166) associates Xochipilli, the "Lord of the South," with high noon, and may account, at least in part, for the apparent confusion at the time of the Conquest of north and south in regard to the location of the land of the dead (see n. 12 above).

RICHARD F. TOWNSEND

State and Cosmos in the Art of Tenochtitlan (1979)

Editors' Commentary

A frequently cited source on Aztec art, Richard F. Townsend's State and Cosmos in the Art of Tenochtitlan *(1979), based on his dissertation of 1974, discussed how ceremonial architecture and monumental sculpture articulated the Mexica concept of a "living structural affinity between the natural and social orders" (1979, 9). After briefly dwelling on methodological disputes between the disciplines of anthropology and art history, Townsend stressed that Mexica iconography is best interpreted within the time frame of the Mexica empire itself—the ninety-two years from expansion under Itzcoatl until the cataclysmic events of 1519. He identifies three major sources for Mexica sculpture—the codices of the Mixteca-Puebla and the lapidary traditions of the Toltecs (specifically, Tula-Hidalgo) and the Huastecs of Veracruz. His discussion of Mexica "cult effigies" introduces Arild Hvidtfeldt's* teixiptla *concept to a broader academic audience (Hvidtfeldt 1958).[1] For Townsend, teixiptlas were objects that "commemorated a lasting relationship between a community…and the animating spirits of the universe" (1979, 34). If the teixiptlas served as social expressions of domestic, conservative religious practices, large-scale sculpture operated in a more historic and political context. Yet Townsend is not as concerned with identifying specific events so much as prying monuments loose from atemporal interpretive frameworks and understanding them anew, as statements of cosmology and imperial power. State-sponsored monuments provided a venue for "history" to be aligned with a larger cosmological order. Townsend moved across media and scale, demonstrating how even small objects encapsulate the same ordering principles as monumental ones. Nonetheless, his focus remained on historiographic discussions and iconographic identifications of four major monuments: the* Dedication Stone, *the* Stone of Tizoc, *the* Teocalli de la Guerra Sagrada, *and the* Aztec Calendar Stone. *In all cases, consistent iconography served to locate Tenochtitlan as the center of the Mexica Empire, often by conflating the earth itself with the space of the ceremonial center. The first three monuments embody the empire's three distinct stages—the religious piety of its early emperors, its rapid expansion, and its "regeneration." Although Townsend does not enter into a debate over exactly when the* Calendar Stone *was carved, his placement of it as the concluding monument of the sequence is telling. Townsend also argues strongly for interpreting the central face of the* Calendar Stone *as a Tlaltecuhtli mask, in keeping with his vision of these monuments as representations of the lands of the Mexica empire.*

Excerpted from Richard F. Townsend, *State and Cosmos in the Art of Tenochtitlan* (Washington, D.C.: Dumbarton Oaks, Trustees for Harvard University, 1979), 63–70. Published with permission. Introductory text by Matthew H. Robb and Khristaan D. Villela.

*   *   *

State and Cosmos in the Art of Tenochtitlan

THE "SUN STONE": TIME, SPACE, AND THE ASCENDANCY OF TENOCHTITLAN

Discovered beneath the downtown plaza of Mexico City in 1790, this large (3.60 meters, diameter), intricately carved disc has been a major subject of scholarly debate since the nineteenth century. Undoubtedly it once occupied a prominent position somewhere in the main ceremonial center of Tenochtitlan, but the name and location of the building where it was originally placed have not been definitively traced. Another related question also remains unanswered: was this sculpture fixed vertically to a wall, as it has been traditionally displayed in the National Museum of Anthropology, or was it set into a floor, perhaps as the center of a circular shrine akin to the Pantheon of Rome, or the Dome of the Rock in Jerusalem? It is beyond the scope of the present study to review the complex architectural data on the ceremonial center, but the question of vertical or horizontal positioning has a suggestive bearing on the immediate problem of iconographic interpretation, as we shall see on the following pages....

But we cannot forget that the Mexica felt the need to assert the validity of their state to their contemporaries as well as to themselves, and that sculptural art communicated these concerns in direct, explicit fashion that left no room for doubt. Therefore it may be surmised that a monument as ambitious as the Sun Stone would make some direct reference to the Mexica state. To set Beyer's argument in the perspective afforded by the other monuments we have seen, let us recall the mosaic shield and the Stone of Tizoc: both are cosmograms with circular shape, and both have motifs indicating the horizontal and vertical divisions of the cosmos. Could the Sun Stone similarly be a "compressed" cosmogram, intended to be set into a floor? Here we return to the argument for a horizontal, as opposed to a vertical position. Curiously, Beyer thought it had probably been displayed horizontally, though not for the same reasons that we shall be concerned with.

The question can be resolved by pointing out that the supposed eagle claws flanking the central mask are really more akin to the five-clawed gloves worn by Tlaltecuhtli and related impersonators. In effect, eagle talons have only four claws, a detail not likely to have been glossed over on this major monument. Seler (1902–23, 2:790) had also observed that the five-clawed gloves suggested jaguar paws, and that the jaguar was an animal traditionally associated with the earth; but Beyer (1921) contested this idea by pointing to a Mictlantecuhtli ("lord of the land of the dead") figure from the Post-Conquest Magliabechiano Codex, shown with four-clawed birdlike talons (see p. 129, fig. 20). Mictlantecuhtli is certainly associated with the earth, and Beyer argued that there was therefore no particular consistency in the number of claws depicted on these images; a five-clawed glove could just as well have served to represent the solar eagle. The argument is unconvincing, for iconographic inconsistencies are more easily apt to occur in Post-Conquest manuscripts than on a monument of the caliber of the Sun Stone. It is highly probable that the five-clawed gloves flanking the central mask do in fact refer to Tlaltecuhtli, and not to the eagle as a sun metaphor. This becomes evident when the mask is compared to similar masks on Tlaltecuhtli effigies and when the flanking position of the gloves is seen in relation to the impersonator's ritual posture of holding the hands upon, or just in front of, the shoulders. The idea that the central mask of the Sun Stone represents the *face of the earth,* and not the face of Tonatiuh, "the sun," is consistent with the enclosing glyph *ollin.* Was it not predicted that the present sun would end in earthquakes, the "movement of the earth?" Moreover, the presence of a Tlaltecuhtli mask is consistent with the iconography of the other commemorative monuments we have seen—and like the Tlaltecuhtli images on the Dedication Stone, the Stone of Tizoc, and the Teocalli, it may also be interpreted as representing both the sacred earth and the territory of the Mexica nation.

Cem anahuac Tenochca tlalpan, "the world, Tenochca (Mexica) land": does this interpretation of the central mask correlate with the rest of the Sun Stone iconography? We may begin by re-examining the four small glyphs which Beyer thought to be esoteric signs for the four directions. With the large rays of the sun already clearly establishing the cardinal and intercardinal directions, what other meaning could these small glyphs have? The first of them, 1-Tecpatl, has been explained as the calendar date of Huitzilopochtli on the Teocalli. Next is the royal diadem with lip plug and a speech-glyph in the shape of an abbreviated sign for smoke or mist (also note the small breastplate of the type worn by warriors below). This assembly refers to the office of Mexica kingship, and communicates its might, fame, and honor. The two bottom glyphs, 1-Atl and 7-Ozomatli, are, like 1-Tecpatl, the names of days in the 260-day divinatory cycle, the *tonalpohualli;* however, the cults to which these two days were ritually dedicated remain somewhat enigmatic (no full account of the ritual cycles and the movable ceremonies using all the primary sources has yet appeared). Nevertheless the day 1-Atl is mentioned as being dedicated to Chalchihuitlicue, and was observed by those who gained their lives in aquatic pursuits. Most probably this cult was of very ancient origin among the lakeshore peoples, and it may have reached Tenochtitlan from one of its allied cities— Tlacopan, for instance. One may speculate that the 7-Ozomatli has similar ritual and sociopolitical implications as the day of the cult of an important community within Tenochtitlan or within an allied city. However incomplete, this reassessment of the four small glyphs indicates that they fall into the general pattern of signs and symbols that we have seen on other commemorative monuments, in that they illustrate matters of immediate historical importance to the Mexica state.

Next to be considered is cosmological orientation, a topic that has already been touched upon in mentioning the counterclockwise reading of the calendrical band and the disposition of the sun rays. It will be recalled that in the Indian frame of reference, the cardinal points were customarily described from a dominant position facing east; and that the north, west, and south quadrants followed in that order. It is therefore to be supposed that the most important region, the eastern place of life, light, and authority, would be emphasized in cosmological compositions. In the present case, east is undoubtedly at the top of the monument, in the position that would normally be assigned to the north in the current European system of orientation. The primacy of east is not only expressed by (1) the counterclockwise movement of the calendrical band which begins at the "top" with the glyph *cipactli,* but also by (2) the compass-like "pointer" that Beyer could not account for, (3) the direction of the dragonlike *xiuhcoatls,* and (4) the significance of the 13-Acatl date.

The curious triangular "pointer" with its elaborately decorated tassel at last becomes meaningful when seen as a directional arrow on the surface of the earth, pointing to the place of the sun's emergence. Read in terms of its association with the other glyphs in this central portion of the Sun Stone, it expresses metaphorically an inseparable association between the earth as Mexica territory, the royal house and official cult of Tenochtitlan, and the sacred (east) place of cosmological authority.

Beyer believed that the two dragonlike *xiuhcoatls* represented mythological animals associated with the celestial sphere, whose task it was to bear the sun across the sky. This interpretation cannot be contested in any major way save to point out that the *xiuhcoatls* should be seen as metaphoric pictograms—as opposed to mythological creatures—of the heat, light, and color of the sky. The notion that they are connected with the path of the sun appears to be borne out by their "downward" movement from the 13-Acatl cartouche; like the "serpent balustrades" that flank the stairways of so many Mesoamerican pyramids, they express the flow of energy or power from one place to the next. And in this respect, their cosmological meaning can be metaphorically correlated with the power of the Mexica nation. This is illustrated by Sahagún's description of the annual Panquetzaliztli festivals, held in honor of Huitzilopochtli; in a concluding episode of the ritual events, a large paper-and-feather *xiuhcoatl* was brought down the steps from the platform of the Main Pyramid, to be presented at an altar on the bottom landing:

> Thereupon likewise descended the fire serpent, looking like a blazing pine firebrand. Its tongue was made of red arara feathers, looking like a flaming torch. And its tail was of paper, two or three fathoms long. As it descended, it came moving its tongue, like that of a real serpent, darting in and out.
>
> And when [the priest] had come [with it], bringing it down to the base [of the pyramid], he proceeded carefully to the eagle vessel. Then he went up [to the eagle vessel] and raised [the fire serpent] also to the four directions. When he had [so] raised it up, then he cast it upon the sacrificial paper, and then they burned. (Sahagún 1950–82, 2:136)

Celestial luminosity, heat, and the generative might of the sun are metaphorically represented by this dragon-like creature; through the east-west orientation of the pyramid, these powers are shown to originate in the direction of the sun's emergence and are brought down to the surface of the earth and presented to the four directions. By analogy, Huitzilopochtli and his chosen people were recognized in terms of these celestial forces.

The last main element of the Sun Stone to account for is the date-glyph 13-Acatl. There can be no doubt about the mythological importance of this date, for it is mentioned in at least two versions of the origin myth as the time of the present sun's creation. Yet the glyph also reoccurs in the calendar cycle to mark a more directly historical year of genesis: 1427, the year of Itzcoatl's accession to power and the cruel beginning of an imperial vision, a time in which the Mexica began to conceive of themselves as great, and to create a sense of historical mission that propelled Tenochtitlan from the position of a backwater tributary city to a position of unparalleled might in Mesoamerica. By illustrating the conjunction of a cyclically recurring date in sacred time with the time of national independence and the first territorial aggrandizement, the rulers of Tenochtitlan sanctified the authority of their imperial office. Placed in the cardinal position of supreme importance, 13-Acatl acts as a validating touchstone linking the cosmic and the social orders.

More than any other single monument, the Sun Stone demonstrates how the vitality and the structure of the natural order were conceived of as models, indeed were automatically equated with the activities and the organization of society. The four quarters of the earth and an imperial territory; divine patronage, imperial sovereignty, and the direction east; the calendar, the present solar era, and Mexica rule; and the generative force of the sun and the might of the Mexica nation—all are inseparably associated in this sculptural relief. In the Mexica vision of the world, the hard aims of secular power were fused with a fundamentally mythopoeic outlook in which every aspect of life was part of a cosmic system. In such a system, the universe was seen as a reflection of relationships between life-forces. In that immensely magic world, perceived objects were automatically translated into another level: the boundaries between objective and perceptive become blurred, dream and reality are one, and everything is alive and intimately relatable.

Note

1. The Nahuatl term *ixiptla* referred to a broad category of images of the sacred, including human impersonators; effigies in stone, clay, wood, and dough; as well as assemblages of costume elements and bundled relics. See Hvidfeldt 1958; and Towensend 1979, 28.

"The *Aztec Calendar Stone:* A Critical History" (1981)

Editor's Commentary

Stacie Graham Widdifield's previously unpublished historiography of 1981 of the Aztec Calendar Stone *focuses on the interpretations presented by Antonio de León y Gama and Alfredo Chavero, the first scientific and the second religious. She argues that León y Gama's description of the* Calendar Stone *as a scientific instrument and as proof of advanced knowledge of astronomy, mathematics, geometry, and gnomonics should be understood as an attempt to answer European writers who depict ancient Mexico as benighted and the Aztecs as barbarians. On the one hand, although León y Gama never approves of the religion of the Aztecs, he feels they were redeemed by the science and rationality so obviously present in the* Calendar Stone. *Chavero, on the other hand, influenced by Darwinism, positivism, and late nineteenth-century Mexican liberalism, argues that the* Calendar Stone *was the product of Nahua civilization, perverted by the fanatical religion and despotic rule of their Aztec descendants. He follows a long line of writers who claim that the Nahuas did not practice human sacrifice (see Alexander von Humboldt, this volume) and they ruled themselves with reason and equality—in short, very close to how Benito Juárez, Porfirio Díaz, and other liberal figures hoped Mexico would be ruled in the late nineteenth century. By contrast, the Aztecs were a superstitious people, driven to bloody and irrational rites by their fanaticism, just as the Roman Catholic Church used to rule Mexico in the colonial period and until the Reforma and the Constitución de 1857. Chavero's explanation later would be echoed by writers on the ancient Mayas, such as J. Eric S. Thompson, who asserts as early as the 1920s that the original Mayas were peaceful and did not practice human sacrifice, an abomination introduced by Mexican or Mexicanized invaders. Widdifield's essay is an important contribution to* Calendar Stone *studies because it refocuses our attention, taking it away from iconography and placing it on the monument's afterlife, and examines how our own prejudices and cultural attitudes shape our explanations of Mexican antiquity.*

*   *   *

"The Aztec Calendar Stone: *A Critical History*"

INTRODUCTION

The 1980 edition of *Travelers Guide to Mexico* states, "World famous, the Museum of Anthropology is not to be missed. Here you'll find the famous Aztec Calendar, the unofficial symbol of the country" (Luhnow 1980). Indeed the *Aztec Calendar Stone,* while never having been officially declared the national symbol of Mexico, has been generally recognized as the symbol of that country. It

---

Excerpted and slightly revised from Stacie Graham Widdifield, "The *Aztec Calendar Stone:* A Critical History," master's thesis, University of California at Los Angeles, 1981. Published with permission. Introductory text by Khristaan D. Villela.

appears in national and international contexts, from travel posters to lottery tickets, and serves as the logo for, among other things, banks and scholarly journals on pre-Hispanic culture.[1]

The *Calendar Stone,* an Aztec Post-Classic period low-relief basalt cylinder, is still the subject of scholarly debate over its pre-Hispanic function and significance. Its role as a national symbol has very definite connotations in this regard. What is the relationship between the stone's pre-Hispanic and post-Hispanic identities? Is the identity of the stone in its pre-Hispanic historical context the same as that which "has come to symbolize for the Mexican people the beauty and complexity of their prehispanic heritage (Klein 1976b, 1)?"

To answer these questions, it is necessary to consider that in the most recent literature on the stone two clearly defined and opposed positions are taken on the stone's original function and significance. The first claims that the stone functioned as a vertically oriented astronomical clock, a work of scientific technology.[2] The second claims that it was a horizontally oriented platform for use in ritual human sacrifice.[3]

This schism between the religious and scientific interpretations of the stone has its basis in the history of nineteenth-century Mexico and is directly intertwined with liberal ideology. Because these two basic interpretations have not been superseded in the twentieth century, this thesis will focus on an analysis of their nineteenth-century origins. In particular, therefore, it will focus on the scholarly interpretations of the stone, first by Antonio León y Gama, who in 1792 first proposed that the stone was an astronomical clock, and, second, of Alfredo Chavero, who in 1875 first proposed that the stone was a sacrificial platform. The subsequent acceptance or rejection of these initial interpretations must be seen in relation to Mexican liberal ideology. The period of acceptance of León y Gama's interpretation corresponds to the first phase of liberal ideology; the acceptance of Chavero's corresponds to the second phase.

In the first phase, roughly between the end of the eighteenth century and the first three quarters of the nineteenth century, liberal ideology was based in Enlightenment philosophy, particularly the notions of science, rationality, and the rights of the individual. This was the ideology of emancipation from theology and the right of a Christian monarchy that, in practice, culminated in Mexico's war for independence from Spain between 1810 and 1821. It was the period when León y Gama wrote his interpretation, and when it was positively received. Around the third quarter of the nineteenth century, liberal ideology shifts to an emphasis on the welfare of the state, which superseded individual rights. It did not, however, shift away from the notion of science as emancipatory; rather, the basis of the state was scientifically justified. It was in this period that Chavero proposed that the *Calendar Stone* was a sacrificial platform, a work used in the service of Aztec religion....

ANTONIO LEÓN Y GAMA'S INTERPRETATION

The first interpretation of the *Calendar Stone* was published in 1792, two years after the stone was discovered beneath the central plaza of Mexico City, in Antonio León y Gama's *Descripción histórica y cronológica....*[4] León y Gama attempted to identify all the images on the stone (1832, pt. 1:90–105). He identified the central image as the Aztec solar deity Tonatiuh; the six-lobed form as the calendric name of the sun, Four Ollin (Four Earthquake or Four Movement); the four images in the square lobes as the calendric signs Four Ocelotl (Four Jaguar), Four Ehecatl (Four Wind), Four Quiahuitl (Four Rain), and Four Atl (Four Water). He termed the images in the round lobes "claws." The four small glyphs encircling the Ollin sign he identified as three calendric glyphs: One

Tecpatl (One Flint), One Quiahuitl (One Rain), Two Ozomatli (Two Monkey), and one non-calendric glyph as a sign related to fire. The twenty small images in the next band he identified as the twenty day signs of the Aztec 260-day calendar, formed by a rotating cycle of twenty thirteen-day weeks. The series of small boxes inscribing five points he identified as numerical units, each box representing five days of the Aztec calendar. Each of the small round arches he identified as numerical signs as well. The pointed arches he viewed as mountains, the large combination motifs as the sun's rays. The flame-like appendages were clouds. León y Gama identified the two serpents as representations of the Milky Way, and the profile faces emerging from the jaws of each serpent as Yohualtecuhtli, the Aztec Lord of the Night. The cartouche at the top of the stone he identified as the date Thirteen Acatl (Thirteen Reed), but he disposed of the images on the outside of the cylinder by claiming that they served no purpose and were purely ornamental.

León y Gama (1832, pt. 1:94–95), moreover, associated the calendric signs in the center, Four Ollin, Four Ocelotl, Four Quiahuitl, Four Atl, and Four Ehecatl, with the Aztec myth of the five cosmogonic or solar ages, as recorded by the sixteenth-century chronicler Alva Ixtlilxochitl and the eighteenth-century chronicler Juan de Torquemada.... León y Gama's work constituted the first synthesis of the calendrical and cosmological information contained in colonial period manuscripts dealing with the Aztecs.

León y Gama's analysis of the *Calendar Stone* was based on the premise that the foundation of the Aztec system of reckoning time was the actual and relative movements of astronomical bodies. This notion is indisputable. It was also on this basis, however, that León y Gama proposed that the stone was a giant sundial or solar clock (1832, pt. 1:91–92). He said that the glyphs on the stone, those in the ring of twenty day signs, the three calendric glyphs in the central zone, and the five solar glyphs, signified the dates on which various ceremonies were to be performed by Aztec priests during the solar year to honor various deities (102). The celebration of such ceremonies was keyed to various solar phenomena, whose occurrence, León y Gama insisted, "served the priests as a rule for their performance" (92).

The graphic symbol or hieroglyph for the movements of the sun, according to León y Gama, took the form of the glyphs for the five cosmogonic ages, the arrow that pierced the central image of the sun, and the two claws to either side of it (1832, pt. 1:92). These images were to be read in order marked on his diagram of the stone: A, I, B, E, C, H, D, F, A. This order signified for him the passage of the sun during the year (93). The term Four Ollin, meaning both Four Movement and Earthquake, thus gained significance for León y Gama as the "sun in its four movements."

León y Gama explained how these movements of the sun were indicated on the stone and how they served to indicate to Aztec priests when ceremonies should have been performed in terms of the function of the stone as a solar clock. To begin with, he claimed that the stone had to have been positioned vertically, with an exact east-west orientation, facing to the south (León y Gama 1832, pt. 1:105). Second, the stone must originally have been a rectangular parallelepiped with a perfectly square base (92). In the square base were, to León y Gama's mind, eight holes, distributed around the perimeter of the cylinder in four parallel pairs (105). These "four" pairs of holes are indicated by the letters XZ, PP, QQ, and SY on his diagram. Into each of these holes he constructed a gnomon or marker. Each pair held a thread, suspended between its two members, that would cast a shadow across the face of the stone and thus across the calendric signs. The shadows cast were so exact that they would indicate the points of the zenith, solstices, and equinoxes (105). León y Gama stated that the hours of noon, 9 a.m., and 3 p.m. were also indicated by these cast shadows (108–9). Each day sign represented on the stone thus corresponded to a particular point in the passage of the sun. Aztec priests could consult this giant solar clock to determine at precisely what time of day a ceremony should be performed by reading the relationship between the shadows cast by the threads and the calendric signs represented on the face of the stone.

Thus, for León y Gama, the *Calendar Stone* functioned as a precise instrument of science. It demonstrated to him not only the degree to which the ancient Mexicans understood, and could monitor and record, the movements of the sun but also their knowledge of geometry required for both of the placement of the holes in the matrix and the concentric patterning of the images on the surface (León y Gama 1978, 5)....

THE CALENDAR STONE AND EARLY LIBERAL IDEOLOGY

By recognizing that the symbols of the five solar ages on the stone were associated with a myth, and that Aztec priests used the stone as a guide for performing ceremonies, León y Gama was, in essence, acknowledging their ritual and mythical associations of the stone. Yet, clearly, it was the stone's scientific characteristics, and the scientific function that he deduced from them, that were of preeminent importance for him. He stated that:

> one ought to consider this stone as an appreciable monument of Mexican antiquity for the use of astronomy, chronology, and gnomonics, leaving aside the other uses to *which* the pagan priests put it for their judicial astrology.[5] (1832, pt. 1:92)

Judging by this statement, the *Calendar Stone* was "an appreciable monument of Mexican antiquity" precisely because it had astronomical, chronological, and gnomonic uses to which it could be put, that is, because it was a solar clock. These uses were emphasized at the expense of the other, judicial astrological uses. León y Gama did not explicitly define the term "judicial astrology," but it was most probably the Aztec practice of interpreting the calendar as depicted in the *tonalamatl* to which he referred. An Aztec priest, for example, would interpret the significance of a child's birth date and predict what would happen in the future. In any case, León y Gama was establishing his preference as to what uses could qualify the *Calendar Stone* as an appreciable monument and which could not. The first uses were scientific in nature, their bases ultimately lying in the observation and recording of the movements of astronomical bodies, that is, in physical fact. The second uses were those based not in fact but in speculative prediction.

That León y Gama was specifically interested in connecting the *Calendar Stone* with a scientific function and significance is demonstrated by his interpretation of another Aztec sculpture, the colossal stone statue of *Coatlicue,* a variant of the Aztec earth deity.[6]... *Coatlicue* seems to have represented for León y Gama the worst aspects of the Mexican past. He even went so far as to say that the *Calendar Stone* was the "greatest, the most particular and instructive" of the two stones (León y Gama 1832, pt. 1:10).[7]

What accounts for this apparent discrimination in León y Gama's treatment of the two monuments? In a letter to a certain Don Andrés Cavo, León y Gama wrote that one of the reasons he felt it important to discuss the *Calendar Stone,* and in general to illuminate the workings of the ancient Mexican calendrical system, was that understanding it would help refute the accusations of barbarism made by Europeans against the ancient Mexicans (1832, pt. 1:viii).[8] These accusations came from a number of eighteenth-century writers who had published works dealing with the New World, in which they described the New World culture as savage and barbaric and inherently inferior to that of Europe, most notably as propounded in Cornelius de Pauw's *Récherches philosophiques sur les Américains* of 1768–69, which proclaimed the so-called degenerate character of all forms of natural and human life in the new world.[9]

Included in the first edition of León y Gama's work on the stone is a letter commending the work, written by Joseph Rafael Olmedo, who held a chair at the Real y Pontificia Universidad de Mexico. Olmedo spoke of the great effect that León y Gama's would have in contesting publications such as de Pauw's, which he even mentioned by name.[10] How would León y Gama's work be able to counter the "calumny" of such writers as de Pauw? Apparently, it was by interpreting the *Calendar Stone* as an object for the use of astronomy, chronology, and gnomonics. The accusations of barbarism and savagery hurled at the New World were based largely on the indisputable fact that the ancient Mexicans, that is, the Aztecs, practiced human sacrifice and cannibalism. Since the conquest of Mexico in the sixteenth century, this fact was used to justify colonization and even in the eighteenth century still served as a rationale for western European colonial expansion. The idea was that native populations needed the intervention of Western civilization and religion to fulfill their human potential. By emphasizing the "great knowledge of our ancient Mexicans," León y Gama was attempting to prove the existence of the same forms of knowledge and pursuits that Europeans valued as hallmarks of civilization....

León y Gama was still faced with the fact that ancient Mexican religion had its judicial astrological, that is, nonscientific, aspects and that sacrifice played no small part in it either. He dealt with these problems by suggesting that one had to distinguish between those ancient Mexican sculptures that referred only to the cult of the gods and those that referred strictly to "history" (León y Gama 1978, 5). Thus, the *Calendar Stone* and *Coatlicue* were already distinguished according to this classification; the latter referred to the cult of the gods and the former to history.[11] The judicial astrological significance of the *Calendar Stone* was by extension of incidental importance. So, moreover, was the fact that the symbols representing the "four movements of the sun," that is, the calendric names of the suns in the central zone, happened to refer to the most fundamental of ancient Mexican religious beliefs, the mythical destruction and recreation of the universe. León y Gama himself disparagingly referred to these beliefs as "fictions" (1832, pt. 1:95). He defended them, however, by comparing the myth of the five solar ages to the ages of man described in the books of one of European civilization's most esteemed writers, Ovid (León y Gama 1832, pt. 1:92). Other eighteenth-century writers dealt similarly with the practice of human sacrifice, while defending ancient Mexican culture against accusations of European writers. In his *Historia antigua de Mexico,* Francisco Saverio Clavigero, for example, confronted the charge of cannibalism and human sacrifice by noting that the same practices had occurred among the Scythians, the Carthaginians, and the ancient Greeks (Keen 1971, 573).[12]...

The promotion of science in Mexico occurred during the reigns of the two Spanish Bourbon kings, Charles III (1759–88) and Charles IV (1788–1808), favored by their policies of reform and Enlightenment. Charles III and Charles IV ordered a number of systematic exploratory expeditions in Mexico; some were directed to carry out reconnaissance in the archaeological zones of Mexico, Chiapas, Tabasco, and Puebla, others to collect and catalog data on Mexico's plant and mineral resources. The promotion of scientific endeavors served to benefit the economy of both Spain and its colony. Gathering information on resources was a first step; exploiting them was a second.[13] The development of science, especially in the fields of geography, mining, and natural sciences, was an aid to the increased exploitation and management of resources.

It is true that the Bourbon kings and the *peninsulares,* or Spaniards born in Spain but living in Mexico, and the *criollos,* Spaniards born in Mexico, viewed the pursuit of scientific endeavors as a means to proving to the enlightened countries such as England and France that Mexico too was enlightened. *Peninsulares* viewed themselves as superior by birth. This was the principal justification for the economic, political, and social monopoly they held.[14] The *criollos* began to seek a way of breaking these monopolies. It is well documented that it was largely the *criollos* who strove for independence.[15]…

By virtue of their birth, *criollos* could not claim a heritage either in Mexico or in Spain. It suited their purpose, nevertheless, to claim a heritage in the former, specifically in the ancient Mexican or Aztec past….

The reform-minded Bourbon kings and their colonial supporters' interest in the study and collection of materials from the ancient past was also evident from their direction of archaeological expeditions. Spanish colonial, that is, viceregal, interest was evident as well. The institution that is now the Museo Nacional de Antropología of Mexico was established during the reign of the Viceroy Bucareli (1771–79) with his order that all documents referring to ancient Mexico be gathered at the university in Mexico City. Viceroy Revillagigedo (1789–94) later ordered all archaeological remains of ancient Mexico to be gathered at the university. Indeed, it was due to Revillagigedo, as well as the chief architect of the cathedral of Mexico City, that shortly after its discovery, the *Calendar Stone* was embedded in the wall of the cathedral, to be preserved for public view (León y Gama 1832, pt. 1:10–11).

Criollos like León y Gama were defending the ancient past and trying to construct from it a laudable heritage as part of their rationale for assuming power in Mexico. But their interests in the ancient Mexican past were quite distinct from their interest in modern Indians. Both *criollos* and *peninsulares* feared that there would be a resurgence of ancient Mexican religious beliefs and practices. When the *Calendar Stone* was found, León y Gama was immediately interested in studying it and just as quickly, fearing that "the stone might suffer from the curiosity and fanaticism of the people," hastened to have an exact copy made (Keen 1971, 302–3).

Indeed the selective appreciation of ancient Mexican artifacts bore this out. While the *Calendar Stone* was physically incorporated into the richest and most powerful institution in Mexico, the church, the *Coatlicue* was buried beneath one of the galleries of the university shortly after her discovery (Bernal 1980, 85). A nineteenth-century source records that she was buried for fear that she "might tempt Indians to their ancient worship" (Ober 1884, 314), and she was not exhumed permanently until 1824 (Bernal 1980, 85).

For the Bourbon regime, the *peninsulares,* and the administration in Mexico, the acceptance of the Enlightenment, which included the sciences and the interest in the pre-Hispanic past (though not a claim to its heritage), was essentially superficial…. The *criollo* interest in science and the pre-Hispanic past, by contrast, was profound. The defense of the ancient Mexican past and the promotion of science were two key elements in the *criollo* justification for independence, in essence a revolt against the Spanish monarchy….

The rationalist, anticlerical position of the early Mexican liberals, among whom must be counted León y Gama, explains his position on the *Calendar Stone.* Because of his pro-science position and his presentation of the stone as an example of the valuable legacy of the ancient Mexicans decried by the *peninsulares,* the significance of the *Calendar Stone* became inextricably linked with liberal ideology.

León y Gama's work on the stone was republished in 1832, edited and annotated by Carlos María de Bustamante, a liberal who had been actively involved in the struggle for independence.[16] It is not known whether León y Gama participated in this struggle; moreover, he died in 1802, several years before the major insurrections of 1810.[17] His work was hailed by Bustamante and even in his own day, was described by another well-known *criollo* scientist, Antonio Alzate y Ramírez, as having been motivated by a patriotic spirit (1831, 2 June 1792). The German liberal, Alexander von Humboldt, praised León y Gama's interpretation, and helped give it international notoriety in his *Vues des Cordillères* of 1810.[18] Until 1875, only a few authors appear to have dealt with the *Calendar Stone,* and all support León y Gama's interpretation.[19] In fact, by 1874, his interpretation was included in a Mexican secondary school textbook on chronology, in which the stone was used to represent the sum of ancient Mexican scientific knowledge (Mendoza and Romo 1874).

ALFREDO CHAVERO'S INTERPRETATION

In 1875, Alfredo Chavero, lawyer and playwright, published his first of several essays on the *Calendar Stone.*[20] He was the first author to challenge León y Gama's interpretation of the stone. He began by noting that León y Gama had become the authority on the subject, accepted by Europeans and Americans alike. He then proceeded to take issue with León y Gama's assertion that the stone was a solar clock, or calendar.[21] Chavero proposed that the stone was a platform upon which sacrifices were performed, requiring it to be positioned horizontally, rather than vertically, as León y Gama had claimed. Chavero believed that the stone was carved in A.D. 1479, during the reign of the Aztec ruler Axayacatl. As evidence, he cited the works of the sixteenth-century chroniclers Diego Durán and Alvarado Tezozómoc.[22] Both chroniclers spoke of a number of large, round, carved platforms for the sacrifice of prisoners of war taken by the Aztecs on their conquests.

Chavero seized as particular evidence the passage from Durán's chronicles…that he believed confirmed that the stone to which Durán referred and the *Calendar Stone* were one and the same. First, the *Calendar Stone* was dug up in the central plaza in 1790, where Durán said Axayacatl's stone had been located and then buried in the sixteenth century. Second, the rationale given by the archbishop for burying Axayacatl's stone—because of crimes of death committed on it—corresponded to the *Calendar Stone*'s assumed function as an Aztec sacrificial platform. Third, that Axayacatl's stone was, according to Durán, carved in the year 1479, two years before the death of the ruler, corresponded to the Aztec year Thirteen Reed, or 1479, indicated at the top of the *Calendar Stone.* Chavero also noted that it was customary for the Aztecs to mark the date of construction on important monuments. Finally, Durán's description of Axayacatl's stone as one carved with the months years, days, and weeks convinced Chavero of its identification as the *Calendar Stone.*

Chavero's proposal that the *Calendar Stone* was a horizontally positioned sacrificial platform, carved for the ceremonial dispatching of Aztec prisoners of war, was in all aspects a function diametrically opposed to León y Gama's interpretation. Indeed, Chavero emphasized in his essay of 1875, as well as in the second edition, published in 1876, and, again in his lengthy articles published in 1877, 1888, 1886, and 1903, that it was precisely over the issue of function that he wanted to establish his differences with León y Gama. The latter's characterization of the *Calendar Stone* as a monument of astronomical science and as an appreciable monument of

Mexican antiquity was evidently based on the assumption that the stone was a vertically positioned solar clock. Its function and significance here seemed to be inseparable. In addition, it was León y Gama who had purposefully dispensed with any "pagan," hence ritual, "or religious uses to" which the stone might have been put, although he knew Torquemada's work of 1723, which discussed sacrificial stones.[23]

Chavero's vehement claim that León y Gama was wrong is difficult to reconcile with the fact that in his own way Chavero also viewed the stone as a testimony to the scientific achievements of the ancient Mexicans. "In no monument of antiquity," he said, "does one find so much science and so many marvels" (Chavero 1876, 15).[24] In order to prove his point, he actually restated a number of the same points that León y Gama had made earlier to prove his own case....

...However, for him, the stone's scientific value appeared to have no relation to the stone's sacrificial function, writing: "This stone, at the same time that it was a monument to the sun, under its multiple manifestations" (referring to the actual movements of the sun)..."was a *cuauhxicalli* for sacrifices" (Chavero 1888, 747).[25] Apparently he was convinced that the *Calendar Stone* could have functioned as a sacrificial platform and still symbolize the scientific achievements of the ancient Mexicans. In fact, on balance, in his interpretations the scientific aspects outweigh the sacrificial ones, supporting his assertion that "the stone (was) principally a manifestation of the movements of the Sun" (747).[26]

LATE LIBERAL IDEOLOGY AND THE CALENDAR STONE

...It would be easy to say that Chavero was able to conclude that the *Calendar Stone* was a sacrificial stone because, he, unlike León y Gama, had access to the copy of Durán's manuscript, which gave very good evidence for such a conclusion. Chavero found Durán's information irrefutable. Yet, León y Gama was also confronted with the fact that the stone had other than scientific uses and chose not to assert them. Human sacrifice was a cultural phenomenon that, for Chavero, fell under the rubric of religion. Religion was, he claimed, a sociological element that had to be taken into account in the development of a people (Chavero 1888, 752). Ultimately, knowledge of religion enabled Chavero to measure social or cultural progress, such progress being measured in stages.

Chavero, like many nineteenth-century liberals, was heavily influenced by the works of the evolutionists, in his case, certainly by Darwin and probably by Spencer (Keen 1971, 427). For them, human universal history had evolved through stages, the completion of each stage marking progress toward the ultimate goal: liberty.[27] Chavero's evolutionist tendency can begin to explain the apparent contradiction between what he saw as the *Calendar Stone*'s function and its significance in the first place. His interpretation of the stone reveals a dichotomy between religious function and scientific significance. In the second place, it reveals a juxtaposition of historic phases. One phase is represented by the scientific significance, the other by the sacrificial function. On the one hand, Chavero specifically stated that the stone "housed the greatest mysteries of nahua science" (1876, 47),[28] not of ancient Mexican or Aztec science; the Nahua were one of the ancestral central-Mexican groups that were to make up the Postclassic period Aztecs. On the other hand, he dated the stone to the Aztec period. The historical, evolutionary relationship between the Nahua and the Aztecs is detailed by Chavero in his *Historia antigua* of 1888.

The Nahua, Chavero said, were a simple, agricultural people whose life was one of communal living and work and from which was born fraternity and virtue (1888, 158). Their social progress was measured by the development of art, science, and the calendar (Chavero 1888, 158). The Nahua had arrived at "the two expressions of human greatness: power through force and riches, and happiness through work and virtue" (Chavero 1888, 158).[29] The Aztecs, by contrast, were a different story. They were a people whose social development had led to distinct class divisions; their subsistence came from agriculture and tribute. Their evolution had led them far away from "the liberty and equality of the tribe," and Aztec social organization "constituted a true despotism" (Chavero 1888, 612). Thus, the Nahua, representing the tribal origins of the Aztecs, constituted a democratic society, whereas the Aztecs represented an autocratic society.

Intertwined with the evolution of social organization was the evolution of religion, thus forcing Chavero to confront it in relation to the *Calendar Stone.* Just as the social organizations of the Nahua and Aztec were radically different for Chavero, so too were their religions. The Nahua professed a religion based solely on the worship of planets that directly influenced their lives, particularly the sun (Chavero 1888, 117); it was a religion in harmony with their subsistence. Moreover, there was no evidence, he asserted, for the practice of human sacrifice (117), adding that Nahua religion was contemplative, based on the universal need of all men to adore a superior being. The Aztecs, on the other hand, had an institutionalized religion that lacked such pacific qualities. Gods took the place of planets: "For a people essentially fanatical, sacrifice and blind obedience to divine will" was unquestionable (540).[30] Divine will was that of the Aztec ruler, who now, turned monarch, was also the image of a god (561). Under the Aztec, moreover, a sacred war was instituted whereby ritual combat with enemy territories was the mechanism for providing victims, that is, prisoners of war, who were ceremonially dispatched with the rationale that they were providing sustenance for the gods. The Nahua, Chavero said, practiced war only in defense of their fields (117).

Consistently Chavero underscored the increase in the "superstitious and cruel fanaticism" of the Aztecs and the increase of despotic rule. Clearly there was a link between the rise in one and the rise in the other. This phenomenon began, he said, with the emperor Motecuhzoma I and increased under Axayacatl, during whose reign Chavero thought the *Calendar Stone* to have been carved. The result of despotism and religious fanaticism was an alienation of the people from the ruler; the emperor became hateful to his people, who lived by sacrificing men of other rulers in the costumes of their gods (Chavero 1888, 563). This, Chavero said, was the "blackest blindfold which covers the light of reason" (563).[31]

Chavero has thus interpreted the *Calendar Stone* in such a manner that: (a) the scientific significance, which was of primary importance for him, was associated with the essentially democratic Nahua, and (b) the sacrificial function was associated with the later Aztec phase characterized by a despotic monarchy and in which religion had become fanaticism and sanctioned human sacrifice in the name of the gods. We are left with the impression that Chavero's attempt to reconcile the function and significance of the stone remains ambiguous, or even a refusal to take a definitive position. His evolutionist interpretation of the stone only reveals this ambiguity; it does not resolve it.

From the time independence from Spain was achieved in 1821 until 1858, there was a constant struggle between Mexican conservative and liberal factions. The conservatives favored a monarchical political structure, an internal market system based on the maintenance of large estates, and tightly controlled national trade networks, backed by the military and the church. The liberals favored a republican form of government, participation in an international market structure, the rupture of land and trade monopolies, the destruction of church power, both politically and economically, and the creation of a middle class of small property owners and merchants. This struggle culminated in the Three Years War, or the War of Reform of 1858–62, from which the Partido Liberal Mexicano emerged victorious. By 1864, the conservatives had put the Austrian Archduke Maximilian in power. Three years later, liberal opposition forced him to surrender the throne and that same year he was put to death by a firing squad. Juárez, who had been in exile since 1855, regained the presidency in 1867—the Partido Liberal Mexicano, the party of reform, had come to power. Various factions of it governed Mexico until the outbreak of the revolution in 1910–11.

One of the most volatile, if not the most volatile, issue of the liberal-conservative clash was that of anticlericalism. The issue was not religion per se but rather the institution of the Catholic Church, which, along with the viceregal administration, had controlled Mexico economically, politically, and theologically since the colonial period. The church had become the major obstacle to liberal control since its power rested specifically on its control of vast areas of land, which the liberals wanted broken up and made available for private ownership. The political and economic power of the church was linked to the viceregal administration, and ultimately to the Spanish monarchy. Interests of the individuals were subordinated to those of God and King.

A parallel between the liberal position on the church and the monarchy in contemporary Mexico and Chavero's own position on the existence of similar institutions in Aztec culture can be made: the progress of Aztec culture was stunted by the evolution of a religion sanctifying human sacrifice and by the despotic usurpation of the power of Aztec rulers, both the result of imperfect social organization. Moreover, like the despotic nature of Aztec culture and its religion of sacrifice, the institution of the church and the monarchy and their conservative backers would necessarily be overcome according to the law of social evolution: the conquering race legitimized its conquest by its social superiority (Chavero 1882, 42)....

The relationship expressed between first, the Nahua and the significance of the *Calendar Stone* and second, the Aztecs and the function of the stone, thus made a statement about the contemporary relationship between liberals and conservatives. Liberal ideology was evidently parallel with Nahua practice, hence the primary importance of the scientific significance of the stone and conservative ideology and practice to the Aztecs, and hence, the adamant claim of the stone's sacrificial function. It appears that Chavero had constructed the historical basis for the liberal ascent to power through his interpretation of the *Calendar Stone.*

In the late nineteenth century, liberal justification for the formation of a secular state, the key to emancipation, had its basis in the philosophy of positivism, in which the notion of historical progress was viewed in terms of three stages: the theological, the metaphysical, and the positive.[32] In Mexico, just as in France, positivism was adopted by a middle class who similarly regarded Mexico's history as having gone through a theological phase, "the era when the clergy and the military held social and political power"; a metaphysical phase, the combative phase during which the theological order had been destroyed and the liberals fought the conservatives to put the Partido Liberal Mexicano into power; and the positive or present phase. The liberals, who saw themselves as the Mexican middle class, identified their interests with those of the entire Mexican nation (Zea 1974, 33).

The doctrine of positivism was outlined in a speech by Gabino Barreda, secretary of instruction under Juárez, who had lived and studied in France.[33]...

Positivism, however, was not a philosophy whose central focus was the individual; rather, it was society as a whole. Liberal ideology of the late eighteenth century and the early nineteenth century focused on the emancipation of the individual. Late liberal ideology, from 1867 on, claimed the scientifically, positivistically based state apparatus as the mechanism of emancipation and progress.[34] The priorities of the late nineteenth-century liberals were the progress and order of the nation, to be achieved by the state. Economically, progress was to be achieved through a reordering of the economic structure....

The achievement of these goals required, however, a strong centralized government that would run the state, not the federal government that the early liberals had called for. While the early liberals had demanded sovereignty, the late liberals demanded sovereignty and unity....

Given this shift in liberal ideology from the individual to the state and the nation, Chavero's apparently liberal interpretation of the *Calendar Stone* appears problematic, since it spoke favorably of early liberal ideology, if only implicitly. In his analysis of the Nahua and the Aztecs, he referred specifically to the concept of the nation. The Nahua, he said, lacked national cohesion, there existed "no interest in the *patria* or nationality" (Chavero 1888, 117).[35] This is a major criticism from the standpoint of a late nineteenth-century liberal such as Chavero but explicable, according to him, by the fact that they "had reached the highest level of progress compatible with the social milieu in which they lived" (158).[36] The Aztecs, he confessed, had distanced themselves greatly from their tribal Nahua origins but, unlike the Nahua, had evolved into an "organized nation"; the center of this nation was the imperial capital of Tenochtitlan, which was for the Aztecs *la patria* (661). The failure of the Aztecs on this score was that they could not unite the people they had conquered: "they did not understand that uniting the interests of all of them into one single interest would have formed a very powerful empire" (661).[37]

These remarks do not demonstrate an inconsistency with late liberal ideology on Chavero's part; on the contrary, they only prove a consistency. While the Aztecs conceived of a *patria*, of a nation, they could not unify their conquered territories into one because of the authoritarian and fanatically religious nature of Aztec rule. The Nahua, though more progressive, due to their more democratic social organization, were limited to their stage of progress because of their agricultural subsistence base. They were not conquerors like the Aztecs, nor did they aim to accumulate power like the Aztecs. Chavero did not object to the accumulation of power or territory on the part of the Aztecs. He objected to the fact that the rationale for conquest was their fanatic religion justifying human sacrifice, for which the ruler, in the end, was responsible. This, Chavero stated, was the "great political error" of the Aztecs (1888, 563). As pointed out earlier, superstition and blind faith proved the Aztec downfall. Had they used reason, an immensely powerful empire might have been theirs....

In view of the character of late nineteenth-century liberal ideology, an ideology that determined Chavero's interpretation of the *Calendar Stone,* what at first appeared as a contradiction between scientific significance and sacrificial function finds its resolve. The *Calendar Stone* proved itself an ideal vehicle for the expression of the justification of this ideology. In his interpretation, Chavero posed a series of oppositions: Nahua and Aztec, science and religion, democracy and despotism, demonstrating the progressive nature of the first element of each of these pairs....

Chavero's claim of the primary importance of the *Calendar Stone*'s scientific significance and his unequivocal assertion of the stone's sacrificial function thus appear quite consistent within the context of late liberal ideology. As an ideologically determined, and supportive, interpretation, it is no wonder that Chavero declared the *Calendar Stone* to be the most important monument of American antiquity (1888, 747).[38]

THE CALENDAR STONE AS NATIONAL SYMBOL: CONCLUSIONS

Chavero declared that the *Calendar Stone* was the most important monument of American antiquity not only because "it enclosed the greatest mysteries of the Nahua race" but also because "of its admirable work in relief, in its execution as well as its geometrical division, and in its bizarre, harmonious and aesthetic design" (1888, 747).[39] It has remained the most important monument of Mexican antiquity for these same reasons up to the present. In fact, by the end of the nineteenth century, the *Calendar Stone* had become the single artifact capable of representing all of pre-Hispanic culture to an international audience. In his trilingual *Monumentos del arte antiguo* of 1890, Antonio Peñafiel said:

> It cannot be asserted that our National Archaeology lacks grand monuments, because as a representative of a great historic era, we need only look at the Calendar stone, which is a compendium of the astronomical knowledge of the Aztecs, who were further advanced in the division of time than the very Europeans themselves.[40] (1890, i)

The national significance of the *Calendar Stone* was explicitly confirmed by Peñafiel. According to him, the stone could represent Mexico's national archaeology and glorious past. "To write about the *Calendar Stone*," he said, was "to describe the most important subject of national archaeology" (Peñafiel 1890, 102).... The *Calendar Stone* had been elevated from just "an appreciable monument of Mexican antiquity," as León y Gama described it, to *the* monument of Mexico.

There is no question that the *Calendar Stone* had become of great national significance in the nineteenth century, as Peñafiel's work demonstrates. The stone's role as national symbol today rests precisely on the same basis as it did for the liberals. This is perhaps best demonstrated by its context in the Museo Nacional de Antropología in Mexico City.

The stone stands upright, against a wall in the Mexica culture hall, centered on the museum's longitudinal axis. This is to demonstrate that it is the most important object in the museum; in addition, it is the only object in the museum enclosed on two sides by walls, one bearing a black and white reconstruction drawing, the other bearing a color reconstruction and a plaque with a lengthy description of the stone. The concluding remarks sum up the stone's significance according to the museum's label of 1980:

> This piece of sculpture reveals profound knowledge of geometry and composition which together with its scientific importance and its masterful carving constitute it as an appreciable relic of Mexica culture.

These words bear an uncanny resemblance to those written by León y Gama and Chavero. The vertical orientation of the stone in the museum has its verbal parallel in León y Gama's work, since he thought the stone was a vertically positioned solar clock....

The wealth of iconographic information contributed by such early twentieth-century scholars as Eduard Seler and Hermann Beyer has been deemed insignificant by those following the work of León y Gama. Enrique Juan Palacios, for example, in his publication of 1922, accused both scholars of expounding a "decorative thesis," that is, of attempting to analyze the iconography of the stone without attributing to it either mathematical or chronological significance.

Palacios's position was that there were no "simply decorative elements in the relief" (1922, 15). It was precisely through such attempts to understand the significance of the "decorative" elements, however, that progress in dating and the understanding of the religious implications of the stone were made by Beyer and Seler. In 1957, Raúl Noriega emphatically wrote (in capital letters) that there is no truth to this "decorative" theory (n.d., 11). Purely decorative elements would evidently undermine Noriega's theory that the stone was used for the computations of the cycles of the sun, the moon, Mercury, Venus, Mars, Jupiter, and Saturn!

The early iconographic studies of Seler and Beyer, considered in relation to Chavero's assertion that the *Calendar Stone* was a horizontally positioned platform, led more recent scholars to attempts to understand the significance of the iconography and the social function of the stone.[41] Only those interpreters making use of Chavero's assertion have confronted, to varying degrees, the more concrete circumstances of the *Calendar Stone*'s production....

While Chavero was critical of the function of the stone, and of the religious rationale given for this function, he did not critique its ideology; rather, his criticisms were themselves ideologically determined. In actuality, he only pitted the virtues of one ideology against another. Progress toward a new understanding of the historical function and significance of the *Calendar Stone* can only be achieved if progress is defined in terms of confronting the human, social forces responsible for the stone's production. It also requires casting off the idealized image that the stone's nineteenth-century interpreters created for it.

This task falls not only to those who have maintained León y Gama's interpretation but also to those who have maintained Chavero's. Even those authors who recognize the stone's sacrificial function have sustained the notion, like Chavero, that it has positive aspects, expressed particularly in terms of its aesthetic qualities.[42]

To admit the stone's sacrificial function on the one hand and to praise its aesthetic qualities on the other is not to confront the stone on a critical level. On the contrary, it is a perpetuation of the stone's nineteenth-century interpretations. Those interpretations have contributed to the transformation of an object used for human sacrifice into a national symbol expressive of a glorified ancient Mexican past. In order to proceed further with a more objective investigation of the *Calendar Stone*'s pre-Hispanic function and significance, a more critical stance must be taken. The *Calendar Stone* must be disengaged from its contemporary symbolic functions, themselves derived from ideological needs.

Notes

1. Journals and publications that bear the *Calendar Stone* as their logo include those of the Museo Nacional de Antropología and the Instituto Nacional de Antropología e Historia; the stone is also used as a commercial logo for various brands of food and the Banco Mexicano.

2. Authors supporting this interpretation include Avilés Solares (1939, 1957), Noriega (n.d., 1954), and Palacios (1918, 1922). Nuttall (1886) presents a variation on the stone's calendrical function and argues that the stone was a regulator of the Aztec periodical market day.

3. Authors supporting this interpretation include Aguilera (1977), Beyer (1921), Caso (1928, 1958), Navarrete and Heyden (1974), Townsend (1979), Klein (1976a, 1976b), and Umberger (1980).

4. Three short articles in the *Gazeta de México* of 1792 noted the discovery of the *Calendar Stone* and the publication of León y Gama's work.

5. "prescindiendo de los demás usos que el hacían los sacerdotes gentiles para su astrología judiciaria." (All translations in this essay are by Stacie Graham Widdifield.)

6. Ignacio Bernal (1980, 85) makes the same comparison.

7. "Esta segunda piedra, que es la mayor, la mas particular e instructiva."

8. León y Gama wrote to Cavo: "¡Cuantas noticias le comunicaría yo, por medio de las cuales, llegaría á hacer manifiestas y claras las luces, y muchos conocimientos de nuestros antiguos mexicanos, y para desvanecer la calumnia de bárbaros, con que los han querido denigrar para con todas las naciones europeas!" (1832, pt. 1:vii).

9. See Keen (1971, 268–73) and Brading (1980, 32–41) for analyses of this work.

10. Olmedo referred to "las fieras y brutos mas estúpidos el Abate Raynal, el Dr. Robertson, Mons. Buffon, Paw [sic] y otros" (León y Gama 1978, n.p.).

11. León y Gama also noted that because the Spaniards could not recognize the difference between the two types of sculptures, they destroyed a number of monuments (1978, 5).

12. León y Gama's concern with the scientific aspect of ancient Mexican culture is due in part to the fact that he was himself a man of science, acclaimed internationally for his astronomical studies. The French astronomer Joseph Lalande praised him highly for his calculation of the eclipse of 6 November 1771 (Gortari 1980, 255). León y Gama was also acclaimed for his part in establishing the latitude and longitude of Mexico City (Gortari 1980, 255). European as well as Mexican scientific societies honored him with memberships, and his works were published in their journals (León y Gama 1832, v–vii). In addition, he taught mechanics, aerometry, and pyrotechnics at the Real Seminario de Minería in Mexico City (Gortari 1980, 255). León y Gama's scientific bent in pursuing the *Calendar Stone,* therefore, could certainly be explained in part by his own academic pursuits.

13. The Mexican economy had expanded and become more stable in the eighteenth century, largely due to trade in textiles, sugar, tobacco, and silver, which were, aside from agriculture, the bases of the economy (Meyer and Sherman 1979, 254–56).

14. See Meyer and Sherman (1979, 274–76) for a discussion of *criollo* status in the late eighteenth century.

15. As Philip Russell notes, it was "restricted access top jobs, inefficient administration which hurt [them] economically, and the monopolistic commercial position of the Spaniard that probably did more to push [the *criollos*] toward independence than any other royal policy" (1977, 12).

16. Bustamante's activities included, among others, participation in the Congress of Anahuac of 1813, organized to declare a constitution; the congress was modeled after the French Assemblée nationale constituante (Cosío Villegas et al. 1974, 74).

17. None of my sources mentioning León y Gama referred to his specific activities in the struggle for independence. Had he actively participated, it would seem that later liberal sources would have mentioned it.

18. Humboldt supported León y Gama's interpretation, but, as a diffusionist, he also tried to prove analogies and contacts between the Old and New Worlds, especially in terms of calendrical and cosmological systems.

19. The authors supporting León y Gama were Mayer (1852), Gallatin (1845), Tylor (1861), Nebel (1963), and Carbájal Espinosa (1862).

20. A second edition of the first essay and a series of articles were published in the *Anales del Museo Nacional de Mexico* in 1877, 1882, 1886, and 1903 (see Chavero 1877a, 1882, 1886, 1903). In addition, Chavero discussed the *Calendar Stone* in his *Historia antigua y de la conquista* (1888).

21. León y Gama never actually called the stone a calendar, but his interpretation prompted later writers to call it this.

22. The works of Durán and Tezozómoc both stem from a single, now lost, manuscript called the *Crónica X;* see Barlow 1945.

23. See Torquemada 1723, vol. 2.

24. "en ningun monumento de la antigüedad se encuentra tanta ciencia y tanta maravilla como en este."

25. "Esta piedra, al mismo tiempo que era un momumento al sol bajo sus muliples manifestaciones, era cuauhxicalli para sacrificios." A *cuauhxicalli* refers to a receptacle for sacrifices.

26. "pero siendo principalmente esta Piedra una manifestación de los movimientos del astra."

27. Justo Sierra, Porfirio Díaz's secretary of instruction, closed his chronicle *The Political Evolution of the Mexican People* with an affirmation of this goal: "Mexican social evolution will have been wholly abortive and futile unless it attains the final goal. liberty" (1969, 368).

28. "piedra es esta que encierra los mas grandes misterios de la ciencia nahua."

29. "Asi llegaron los nahoas a las dos expresiones de la grandeza humana: el poder por la fuerza y la riqueza, y la felicidad por el trabajo y la virtud."

30. "para un pueblo esencialmente fanática, no era discutible el sacrificio y la obediencia ciega a esa voluntad divina."

31. "Tan cierto es que negra la superstición que cubre la luz de la razón."

32. My primary source for the discussion of positivism, derived from Auguste Comte's philosophy, is Leopoldo Zea (1974).

33. In 1867, at the moment of restoration, Barreda delivered his "Oración Cívica" in Guanajuato, proclaiming the value of this philosophy for the progress of Mexico, which was entering this new, positive phase of its history. He asserted the need to develop a group of leaders who would originate in the middle class and who would guide Mexico through this

positive phase. They would be trained in the practical application of positivism (Villegas 1972, 41–75). Juárez appointed a committee to restructure the educational system in primary and secondary schools under the supervision of Barreda, whose curriculum was adopted by the Mexican congress in 1867 (Meyer and Sherman 1979, 407). Heavy emphasis was placed on the disciplines whose practical application would most benefit the material base of Mexico—that is, the physical, natural, and mechanical sciences. During the regime of Porfirio Díaz, which saw the greatest fulfillment of the positivist desires of the liberals, a scientific education was just as important. Justo Sierra, official historian and secretary of instruction under Díaz, spoke of the necessity of scientific training for all careers, "for the constant exercise of this positivist method (and) for the systematic observation of contemporary society" (1991, 105).

34. See Hale 1965 for an in-depth analysis of the shift in nineteenth-century liberalism in Mexico.

35. "lo repetimos, no existía el interés de patria o nacionalidad."

36. "pudo alcanzar el mayor grado de progreso compatible can el media social en que vivía."

37. "no comprendieron que uniendo los intereses de todos ellas en un solo interás habran formado un imperio poderosísimo."

38. Larráinzar (1875–78), Orozco y Berra (1880), Rivera Cambas (1880–83), and Mendoza and Sánchez (1882) acknowledged the stone's sacrificial function. Batres (1888), Abadiano (1889), and Peñafiel (1890) sided with León y Gama. The reasons for this apparent shift in support from Chavero to León y Gama at the end of the century requires a detailed historical analysis that cannot be done within the confines of this thesis. It may correspond to another shift in liberal ideology or to ideological differences between various liberal factions.

39. "Aquí damos por primera vez la descripción y explicación completas de tan prodigioso monumento, que creemos el mas importante de la antigüedades americana, y encierra los mas grandes misterios de la raza nahua, y par su admirable trabajo de relieve, tanto en su ejecución en su división geométrica y su dibujo bizarro, armonioso estético."

40. Peñafiel's book was published by Díaz's secretary of development, in conjunction with other preparations made by Mexico's delegation to the Columbian Exposition to be held in Madrid in 1892. These preparations included the construction of a Mexican pavilion and the reproduction of numerous pre-Hispanic artifacts. The *Calendar Stone* was sent as a reproduction in papier-mâché, but, as *El monitor republicano* reported, it arrived as a wet mass because the crate in which the stone was packed leaked (22 October 1892).

41. See, for example, the studies by Townsend (1979) and Umberger (1980).

42. For example, the *Calendar Stone* is described as "unquestionably one of the most successful examples of intricate patterning in the history of art. The most famous of all artistic productions of the American Indian constitutes a magnificently conceived basaltic hymn to the sun, whose thirst and appetite must needs be constantly slaked and satisfied with man's most precious offering, the blood of his veins and the very seat of his life" (Nicholson 1971a, 132). See also works by Caso (1958) and Klein (1976b).

"A Reconsideration of Some Hieroglyphs on the Mexica *Calendar Stone*" (1988)

Editors' Commentary

In this article, first delivered in 1979 at the XLIII International Congress of Americanists, Emily Umberger addresses the five hieroglyphs carved above and below the central deity on the Calendar Stone, *arguing that they can be best understood in light of historical and dynastic considerations, in addition to their mythological import. Beginning with her dissertation of 1981, Umberger has consistently examined the relationship between history and mythology in Aztec art, particularly as reflected in its style and iconography (1987a, 1987b, 2003). In* Calendar Stone *studies, the assessment of the meaning and function of the five hieroglyphs carved on the monument often has been eclipsed by efforts to identify the central face. This is partly because four of these hieroglyphs seem to be dates, but we do not know if a day, year, or personal name was meant; nor do we know to which fifty-two-year cycle they pertain, if they are indeed dates. Umberger argues that 13 Reed, 1 Flint, and the other dates on the* Calendar Stone *were selected precisely because they referred not only to mythological events, as Eduard Seler asserts, but also to key moments in Aztec history, thus establishing symmetries between cosmic and historical time. Contributing to a debate on the patronage of the monument that stretches back to Chavero (1875), Umberger amasses stylistic and iconographic evidence that Motecuhzoma II commissioned the* Calendar Stone. *She notes that there is no clear indication that the headdress glyph represents "the spirit of the dead warrior," as Seler and Hermann Beyer think. The style of the monument and a passage in Fray Toribio de Benavente Motolinía's* Memoriales; o, Libro de las cosas de Nueva España y de los naturales de ella *(1971) also support her contention that Motecuhzoma II was its patron.*

✳   ✳   ✳

"A Reconsideration of Some Hieroglyphs on the Mexica Calendar Stone"

The purpose of this paper is to interpret and analyze the interrelationship between the five hieroglyphs on the Calendar Stone: the 13 Reed date at the top and four small glyphs above and below the sun's face, especially 1 Flint and the noncalendric glyph facing it (fig. 1).[1] In previous studies these glyphs have been given a variety of meanings. Thirteen Reed and 1 Flint have been interpreted variously as referring to the distant ("mythological") past, the more recent past, and the present (the date of the monument's creation). The noncalendric glyph has been interpreted as a

---

Excerpted and reprinted from Emily Umberger, "A Reconsideration of Some Hieroglyphs on the Mexica *Calendar Stone*." In J. Kathryn Josserand and Karen Dakin, eds., *Smoke and Mist: Mesoamerican Studies in Memory of Thelma D. Sullivan*, 1:345–88. Oxford, England: B.A.R., 1988. Published with permission. Introductory text by Khristaan D. Villela and Matthew H. Robb.

Fig. 1.
Drawing of the *Aztec Calendar Stone,*
modified by the author after Noriega
1959

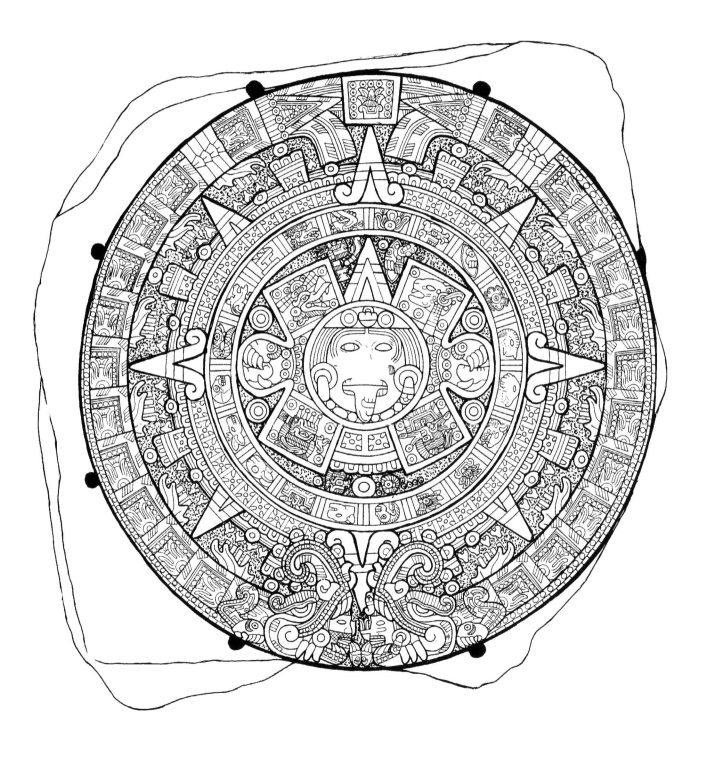

king's name, kingship in general, and the "soul of the dead warrior." In addition, the four small glyphs as a group have been interpreted as the four directions of space.

Most of the differences between interpretations involve decisions between possible mythological and religious meanings, on the one hand, and historical, dynastic, and political significance, on the other. Historical interpretations of hieroglyphs on Aztec sculptures, which were attempted by several nineteenth-century scholars, became unpopular after the time of Eduard Seler (mostly because of his influence), except for the most obvious examples, like the Stone of Tizoc. In this study, I am following Richard Townsend's (1979, 63–70) example in reconsidering the Calendar Stone as a commemorative monument on which religious, historical, and political meanings are intertwined.

I am focusing in particular on the date 1 Flint, which, although not featured in a cartouche like 13 Reed, is a pivotal glyph in the Calendar Stone's composition and is symbolically the most important date in Mexica thought. I am also arguing that the noncalendric glyph, which I call the headdress glyph, is the name sign of Motecuhzoma II, as Peñafiel first suggested in 1890 (1:101–2, 108 <English text>).[2] Although seemingly uncomplicated, especially in comparison to Maya glyphs, hieroglyphs on Mexica sculptures can refer to multiple, related ideas; and their placement, framing, size, and decoration on late sculptures are purposeful. The Calendar Stone is the most intricate in this respect, and its study reveals a great deal about the function of glyphs on state monuments.

THE GREAT SACRIFICIAL STONES

… By the mid-fifteenth century Tenochtitlan was fast becoming the politically dominant city of the alliance and taking on the appearance of an imperial capital, with a great ceremonial precinct, temples, and palaces.

It was at this time that the creation of major stone monuments became very important to the Mexica. Of special interest are the large round sacrificial stones, whose conception, carving, and ceremonial use are described in the histories of Durán and Alvarado Tezozómoc (cognate histories for which Barlow [1945] hypothesized a lost prototype, the *Crónica X*). As is well known, the Mexica waged constant warfare and sacrificed the prisoners of war as offerings to the sun, because they thought that without the nourishment of human hearts and blood, the sun would not continue to move through the sky. The sacrificial stones were thus the focal points of great state ceremonies.

Two types of round sacrificial stone are described by the chroniclers. The *temalacatl* (round stone) was the stone of gladiatorial sacrifice and it supposedly had a place in the center for attaching the rope to which the victim was tied.[3] One small surviving gladiatorial stone (none of the great ones remain) has a bar across the central hole for this purpose (Beyer 1955a). The *cuauhxicalli* (eagle's <sun's> vessel), or Stone of the Sun, usually had a hollow in the center to hold hearts and blood offerings to the sun, but not always.[4]

New sacrificial stones were carved periodically by various kings (perhaps by every king). It seems that at different times the two great stones were placed either on platforms in the same courtyard (Durán 1967, 1:98) or on the platform of the Great Temple of Huitzilopochtli (Alvarado Tezozómoc 1975a, 415–16). Both types of stones were inaugurated with sacrificial victims captured during specified military forays. The gladiatorial stone was used during the Tlacaxipehualiztli (Skinning of Men) ceremony, the main festival celebrating warfare, conquest, and Mexica rule.

The *cuauhxicalli* was used for the final dispatch of the victims after gladiatorial sacrifice (Durán 1967, 1:98) and also on a variety of other occasions, for instance the sacrifice of the messenger to the sun on the day 4 Movement (Durán 1967, 1:107; 2:194) and sacrifices of prisoners-of-war by the king and prime minister (Durán 1967, 2:193).

As for the iconography of the great stones, the *cuauhxicallis* are described as having had the image of the sun on the upper surface and at least one gladiatorial stone, that of Motecuhzoma I, bore carvings commemorating an important victory.[5] However, the imagery on the two types of stones may not have been as different as this implies. The small *temalacatl* mentioned above likewise has solar rays on the upper surface (Beyer 1955a), and the Stone of Tizoc, one of the great *cuauhxicallis,* has scenes commemorating Mexica conquests around the sides. Thus both types of stones probably combined solar imagery with allusions to military victories, and sacrifice was performed on the sun itself.

According to the *Crónica X* tradition, two great sacrificial stones were carved in the time of Motecuhzoma I (1440–69).[6] The first, a *temalacatl,* was made to celebrate victories in the Huastec area of Veracruz (which occurred sometime in the 1450s). Although celebrating a recent conquest, the reliefs on the stone are described as commemorating events that had occurred over two decades earlier: the death of Chimalpopoca and the war of independence from the Tepanecs (Durán 1967, 2:171–75; Alvarado Tezozómoc 1975a, 318–23). A *cuauhxicalli* was carved later in Motecuhzoma's reign for the immolation of prisoners from Coixtlahuaca in Oaxaca (Durán 1967, 2:188–95; Alvarado Tezozómoc 1975a, 338–39). Supposedly two more stones were carved in the time of Axayacatl (1469–81). The gladiatorial stone was initiated with victims from Tollocan (Toluca) and Matlatzinco, and the later *cuauhxicalli* was to be inaugurated with Tarascan prisoners from Michoacan. This important campaign having failed, however, the Mexica initiated the stone with victims from Tliliuhquitepec, a much less significant conquest (Durán 1967, 2:267–80 passim, 292–93; Alvarado Tezozómoc 1975a, 398–400, 409–19 passim, 429–30). The chronicles do not mention any sacrificial stones for Tizoc (1481–86) or Ahuitzotl (1486–1502) (although there is a reference to a sacrificial stone established in Tenochtitlan in 1498 in another source (Chimalpahin Cuauhtlehuanitzin 1965, 225). They do, however, tell of a great *temalacatl* which Motecuhzoma II (1502–20) ordered carved…(Durán 1967, 2:485ff; translation, Durán 1964, 250).[7] Durán calls the stone a *temalacatl,* but Alvarado Tezozómoc does not identify it by type.

The Stone of Tizoc and the Calendar Stone are two large round stones that are usually thought to have served as sacrificial platforms and specifically as *cuauhxicallis* (Beyer 1965d, 137–48).[8] Both have sun discs on top and both, as we will see, commemorate Mexica victories. The Stone of Tizoc has a sun disc on its upper surface (fig. 2) with a hollow for blood in the center, and scenes representing Mexica conquests around the sides.[9] Although the chronicles do not mention a sacrificial stone from Tizoc's time, his hieroglyph next to one of the conquering figures (the only one with a personal name sign) dates the monument to his reign.

The Calendar Stone is a flat relief depicting a very elaborate version of the sun disc. In the center is the face of the sun of the fifth and final era of time.[10] Framing the face is the date 4 Movement, the sun's calendric name.[11] In the arms of the Movement sign are the names of the suns of the previous world ages: 4 Jaguar, 4 Wind, 4 Rain, and 4 Water. In the areas between the arms the four small hieroglyphs represent: the day signs 1 Rain and 7 Monkey below the sun's face; and the date 1 Flint and the noncalendric glyph in the form of a ruler's headdress above the sun's face. Surrounding the central area are a series of rings. In the first ring are the 20 day names of

Fig. 2.
Stone of Tizoc
Mexico (Tenochtitlan), 1481–86, stone,
basalt, height: 90 cm (35½ in.), diam.:
270 cm (106¼ in.)
Mexico City, Museo Nacional
de Antropología

the Aztec calendar. In the next ring are symbols representing precious greenstones, and beyond these are a stream of blood, greenstone pendants, and the rays of the sun. Framing the stone are two fire serpents from whose mouths emerge human heads; these heads are identified by Beyer (1965d, 237–47) as (left) Xiuhtecuhtli, the god of fire and time, and (right) the sun god, who is also represented in the center. At the top of the stone the date 13 Reed is framed by a square cartouche.

VARIOUS INTERPRETATIONS OF THE GLYPHS

Aztec date glyphs consist of a day name plus a numeral and are usually not difficult to read. It is, however, difficult to know what they signify: whether they represent days or years and in what cycles they occur. The Aztec calendar was based on a 260-day count which consisted of 20 day signs intermeshing with the numbers one through thirteen. Four of the day names—Rabbit, Reed, Flint, and House—were also year bearers.[12] The year had 365 days. The "century" consisted of 52 years, beginning with 1 Rabbit[13] and proceeding thirteen times through the four year names plus the numbers one through thirteen (four times) until 1 Rabbit was reached again. The four quarters (*tlalpilli*) of this 52-year cycle, beginning with 1 Rabbit, 1 Reed, 1 Flint, and 1 House, respectively, were important divisions of time.

Because the names of years were also the names of days, it is sometimes difficult to distinguish between the two in hieroglyphic inscriptions. In most cases cartouches frame year dates, but in a few important examples year dates are not framed. Because 13 Reed on the Calendar Stone

is in a cartouche, it is usually interpreted as a year; 1 Flint, however, is unframed and has been interpreted as either a year or a day.[14] The other problem with inscriptions on sculptures is that the Aztecs did not distinguish between days and years in various cycles. For this reason, both 13 Reed and 1 Flint have been interpreted as referring to events in different cycles.

The Calendar Stone has been the subject of a great deal of scholarly writing since its discovery in 1790. The major interpretations of its hieroglyphs are those of León y Gama (1832), Chavero (1875), Peñafiel (1890), Seler (1960a <1904>), Beyer (1965d <1921>, 1965e <1922>, and 1965a <1923>), and Townsend (1979). León y Gama (1832, pt. 1:91–102) connected the monument with the myth of the five suns and identified the calendric names of the suns. Chavero (1875, 1–5) suggested that the Calendar Stone was the sacrificial stone that Durán described as carved in the reign of Axayacatl. He interpreted 13 Reed as the year 1479, which occurred near the end of that king's reign. Peñafiel (1890, 1:101–2, 108 <English text>), on the other hand, identified the head-dress glyph as the name sign of Motecuhzoma II and therefore dated the monument to his time (even though the year dates on the monument did not occur in Motecuhzoma's reign).

Seler (1960a, 795–801) did not attempt to resolve the differences between Chavero's and Peñafiel's interpretations; he did not discuss the dating of the monument at all or possible allusions to recent history. Rather he interpreted both 13 Reed and 1 Flint as years in which important events took place in the distant, mythic past. Thirteen Reed was the year of the sun's birth and 1 Flint was the first year of Mexica history (the year they left their homeland, Aztlan). Although Seler acknowledged the resemblance of the headdress glyph to the name glyph of Motecuhzoma, he rejected the possibility that it represented the ruler's name, preferring instead to interpret it as a symbol of the "spirit of the dead warrior," because royal paraphernalia are also the accoutrements of mummy bundles in the pictorial manuscripts.[15] In addition, he (Seler 1960a, 799–800) thought that this glyph and the other three dates around the Movement sign represented the four world directions. The headdress glyph thus referred to the East because the spirits of dead warriors accompanied the sun through the eastern part of the sky to the zenith. One Flint was assigned to the North, 1 Rain to the South, and 7 Monkey to the West.

Beyer (1965a, 1965d, 1965e), whose discussions are still the most thorough on all aspects of the Calendar Stone, accepted Seler's interpretation of 13 Reed as referring to the birth of the sun and the four small glyphs as the four directions (Beyer 1965d, 188, 247–48). One Flint he further interpreted as a day related to the god Tezcatlipoca, Smoking Mirror, because of the smoking mirror appended to it (Beyer 1965d, 189–90). He did not mention Seler's reading of the date as a year at the beginning of history. He did, however, reiterate Seler's interpretation of the head-dress glyph as the "spirit of the dead warrior," adding that the emblems appended to the glyph are those of the fire god Xiuhtecuhtli (Beyer 1965d, 190–95). Although not adding substantially to the interpretation of the glyphs, Beyer (1965a, 264–65) did discuss the date of the monument. Like Peñafiel, he thought that the Calendar Stone must post-date the Stone of Tizoc and that it was made in the time of Motecuhzoma II (although not acknowledging the resemblance of the headdress glyph to that king's name glyph). According to the *Crónica X* tradition (Durán 1967, 2:485–97; Alvarado Tezozómoc 1975a, 662–67), the stone fell off a bridge on the way to Tenochtit-lan and then returned miraculously to the quarry but, according to a related passage in Torque-mada (1969, 1:214–15), the stone was retrieved, carved, and set up as a sacrificial stone in the tenth year of Motecuhzoma's reign. Beyer identified the Calendar Stone with these passages (although the monument was actually supposed to have been a *temalacatl*) and dated it to 1512.

Fig. 3.

Hieroglyph of the name Motecuhzoma
in codices, drawings by the author
a: Motecuhzoma II in battle costume,
after *Codex Vaticanus A,* fol. 83v,
from Seler 1960–61, 2:675, fig. 4), b:
Motecuhzoma II, after *Codex Mendoza,*
fol. 15v, c: name glyph of Motecuhzoma
I, after *Codex Telleriano Remensis,* fol.
34v, d: name glyph of Motecuhzoma II,
after *Codex Telleriano Remensis,* fol. 41r

Of special interest in Townsend's (1979, 63–70) interpretation of the Calendar Stone is his discussion of the date 13 Reed. Townsend states that, in addition to being the date of the sun's birth, 13 Reed was also meant to refer to the year 1427, the first year of the reign of Itzcoatl (after the assassination of Chimalpopoca), which the Mexica conceived of as the beginning of their rule. By putting these events in the same year, the Mexica were comparing the beginning of the empire to the birth of the sun and thus validating their rule. Townsend further interpreted 1 Flint as the calendar date of Huitzilopochtli, the Mexica tribal and war god, and the headdress glyph as a symbol of kingship.

THE HEADDRESS GLYPH

The basic elements of the headdress glyph are the crown, hair, earplug, and noseplug of a lord or ruler. These same elements characteristically form the hieroglyph of the name Motecuhzoma in the codices (figs. 3, 4). Motecuhzoma means "angry lord" or "the lord grows angry," and the royal paraphernalia represent the word *tecuhtli,* "lord." The glyph on stone sculptures, however, has been more often than not read by scholars as something other than the name Motecuhzoma, in part because of the elaborations on the different versions.

The glyph occurs in three variations on eight Mexica sculptures.[16] The simplest version, Type I, is found on two boxes (fig. 5a, d), one in the National Museum in Mexico City (Seler 1960d, 742–45) and the other in Berlin (unpublished). It also occurs on a greenstone fire serpent (fig. 5b) at Dumbarton Oaks (Benson and Coe 1963, no. 107), and on the back of a sculpture of Tlaloc (fig. 5c) in the Santa Cecelia Acatitlan Museum (Solís Olguín 1976, 6, figs. 5, 6, illustrates the sculpture, but not the glyph). The outlines of a fifth example (fig. 5e), formerly identified as an animal head, can be made out among the glyphs to the left of the relief portrait of a Mexica ruler at Chapultepec. The only elaborations on Type I are the speech scrolls on three examples. At Chapultepec, the speech scroll is the *atl-tlachinolli* symbol of sacred warfare.[17] On examples A and B the speech scroll is similar to another, G, that is clearly a feathered serpent head.

Fig. 4.
Motecuhzoma I posing for his portrait at Chapultepec, from *Durán Codex*, fol. 91v
Mexico, ca. 1581, watercolor on European paper
Madrid, Biblioteca Nacional de España

Fig. 5.
Headdress glyph (Motecuhzoma II's name glyph) on Aztec stone sculptures, drawings by the author
Type I, a: box, Mexico City, Museo Nacional de Antropología, b: fire serpent, Washington, D.C., Dumbarton Oaks, c: Tlaloc, Museo de Santa Cecelia Acatitlan, d: box, Berlin, Museum für Völkerkunde, e: Chapultepec rock sculpture. Type II, f: *Teocalli de la Guerra Sagrada,* Mexico City, Museo Nacional de Antropología, g: *Hackmack Box,* Hamburg, Museum für Völkerkunde. Type III, h: *Calendar Stone*

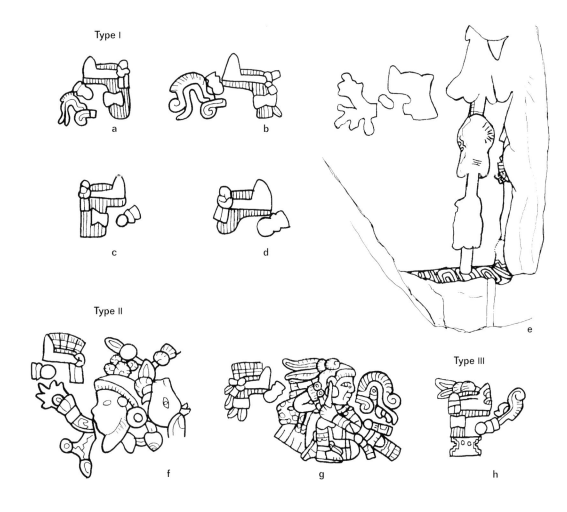

Type I

a

b

c

d

e

Type II

f

g

Type III

h

Type II occurs on the pyramid model called the Temple of Sacred Warfare [*Teocalli de la Guerra Sagrada*] (fig. 5f) in the National Museum in Mexico (Caso 1927 discusses glyph on 39–48) and on the Hackmack Box (fig. 5g) in Hamburg (Seler 1960d, 731–42). In Type II some upright elements are added to the top of the crown. This type of headdress is also worn by the fire priests in the depiction of the New Fire Ceremony in the *Codex Borbonicus.* Since both sculptures probably date from the time of the New Fire celebration in 1507, this addition is not surprising (the Hackmack Box, possibly 1 Rabbit <1506>; the Temple of Sacred Warfare, 2 Reed <1507>). On both the speech scroll emanates from the figure rather than the glyph. (The same paraphernalia apparently can decorate either). On the Temple it is the speech scroll of sacred warfare; on the box, it is the one that resembles a feathered serpent's head.

Type III occurs only on the Calendar Stone (fig. 5h) and is the most elaborate version. There is a feather decoration on top, a face on the front of the crown, a speech scroll attached to the noseplug, and a stepped breastplate, which Beyer (1965d, 192) identifies as that of Xiuhtecuhtli, below the headdress. Two of these motifs, the feather decoration and the serpent-like speech scroll, also pertain to the figure with the headdress glyph on the Hackmack Box (see fig. 5g).

The headdress glyphs on the other seven sculptures have been given the same variety of interpretations as the one on the Calendar Stone. Peñafiel (1890, 1:23, 105 <English version>) identified the glyph on the National Museum Box as the name of the Tetzcocan king Nezahualpilli (apparently he thought it was a different glyph from the one on the Calendar Stone, which he interpreted as Motecuhzoma's name). Alcocer (1935, 60) identified the glyph on the Temple of Sacred Warfare as Motecuhzoma's name, but Caso (1927, 43–48) thought rather that it represented a deity's name. These conflicting interpretations persist to the present.

The individual elements of the headdress glyph do represent different concepts in other contexts (Nicholson 1967b, 71–72, lists most of the following examples). In the manuscripts (all of which are actually postconquest) royal crowns are used as hieroglyphs to represent high political offices, months, and place names (like Tecutepec) that have the root *tecuhtli,* "lord." The royal paraphernalia are worn by gods like Xiuhtecuhtli, as well as kings, lords, and mummy bundles. There is no real evidence, however, for the existence of a hieroglyph representing the "spirit of the dead warrior." Nor is it likely that a noncalendric glyph would accompany a deity on stone sculptures, where they are usually identified by their costumes and are occasionally accompanied by calendric names (fig. 6b).

It is also unlikely that the headdress glyph is the symbol of the direction East, as Seler suggested. It may be true that the glyphs on the Calendar Stone (the dates of the four suns as well as the four small glyphs) are aligned with the directions, but there is no evidence that any one set symbolizes the directions themselves. All have other, more important meanings. In the composition, the four small glyphs look like a group, but in some ways they are two separate pairs. The lower pair are simple, unelaborated day signs that are also smaller and in lower relief than the other two. The upper pair, in addition to being more elaborate, are different in type: 1 Flint is a year bearer and the headdress glyph is not even a date.

The elaborations on the different versions of the headdress glyph should not be considered as changing its basic meaning. Hieroglyphic dates on sculptures can likewise be decorated with different ritual paraphernalia; jaguar spots, ropes, and other attributes. A Flint date, for instance, can be a plain flint knife or it can be more elaborate, with the smoking mirror of the god Tezcatlipoca on the upper part and a speech scroll emanating from the face (fig. 7). Elaborate

Fig. 6.
Hackmack Box; Hamburg, Museum für
Völkerkunde; drawings of details by
Eduard Seler (German, born Prussian,
1849–1922)
a: headdress glyph representing the
name Motecuhzoma, b: 1 Reed glyph
representing the calendric name of the
god Quetzalcoatl

a

b

Fig. 7.
Various Flint dates, drawings by
the author
a: 8 Flint on rim of *Bilimek Pulque
Vessel,* Vienna, Museum für
Völkerkunde, after Seler 1960–61, 2:922,
fig. 23, b: 1 Flint on side of the *Teocalli
de la Guerra Sagrada,* Mexico City,
Museo Nacional de Antropología, c:
1 Flint on *Aztec Calendar Stone,* Mexico
City, Museo Nacional de Antropología,
d: 11 Flint on box, Mexico City, Museo
Nacional de Antropología, after Seler
1960–61, 1:744, fig. 30

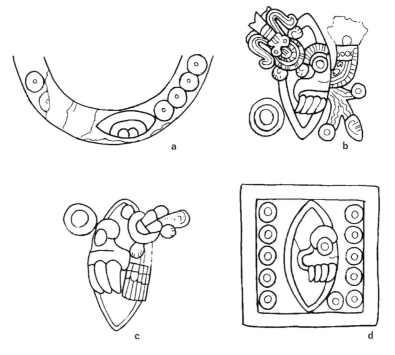

versions of dates can even occur together with simpler ones on the same sculpture. On the Calendar Stone the dates in the central area are more elaborate than the ones in the ring of day names. If date glyphs are thus added to, then it follows that the name of the ruler likewise can assume the paraphernalia of the deities with whom he was identified on different occasions.

Finally, the headdress glyph on Mexica sculptures should be interpreted as the name Motecuhzoma because of its context. On the Hackmack Box, the Chapultepec sculpture, and the Temple of Sacred Warfare, both glyph Types I and II accompany a figure. The figure at Chapultepec is known from the chronicles to be the portrait of a ruler; both Durán (1967, 2:245–56, 489–90, and elsewhere) and Alvarado Tezozómoc (1975a, 368–69, and elsewhere) describe the carving of rulers' portraits at the site. Although unaware of the hieroglyph, Nicholson (1959) identified the figure as Motecuhzoma II on the basis of the descriptions, the dates next to the figure, and some unfinished carvings nearby, which he suggests were interrupted by the Conquest. That the glyph represents the name Motecuhzoma is especially clear when the sculpture is compared to Durán's illustration of Motecuhzoma I posing for his portrait; the name glyph is also on the rock to the left of the figure (see fig. 4).[18]

On the Temple of Sacred Warfare, the glyph accompanies a figure in a characteristic dynastic composition, comparable to the well-known Dedication Stone (figs. 8, 9). In both reliefs, two figures face over a central cult object—a grass ball in one, a solar disc in the other.[19] On the Dedication Stone, the hieroglyphic names of the rulers Tizoc and Ahuitzotl are located next to their heads. The glyph on the Temple of Sacred Warfare is also next to the figure's head, and one can assume that it too is a ruler's name. In summary, the headdress glyph, like hieroglyphic dates on stone sculptures, occurs in several variations, with different speech scrolls and ritual paraphernalia. Examples of both Types I and II are situated in contexts in which they should be interpreted as a ruler's name. Type III on the Calendar Stone must, by extension, also represent the name of a king. The dating of the monument to the time of Motecuhzoma II will be discussed later.

Fig. 8.
Huitzilopochtli and Motecuhzoma
on the *Teocalli de la Guerra Sagrada*;
Mexico City, Museo Nacional de
Antropología; drawing by Enrique Juan
Palacios, 1929

Fig. 9.
Rulers Tizoc and Ahuitzotl with
hieroglyphic names on the *Dedication
Stone*; Mexico City, Museo Nacional de
Antropología; drawing by Eduard Seler
(German, born Prussian, 1849–1922)

Although not really paired on the Calendar Stone, 13 Reed and 1 Flint are linked by the "arrow" above the central face, and since they do occur together on other sculptures, it is important to understand the relationship between them. Sculptures featuring these dates include a Teotihuacan-style figure in Hamburg (Danzel and Fuhrmann 1922, vol. 2, pl. 67), which was recarved in Post-classic times with 1 Flint and 13 Reed on its chest,[20] and a stela from Castillo de Teayo, an Aztec site in the Huastec area of Veracruz.[21] The dates 13 Reed and 1 Flint as a pair are significant in several contexts: 1) they are the dates of important events in the distant, "mythological" past, 2) they are the dates of related events in recent history (which were therefore prefigured by the mythological events), and 3) they have very significant positions in the 52-year cycle; and it is for this last reason that they were made the dates of the events in question.[22]

As we have seen, Seler identified 13 Reed and 1 Flint as the dates of two very important events in the distant past. According to the myth of the suns, four world ages came and went, each with its own sun and each destroyed by a cataclysm. The Fourth Era ended in the year 1 Rabbit when the sky fell and the earth was flooded. The Fifth Era began in the same year with the restoration of the earth and sky, but all was in darkness because there was no sun. It was not until 26 years later, in the year 13 Reed, that the gods gathered at Teotihuacan for the creation of the 4 Movement sun.[23] Several cycles later, in the year 1 Flint, the Mexica left Aztlan setting out on their migration under the guidance of Huitzilopochtli, their tribal god (fig. 10). At one point during their journey they settled near Tula, the capital of the ancient Toltecs (ca. 900–1200)—which was probably pretty much abandoned by this time.

After further wandering from place to place, the Mexica arrived in the Basin of Mexico and finally settled on the island of Tenochtitlan, where they were under the domination of the Tepanecs until the mid 1420s. In 13 Reed (1427) the Tepanecs assassinated Chimalpopoca and Itzcoatl acceded to the throne, and in the following year, 1 Flint (1428), the Mexica overthrew the Tepanec capital of Azcapotzalco.[24] Thus the years that mark the end of the old era and the beginning of the Mexica's rise to empire have the same names as the years the sun was born and their ancestors left Aztlan in the distant past (as Townsend noted in the case of 13 Reed). This could not be a coincidence.

It is well-known that the Mexica reconceived (that is, "rewrote") history on occasion. The best documented example of this occurred after the Tepanec War in the reign of Itzcoatl, when they burned the old "books" and rewrote them (Sahagún 1950–82, 10:191). This history, which has come down to us in later versions, was an idealized, official history in which, I believe, the dates of events played an essential part. Several aspects of the Mexica's concept of history and use of dates are of interest here. In the first place, as López Austin (1973, 96–106) has pointed out, Mexica history is cyclical. Dates of the same name have certain associations; and particular types of events were expected, or made to happen, on these dates. One Rabbit, for example, was associated with famine; and whenever that date came around, the Aztecs prepared for bad times.

In addition, as I have demonstrated elsewhere (Umberger 1981a, 209–13; 1981b), the most important events of the past were assigned particular dates on the basis of their relative positions in the 52-year cycle, and the purpose of this schema of dates was to express the relationship between the cosmos and the state. In 1 Rabbit, the first year, the flooded earth was restored and the Fifth Era began; in 2 Reed, the second year, fire was created; in 1 Reed, the first year of the second quarter, the legendary Toltec king Topiltzin Quetzalcoatl was born (according to different sources, he also died or left Tula in 1 Reed 52 years later); in 13 Reed, the last year of the first half of the cycle, the sun was born; in 1 Flint, the first year of the second half, the Mexica left Aztlan; in 2 House, the next year, they founded Tenochtitlan; and finally in 1 House, the first year of the fourth quarter, some of their number moved to the island to the north and founded Tlatelolco, Tenochtitlan's twin city.[25]

Thus the dates of the most important events of cosmic and tribal history were placed at the junctures between the quarters of the cycle, and as the cycle progressed they recurred in a symbolically significant order. Although the actual events were separated in the histories by several cycles in some cases (and two events, the birth of the sun and Quetzalcoatl's activities, were actually in reverse order), the names of the years form this pattern within a single cycle. The departure from Aztlan actually occurred many years after the birth of the sun, but in the 52-year cycle 13 Reed and 1 Flint are two consecutive years. These two dates, in fact, have the most important positions, in the exact middle of the cycle, and divide it in half. The first half was the sunless, pre-Mexica half and the second, light half was under Mexica domination. In this way, the close relationship between the sun and the Mexica state (and Huitzilopochtli) was emphasized, and the Toltecs and Quetzalcoatl were placed in the time of "darkness."

Fig. 10.
Departure from Aztlan, *Codex Boturini*
(*Tira de la peregrinación*), fol. 1.
Mexico (Tenochtitlan), 1450s–1520s,
paper
Mexico City, Museo Nacional
de Antropología

Likewise in more recent history, the dates 13 Reed and 1 Flint marked the boundary between the periods of Tepanec and Mexica rule. For the Mexica the sun was a general metaphor for political power; and a change in leadership through death or conquest was compared to the darkening and reappearance of the sun.[26] Townsend's suggestion that the Calendar Stone links the birth of the sun with the beginning of Mexica rule is therefore appropriate in a general sense. It is not, however, the date 13 Reed that is specifically associated with the rise of the Mexica. Rather it is 1 Flint, the following year, a date related to warfare, conquest, and the empire.

The Mexica must have conceived of the conquest of Azcapotzalco as a second beginning, the realization of a destiny which had been born when they left their homeland long before. The *Historia de los mexicanos por sus pinturas* indicates how the departure from Aztlan was seen as similar to the later conquest: "... their count started with that first year when they set out, ... the year in which the Mexicans agreed to go in search of lands to conquer" ("Historia de los mexicanos por sus pinturas" 1973, 39; my translation). The *Crónica mexicáyotl* says likewise: "... when they came in search of lands, when they came to win lands, here to the great settlement of the city of Mexico Tenochtitlan, their place of fame, ..." (Alvarado Tezozómoc 1975b, 3, my translation). One could say then that the armies setting out from Tenochtitlan were like the ancestors leaving Aztlan in search of lands, in both cases under the guidance of Huitzilopochtli. With the achievement of independence, the Mexica were again following their destiny and 1 Flint was the symbol of that destiny.

In sum, the dates 13 Reed and 1 Flint, when they appear together, refer to linked events, the birth of the sun and the birth of the empire on which the sun depended for sacrifice and sustenance. According to myth (Sahagún 1950–82, 7:3–9), after the sun was born, it was very weak and could not move until the gods had sacrificed themselves. This was the example mankind was to follow and the Mexica were chosen to do so. Although 13 Reed is the featured date on the Calendar Stone, the proximity of the two dates was meant to recall the tie between them.

THE DAY SIGNS AND MEXICA CEREMONIES

The Calendar Stone must have been used on a number of different ceremonial occasions, probably on all the dates inscribed on it. Ceremonies are known to have occurred on the days 4 Movement, 1 Flint, and 1 Rain, and I would guess that there were also ceremonies on 13 Reed and 7 Monkey, although there is no direct evidence in the sources.

Four Movement is the day on which, Durán (1967, 1:105ff) tells us, the messenger to the sun was sacrificed at high noon. Thirteen Reed may also have been a ceremonial day in relation to the sun's birth. Caso notes (1927, 35–36) that 13 Reed must have been the day as well as the year of the sun's birth. The sun did not begin to move until 4 Movement, four days after its birth, and 4 Movement is four days after 13 Reed.

Interpretations can be suggested for the two glyphs below the Movement sign that complement those suggested for the two glyphs above. One Rain, below Motecuhzoma's name glyph, was the day on which sacrifices were made to increase the king's strength (Motecuhzoma, like the sun, apparently needed human sacrifice to renew him).[27]

> And then also at that time died those who were in jail, ... Also of the captives some then died.
>
> It was said that through these <Motecuhzoma> received life. By them his fate was strengthened; by them he was exalted, and on them he placed the burden. So it was said that

it was as if through them once more he were rejuvenated, so that he might live many years. Through them he became famous, achieved honor, and became brave, thereby making himself terrifying. (Sahagún 1950–82, 4:42)

Seven Monkey, below the 1 Flint date, was a day in the section of the day count beginning with 1 Snake, a special day for merchants and long distance travelers. War was declared on 1 Snake and armies and merchants (the forerunners of the army) set out for foreign parts on that day (Sahagún 1950–82, 4:59–60, 70). Seven Monkey was a propitious day (Sahagún 1950–82, 4:73–74) and may have had a significance similar to that of 1 Snake. If so, it would relate to the departure and conquest associations of 1 Flint.

1 FLINT AS A CEREMONIAL DAY

One Flint was an important ceremonial day as well as an important year in history. Seler (1960a, 798–99) discussed the date on the Calendar Stone as both a day and a year, and although he does not explain why, he was essentially correct in doing this. A number of dates were important as both days and years of related significance. For example, both the day 1 Rabbit and the year 1 Rabbit were associated with hunger and famine. The day 2 Reed was dedicated to Tezcatlipoca (Sahagún 1950–82, 4:56), the creator of fire, and the year 2 Reed was the New Fire year. One Flint, according to Sahagún (1950–82, 4:77–79), was the day when sacrifices were made to Huitzilopochtli. The significance of the day 1 Flint therefore is related to the events of the years of that name. In 1 Flint years Huitzilopochtli led the Mexica from Aztlan and later to victory over the Tepanecs. Beyer (1965d, 189–190) links the date 1 Flint on the Calendar Stone with Tezcatlipoca because of the smoking mirror attached to it. But the smoking mirror was also an attribute of Huitzilopochtli (no doubt appropriated from Tezcatlipoca), and is depicted as a head decoration on representations of the god (see fig. 8) as well as being attached to his date glyph.

Considered in relation to the other day signs on the Calendar Stone then, 1 Flint refers to the ceremonial day of Huitzilopochtli.

1 FLINT AS THE CALENDRIC NAME OF HUITZILOPOCHTLI

Although I do not know of any place where Huitzilopochtli is actually called Ce Tecpatl (1 Flint), he was said to have been born in 1 Flint (Alvarado Tezozómoc 1975b, 36), and 1 Flint should be considered his calendric name (Caso 1967, 197). And it seems logical to interpret 1 Flint as Huitzilopochtli's name in relation to the name glyph of Motecuhzoma, which it faces above the sun disc on the Calendar Stone. The god and the king likewise face each other over the sun disc on the Temple of Sacred Warfare (see fig. 8). In addition, the pairing of a king accompanied by a name glyph and a deity accompanied by a calendric name occurs on the Hackmack Box (see fig. 6a, b). (On the Temple, 1 Flint is actually on the side of the pyramid next to the figure of the god).

There is an interesting passage in Motolinía's *Memoriales* that may allude to the Calendar Stone and the connection between Motecuhzoma and Huitzilopochtli that is expressed in its iconography. "Panquetzalistle <Panquetzaliztli>. This feast was the birth of Uichilobos <Huitzilopochtli>…, and one <prisoner taken in war> they dressed in blue and painted the face blue with two yellow stripes and they killed him on the stone of Mutizuma <Motecuhzoma>,…" (Motolinía 1971, 53, my translation).

In summary then, 1 Flint was a special date with multiple meanings in Mexica thought, and in the composition of the Calendar Stone these various meanings are expressed in its relationship to the other glyphs around it. In relation to 13 Reed, 1 Flint refers to important years in myth and recent history. In relation to the days of Mexica ceremony, it is the ceremonial day of the tribal god Huitzilopochtli. And in relation to the glyph of Motecuhzoma which faces it, 1 Flint probably represents the calendric name of Huitzilopochtli. As a special glyph with multiple meanings it does not require a cartouche. In fact, 1 Flint is not framed on any Aztec sculpture known to me.

THE DATE OF THE CALENDAR STONE'S CREATION

One set of parallel passages in the *Crónica X* accounts describe a sacrificial stone from the time of Motecuhzoma I that may have had some of the same hieroglyphs on it as the Calendar Stone. After the conquest of the Huastec area in the 1450s, the king had a great stone *temalacatl* carved to commemorate the events of the Tepanec War. According to Durán:

> Tlacaelel <the prime minister> then reminded King <Motecuhzoma> of the work on the temple, …and said that it was necessary to carve a wide stone to serve as an altar or table upon which sacrifice would be made…and that in its carvings appear the war of liberation of their forebears from Azcapotzalco, so that this war might be given perpetual memory. (Durán 1967, 2:171; translation, Durán 1964, 109–110)

In Alvarado Tezozómoc's version, Motecuhzoma proposed a *tajón* (sacrificial stone),

> …on which were to be killed the slaves taken in war and in memory of the king Chimalpopoca, who began what would be a just cause. Cihuacoatl Tlacaeleltzin answered that he well agreed, and that the *tajón* would not be made of wood but a round stone hollowed in the center for the hearts…, and that this stone would not be carved by the Huastecs but by Azcapotzalcas and Coyoacanos <other Tepanecs>, excellent stone workers, carving on the stone the war of their own towns when they were conquered and killed and subjugated to this our Mexican rule. (Alvarado Tezozómoc 1975a, 318–319, my translation)

The hieroglyphs on the Calendar Stone could refer both to these events and to the name of the ruler, but this was probably not the monument carved in the time of Motecuhzoma I. Because of its elaboration and the complexity of its inscriptions, it would be difficult to date it to the 1450s, thirty years before the Stone of Tizoc, as Beyer (1965a, 264) noted. I believe, in fact, that all eight sculptures with the Motecuhzoma name glyph relate in style to sculptures dating from around 1500, late in the reign of Ahuitzotl,[28] rather than to earlier pieces like the Stone of Tizoc (1481–86) and the Dedication Stone (1487). The Stone of Motecuhzoma I, as described by the *Crónica X* sources, was more likely to have included explicit scenes of capture like those on the Stone of Tizoc and the rock carving at Peñon de los Baños. (The date 1 Flint below a conquest scene on the latter probably refers to the defeat of the Tepanecs).[29]

Originally it bothered me to attribute the Calendar Stone to a king in whose reign the featured date, 13 Reed, did not occur. Often one date on a monument commemorates a contemporary event or the anniversary of an event. However, according to the *Crónica X* passages, Motecuhzoma I's *temalacatl* commemorated the Tepanec War, although the anniversary of that event did not fall in his reign. In fact, although it appears that every king created a stone of the sun, only one, that of Axayacatl, could have commemorated the anniversary of the beginning of the war or the birth of the sun (in 13 Reed 1479 and 1 Flint 1480). In conclusion, it would be preferable to attribute the Calendar Stone to the reign of one of the Motecuhzomas on the basis of the hieroglyphic name than to the reign of Axayacatl on the basis of the date. Because of the late style of the monument, I feel that it should be dated to the time of Motecuhzoma II and seen as a descendant of the stones of the earlier rulers.

Notes

1. This is an expanded version of a paper entitled "Myth, History, and the Calendar Stone," which was delivered at the XLIII International Congress of Americanists, University of British Columbia/Simon Fraser University, Vancouver, British Columbia, in August 1979. I have profited greatly from the advice and criticism of Betty Brown, Diana Fane, Cecelia Klein, H. B. Nicholson, and Esther Pasztory. I am also grateful for the following research support: A Rudolf Wittkower Fellowship from the Department of Art History and Archaeology, Columbia University, 1978–79, and a Faculty Grant-in-Aid from Arizona State University, 1984.

2. Proskouriakoff (1968) suggested that the elements of Maya hieroglyphic writing be called "graphemes," units of form of unknown meaning, until their meaning is known, in which case they become "signs" (see also Nicholson 1973c, 2n4). In the case of Aztec writing, one might add that a grapheme's meaning can vary according to context and that a sign is a grapheme whose meaning is known in a particular context. The headdress glyph is a grapheme with various meanings in Colonial period manuscripts. However, as I will demonstrate, on preconquest stone sculptures, it is always the name sign of Motecuhzoma.

3. See Beyer 1955b; and Nicholson 1955.

4. See Beyer 1965d, 137–48; Seler 1960c.

5. The *Crónica X* sources describe several of the other great stones, but the descriptions seem not to come from the original oral tradition but rather are descriptions of the Stone of Tizoc and the Calendar Stone, both of which were visible for years after the Conquest.

6. The generally accepted dates of the reigns of Mexica rulers from Chimalpopoca on were proposed by Orozco y Berra (1975, 151–222) in his 1878 comparative study of the lengths of reigns in various written and pictorial sources. He (Orozco y Berra 1975, 204–5) found that part 1 of the *Codex Mendoza* (the historical section) is the source that comes closest to what he (passim) implies was the official version of Mexica history after the foundation of Tenochtitlan.

7. See also Alvarado Tezozómoc 1975a, 662ff.

8. In the first scholarly study of the Calendar Stone, León y Gama (1832, pt. 1:91ff) suggested that the monument was set up vertically and served as a sort of sun dial. It is, however, more commonly believed that the Calendar Stone was a sacrificial stone and that it was set horizontally on a low platform or pyramid, as Chavero first suggested in 1875 (1–5). See Orozco y Berra 1880, 1:176–81; Seler 1960a, 797; Beyer 1965d, 143; Alcocer 1935, 40; Navarrete and Heyden 1974, 3/3–/4; and Townsend 1979, 69.

9. See Wicke 1976.

10. The identity of the central face has been the subject of controversy in recent years. Formerly it was identified as Tonatiuh, the day sun. Because it has some characteristics associated with the earth monster (e.g., the clawed hands and flint knife tongue), Navarrete and Heyden (1974) and Townsend (1979) believe it is the face of the earth, Tlaltecuhtli; Klein (1976b) argues that it is the dead night sun in the earth and underworld.

11. A calendric name was supposedly the date of one's birth, but it could be a more propitious date a few days later (Soustelle 1975, 112). The fifth sun's calendric name, 4 Movement, is associated with both its beginning and end. According to the "Leyenda de los soles" (*Codex Chimalpopoca* 1975, 119–21), the four previous suns ended on the days of their names (e.g., the 4 Water sun ended on the day 4 Water). From this it has been assumed that the 4 Movement sun would end on the day 4 Movement, although it is not stated. Caso (1927, 35–36) connects the date also with the beginning of the sun's existence. He quotes Muñoz Camargo's (1892, 132) statement that after the sun was created, it did not move until 4 Movement four days later. Soustelle (1975, 95–96) summarizes the relationship between the fifth sun and the date 4 Movement: "Each of these 'suns' is shown on monuments…by a date, a date which is that of its end and which evokes the nature of the catastrophe which ended it.…Our world will have the same fate: its destiny is fixed by the date which has, as one might say, branded it at birth—the date *naui ollin* (4 Movement), at which our sun first began to move. The glyph *ollin*…which shares the center of the Aztec calendar with the sun god's visage, has the double sense of 'movement' and 'earthquake.' It symbolizes both the first motion of the heavenly body when our age began and the cataclysms that will destroy our earth."

12. A year bearer was the day which gave its name to the year. The location of this day within the year is uncertain (see Broda de Casas 1969, 35–36).

13. Although 1 Rabbit was the numerical leader of the years, 2 Reed was the year of the New Fire Ceremony, which initiated the new cycle (see Umberger 1987b, appendix).

14. It is generally thought that the purpose of the cartouche was to distinguish years from days in Aztec inscriptions (Caso 1927, 13). This is a rule that was not strictly observed, however. Dates in a true cartouche (a square frame with unbroken lines) are usually year bearers, but there are a few day names in cartouches, and conversely dates which one would expect to refer to years are not always in cartouches. Two stone year bundles have the day sign 1 Death on the front in a cartouche (Caso 1967, 139, fig. 11, illustrates one), but on another year bundle the same date is unframed (Historisches Museum Frankfurt am Main 1960, no. 189, pl. 24). Unframed dates that must represent years include the most important dates in Mexica history, like 1 Rabbit and 2 Reed. On the Temple of Sacred Warfare these two dates in cartouches on the front (Townsend 1979, fig. 22b) signify the first two years of the Fifth Era of time and also the first two years of the 52-year cycle. The same two dates on the Acacingo Cliff relief (Krickeberg 1969, figs. 79, 80) are unframed.

Another interesting example of the same date in the same context, but with different framing, is the 12 Reed date above the skull on the back of both the great Coatlicue and the Yolotlicue (Umberger 1981a, fig. 28A <c and d>, a pair of sculptures that belonged to a "set" (Boone 1973). On the Coatlicue the date is unframed, whereas on the Yolotlicue it is in a cartouche. Does this signify that 12 Reed was important as both a day and a year? It is apparent in yet other inscriptions that a single date was meant to refer to both a day and a year. For instance, on one well-known year bundle with three dates (Seler 1960a, 877–79, fig. 77) 2 Reed in a cartouche on the front probably refers to both the year 2 Reed and to the day 2 Reed, judging by its relationship to the day signs on either end of the bundle (see Umberger 1981a, 122–24).

On a number of Aztec sculptures in the late fifteenth- and early sixteenth-century style, framing, composition, and elaboration seem to be very carefully used to differentiate between glyphs. On the Calendar Stone, for instance, distinctions are made between the 13 Reed year date with its true cartouche and the day signs, where framing is with broken lines.

In conclusion, despite some obvious exceptions, a date in a cartouche should be considered as referring to a year. However, a number of dates which encompass several meanings may or may not have a cartouche. One Flint is the most important date of this type. See also Nicholson (1966) and Caso (1967, 166–86) on year signs in Central Mexico.

15. See also Seler 1960d, 731–38, where he develops this argument.

16. See Nicholson (1973c, 7), who lists all but two of these sculptures.

17. See Seler 1960b.

18. The picture in Durán is supposedly of Motecuhzoma I posing for his portrait, but the sculpture at Chapultepec is of Motecuhzoma II.

19. Other Mexica sculptures feature this composition, including the Stone of the Warriors and the Bench Relief (both in the National Museum of Mexico and published by Beyer <1955a>). Both have processions of warriors with the leaders facing each other over a grass ball. This part of the Stone of the Warriors is badly damaged (all that is visible are the faces of the two figures and the top of the grass ball). On the Bench Relief, however, the ruler wears a crown and the smoking mirror of Tezcatlipoca at the temple and replacing one foot. There is no name glyph, but this is probably because the sculpture is earlier in date than the reliefs in which rulers are named. Beyer (1955a, 37) thought the ruler on the Bench Relief might have been Itzcoatl. The recent excavations at the Templo Mayor (Great Temple of Tenochtitlan) tend to confirm this identification. The level where the reliefs were discovered in 1913–14 is now designated as Phase III, which is associated with the date 4 Reed (1431) and was covered by Phase IV, which is associated with the date 1 Rabbit (1454) (Matos Moctezuma 1981b). This gives a rough estimate of the date of the Bench Relief as between 1431 and 1454; Itzcoatl ruled from 1427 to 1440.

20. Although the figure is in the Teotihuacan style, the dates are certainly Postclassic. The flint knife could be either Mixtec or Aztec, but the Reed date is more in the Mixtec mode, representing two full-length arrows. The usual Aztec Reed date consists of a single arrow shaft framed by leaves and set into a U-shaped vase (seen in section). There exist, however, two late Aztec-style sculptures with Reed dates formed by arrows (Caso 1967, 68, fig. 20; Nicholson 1955, 114–15, and fig. 3).

The Mexica did on occasion imitate foreign and archaic styles. A good example of the use of an archaic style in a date inscription is on the bottom of several *xiuhcoatl* (fire serpent) sculptures, where the frame of the 2 Reed date is in the style of Xochicalco (Nicholson 1971a, 120, and fig. 32). Nor is the recarving of an ancient object by the Aztecs unknown. An Olmec bib-head pendant, now set into an eighteenth-century European "niche" in the Schatzkammer der Residenz München, is thought to have been recarved in the cheek and mouth areas by an Aztec artist (Easby and Scott 1970, no. 307). A number of ancient objects in Teotihuacan, Toltec, and even Olmec styles have been discovered in the recent Templo Mayor excavations (Matos Moctezuma 1981a, nos. 11, 12, 37, 90), as well as an archaizing Mexica sculpture carved in imitation of a type popular in Teotihuacan times (Matos Moctezuma 1981a, no. 95) and Mixtec and Guerrero objects. All of these examples provide evidence of the Mexica's interest in the art of their predecessors and non-Aztec contemporaries, both in the collection of the actual objects and in the making of imitations.

The Teotihuacan figure was probably recarved in late Aztec times; the inscription certainly reflects Central Mexican rather than Mixtec concerns. And although the two dates were probably associated and had similar symbolic significance in pre-Aztec times, to my knowledge speech scrolls are appended to dates only on Aztec sculptures.

21. The other two dates on this stela also relate to the Calendar Stone. They are 1 Crocodile and 13 Flower, the first and last days of the 260-day count. On the Calendar Stone the day names Crocodile through Flower are in a ring around the central area. In both, the dates encompass the whole count, or all time. Like the inscription on the Teotihuacan figurine, these glyphs are in a variant style, here a local Veracruz-Aztec style. As Seler first suggested. 13 Reed and 1 Flint refer to the birth of the sun and the birth of the Mexica empire. The inscription of these dates on the Teotihuacan figure is appropriate because, according to myth, the sun was born at Teotihuacan, and on the Castillo stela because Castillo de Teayo was in conquered territory.

It is curious that these inscriptions are in variant styles. Perhaps the point was to make captured peoples inscribe the symbols that justified their conquest. We know from Durán and Alvarado Tezozómoc that the Tepanecs were made to carve a monument celebrating their own defeat, which, by the way, could also have featured the dates 13 Reed and 1 Flint, the years at the beginning of the Tepanec war, or at least 1 Flint, the date of the overthrow of Azcapotzalco (see quote from Durán and Alvarado Tezozómoc in the last section of this paper).

H. B. Nicholson (personal communication) has called my attention to two other objects with the dates 13 Reed and 1 Flint: two boxes discovered at an archaeological site on a hill near Tolcayuca, Hidalgo (published by Cossío 1942, 23–28, figs. 8, 11–14), one with 1 Flint on the lid and the other with 13 Reed on the side. These are even more unusual carvings than the Hamburg figure and the Castillo stela. The 1 Flint date is presented frontally (!), and the numeral of the 13 Reed date is formed by two bars and three dots (Aztec numerals usually do not have bars). (The published photographs are so indistinct that it is difficult to say anything further about the inscriptions). The context of the boxes is unclear, because archaeologists were not called to the site until after local people had excavated the objects. The 1 Flint box was found in a burial, but the original location of the 13 Reed box is not known. Eduardo Noguera's analysis of the ceramics associated with the finds revealed mostly Toltec-period wares and a lesser number of early Aztec ceramics (Aztec II) (Cossío 1942, 33–34), so it is probable that the boxes are pre-Mexica. I would suggest that, given the dates on them, they should be seen as a pair.

22. See Umberger 1981b on the use of dates in Mexica history.

23. See Elzey 1976 and Moreno de los Arcos 1967 on the myth of the suns.

24. According to Davies (1973, 159, and table A, facing 210), the official account of Tenochtitlan's history seems to have put the death of Chimalpopoca in 13 Reed (1427), the accession of Itzcoatl in 1427 or 1428, and the defeat of Azcapotzalco in 1 Flint (1428). The sources of these dates are: Chimalpahin's Third, Sixth, and Seventh Relations; the *Crónica mexicayotl*; the *Codex Mendoza*; the *Anales de Tlatelolco II* (Berlin-Neubart and Barlow 1948); and others.

25. The dates given here for the important events of Mexica history are those that are given most often in the sixteenth-century annals. The suggested schema exists almost *in toto* in several sources. No single annal gives every date, due to omissions and what are probably errors, but two come close to giving the whole schema (the *Historia de los mexicanos por sus pinturas* and the *Leyenda de los soles*), and three others which start at the departure from Aztlan give the schema pretty much date for date after that point. These are: Chimalpahin's Third Relation; the *Crónica mexicayotl* (Alvarado Tezozómoc 1975b), which was also written in part (perhaps mainly) by Chimalpahin (Gibson and Glass 1975, 346); and the *Anales de Tlatelolco* (see Umberger 1981a, 211–13).

26. See Umberger 1987b.

27. One Rain also appears on the side of a stela fragment representing the lower body of a standing man (ruler?) in the Philadelphia Museum of Art (Kubler 1954, no. 50). It is associated with the solar disc on a sacrificial vessel in the British Museum (Joyce 1912, pl. 2b).

28. In my dissertation (Umberger 1981a), I deal with the dating of a number of sculptures to events late in Ahuitzotl's reign (the flood of 1499, ceremonies to stop the flood in 1500, and the death of Ahuitzotl in 1502) and their stylistic similarities to a number of the Motecuhzoma monuments, which should therefore be dated to the reign of Motecuhzoma II (1502–20).

29. [The *cuauhxicalli* of Motecuhzoma I was discovered in 1988. As Umberger predicted, it features scenes of conquest, like the Stone of Tizoc.]

"The *Stone of the Sun*" (1992)

Editors' Commentary

Since the late 1970s, Michel Graulich, a professor at the Université libre de Bruxelles, has been a prolific author on many aspects of ancient Mexico, writing major works on mythology (1997a), festivals, rites (1999), and human sacrifice (2005). In the article below, and in another, later work (1997b), Graulich argues that the central face on the Calendar Stone *represents the god Xochipilli, or the sun at midday, at the moment when it is between the rising eagle sun and the setting jaguar sun. He makes the case that those who believe the* Calendar Stone *represents either the day sun or the night sun are in error because the ancient Mexican day began at midnight, not at dawn, and ended at noon, rather than at sunset. Accordingly, the key moments of the day were midnight and midday, rather than dawn and dusk. Graulich also reasons that the order of the suns on the monument expresses Aztec imperial ideology, since the Aztecs changed the order of the eras and added a fifth sun.*

✳   ✳   ✳

"*The* Stone of the Sun"

…The work represents the sun in its diverse aspects in Mexica thought: as the heavenly body that marks time and defines space, as that which realizes the union of opposites, as that which constitutes the afterworld of the glorious dead, as that which requires blood and human hearts to continue to move, and naturally, as the star that drives away the darkness by casting its rays.

In the first place, the sun marks and divides time. It defines and constitutes the day and the year, as well as the other main divisions of time that are shown on the monument: the "month" of twenty days in the third ring from the inside and the "century" of fifty-two years represented by the forty quincunxes, to which should be added thirteen others that are hidden behind the sun rays with volutes [sic, 40+13=53]. The quincunx was the glyph for turquoise, *xihuitl* (Seler 1902–23, 1:191), and a word that also refers to the year. In the *Codex Borbonicus,* similar glyphs mark the braziers and also the priests and temple of the New Fire lit at the end of a fifty-two-year cycle. With respect to the ages or suns, for most Mesoamericans the present age was the fourth. Its calendrical name was 4 Jaguar and would end when these beasts would descend to devour the humans. The preceding ages, 4 Water, 4 Wind, and 4 Rain [of fire], were named according to the kind of cataclysm that destroyed them. After they seized power in the central highlands, the Aztecs changed the order of the suns and introduced a fifth sun, named 4 Movement.

Excerpted and translated by Khristaan D. Villela from Michel Graulich, "La *Piedra del Sol*," in José Alcina Franch, Miguel León-Portilla, and Eduardo Matos Moctezuma, eds., *Azteca-mexica: Las culturas del México antiguo* (Madrid: Lunwerg, 1992), 291–95. Published with permission. Introductory text by Khristaan D. Villela and Matthew H. Robb.

The days, the years, the cycle of fifty-two years, and the suns: the divisions of time generated by the sun are thus clearly illustrated and announce the new doctrine of the Aztecs: the four past suns are situated around the face of the present sun and in the new Aztec order, beginning with Jaguar; furthermore, they are framed by the glyph of the Fifth Sun, of the age of synthesis, and of the "fifth element" (4 Movement).

The image of the sun god is also an image of synthesis. Its identity is disputed: some feel this face should be identified as that of Tonatiuh, the personification of the sun. However, certain similarities with images of Tlalteotl, goddess of the earth and of death, have led various researchers to identify it rather with her, or with the night sun, related to Tlaloc, the male aspect of the earth (Navarrete and Heyden 1974; Klein 1977, 1980).[1] But this interpretation as a "night sun" is unsupportable: the traditional view that opposes the day sun (east-zenith-west) with the jaguar or night sun is incompatible with Mesoamerican beliefs about the sun. According to these beliefs, a vertical dividing line sets the rising eagle sun (from midnight to midday) in opposition to the descending jaguar sun. In the myths, the sun is born at midnight and the night is born at midday. Mesoamericans believed that the true sun appeared only during the morning hours. Once the zenith was reached, it returned to the east, and what was seen after this time was only the light of the sun, or, better, its reflection in a (black) obsidian mirror. This mirror was the same as at night for the moon at zenith [*similar a la noche y a la luna cenicienta*], which also received its light from the sun. What was seen in the afternoon, the light of the sun in a mirror, was a false sun, a lunar sun, a heavenly body that united night (the black mirror) and day, the masculine sun and feminine moon, the sun of the union of opposites. This is why the western sun is represented in the codices partly as the earth god Tlaloc (e.g., *Codex Telleriano Remensis* 1899, fol. 20r). This also explains why it was the dead heroic warriors who accompanied the true sun from the east to midday, while women who died in childbirth and were deified, the warrior women, male and female at the same time, accompanied the reflected sun (Graulich 1990, 77–78).

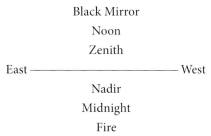

Black Mirror

Noon

Zenith

East ———————————————— West

Nadir

Midnight

Fire

Thus the key moments were midnight, when the sun was reborn, as in mythic times, and midday, when the black mirror—the night—appeared and when a false lunar and earthly sun replaced the true sun.

Now the identity of the central face of the *Piedra del Sol* is obvious: it is the meridian sun, or of the union of opposites, also called Xochipilli, "Prince of Flowers," because in the afternoon the dead warriors transformed into birds and butterflies that drank the nectar of flowers in the solar-lunar paradise of Tlaloc (Sahagún 1950–82, 6:13; Graulich 1990). Certain elements refer to his solar aspect: the location at the center of the disk, the typical curved lines that surround his eyes, the tubular jade bead in his septum. Other features point to a connection with the night, the earth, and death: the defleshed mouth, with the tongue protruding and transformed into a sacrificial knife, the claws rendered as faces by means of an eye, and the green stone jewels. Skulls with flint blades in the mouth and nose have been discovered in various offerings, and they also appear like this in the codices. They symbolize death and rebirth, since the flint contains a spark and the spark is life (Sahagún 1950–82, 6:175, 183, 201). Moreover, in Mesoamerican thought the flint is equivalent to bones on account of its appearance and because of its relation to death, and human bones are thought of as seeds, like the pits of fruits. The two are interchangeable. According to a myth, humans were created from crushed bones (in a variant [account], from crushed maize kernels).

The claws-faces with hearts are characteristic of earth goddesses. Tlalteotl was described as a savage beast "full of eyes and mouths at all of her joints," who "refused to bear fruit unless she was watered with blood" and fed with human hearts ("Histoyre du Méchique" 1965, 108). On the other hand, the sun also required blood and hearts to follow its path, which explains the blood around the disk....

The image of the solar disk also represents the union of opposites. Eight sun rays alternate with eight jade pendants. The *chalchihuitl* was considered to be a substance that attracted moisture and also as the flesh and spirit of the Tlaloque. Fire and jade were opposed like sky and earth, or like conquerors and conquered (Sahagún 1950–82, 11:223, 69; Graulich 1990; 1988, 10).

This is because the rays refer to the eastern sun, the true sun of the morning, and the jade pendants to the western sun, for which reason there is a sun ray above the central face, that is, in the east, and a *chalchihuitl* pendant beneath it, that is, in the west. The upper half of the stone thus corresponds to the east and the lower to the west. For the Aztecs, the east was the direction of beginnings, and in iconography it is always placed in the upper position. Consequently, the glyph 13 Reed, the year of the birth of the sun and of the present age, is located in the upper half. The glyphs that flank the central ray, between the 4 Jaguar and 4 Wind suns, are also related to the east and to beginnings. On the right, we have the date 1 Tecpatl or Flint. We already know that flint represents the spark of life, the seed and thus the absolute beginning. It was in a year 1 Flint that a celestial flint fertilized the earth and that the Aztecs left (were born from) Aztlan (Mendieta 1945, 1:83; Graulich 1990, 117–18). It was also in 1 Flint that the first Toltec king was enthroned, also the first Aztec king, and the first rulers of Cuauhtitlan (Davies 1973, 209). The Aztec empire was actually born, according to the information in the codices, in a like-named year. Finally, 1 Tecpatl was the birthday of Huitzilopochtli, the (rising) sun god of the Mexicas.

Between the east and midday is found a very important afterworld, the House of the Sun, where the dead heroes went to accompany the sun in its ascent. This primary aspect of the sun was not forgotten on the most important monument dedicated to it. On the other side of the central sun ray, to the left of 1 Flint, we find hair with the *xiuhuitzolli* crown and eagle feathers, a nosepiece, and a pectoral shaped like a stylized butterfly. These emblems surely refer to the heroic dead (Seler 1902–23, 2:683, 736). The eagle feathers were a characteristic attribute of warriors, and the butterfly pectoral belonged to the prototypical warriors referenced in the myths, the Mimixcoa.

If the upper part refers to the east, to the birth of the sun and to beginnings, and the central part to midday, when the lunar sun replaced the authentic sun, the lower part must be related to the west and to the women who died in childbirth. First we see the glyphs that flank the jade pendant beneath the central face: 1 Rain and 7 Monkey. "1 Rain" is the calendrical name of the "divine women" who died in childbirth and of the old woman goddess Ilamatecuhtli (Caso 1967, 198). It was also on this day that they made sacrifices to strengthen the power of the rulers; a kingdom was comparable to a day, and it was the sun and the king in decline who were most in need of this kind of sacrifice to be "rejuvenated" (Sahagún 1950–82, 4:42; Umberger 1981a, 204). Once again, we note the connection to the afternoon and the west.

We lack specific information about the date 7 Monkey. Although we must be satisfied with exploring the connotations of the day Monkey in general, we will see that they perfectly confirm the suggested hypothesis. Accordingly, all the deities who have this calendrical name are associated with the afternoon: one of the divine women was called 1 Monkey; Chalchiuhtlicue, the goddess of water, or Chicomecoatl, the goddess of maize germination, 3 Monkey; the moon god, 6 and 8 Monkey; the warrior goddess Itzpapalotl, 9 Monkey; and Huehuecóyotl, god of sexuality, music, and dance, 12 Monkey. The evening star was also related to the monkey (Caso 1967, 194–95; Seler 1902–23, 3:392; Thompson 1970, 361). Additionally, in metaphorical terms, the monkey was closely associated with the afternoon. The relationship between the lunar sun and the true sun was comparable to the relationship between the monkey and the human: the monkey and the lunar sun are both false reflections. The monkey was closely related to Xochipilli, the afternoon sun, and the most famous statue of the god shows him with a mask of this animal (Graulich 1979, 700–709). In his aspect as the deity of flowers, of music, and of dance, Xochipilli also has much in common with monkeys, who are often depicted singing and dancing.

Two fire serpents facing downward surround the image of the sun, which confirms the sense of the reading of the monument. We have already seen that *xiuhcoatl* means "turquoise serpent" (the fire god was called "Lord of Turquoise") or "Year Serpent" and that its body is covered with fire-butterflies and by flames. They also have on their nose a curved appendage decorated with star-eyes that represents the constellation *xonecuilli*. Their symbolism relates them to the year, the fire, the sky, and the stars. More precisely, they ought to represent the night sky or one of its aspects. The celestial fires represented by the butterflies may correspond to the stars, described in one myth as lit by the god Tezcatlipoca ("Historia de los mexicanos por sus pinturas" 1965, 33), who is sometimes represented in sculpture as a fire serpent. The flames on the back would be comets. According to the "Historia de los mexicanos" (1965, 69), the fire serpents lived in the fifth sky and from them "came the comets and other celestial omens." The nocturnal character of the creature is confirmed by two details taken respectively from the myths and rituals: it was at night that Huitzilopochtli vanquished his enemies with the xiuhcoatl weapon, and the making of new fire at midnight every fifty-two years was called "the descent of the fire serpent" (*Codex Azcatitlan* 1949, pl. 6).

In the lower part of the *Piedra del Sol,* the serpent heads meet and swallow the face of the sun, Tonatiuh, and that of the fire god, Xiuhtecuhtli. Here they symbolize the starry night sky and the place of the night earth where the sun sinks upon setting and where it transforms until the point where it merges with the fire god (Graulich 1988).

In conclusion, the *Piedra del Sol* thus represents this heavenly body in an exhaustive manner, since the image of the deity had to be both effective and functional. The sun appears as the god that [both] is and creates the days (and their divisions of morning, midday, and afternoon), the years, and the suns or eras of the world. It emphasizes the concept of the fifth sun as the synthesis of the previous eras. The heavenly body is that of midday, the sun of the union of opposites, and for this reason his face is partly solar and partly earthly and skeletonized, while on the disk solar rays alternate with *chalchihuites* of Tlaloc.

The sun also demarcates the cardinal points and, from those, all of space. The upper part of the monument corresponds to the east, the face to the center, and the lower part to the west.

And the sun is space: during the morning, the House of the Sun of the heroic warriors, and in the afternoon, the sun accompanied by the women who died in childbirth, and, in its lunar aspect, the paradise of Tlaloc, located on the moon.

The sun is that which illuminates and drives away the darkness, represented by the fire serpents and by the celestial band on the profile, but they also swallow it. And finally, the sun must be fed, and consequently and for this reason, it has hearts in its claws and is surrounded by blood.

Note
1. See also Townsend 1979, 67; and Pasztory 1983, 170.

H. B. NICHOLSON

"The Problem of the Identification of the Central Image of the *Aztec Calendar Stone*" (1993)

Editors' Commentary

H. B. Nicholson (1925–2007), a longtime professor of anthropology at the University of California at Los Angeles, was the "dean of Aztec studies" since the late 1950s. His interests in the Aztec and other peoples of central Mexico covered subjects as broad as history, ethnohistory, iconography, Nahuatl-language sources, and the study of pictorial manuscripts. Like Eduard Seler, about whom he wrote (1973a), Nicholson mastered both the Mexican codices and the imagery of Aztec monuments. He published one of his first articles on Aztec iconography in 1955 in El México antiguo, *the same journal that would later reprint Hermann Beyer's work on the* Calendar Stone *(1965a–g). In addition to authoring two important works on Topiltzin Quetzalcoatl (1957, 2001), Nicholson wrote or edited books and essays on the Chapultepec cliff carving (1959), the Mixteca-Puebla style (Nicholson and Quiñones Keber 1994), and the religion and the iconography of Aztec Mexico (1971a, 1971b, 1973b), as well as another short contribution on the* Calendar Stone *(1996). Nicholson tried to visit every Aztec archaeological site and familiarize himself with every Aztec object in both public and private collections, an interest that is clear from his curatorial activities, especially his exhibition of 1983,* Art of Aztec Mexico, *organized with Eloise Quiñones Keber at the National Gallery of Art, Washington, D.C. In the article below, which appeared in Nicholson's Festschrift (Cordy-Collins and Sharon, eds., 1993), he argues that in spite of the arguments of Carlos Navarrete, Doris Heyden, Cecelia Klein, Ariane Fradcourt, and others, the central face on the* Calendar Stone *represents the Aztec sun god Tonatiuh.*

*   *   *

"The Problem of the Identification of the Central Image of the *Aztec* Calendar Stone"

Pluralites non est ponenda sine necessitate.[1]

...After careful consideration of these various recent suggestions for rejecting or significantly altering the traditional identification of the central image of the Calendar Stone as the *en face* visage of the diurnal sun deity, Tonatiuh, I find none of them very convincing.[2] In my view, Hermann Beyer presented a very cogent case for the Tonatiuh identification, certainly the best that had been presented up to that time—and I believe it can be even further strengthened. In his Figure 36 (see p. 127, fig. 17), Beyer provided a line drawing of his reconstruction of the central image, with

Excerpted from H. B. Nicholson, "The Problem of the Identification of the Central Image of the *Aztec Calendar Stone*," in Alana Cordy-Collins and Douglas Sharon, eds., *Current Topics in Aztec Studies: Essays in Honor of Dr. H. B. Nicholson* (San Diego: San Diego Museum of Man, 1993), 3–15. Published with permission. Introductory text by Khristaan D. Villela and Matthew H. Robb.

Fig. 1.
Aztec Calendar Stone, drawing by
Raúl Noriega, 1954

hatchings to indicate the original coloration, which I reproduce in Figure 3 (cf. front cover [of Cordy-Collins and Sharon, eds., 1993], the version of Sieck Flandes [1942], who largely followed Beyer) (see pl. 15). In spite of the post-Conquest mutilation of the central portion of the image, Beyer's reconstruction can be accepted for the most part. The nose bar, although largely effaced, seems highly probable, and the only significant question concerns the possibility of a horizontal line at the level of this nasal ornament. Beyer omitted it, while some subsequent reconstructions (e.g., see pl. 15; and fig. 1, which also appears as the frontispiece to Noriega 1954) have included it. If present, it would have divided the face into two separate chromatic fields, of which more below.

The most significant features of this visage are: a headband studded with three "jewels" of precious greenstone, *chalchihuitl,* the central one of the more complex pendant type and the two flanking ones of the simpler circle-within-circle type; double curving bands that flank the eyes; the hair indicated by five parallel strands on each side; a long nose bar tipped with the typical *chalchihuitl* edging motifs; circle-within-circle ear spools with *chalchihuitl* pendants issuing from their centers; open mouth with prominent teeth and with a protruding stone sacrificial knife, *tecpatl,* decorated with the usual "demon face," serving as a tongue; and a necklace of alternating globular and lozenge-shaped precious greenstone beads.

Most of these features are typical and diagnostic of the solar deities in Aztec iconography, as Beyer demonstrated by illustrations from the pictorials—and which could be substantially expanded (e.g., figs. 2–4; see p. 126, fig. 16; p. 128, fig. 18; p. 129, fig. 21).

Fig. 2.
Tonatiuh, one of two deity patrons (with Mictlantecuhtli) of the tenth *trecena,* commencing 1 Tecpatl (Stone Knife), of the 260-day divinatory cycle, *tonalpohualli, Codex Borbonicus,* fol. 10 (detail)
Central Mexico, sixteenth century, probably ca. 1521, watercolor on deerhide
Paris, Bibliothèque de l'Assemblée nationale

Fig. 3.
Ceramic plaque with representation
of Tonatiuh
Ca. 1500, terra-cotta, 13.2 × 13.1 × 1 cm
(5⅕ × 5⅕ × ⅔ in.)
Lyon, Musée des Confluences

Fig. 4.
Tonatiuh, fourth of the Thirteen Lords,
patrons of successive *tonalpohualli* days,
with quail, fourth of the Thirteen Sacred
Birds, *Codex Borbonicus,* fol. 6 (detail)
Central Mexico, sixteenth century,
probably ca. 1521, watercolor on deerhide
Paris, Bibliothèque de l'Assemblée
nationale

Perhaps the most unusual element is the "stone knife tongue." As Beyer recognized . . . this is a common feature on sculptures of coiled feathered serpents and, in pictorials, skulls. It is standard on the gape-jawed earth monster images (often multiple, e.g., Seler 1902–23, 2:735, fig. 25), as well as on those with the *en face* visage of the earth/fertility goddess (see p. 189, fig. 7). Those who prefer the Tlaltecuhtli identification, beginning with Navarrete and Heyden, stress the similarity in appearance of the Calendar Stone image and these "faced" examples of this creature. They share frontal countenances with toothy open mouths from which extrude stone knife tongues, but the differences are also quite evident. The jewel-studded fillet diagnostic of the solar deities is never present on the earth monsters with human faces, nor are the even more diagnostic curved bands flanking the eyes. The ear spools and the necklaces, when present, are often similar, but these are generalized features with little identificatory diagnostic value.

As for the stone knife tongue, this feature is repeated on the two profile faces that emerge from the gaping jaws of the pair of *xiuhcoatl,* "fire serpents," that encircle the solar disk. Beyer convincingly demonstrated that the face on the left is that of Xiuhtecuhtli, the fire deity, and the one on the right that of Tonatiuh. It is also worth noting that the deities Xolotl and Xochiquetzal, in the *tonalamatl* of the *Codex Borbonicus* (1974, 16, 19), display this feature.

The significance of these *tecpatl* tongues is somewhat debatable. Seler (1902–23, 2:715) interpreted the ones emerging from the gaping jaws of the earth monsters as symbols of light. This was accepted by Beyer and applied to the Calendar Stone—and has since been followed by others. This identification could be supported by the presence of these sacrificial knives on the celestial bands, including those on the edge of the Calendar Stone, where they were interpreted as connoting "el rayo solar" by Beyer (1921, 122). Other connotations might also be involved, including a more general sanguinary sacrificial significance. In any case, they are not confined to earth monsters.

Features that sometimes occur on the Tlaltecuhtli faces, the darkened lower face, indicated by a striated field, and, more frequently, a circle-within-circle on each cheek (see p. 189, fig. 7), deserve special comment. Both are diagnostic of the earth goddesses, especially Teteoinnan/Tlazolteotl (Seler 1902–23, 2:468–69). The faces of the solar deities are sometimes divided into two fields, upper: light red or yellow, lower: darker red (e.g., see figs. 2, 4; p. 126, fig. 16). As noted, this might have been the case on the Calendar Stone, but is uncertain due to its damaged condition. However, even if the bicolored facial layout is accepted, it would only superficially resemble that on the Tlaltecuhtli faces because the color scheme in the case of the earth goddesses, as known from the pictorials, is upper: white, lower: black. As for the circles on the cheeks, the solar deities occasionally display this feature (e.g., see fig. 4; fig. 5), but they are red, while those on the earth goddesses are black.

Flanking the central face of the Calendar Stone, in two projecting "lobes" on either side of the "wings" of the large Ollin sign that occupies the central part of the solar disk, are claws, with "demon faces," clutching human hearts (see p. 128, fig. 19). This feature appears to provide support for those who favor the Tlaltecuhtli identification, for these creatures always display prominent sets of claws of this type (e.g., Beyer 1921, fig. 43). On the Calendar Stone, these claws have been identified by some as eagle claws, by others, as jaguar claws. Beyer (1921, 23–24) addressed the issue, opting for an identification as the claws of the mythological "dragons," the *xiuhcoatl,* that rim the disk. In support, he cited a representation of a flying "Turtle-Xiuhcoatl Sacrificer" on *Codex Zouche-Nuttall* (1987, 69) (see p. 129, fig. 21), a *yahui* (Nicholson and Quiñones Keber

1983, 172, 176–77; Smith 1973, 60–64), with a human profile face peering from the gaping jaws, clutching a sacrificed human heart. In any case, similarly configured claws are a feature of various supernatural creatures and beings in the Aztec iconographic repertoire and are not by any means confined to terrestrial beings. It is also worth noting that another Aztec monument that features a prominent 4 Ollin date, a cubical stone that was employed after the Conquest as a base for a cross in Nativitas, near Xochimilco, depicts human hearts with "demon faces" in the same position and in virtually the same configuration as the "demon faced" claws clutching human hearts on the Calendar Stone (Nicholson 1958, fig. 6, printed upside-down!).

Finally, the issue of the frontality of this central image of the Calendar Stone, which particularly influenced Klein in developing her "nocturnal sun/Venus" hypothesis, must be addressed. The profile depiction of Tonatiuh (complete figure or just the head) in the center of solar disks is a standard feature of Aztec and Mixteca-Puebla iconography. Various examples were illustrated by Beyer (see p. 126, fig. 16; p. 128, fig. 18) to which others could be added (e.g., see fig. 5; fig. 6). The Calendar Stone image is unusual in its *en face* format. Beyer could cite only one other example, a crude, Europeanized image in the illustration of the celestial and terrestrial tiers on *Codex Vaticanus A* (1900), fol. 1 (fig. 7). An even less satisfactory example might be cited, a

Fig. 6.
Tonatiuh figure within solar disk
on back of image of skeletal deity
Central Mexico (Aztec), ca. 1440–1521,
blue-green stone, 22.8 × 12 cm
(9 × 4¾ in.)
Stuttgart, Wurttembergisches
Landesmuseum

Fig. 7.
Tonatiuh image in the fourth celestial
tier, Ilhuicatl Tonatiuh, drawing
by Hermann Beyer after *Codex
Vaticanus A*, fol. 1

Fig. 8.
Tonatiuh image (*ixiptla*) featured in 4
Ollin ceremony, Bernardino de Sahagún,
Florentine Codex, vol. 1, bk. 2, fol. 135r
Mexico (Tenochtitlan), ca. 1575–77,
watercolor on European paper
Florence, Biblioteca Medicea
Laurentiana

Europeanized depiction in the Sahaguntine *Florentine Codex* (Sahagún 1979, vol. 1, bk. 2, fol. 135r) of a Tonatiuh image during the propitiation of the sun on his special day, 4 Ollin. The illustration shows a standing man nearly covered by a large circular device with a European style multi-rayed sun face (the usual manner of depicting the sun in the codex) in the center, surrounded by a wide, ticked border, equivalent to the more standard form of the solar disk (fig. 8). Designated *ixiptla* in the Nahuatl text (Sahagún 1981, 216–17), the native artist obviously assumed that a human impersonator was involved, but the passage can perhaps be more satisfactorily interpreted as referring to a painting or a sculpture of the solar image. This is supported by Sahagún's Spanish translation (Sahagún 1988, 1:196–97). In any case, apart from the possible misunderstanding of the artist, the illustration is so Europeanized that it is of dubious value in deciding whether it represents a genuine continuation of a pre-Hispanic mode of depicting the solar disk.

Klein (1975, 76–78; 1976a, 178–80; 1976b) based much of her "Yohualtecuhtli hypothesis" on this illustration and the text that accompanies it. Although in Sahagún's paraphrastic Spanish translation of this text, the great annual ceremony to propitiate the sun that fell on the day 4 Ollin is attributed to Yohualtecuhtli, designated just before as being greeted with incensing at the onset of nocturnal darkness (along with Yacahuiztli, omitted in the translation), this attribution is lacking in the Nahuatl. With some trepidation, therefore, I venture to suggest that "the father of modern ethnography" misunderstood here the referent for *in ilhuiuh,* "the feast day" (of 4 Ollin), which was clearly that of the diurnal sun, Tonatiuh, not Yohualtecuhtli, whom he elsewhere (Sahagún 1950–82, 8:60) identified with a star, apparently Castor.

There are extant, however, at least two examples of indubitably pre-Hispanic examples of representations of solar disks with *en face* central images of solar deities. One, although from Oaxaca rather than Central Mexico, can be assigned to the Mixteca-Puebla stylistic/iconographic tradition that in its broadest definition would include Aztec as a major sub-tradition (Nicholson 1982). It is the gold pectoral, featuring the solar disk, that was found in 1962 by Roberto Gallegos Ruiz in Zaachila Tomb 2 (Gallegos Ruiz 1978, 102, 114, 118, fig. 78). In the center of the disk is a frontal figure, with a bell-shaped body, of the Mixtec version of the solar deity (Caso 1959; 1969, 212–13), who shares iconographic features with the Central Mexican versions, including the long nose bar and the jeweled fillet (fig. 9).

A more relevant example is a polychrome vessel discovered in Mexico City in 1900 during the Calle de las Escalerillas sewer excavation that passed through a portion of the Tenochtitlan Templo Mayor precinct (Batres 1902, 22; Castañeda and Mendoza 1933, 519–23, figs. 70, 71, pl. 14; Seler 1902–23, 2:867–68). The tall vase, which Castañeda and Mendoza reconstructed from numerous fragments and believed functioned as a drum, features a painted and sculpted frontal image of a solar deity, the upper portion of whose body is surrounded by a solar disk (fig. 10). The figure displays various of the iconographic elements characteristic of the solar deities, including: the jeweled fillet; long nose bar; the face divided into two horizontal fields, the lower one darker red; and a broad jeweled collar edged with a disk bearing the interlocking symbol for gold (cf. figs. 3, 5). The mouth, serving as an air duct for the drum, is open and displays a prominent row of upper teeth. The overall image shares many features with that on the Calendar Stone. If nothing else, this piece does provide at least one instance of a pre-Hispanic Central Mexican *en face* depiction of a solar deity within a solar disk.

My own view concerning the identification of the central image of the Calendar Stone can be simply stated. Despite all of the recent efforts on the part of many serious students to refute

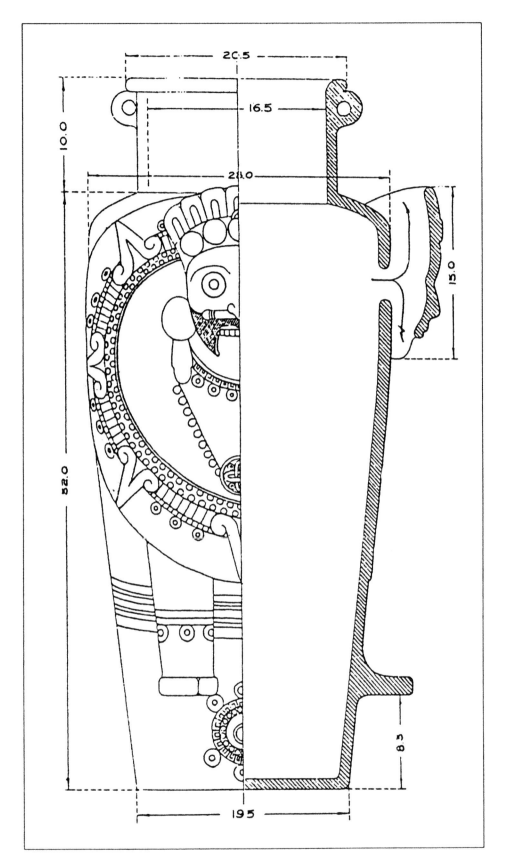

Fig. 9.
Pectoral with image of Mixtec
solar deity, cognate with Tonatiuh,
within solar disk, from Tomb 2,
Zaachila, Oaxaca
ca. 1450–1500, gold, height: 10 cm (4 in.)
Mexico City, Museo Nacional
de Antropología

Fig. 10.
Polychrome vessel displaying frontal
figure of Tonatiuh with surrounding
solar disk; Mexico City, Museo Nacional
de Antropología; drawing by Daniel
Castañeda and Vincente T. Mendoza,
ca. 1930

or significantly modify the traditional view that this visage represents Tonatiuh, the diurnal solar deity, I believe the best evidence still supports this identification.

The case for Tlaltecuhtli, apart from the generalized resemblance of the *en face* Calendar Stone countenance to those on one type of this terrestrial creature, is based mainly on the "stone knife tongue" and the flanking claws, both features typical of representations of the monstrous aspect of the Lord of the Earth. As was noted, however, stone knife tongues are not limited to Tlaltecuhtli images; they are depicted on snakes, skulls, and other deities—and on the Calendar Stone itself they are also a feature of the profile faces of Xiuhtecuhtli and Tonatiuh in the jaws of the two *xiuhcoatl* that rim the solar disk. As for the "demon-faced" claws clutching human hearts, whether Beyer's view that they can be best interpreted as those of the *xiuhcoatl* is correct or not, they clearly belong within the structure of the 4 Ollin date (see p. 123, fig. 10) and should not necessarily be interpreted as the claws of the being represented by the central image. In any case, they could be considered appropriate elements of any 4 Ollin, the date that connoted the current sun, Tonatiuh, who was fed with sacrificed hearts—and, as was noted earlier, anthropomorphized hearts, *sans* claws, were depicted in these same positions on the 4 Ollin of the Nativitas monument.

I regard Klein's Yohualtecuhtli, "nocturnal sun," hypothesis as equally unconvincing, reflecting an over-reliance on Seler's somewhat speculative identifications of certain images on *Codex Borgia* 35 and 40 as depictions of Yohualtecuhtli and a passage in the *Florentine Codex,* discussed above, that I doubt really indicates that the great annual 4 Ollin ceremony was dedicated to Yohualtecuhtli rather than Tonatiuh. Yohualtecuhtli was certainly stellar; that this poorly documented deity was also identified with the nocturnal sun is not supported by any primary source. As indicated, spatial limitations preclude adequate discussion of Klein's complicated hypothesis. Suffice it to say, I regard as dubious some other of her arguments, particularly her defining the young solar deity Xochipilli/Piltzintecuhtli, the patron of various artistic and pleasurable activities, as "the dead sun at night at the navel of the female earth monster."

Finally, I also find it hard to accept the views of those, such as Graulich and Fradcourt, who interpret the Calendar Stone's central visage as a hybrid image, combining diurnal solar with nocturnal terrestrial elements. I see no reason to accept this complication. The circumstance that the Calendar Stone version of Tonatiuh displays some features hitherto not encountered on other depictions of this deity does not necessarily compel the conclusion that it must represent a different deity, is a special aspect, or that it is combined with the features of other supernatural beings. So much of the available data on Aztec iconography is based on the accidents of survival and the happenstance of discovery that considerable interpretative caution would seem advisable, particularly the assumption that there is something unusual about this image of Tonatiuh that demands explanation because no other precisely similar image has yet been discovered.

Innovative interpretative hypotheses are certainly welcome in a field that is crucial to a better understanding of the ideological component of pre-Hispanic Mesoamerica's best documented civilization. But any new interpretations, particularly if they overturn or significantly modify one that has long been accepted by leading scholars, must be subjected to thorough appraisals. And in my opinion, for the reasons I have given, none of the recent anti-Tonatiuh hypotheses can successfully stand up under critical examination.

On the other hand, the issues involved here well exemplify the types of problems frequently encountered in the interpretation of Aztec sacred art. Progress in this major field of

Mesoamerican research can only be made within the context of open, critical discussion, with frank exchange of differing views. I have reaffirmed here, wielding "Ockham's razor," the case for the traditional identification of Tonatiuh in the center of the Calendar Stone. I invite those with differing views to present additional arguments, or new data, in support of their positions. New data would, of course, be especially welcome. Fresh discoveries in the subsoil of Mexico City or elsewhere may someday clarify some of the identificatory and interpretative problems that continue to preoccupy students of this remarkable monument.

This article has focused explicitly on the question of the identity of the central image of the Calendar Stone. I agree with the point made recently by Fradcourt (1988a, 15), that a preferable methodology would be to examine this question within the broader context of the significance of the entire iconographic program of the monument. However, this would require a much more extensive discussion than is possible in a paper of this length. I am hopeful that even the necessarily restricted focus here on a single—but very basic—question of identification has contributed something useful to the ongoing, seemingly perennial dialogue concerning the symbolic connotations of one of the most fascinating and beautifully carved stones of ancient America.

Notes

1. "Multiplicity ought not to be posited without necessity" (Ockham's Razor).

2. A preliminary version of this paper was presented under the title "Problems in the Interpretation of Aztec Art" in the session "Mexican Symbolic Art," moderated by Leslie Offutt, II International Symposium on Latin American Indian Literatures, 27–28 April 1984, George Washington University, Washington, D.C. The abstract was published in the *Latin American Indian Literatures Association Newsletter* 3, no. 1 (1984): 21.

"New Insights on the Interpretation of the *Aztec Calendar Stone* (with Notes on Skeletonization)" (1993)

Editors' Commentary

Ariane Fradcourt is the deputy general director of the Service des arts plastiques ministère de la communaute française in Belgium. In this essay, presented in 1988 at the International Congress of Americanists, she argues that the central face on the Aztec Calendar Stone *is a skeletonized form of the sun god Tonatiuh, an idea she advanced much earlier, in an undergraduate thesis at the Université libre de Bruxelles (1982). "New Insights on the Interpretation of the* Aztec Calendar Stone" *was in press for five years, during which time Fradcourt published her findings in* Art and Fact, *a journal of the Université de Liège (1988b, 1991, 1992). Her proposals had a significant impact on* Calendar Stone *studies and many were soon adopted by Michel Graulich (1992) and others.*

After an extended discussion of the iconography of the concentric rings on the Calendar Stone, *Fradcourt focuses on a close, structured reading of the iconographic possibilities presented by the central face. She relies on Cecelia Klein's critical insight that for the Mexica, the sun contained multiple personae, one for each main part of the day (of course, Carlos Navarrete and Doris Heyden also point this out). For Fradcourt, the* Calendar Stone *most likely represents the setting or night sun; its skeletal appearance relates to the skeletal iconography of Mictlan, the Mexica underworld. It therefore describes a liminal space, a moment of transition from death to rebirth. In this respect the* Calendar Stone *becomes a unifying container for two opposing, cyclical forces.*

*   *   *

"New Insights on the Interpretation of the Aztec Calendar Stone *(with Notes on Skeletonization)"*

INTRODUCTION

The purpose of this paper is to provide new insights on the interpretations of the central figure of the Aztec Calendar Stone and of the whole sculpture in general (fig. 1). The identity of the central figure has been much debated these past years. It was first identified as Tonatiuh, the Sun god, more than a century and a half ago. Recently, it has been proposed that the Earth goddess is seen in it (Navarrete and Heyden 1974), and still more recently, it has been interpreted as Yohualtecuhtli, a fusion of Venus as Evening Star and the Night Sun (Klein 1977).

   In a former study (Fradcourt 1982, 1991), I have reviewed the arguments for these three hypotheses and I undertook a new study of the iconography. That study relied exclusively on the comprehensive analysis of each individual motif composing the central figure, leaving aside the

---

Excerpted from Ariane Fradcourt, "New Insights on the Interpretation of the *Aztec Calendar Stone* (with Notes on Skeletonization)," in Jacqueline de Durand-Forest and Marc Eisinger, eds., *The Symbolism in the Plastic and Pictorial Representations of Ancient Mexico: A Symposium of the 46th International Congress of Americanists, Amsterdam 1988* (Bonn: Holos, 1993), 203–31. Published with permission. Introductory text by Khristaan D. Villela and Matthew H. Robb.

Fig. 1.
Reconstruction of the *Aztec Calendar Stone* in situ
Model by Ariane Fradcourt based on illustrations and data from Abadiano 1889, Beyer 1965a, 1965b, fig. 1; Caso 1928; Noriega 1954; and Schmidt 1965, 17

interpretations of the other surrounding motifs. This was done exclusively in the frame of reference of the Aztec iconographic documentation. Basing myself on those criteria, I was able to establish firmly the following characteristics: the central figure shows in its top part typical solar attributes such as almond-shaped eyes, double semicircles around the eyes, orderly hair and a solar headband. The frontal presentation, the lateral claws and the lower part of the face (skeletonized mouth with a protruding flint knife) are, on the contrary, typical attributes of the Tlaltecuhtlis, the Earth Monsters. The collar is a nondistinctive feature.[1] The central deity is surrounded by a sun disk. In other words, *the central figure represents the Sun god with skeletonized features and hands with claws.*

With this clarification of the iconography, we can now try to interpret it and attempt to explain the peculiarity which is surprising, given our current state of knowledge of Aztec iconography. However, it should be noted that the seemingly strong concern with the identity of the central deity is mainly due to the recent controversy that surrounds it (Navarrete and Heyden 1974; Klein 1977). It is the explanation of the whole sculpture, of the presence and of the combination of its composing motifs, which is important. For this reason, I review first the interpretations of the other motifs, before moving to the interpretation of the central figure....

SYMBOLIC READING OF THE STONE

I suggested before (Fradcourt 1982, 67; 1988b, 16) that we could divide the Stone symbolically into two vertical halves opposing each other: the glyphs of the eras 4 Wind (associated with the element "Air") vs. 4 Jaguar ("Earth"), and the glyph 4 Rain of Fire ("Fire") vs. 4 Water ("Water"); the small glyph of Xiuhtecuhtli-Old Fire-Venus vs. Huitzilopochtli (young new fire, Sun god), and the ones of Ilamatecuhtli (1 Rain), old Venusian fire goddess vs. Xilonen (7 Monkey), young Venusian solar goddess; the two fire serpents and the deities in their mouths (corresponding to the upper small glyphs), and the "disjunction" seen in the cycle of the day glyphs. It could also be divided into two horizontal halves whose axis would pass through the middle of the central face. The upper part located to the East with the representation of the living part of the central god, the upper small glyphs of male deities, the solar ray of the 4 Ollin glyph, the date 13 Reed of the creation of the Sun would be opposed to the lower part of the sculpture located to the West and comprising the skeletonization of the central face, the glyphs of the "light" eras (4 Wind and 4 Fire) vs. the "heavy" eras (4 Jaguar and 4 Water), the small glyphs of the female deities, the jade pendant of the 4 Ollin glyph, and the skeletonized deities in the fire serpents. However, this interpretation gives rise to some problems (see below).

THE CENTRAL FIGURE

Let us now return to the interpretation of the central deity.

It is worthwhile underlining the fact that before Klein's thesis, nobody seemed to have drawn attention to the fact that there were different Suns in Aztec mythology, according to the cycle of the divine celestial body in the sky. The cycle of the Sun was the following (fig. 2) (Graulich 1987, 277): the Sun rose in the East (equivalent to Tonatiuh) and was accompanied by the deified dead warriors until Noon, when he entered a descending phase where he was taken charge of by the divine women. At Sunset, he began his journey under the Earth. At Midnight sacrifices took place to recreate him and to allow him to rise again, in the East.

Theoretically thus, the central figure could be interpreted in four ways:

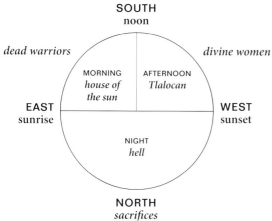

SOUTH
noon

dead warriors   *divine women*

MORNING
house of
the sun

AFTERNOON
Tlalocan

EAST
sunrise

WEST
sunset

NIGHT
hell

NORTH
sacrifices

Fig. 2.

Cycle of the sun, diagram by the author
after Graulich 1987, 277

Fig. 3.

Tonatiuh from terra-cotta relief; Lyon,
Musée d'Histoire Naturelle; drawing by
the author

1. as the Morning Sun,

2. as the Sun at Noon,

3. as the setting Sun,

4. as the Sun at Midnight.

We shall also consider two other hypotheses (5 and 6) which are not directly related to that schema.

We can discard *hypothesis 1* since frontality, the claws and skeletalization are incompatible with Tonatiuh (fig. 3), as being identified as the young Sun god of the daytime sky. The other three hypotheses would all imply a *"transformational process"*[2] which the earth attributes of the Sun god can account for. It is clear that *we have to look for a solar deity who takes up attributes of the earth,* of the dead. Let us first see which representations could fit that criterion.

Tlalchitonatiuh, representing the setting Sun, is swallowed by the Earth monster (fig. 4, which I identify as such). On figure 5 the Sun god adopts the shape of Tlaloc recognizable by his goggled eye and his fangs. On figure 5 his body is made of a solar disk and it is already transformed into a mummy bundle on the right. On the left, there are skulls and bones recalling the skirts of the Tlaltecuhtlis. The figure of Tlaloc receives an arrow in the mouth.

Fig. 5.
Tlalchitoniatiuh, *Codex Borbonicus,* fol. 14 (detail)
Central Mexico, sixteenth century, probably ca. 1521, watercolor on deerhide
Paris, Bibliothèque de l'Assemblée nationale

Fig. 6.
Tlalchitonatiuh, *Codex Borgia*, fol. 43
(detail)
Mexico (Tenochtitlan), sixteenth
century, perhaps before 1519, watercolor
on deerhide
Rome, Biblioteca Apostolica Vaticana

In the Codex Borgia, what Klein regards as the Night Sun (fig. 6) looks in fact much more similar to Tlalchitonatiuh than to a dead Sun god, as she claims. The representations have the attributes of Xolotl-Evening Star (note the typical shape of the earring and the dog's mouth) and one of them is fecundating the Earth lying at his feet, which would rather correspond to the representation of the setting Sun who penetrates the Earth. As a general comment however, I think that we should try to avoid as much as possible comparisons with documents which do not belong to the Aztec system of iconography when such precise iconographic questions are at stake.

Tonatiuh can also receive an arrow in his mouth, as with Tlalchitonatiuh, which could be interpreted as his death or imminent decline (fig. 7).[3]

On figure 8 we see the figure of a warrior represented in the middle of a sun disk. He wears a belt adorned with two skulls, recalling the same type of ornament worn by the Tlatecuhtlis. His hair is in large curls (a feature typical of Earth deities), his heart is excised, and his legs are skeletonized. He also receives in his mouth what could be interpreted as an arrow[4] and he takes on attributes that are clearly death-related.

Thus, those solar figures can take on earth and death characteristics or be associated with Tlaloc. The god of pulque on the vase of Bilimek (fig. 9) is also represented dying (note his skeletonized mouth and the two ranges of curly hair), being swallowed by the Earth monster located below.

This quick review shows that the difficulty of interpretation of the central figure of the Aztec Calendar Stone lies in its *iconographic uniqueness* with respect to the Aztec documents available. We are not accustomed to seeing solar figures associated with death (see also the figures

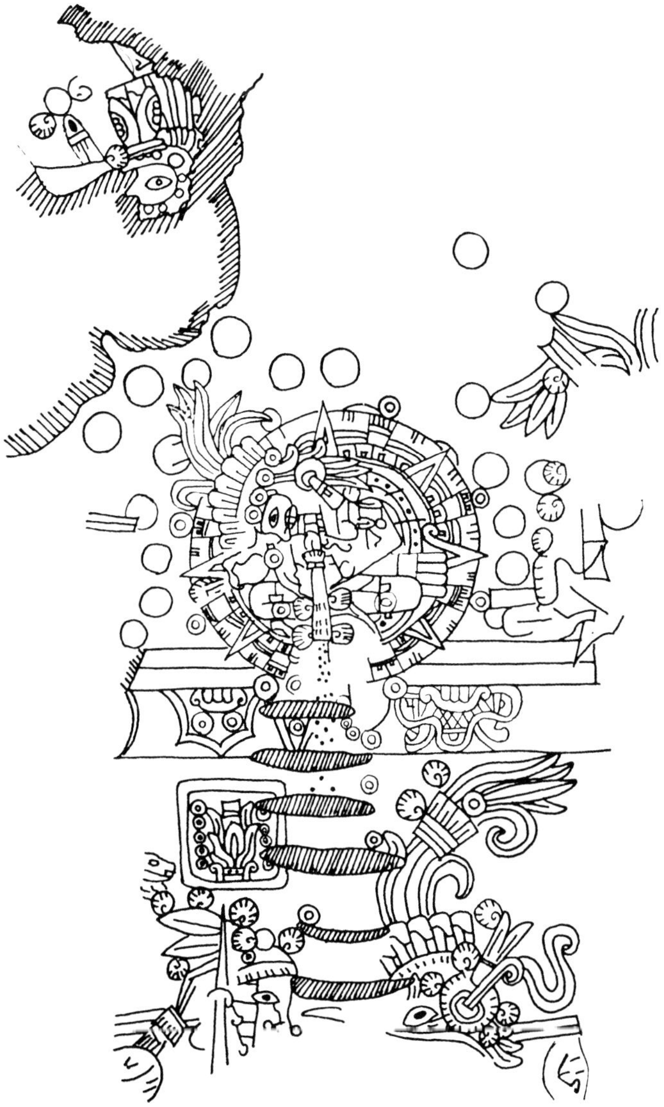

Fig. 7.
Drawing of Tonatiuh receiving an arrow in his mouth, after Cepeda-Cárdenas and Arana 1968

Fig. 8.
Solar skeletonized figure, drawing by the author

on the sides of the Teocalli of the Sacred War (fig. 10) or the ones in the cavity of the stone Jaguar (fig. 11), and none of them really fits our case: they lack the flint knife and the claws.

The closest figures are the two gods in the fire serpents' jaws, and especially the right one representing Tonatiuh. Although they are not displayed frontally as is the central figure and do not have claws, I believe that their interpretation must be related to and consistent with the one of the central figure.

In *hypothesis 2,* the central figure would be the Sun at Noon and would be represented with claws, like a falling Tzitzimitl. But he [has] neither lunar, "tlalocoid" attributes, which we could expect him to bear when becoming the Afternoon Sun god, nor similar attributes (e.g. an arrow) to figures 7 and 8 which could be metaphorically equated with Afternoon Sun gods. Frontality, skeletonization, the claws, and the flint knife would supposedly make our figure much closer iconographically to the Earth than we can speculate that a Sun at Noon (at the very beginning of its decline) would be.

Fig. 9.
Bilimek Pulque Vessel
Fifteenth or early sixteenth century,
greenstone, 36.5 × 17.5 × 25.5 cm
(13⅜ × 6⅞ × 10 in.)
Vienna, Museum für Völkerkunde

Fig. 10.
Sides of the *Teocalli de la Guerra
Sagrada,* drawing by Enrique Juan
Palacios, 1929

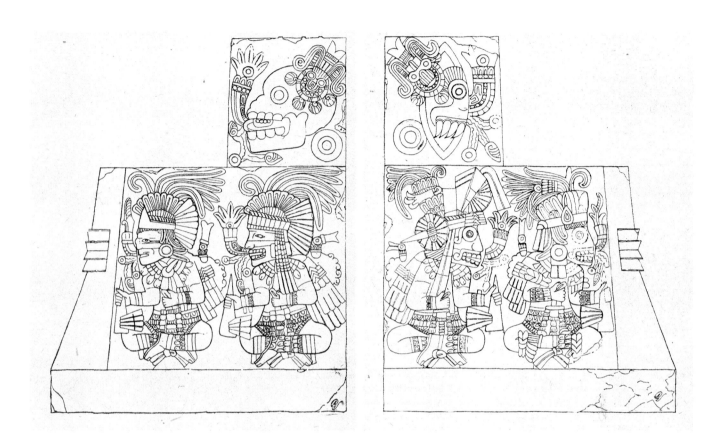

Hypotheses 3 and 4 look, in our state of knowledge, to be the most plausible ones. In *hypothesis 3,* the setting Sun of the Aztec Calendar Stone is represented in the process of transforming himself into the Earth, being swallowed by her, as was the case with the pulque god. The upper part of the face being alive, the lower one being dead, the god would be represented dying, being half-Sun, half-Earth. The claws as attribute of Tlaltecuhtli could also mean that he is a falling Tzitzimitl. 4 Ollin, interpreted as the date of destruction of the Fifth Sun, would fit well into that type of interpretation, as well as its central position on the Stone.[5]

As far as the general interpretation of the sculpture is concerned, we would then have the representation of the Fifth era in its totality, with the date of its beginning (13 Reed) and its end (4 Ollin). The upper part of the stone with the solar motifs (cf. "Symbolic reading of the Stone") would be located to the East and related to birth, whereas the lower part with the two skeletonized gods, also represented dying, as well as the female and earth-related motifs would symbolically be located in the West, in the realm of Death. Such was the thesis I first defended (Fradcourt 1982, 47, 55, 56; Fradcourt 1988b). A somewhat similar interpretation has recently been given by Pasztory (1983, 170), although the central figure is interpreted as being the Earth goddess.

Fig. 11.

Skeletonized Huitzilopochtli and
Tezcatlipoca inside of the Earth-jaguar,
drawing by the author after Beyer 1965g,
fig. 1

However, I noted that this interpretation of the Aztec Calendar Stone in binary terms, dividing it symbolically into vertical and horizontal halves, did not answer some questions, nor did it solve some problems. One may wonder why the central god who would represent the setting Sun has attributes (frontality, claws) which make him look more "earthly" than the two gods below, who should be, in this interpretation, the true chthonic, death figures, at the complete opposite of the 13 Reed glyph of the creation of the Sun. Also, there remains the problem of giving a satisfactory explanation for the presence of the *two* fire snakes in this context. The very reason why the *two* xiuhcoatls, the *two* gods in their jaws were figured remains unclear (or seem superfluous) again. Finally, if the Mexica artists wanted to represent the setting Sun god, why would not an iconographic rendering closer to the existing ones have been chosen, such as the carving of a Tlaloc face in the middle of a sun disk, for example?

Returning to the purely iconographic aspects of hypothesis 3, we can notice that our central figure does not correspond to figures 7 and 8, nor to Tlalchitonatiuh, the setting Sun: the latter have arrows in their mouths (which would mean death) instead of a flint knife (that would mean rebirth).[6] The central figure does not have lunar attributes (i.e. goggled eyes, dog's mouth or long lip), but, on the contrary, does have claws. The companion of the setting Sun in the Codex Borbonicus is Xolotl, who has claws and a flint knife in the mouth but it would be abusive to equate the dying Sun god to Xolotl. The pulque god is swallowed by the Earth just as the setting Sun and has a skeletonized mouth, but the flint knife and the claws are missing again.

Let us note that the closed eye found in the middle of simpler versions of the 4 Ollin glyph (which is replaced here by the Sun god's face) is the representation of a star, of a *light* symbol (Seler 1902–23, 4:47; Beyer 1965f, 493).

Up to this point, we are still confronted with the impossibility of arriving to a satisfactory conclusion because of the lack of adequate iconographical comparisons. The available Aztec documents can be interpreted in different ways which cannot be verified.

As already stated above, we tend to focus our attention on the central figure of the Aztec Calendar Stone because of the recent controversy which has developed around it. Exploring the field of the possible interpretations could well be more rewarding if we tried to look at the *general context* of the Stone, i.e. if we paid more attention to the surrounding motifs. Adopting this approach could give a more complete view of the whole monument, and possibly a closer approximation to the identity of the central figure itself.

If we look at the other motifs, they all seem to converge to express some general themes. We can find six of them. The first one is *Time* and *cycles* and can be seen in:

1. the ring of the glyphs of the days representing the calendar and the passing of Time;

2. the glyphs of the eras alluding to the past eras and world cycles, the fifth (4 Ollin) being the last one, inscribed in that way in the cycles of world continuity;

3. the two xiuhcoatls composed of *13* segments who would represent two cycles of time;

4. the small glyphs of Xiuhtecuhtli-Mixcoatl and of Huitzilopochtli on top and of Ilamatecuhtli and Xilonen below, the latter two deities helping the passage from the rainy season to the dry season.

The second important theme is the one of *life and rebirth* rather than pure and simple destruction:

1. the date of 13 Reed, which signifies the *creation* of the Fifth Sun;

2. the presence of the xiuhcoatls who are light symbols (flames on their bodies), who in the myths help the Sun-Huitzilopochtli at his birth on the Coatepec, destroying the forces of chaos (the Huitznahuas) and who played an important role during the Panquetzaliztli festival which was the re-enactment of the creation and birth of Huitzilopochtli;

3. the magnificent solar disk so richly adorned (note especially the blood drops, symbols of *life*);

4. the presence of the calendar which presides over the passing of time and of the *life cycle* (years, seasons, etc.);

5. the glyph of Huitzilopochtli, the new Sun god of the Mexicas;

6. the presence of Tonatiuh in the right *xiuhcoatl;*

7. the eras themselves which make reference to the successive rebirths of the world;

8. the presence of the glyphs of Ilamatecuhtli and Xilonen who gave birth to Xiuhtecuhtli and Huitzilopochtli, since they are assimilated to their mothers.[7]

The third theme revolves around *fire,* which is itself connected to the theme of life:

1. the fire serpents with two different types of flames;

2. the presence of the two fire gods in their mouths;

3. the sun disk;

4. the igneous gods (and goddesses to a lesser extent) represented by the small glyphs.

We now turn to *hypothesis 4.* Throughout our attempts to try to find relevant iconographic comparisons with the central figure of the Aztec Calendar Stone, we have been confronted with skeletonization and what it would mean exactly. This aspect could also give some insights to the *raison d'être* of the first two major themes described above.

[In contrast] to the Maya area where we have texts (e.g. the Popol Vuh) and abundant iconographic documents on the Sun in the Underworld, the Mexica record is relatively scarce. However, we know that everybody on his or her death had to pass through *Mictlan,* the Place of the Dead. There is mention of warriors who died heroically and who went to Hell, and of princes who were transformed into skeletons in *Mictlan* (Garibay Kintana 1964–68, 1:86–87; 2:5–6, 64–67; León-Portilla 1972, 66; Alvarado Tezozómoc 1878, 380, 472, 632). In the myth of Teotihuacan, Quetzalcoatl-Nanahuatl had also to go through the Underworld before becoming the Sun god (*Codex Chimalpopoca* 1945, 11, 120). Huitzilopochtli also died and went to the Place of the Dead and became the prototype of dead warriors.

These data support the idea that the central figure is also engaged in a *transformational process,* due to *passage in the Underworld,* in a way similar to the worldwide rites of passage that imply the passage from life to death and vice-versa at the occasion of an ordeal (see van Gennep 1909; Eliade 1964, 60–63).

It is also worthwhile stressing that for the Mesoamericans, death was not viewed as a final phase as many of us tend to see it from our Occidental point of view, but was on the contrary closely related to life, as J. Furst has underlined in her study of Mixtec codices: "…skeletal images [are] symbols of fertility in accordance with old shamanistic concepts of bones as the seat of life and source of regeneration" (Furst 1982, 222). Is not Huitzilopochtli said to be born skeletonized and have turned into a Tzitzimitl at his emergence on Coatepec (Alvarado Tezozómoc 1949, 35)?

On the Aztec Calendar Stone, indeed, we can find the life and solar symbols (which we pointed out before) closely related with (and opposed to) other motifs which, in turn, signify *death,* past, and old deities:

1. skeletonization and flint knives for the three human figures (but which would also refer to their life-sustaining qualities);

2. the small glyph of Xiuhtecuhtli under his aspect of Mixcoatl that we find represented in flesh and blood at the bottom, as the old Sun opposed—but complementary to—the glyph of Huitzilopochtli and the representation of Tonatiuh, the Sun god at the bottom, as the new Fire, the new Sun. The same schema would apply to Ilamatecuhtli (old goddess of Fire) opposed to Xilonen (young solar goddess).

The conjunction of the motifs also seem to designate *Midnight* and the *passage from one time cycle to another:* the glyphs of the old deities opposed to the new young ones we just talked about; the 13 Reed glyph referring to the creation of the Sun at Midnight; the xiuhcoatls that represent the Pleiades that culminated at Midnight during the New Fire Ceremony; the central position of the central figure that could be related to midnight;[8] one of the engravings on the stone base which represents the constellation Mamalhuaztli according to Aveni (1980, 32–33) which is mentioned with the Pleiades as appearing at Midnight, at the beginning of the 52-years cycle; the 52 quincunxes referring to the binding of the years (Dieseldorff 1930) and possibly the counter-clockwise reading of the day glyphs.

Therefore, the motifs and their disposition show a transition from one state to another, the passage through the Underworld, and a *renewal.* In my opinion, it is not therefore exclusively life (as implied in the Tonatiuh thesis) which is represented—although it is clearly that aspect which is emphasized—nor Death and destruction (as implied in the Earth goddess and Yohualtecuhtli theses) which we are dealing with, but rather with a *rebirth,* a *re-creation* that is to be understood in a conception of cyclical time and most probably in the context of a New Fire Ceremony.

Supporting this interpretation is the presence of *two* fire serpents, which is rare in Aztec and Central Mexican iconography in general. It is interesting to note that we find similar pairs of fire snakes in the Codex Borgia where they are precisely associated with the Night Sun and the glyphs of the calendar. In Aztec art, we also find a pair of fire snakes in the guise of sacrificial papers on the top of the backrest of the Teocalli of the Sacred War, which can also be related to the New Fire Ceremony (e.g. Pasztory 1983, 167). Also, for Seler, the eye found on the usual representations of the 4 Ollin glyph (and replaced here by the central god's face) represents in fact *a celestial body which moves back and forth from the Light realm to the Dark one,* from the Sky to Earth, and vice-versa. The whole Ollin sign represents the movements of the big celestial bodies and alternatively, their rising and setting, their triumphs and deaths (Seler 1902–23, 4:47, 5:475). Taking an astronomical approach, Milbrath (1980, 1:294, 297) draws some interesting inferences on the death and rebirth of the sun at midnight as referring to the nadir sun of November prior to its rebirth at the winter solstice, in relation with the New Fire Ceremony.

If the central figure represents the Sun god in the Underworld we could put forward *hypothesis 5* in which the Night Sun would not be a Sun god ready to be born again, but, to the contrary, a Sun god who would be completely dead. This hypothesis would then correspond to C. Klein's where 4 Ollin would represent the cataclysmic death of the Sun and of the Era. Apart from the contextual arguments we talked about before and also apart from the presence of the two xiuhcoatls which remains to be explained—all of which are elements that go against such an hypothesis—we might wonder why a simpler or more obvious iconographic formula would not have been used. In fact, we may think that it would have been possible to represent the "dead and buried" Sun god under the features of a Tlaltecuhtli with an anthropomorphic face (Tlaltecuhtli of type 1) and surrounded by a sun disk, following the example of the setting Sun god who completely adopts the features of a Tlaloc face wearing the sun disk behind him (cf. fig. 5). It would also have been possible to represent the dead Sun god by a complete human skull (Tlaltecuhtli of type 2) inside of a sun disk. This is not an iconographic hypothesis devoid of sense, since we find such an iconographic formula some seven centuries before, in a Teotihuacan sculpture which could be interpreted as a completely skeletonized Sun god.[9]

In *hypothesis 6,* the living and dead parts (plus the claws) of the central figure would be a means of representing the different states (from life to death) through which the Sun god has to pass during his lifetime. This would be a complete, "synthesized" representation of his very being, of all the different aspects he can take on and which characterize him. In reality, and if we want to be accurate, only two of these aspects are figured (as a young triumphant Sun god and as the Night, monstrous Sun god). The "tlalocoid" aspect of Tlalchitonatiuh-setting Sun is not represented by any element on the Stone (elements such as goggle-eyes, a curved lip, curved earrings or fangs, which would have been easy to integrate). However, we could push forward the hypothesis and consider that these two aspects are the major aspects of his personality which would implicitly summarize the totality of all the different aspects he can take on, of the different stages through which he can pass.

The interpretation of the other main motifs on the Stone can therefore give rise to a series of more general interpretations which turn out to be close to each other:

With 13 Reed and 4 Ollin, each representing the birth and the (coming) death of the Sun of the Fifth Era, we would have the central face representing all the aspects of the Sun god during his life within the era. His skeletonization would refer more specifically to his coming death. But if 4 Ollin is an allusion to the coming death of the Sun god, we may wonder what the two xiuhcoatls are doing there (as well as the two gods inside them); this problem inevitably brings us back to the re-creations and therefore to hypothesis 4.

If 4 Ollin is not a direct reference to the apocalyptic death of the Sun, but rather more simply to his name, the central figure would represent all the aspects of the Sun god during the duration of the era, aspects through which he has to pass every day and, by extension, every 52 years. In this case, the presence of the two fire snakes becomes explicable. Still, there remains the problem of the skeletonization of the two lower gods (Tonatiuh and Xiuhtecuhtli).

I think we should insist on keeping the interpretation of their skeletonization consistent with the one of the central figure. Let us recall once again that the lower Tonatiuh is (apart from the claws and some minor details) the profile version of the central figure.

If the central Tonatiuh metaphorically represents the Sun god under all his aspects, should the Tonatiuh in the *xiuhcoatl* represent the same thing? And what about Xiuhtecuhtli? Should he also be represented there under all his aspects? If we go further with the reasoning, should all the existing representations of skeletonized figures in Aztec art (cf. figs. 9–11) also mean that these figures are represented under all their aspects? This thesis seems of course hard to support. Although it is true that Xiuhtecuhtli is the Lord of Time (and could therefore be represented here under all his aspects), there exists, however, in Central Plateau iconography other representations of deities emerging from xiuhcoatls and which are definitely alive. It would be a misinterpretation to sustain that these gods "in flesh and blood" are represented under a particular aspect of their being. To my mind, it is exactly the contrary, i.e. it is skeletonization which shows a particular state, a particular aspect of the deities, the living face being the usual, "normal" aspect of the deities which do not belong to the Underworld, to Death.

Finally, it would not be very coherent to make a distinction between the interpretation of the central Tonatiuh (which would be represented under **all** his aspects) and the other two gods (which would be represented under **one** of their particular aspects). We would look in vain to justify such a difference of interpretive treatment for similar motifs on the same monument.

Having explored these different tracks, I arrive to the conclusion that the skeletonization of the central figure and of the two lower gods makes reference to a specific state or a particular aspect of those deities.

CONCLUSIONS

After a detailed and strictly iconographic study of the central figure which established that it represented the Sun god with skeletonized features and hands with claws (Fradcourt 1982, 1991), we could then move on to the interpretive part of its identification, trying to keep to the *iconographical* reality as closely as possible. We retained the two most plausible hypotheses which relate the central figure to the setting Sun or the Sun at midnight. The iconographic arguments were not decisive for the determination of the nature of this central god due to the lack of comparative material which would have corresponded in all respects to our deity. However, they contributed to reducing the range of possibilities. In that respect, the hypotheses of the setting Sun and of the Sun at Midnight looked to be the most plausible ones. It is also true that the concepts of the setting Sun and the Sun at Midnight seem to have such an "ontological proximity" in our eyes (as do the concepts of creation and birth) that it is difficult to attribute iconographic characteristics to one or the other. Faced with this situation, we then relied on *contextual* arguments, taking the other motifs into account.

After all, we should consider that *it is the general context, the presence and combination of all the motifs taken together which actually are really important.*

The Sun Stone is made of a series of redundant motifs from which we can draw six major themes: fire, life (opposed and complementing death), cyclical time, Midnight, and the passage from a cycle to the other.

Given all the above mentioned considerations, we can now attempt to give a *global interpretation* of all the motifs carved on the Stone and of the relationships between them. In so doing, this would constitute the first attempt at such an all-encompassing interpretation, in symbolic terms.[10]

In conclusion, the Aztec Calendar Stone represents the Sun god with earth attributes which, beyond a temporary death, connote his regenerative and life-sustaining qualities. The central figure is the Sun at Midnight, at his (re)creation, in a context of rebirth.[11] He is inscribed in the 4 Ollin glyph, name of the present-day era in which the four preceding ones are located which reassert that we are indeed in the fifth historical era and underlines the fact that the present-day Sun is inscribed in the unfolding of world-history, as its perfect outcome.[12] Together with the glyphs of the days (whose location would indicate a rupture in time), the eras are a reference to sacred time and to cyclical time in which regular passages from life to death and vice-versa take place. Those motifs are in turn inscribed in an exceptionally decorated solar disk filled with preciousness[13] and life symbols, showing the force, glory and the importance of the central god and surrounded (or carried) (Beyer 1965d, 235) by two fire snakes who symbolize the Pleiades, the Light that rejects Darkness and the chaotic forces of the Night, and which preside over the creation and cyclical recreations of the Sun. They originate from the date 13 Reed[14] of the creation of the Sun of the Fifth Era, represented here, since we are mythically and symbolically back in primordial times, in the very beginning of the era, in the re-enactment of the creation of the Sun.[15] The fire snakes would also refer here to a period of time, i.e. to the old and new cycles of the New Year Ceremony. They carry in their mouths the representations of Xiuhtecuhtli-Venus (the predecessor and precursor of the Sun, old Sun, Fire and cycle) and of Tonatiuh (young Sun, new cycle), i.e. the representation of the actors in the recreation or rebirth itself, and of the passage of one time cycle to another, embodied in these two gods. Both are skeletonized because they passed through (or still are) in the Underworld. The speech scroll of Tonatiuh could be interpreted as meaning that the god has successfully passed the ordeal. The deities represented by the four small glyphs are the counterpart of the gods in the fire serpents (for the upper glyphs of Xiuhtecuhtli-Venus and Huitzilopochtli)[16] and would help the passage from the past cycle to the new one, as do the female deities represented by the lower glyphs from the passage of the rainy season to the dry one.

Notes

1. Similar earrings can be found on the Sun god below, in the jaws of the right fire snake.

2. Not for hypotheses 5 and 6.

3. Although it may just refer to a mythical episode unknown to us. It vaguely recalls the myth where Tlahuizcalpantecuhtli shoots arrows at the Sun (*Codex Chimalpopoca* 1945, 122).

4. The object in the mouth has been interpreted as a pipe or a horn (Pasztory 1976, 40). It is also possible to see in it a sacrificial spine with paper bands attached to it.

5. Cf. Klein 1977.

6. See Graulich 1987, 109–10; and Fradcourt 1982, 32–35.

7. See Fradcourt 1988b.

8. Cf. Klein 1977.

9. This sculpture probably represents the Night Sun god in the Underworld. It probably constitutes the iconographic prototype of the central figure on the Aztec Calendar Stone (note especially the central figure inscribed in concentrical rings, the solar disk around the central face, frontality, skeletonization (fully completed here) and the "tongue" sticking out of the mouth). I thank Dr. Hasso von Winning for his critical comments on that piece.

10. The interpretations of the motifs in astronomical and calendrical terms are the only ones to give a complete and "structured" interpretation of all the motifs. However, they present fundamental methodological flaws. The "world-view" approach only interprets the Stone in extremely imprecise and vague terms grouped under one concept, or limits itself to just a few motifs (see Fradcourt 1987). In the symbolic approach, Beyer (1965d), whose study remains essential for the identification and interpretation of most of the motifs, surprisingly did not give an overall interpretation of them. Pasztory (1983, 170) attempts to give such a type of interpretation but not in an exhaustive manner.

11. We would apparently reach a conclusion similar to Klein's (1977). However, the method used to reach this conclusion is completely different. Moreover, I see a context mainly related to life and rebirth, whereas Klein's interpretation is based on destruction and cataclysm. Also, the Night Sun god in my study is just a single deity, whereas Klein saw in it the fusion of two gods.

12. I do not discard completely the hypothesis that the glyphs of the eras on the Calendar Stone refer to the former and present-day destructions of the world, but that reference would only be on a *secondary level,* since of course, when it comes to a question of renewal, cyclical conception of time and the passage from the old to the new are also alluded to. Thus, a "destruction"—or rather, a death, is implied here—but it is, above all, rebirth which is celebrated.

13. Given the chthonic nature of the central god, it would be possible to interpret the jade ornaments of the sun disk as referring to his lunar or earth aspects. Nevertheless, this does not seem to be the case, since the jade pendants are common on the solar stones and since jade quincunxes are also found on the Stone of Tizoc or the square Stone of the Suns. These ornaments would thus simply refer to the concept of preciousness. The same comment can be applied to the jade ornament on the headband, which we also find on many other representations of Tonatiuh.

14. As Umberger (1981a, 49–50) remarks, the sculptures associated with the New Fire Ceremony usually bear the date 2 Acatl. This anomaly could be explained, according to her, if the 2 Acatl date had only been introduced as the first year of the 52-years cycle *after* 1507.

15. See especially the comments on New Year ceremonies in general by Eliade (1949, 83–114) and particularly his ideas on the periodic regeneration of Time, the new creation viewed as a repetition of the original cosmogonic myth, the dead coming back to life, the close relationship with concepts of creation (floods, rains).

16. Let us recall that Beyer had first identified the right figure in the fire snake as Huitzilopochtli. Indeed, it seems more "logical" to have this god there, instead of Tonatiuh, because of his typical nagual (the fire serpent), because of the small glyph 1 Flint knife located above, and because of the close relationship of the sculpture with the New Fire Ceremony. We might ask ourselves why Huitzilopochtli was not represented in flesh and blood. Possibly because in the New Fire Ceremony occurring every 52 years on Panquetzaliztli, it was above all the Sun god in his quality of celestial fire who was to be recreated, and not of Huitzilopochtli who was more specifically the Sun in his quality of tribal god of the Mexicas? Also, in 13 Reed, it is Quetzalcoatl-Nanahuatl who became the Sun and we know that Quetzalcoatl had become Venus for the Mexicas and had been replaced by Hiutzilopochtli (Gardner 1979, 53; Graulich 1987, 347–48). If it is Tonatiuh who is represented, it is perhaps because it was impossible to represent Quetzalcoatl on the one hand (since the Mexicas had usurped him), and Huitzilopochtli on the other hand (since he was not the true actor of the original myth). Nevertheless, Huitzilopochtli is present with his glyph above, corresponding to Tonatiuh below.

FELIPE SOLÍS

"The *Stone of the Sun*" (2000)

Editor's Commentary

Felipe Solís was the director of the Museo Nacional de Antropología in Mexico City from 2000 to 2009 and also the curator of its Aztec collections. He published in fields as diverse as the archaeology of the Bosque de Chapultepec and Pre-Columbian gold and produced surveys of the Museo Nacional de Antropología (Solís Olguín 1998; Solis Olguín et al. 2004) and several catalogs of international exhibitions on the Aztec and ancient Mexico (Solís Olguín 1993a; Solis Olguín, ed., 2004; Matos Moctezuma and Solís Olguín 2002; Solís Olguín and Leyenaar 2002). These exhibitions, and the many articles Solís wrote for general audiences, especially in Arqueología mexicana, *have contributed to a resurgence of interest in Aztec art and culture during the past twenty years.*[1]

Solís wrote several works on the Aztec Calendar Stone *and its imagery, including the book* The Aztec Calendar and Other Solar Monuments, *coauthored by Eduardo Matos Moctezuma (2004), and articles on Antonio de León y Gama (Solís Olguín 1993b) and the imagery of the sun god Tonatiuh. In* The Aztec Calendar, *and in the earlier article that appears below, Solís argues that the* Calendar Stone *should be considered both a* cuauhxicalli *and a* temalacatl *and that its imagery can be best explained by remembering that it was unfinished and likely would have resembled the* Stone of Tizoc *or the recently discovered* Stone of Motecuhzoma I. *Solís reviews the several proposals for the identity of the central face, from León y Gama to Michel Graulich, and concludes that the* Calendar Stone *and the* Stone of Motecuhzoma I *share imagery that identifies the central face as Xiuhtecuhtli, the god of both fire and the center direction in ancient Mexican thought. This article also presents the results of a new study of the original colors of the* Calendar Stone, *which showed that red and yellow dominated its color scheme, rather than the multihued naturalism proposed by Roberto Sieck Flandes (1942).*

*   *   *

"The Stone of the Sun*"*

In 1885, the inhabitants of the Mexican capital watched with astonishment the efforts undertaken by a group of soldiers to dislodge the famous monolith known as the *Calendario Azteca* from the western side of one of the towers of the Catedral Metropolitana (see pls. 1, 17). The purpose was to transport it to the Museo Nacional, at the time still new. It was located—from the time of the unfortunate reign of Maximilian—in a colonial palace, remodeled in the time of Philip V, where precious metals were melted and coins minted.

Translated by Khristaan D. Villela from Felipe Solís Olguín, "La *Piedra del Sol*," *Arqueología mexicana* 7, no. 41 (2000): 32–39. Published with permission of Editorial Raíces and the Solís estate. Introductory text by Khristaan D. Villela.

During several decades of the last century, interested parties and students of Mexican antiquities, the founders of our archaeology, eagerly urged the successive governments to shelter and protect this significant monument of the pre-Hispanic past from the ignominy that it had suffered. According to the chroniclers of the period, when it was displayed, the ignorant masses hurled filth and rotten fruit at the calendrical relief. Even the soldiers who at a certain time occupied the center of Mexico City—because of the constant violent tumult and foreign invasions that characterized nineteenth-century Mexico—killed time by target practice aimed at the face of the deity.

And so, finally, in that year the Porfirian government, acceding to the requests, decided to place it on a pedestal in the main exhibition hall of the Museo Nacional, located at the back of the courtyard.

With the arrival of the *Piedra del Sol* at the old Museo Nacional on the Calle de la Moneda, the institution made an effort to assemble around such an important monument the principal pre-Hispanic sculptures that had been gathered in the capital by that time. Thus, in 1887, President Díaz inaugurated the great Galería de los Monolítos, and thenceforward the monument stood out as the center, nucleus, and heart of the Museo Nacional.

As is well known, the *Piedra del Sol* was discovered on 17 December 1790 on the southern side of the Plaza Mayor of Mexico City, in an area close to the acequia that flowed by the southern side of the Palacio Nacional. The discovery was accidental and was made by workmen who were excavating earth for the paving of the plaza. The monolith was discovered with the relief facing downward, so that at first sight only the blank stone was visible, which leads us to believe that the sculpture was not discovered in situ. For this reason it has been said that it was removed from its original location, and moreover, that after the conquest of the indigenous city by the Spanish, the survivors of the massacre protected its carvings with a layer of volcanic ashes or sand, which saved it from immediate destruction.

Since its discovery, the question of its original position, significance, and function has inspired numerous proposals, and it is our intention to present a brief review of the most outstanding studies. Although the publications that have resulted from the study of the *Piedra del Sol* are quite numerous, it is not appropriate to fill this limited space solely with a vast bibliography. Therefore we recommend to interested readers the articles by H. B. Nicholson (1993) and Michel Graulich (1992).

THE POSITION

Antonio de León y Gama, who in 1792 published the first study of the *Piedra del Sol,* thought that it ought to have been situated vertically, "being thus able to easily show everything that is carved on it." Later, Alfredo Chavero advanced the idea that it ought to have been located "on a platform twenty fathoms [*brazas*] around, in such a way that it was lying horizontally." Until our times, these two proposals have dominated the discussion of various investigators [concerning the original position of the monument]. For clarification, we should only like to note that Hermann Beyer, in his classic study of 1921 of the *Calendario Azteca,* mentioned that the monument was unfinished and that it was surely the idea of the sculptors to make a monument similar in form to the so-called *Stone of Tizoc,* or the recently discovered *cuauhxicalli* of Motecuhzoma Ilhuicamina. According to Beyer, the work was never completed, since when "they had already carved the circular surface, a large piece broke from the left [*sic*] side, making it impossible to complete the original plan. Then there was no other solution but to carve the relief on the side [profile; *lateral*] only to the break." Beyer is correct, since this relief is complete around the whole circumference, with thirty-two symbols of Venus, accompanied by sacrificial knives (see pl. 3). All of this suggests that the position of the *Piedra del Sol* ought to have been horizontal and that it displayed the solar relief just as on many other known cylindrical monuments.

FUNCTION

Since Chavero's study in the last century, it has been thought that in a horizontal position the *Piedra del Sol* could have been used as a ceremonial platform upon which various kinds of sacrifices were carried out. To prove this theory, it is only necessary to remember the image painted by the *tlacuilos* [native artists] of Father Durán, in his *Historia de las Indias de Nueva España e islas de la tierra firme,* in a section on the reign of Axayacatl, in which the high priest extracts the heart of a victim upon a similar monument (Durán 1990–91, 108) (see pl. 20 and Diego Durán, this volume).

Since then it has been debated whether the monolith functioned as *temalacatl* specifically intended for gladiatorial sacrifice, or if, as Beyer says, it was a *cuauhxicalli,* in which they would deposit the sacred food of the gods. Some authors disagree and consider a *temalacatl* only those circular stones that had a hole [*travesaño*] in the center to which the prisoner was tied with a white cord during the festival of Tlacaxipehualiztli. Some of us think, after closely reading the work of Father Durán, that this class of large-scale monuments, like the *Piedra del Sol,* the *Stone of Tizoc,* and the monolith of the ex-archbishopric [*Stone of Motecuhzoma I*], was a platform that functioned like a *temalacatl* but also, when it received the blood and hearts of the victims, was a *cuauhxicalli* receptacle and thus fulfilled both functions simultaneously (Solís Olguín 1992).

SYMBOLIC CONTENT

Almost all of the authors who have studied the *Piedra del Sol* agree that it is a solar monument that displays themes related to the passage of time; it is in effect a complex calendrical relief (see pl. 2). The identity of the deity in the exact center of its composition has caused much debate, which continues to the present day (see pl. 6). One group of scholars identifies it as Tonatiuh, the sun god, Xiuhtecuhtli, and even Huitzilopochtli (León y Gama, Chavero, Seler, Beyer, Caso, etc.). Navarrete and Heyden (1974) proposed that it is a deity of terrestrial character, and they argue that the face is very similar to that of Tlaltecuhtli. Proceeding from [Navarrete and Heyden], a group of investigators argues that the image in the center of the *Piedra del Sol* has to do with the underworld, with the earth, or that it is actually the night sun (Klein 1976b; Ibarra Grasso 1978; Townsend 1979; Pasztory 1983).

Michel Graulich has recently argued that the interpretation of the central face as the night sun cannot be supported; for him, "it is the midday sun, or of the union of opposites," also called Xochipilli, "prince of flowers" (1992). Nicholson (1993), in a new treatment of the problem, accepts that it is an unusual version of Tonatiuh. We think that a comparative analysis should be undertaken of the central face of the *Piedra del Sol* and that of the new *cuauhxicalli,* discovered in the foundations of the ex-Arzobispado. Both faces share elements like the earflares, the bar-shaped nose plug, the defleshed mouth and essentially, the headdress, which consists of a band with two disks, or *chalchihuites,* and the *xiuhtótotl,* or blue bird (we do not accept that the object in the center of the headband on the *Piedra del Sol* is a human heart, as has been argued). All of these elements are also related to Xiuhtecuhtli, the god of the center of the universe, whose image has hybrid characteristics of the earth and underworld.

THE COSMOGONIC SUNS

The central element carved in the first ring, immediately beyond the face of the deity, corresponds to Nahui Ollin, 4 Movement, the calendrical name of the fifth sun, which is formed by the *ollin* glyph in the shape of an x with four compartments, around the first circle, and it is completed by four small disks, which form the number. We should read them counterclockwise, beginning in the upper right. In this way, we have: Nahui Océlotl, 4 Jaguar, the first sun (see pl. 7); Nahui Ehécatl, 4 Wind, the second sun (see pl. 4); Nahui Quiahuitl, 4 Rain (of fire), the third sun (see pl. 5); and Nahui Atl, 4 Water, the fourth sun (see pl. 8). Between the two lower compartments is a large sacred perforator that passes vertically through the face of the deity, with the point above, and the end with feathers and jade below. Flanking the point and the end are three dates and a sign: the date 1 *tecpatl* or Flint, the *xiuhuitzolli* or *copilli,* the crown of a lord, above; and the dates 1 Rain and 7 Monkey below. The upper elements, according to Graulich, have to do with the birth of Huitzilopochtli and the House of the Sun in the east, while those below are related to the west and to women who died in childbirth.

Continuing, in the next circular band are the twenty signs of the native calendar: *cipactli,* crocodile; *ehecatl,* wind; *calli,* house; *cuetzpallin,* lizard; *coatl,* snake; *miquiztli,* death; *mazatl,* deer; *tochtli,* rabbit; *atl,* water; *itzcuintli,* dog; *ozomatli,* monkey; *malinalli,* divine herb; *acatl,* reed; *ocelotl,* jaguar; *cuauhtli,* eagle; *cozcacuauhtli,* vulture; *ollin,* movement; *tecpatl,* flint knife; *quiahuitl,* rain; and *xochitl,* flower. Together these elements connect the movement of the sun with the form of the calendrical cycle.

SUN RAYS AND SACRIFICIAL PERFORATORS

The four pointed sun rays rest on the ring with the calendrical glyphs and are part of another band, with a series of quincunxes, small squares with five points, one in the center and the others at the four corners, which symbolize the universe and the heat of the sun, which extends in all directions. In the next circular band are the points of four sacred perforators alternating with eight [perforator] ends, each elaborately ornamented with a quincunx, three feathers, and a jade bead. The design harmonizes rhythmically with the sun rays and shows that the sun disk is equivalent to a magnificent *zacatapayolli,* the ball of moss where the autosacrificial perforators used in supreme devotion to the gods were stored. The circular design is complemented by rows of short eagle feathers, streams of blood, bands with *chalchihuitls* and inverted V [*remates*] signs that symbolize blood, all of which confers on the disk great preciousness and recalls the vital liquid that allows life to continue.

THE TWO XIUHCOATLS

On both sides, the solar disk is encircled by two fire serpents, or *xiuhcoatls,* whose bodies are composed of a series of small squares with flame elements (stylized versions of butterflies); the same flame signs appear in profile view on their backs. The pointed tails of the reptiles end in the upper part of the stone, according to the position of the monument today, and between them is the square with the date 13 Reed, which according to the principal chroniclers was the year in which the fifth sun, Ollin Tonatiuh, was born (see pl. 9). In the lower half we can see the arms with claws of these mythological animals and the enormous heads, which each end with a kind of horn with seven stars (see pl. 10). The animals open their jaws, from which emerge the profiles of two opposing deities. Graulich identifies them as Tonatiuh, the sun god, and Xiuhtecuhtli, the fire god, who "symbolize here the starry night sky and the place of night-earth, to which the sun descends when it sets and where it transforms until it is indistinguishable from the fire god."

The *Piedra del Sol* may have functioned as the basis of the solar and ritual calendar systems and as the starting point for complex astronomical observations. Since the first interpretation of the monument, made by León y Gama, until our times, dozens of books have been published that make proposals about the numerical value of each element in the relief, so that, as a result of complicated mathematical operations, the stone is supposed to represent the sum of astronomical observations and the result of complex calendrical calculations. The works of Avilés Solares (1957) and Noriega (n.d.) stand out for the complexity of their assertions.

THE COLORS

In 1939, Roberto Sieck Flandes published his reconstruction of the colors of the *Piedra del Sol*. According to his account, after cleaning and moistening the stone he observed that it had red pigment on the light rays and even "other colors." Sieck proposed a polychrome image of the monument based on data taken from the codices and from some archaeological objects that were exhibited in the old Museo Nacional. This highly colored image has been the delight of tourist guidebooks for decades. Recently, as part of the work that we have undertaken to prepare for the opening of the new Sala Mexica in the Museo Nacional de Antropología in 2000, a detailed cleaning of the monument was completed by a team of conservators consisting of José R. Ramírez Vega, Ana J. Ruigómez, José Luis Muñoz, Miguel Villeda, Vida Mercado, Gabriel Moreno, and Ma. del Carmen Castro Barrera, who, in addition to cleaning the monument, took microscopic samples of the vestiges of paint and discovered that the *Piedra del Sol* was originally painted only (and not on all of its surface) with red and ochre, hues that agree with its symbolism (see pl. 11). The reconstruction of the original coloring was completed by Víctor Manuel Maldonado and will allow the correct appreciation of the monolith in the planning for the new museum installation.

Note

1. See, for example, Solís Olguín 1995, 1997.

The Aztec Calendar and Other Solar Monuments (2004)

Editor's Commentary

Since the late 1960s, Eduardo Matos Moctezuma has been a prolific writer on ancient Mexico and one of the most prominent figures in Mexican archaeology. A key figure in almost every archaeological project in downtown Mexico City for the past thirty years, Matos oversaw the Templo Mayor archaeological project and also served as the director of the Museo del Templo Mayor, founded after the excavations. He has written about Teotihuacan (1990) and the earth god Tlaltecuhtli (1997b); the archaeology, art, and symbolism of the Templo Mayor (e.g., 1982, 1984, 1987, 1988a, 1988b); and Antonio de León y Gama and the history of Mexican archaeology (1997a, 1998a, 1998b, 2002a, 2002b).

The article excerpted below was published after two earlier works on the Calendar Stone *(1992, 1999), the former notable because it includes a photographic reproduction of León y Gama's pamphlet of 1792. Matos follows Alfredo Chavero in attributing the* Calendar Stone *to the reign of Axayacatl and emphasizes that its imagery must be understood as deriving from both its function as a sacrificial vessel and from Aztec beliefs about the sun and its progress through the day. More than many authors, Matos emphasizes the male and female associations of symbolism, the cardinal points, and solar mythology.*

✳   ✳   ✳

The Aztec Calendar and Other Solar Monuments

THE SUN STONE

In view of everything that has been discussed so far, we are working from the assumption that the monument was placed in a horizontal position, precisely as described in the *Durán Codex*. In addition to this, we must take into account.... [its function] as a sacrifice stone, where, once the captive warrior had been sacrificed, Tonatiuh, represented there, was nourished with the victim's blood and heart. Therefore, its main purpose was to feed the Sun so that it would not stop moving. Thus the presence of the previous suns and the days, since these suns were created by the action of creation-destruction generated by the struggle between the gods. This is why the fight had to be between the enemy warrior and the Aztec warrior, in representation of the gods, re-enacting their legendary feats. The symbol of the Fifth Sun, or Nahui Ollin, the Sun of Movement, in the middle of the sculpture, must be fed so as not to detain its movement. This was also why the stone must have had an East to West orientation, reflecting the sun's movement, that is with the tails

Excerpted from Eduardo Matos Moctezuma and Felipe Solís Olguín, *The Aztec Calendar and Other Solar Monuments*, translated by H. J. Drake et al. (Mexico City: Conaculta-Instituto Nacional de Antropologia & Historia, Grupo Azabache, 2004), 63–64, 70. Published with permission. Introductory text by Khristaan D. Villela.

of the two Fire Serpents, the Xiuhcoatl, towards the East and their heads facing West, where the Sun is finally to be devoured by Tlaltecuhtli. The 13-Reed numeral between the two serpent tails is also explained, given that it was the year when the Sun was born, according to the *Anales de Cuauhtitlan,* although it may also be related to the date it was carved, during Axayacatl's rule.

Having said this, the stone's purpose was to supply the Sun with food—blood and hearts—so there would be night and day. So it is no surprise that night, with flint knives and circles as stars—the symbols of Venus—is represented on the rim of the stone. The sun will also penetrate into the night, after being devoured by Tlaltecuhtli in the West, the feminine side of the Universe. And here we can see something very important: when it is gobbled up by the *vagina dentata,* with its huge, sharp teeth, the Sun passed into the terrestrial, nocturnal, female womb, where its new birth was gestated. It was a type of rite of passage where the Sun was reborn from the earth's womb the following morning. It has always been said that the solar star illuminated the Mictlan, but it was not only that. Remember that the Mictlan is described as a dark, windowless place apart from being the womb where the bones of the dead were kept. So, the Sun goes into the terrestrial womb to be reborn through battling with the female nocturnal powers, represented by the night, the Moon and the stars. As we have said, it is the myth of the fight of Huitzilopochtli (the Sun) against Coyolxauhqui (the Moon) and the centzonhuitznahuas (the stars of the South), that talks about this important moment when the sun arms itself with the Xiuhcóatl to beat its enemies and be born from Coatlicue (the Earth). It is, yet again, war as the element of renewal and the presence of the supreme duality: life and death....

THE CENTRAL FACE

The essential features of the central face may be described as follows: the eyes are somewhat sunken as they must have had inlaid shell and black obsidian to make them look more real; they are surrounded by a double line ornament which some people consider characteristic of Tonatiuh, as seen on the face of the Sun God depicted in certain codices, such as the *Aubin Tonalámatl* (Seler 1900, 9, 11, 13), the *Cospi* (*Codex Cospi* 1968, 12), and the *Borgia* (*Codex Borgia* 1993, 66). The hair falls neatly on both sides of the face, unlike the deities associated with the underworld and the earth (Mictlantecuhtli, Tlaltecuhtli), who have curly, tangled locks. Tonatiuh has perfectly straight hair, as seen on the sun stone. The lower part of the face is not fleshless, as some observers believe, because if you look closely, you can see that the round cheeks have skin and the mouth is, in fact, slightly open. Between the teeth—or what remains of them, since the nose and upper part of the mouth are badly deteriorated—emerges a knife for sacrifice, or técpatl, where traces of a facial profile with fangs, typical of these large knives, can still be detected. This is how they have been found in offerings in the Templo Mayor and the way they are depicted in some codices. I believe the sacrifice knife indicates that through it, death is achieved so the Sun may be nourished. If we believe in the image of human body in the *Codex Vaticanus A* (1900, 54, overleaf), it is associated with teeth. Indeed this trait has been connected with Tlaltecuhtli, although it must be remembered that of the four variations of this god, the flint knife can only be seen in some of his female representations. In other words, it is not common to all its images and less so to the male ones. Several anthropologists associate the flint knife in the central face with Tlaltecuhtli himself, but strangely enough they do not do this when they see the same flint knives emerging from the mouths of the two encircling serpents that represent Xiuhtecutli, Quetzalcóatl or Tonatiuh himself. On his forehead he wears a band with three ornaments, which Beyer identified as green stones, or chalchihuites; the middle one may be a bird, as seen in many representations of Tonatiuh, for example on pages 66 and 71 of the *Borgia Codex* (*Codex Borgia* 1993) (where there is also a long nose ring, similar to the one on the stone, and the face is never fleshless). A necklace of round tubular beads and the earspools complement Tonatiuh's ornaments. Figures of the Sun God with these features can be seen in several of the codices, particularly the *Borgia* and the *Codex Borbonicus.*

This is, then, the Sun God but represented in the different stages it passes through on a day's journey. It begins in the East, where it is born of the earth, when it is a young, vigorous, masculine, warrior sun, like a rising eagle that has triumphed over the nocturnal powers. It is accompanied by those who died in war or sacrifice, until it reaches the zenith. At that point, it starts to decline towards the West, towards the female side of the Universe, where it is accompanied by women who died in childbirth, female warriors. Finally, it is devoured by Tlaltecuhtli. The Mesoamerican pyramid is the expression of this rising-descending movement and the high temples at Tenochtitlan and Tlatelolco, the two Mexica cities, have this Westward orientation.

We have already mentioned several times that the claws gripping the hearts do not belong to the god Tlaltecuhtli, as the heart is destined for the Sun. The claws of the god of the underworld grip skulls, which also adorn his ankles and forearms, more in tune with his nature as devourer of cadavers; his role is to eat the flesh and blood, leaving only the skeleton. It must also be said that the liver is the organ associated with the underworld and its gods. The claws may be those of an eagle, as some researcher has already suggested, since the monolith serves as a cuauhxicalli.

CIRCLE OF THE FIVE ELEMENTS

[The ring outside the day signs] is made up of small squares with a central point and four elongated elements in the corners. Enrique Juan Palacios considered this "quinary", as he called it, the Venus glyph. For Beyer, the "quinternion", the term he preferred, together with the other ornaments that accompany it, are more chalchihuites, or precious green stones, associated with the Sun. In the case of the six prominent figures with a ring on top and the famous sole quinternion below, he suspects they may be related to the "day" glyph ilhuitl. Indeed, this element, alternating with the sun's rays, also appears on the Stone of Tízoc and other solar representations. I myself am reminded, moreover, of the barbs used in sacrifice and we must not forget that the sun rose after the immolation and penitence of the gods.

The square shapes with the five points resemble the symbol of the old Fire God, Xiuhtecuhtli-Huehuetéotl. If the five raised points are in fact to give shape to the sunken part, we have a cross that symbolizes the four directions of the Universe with its center, the place where this god dwelt. By the way, this cross confused the 16th century friars, who thought it was associated with the Christian cross.

Another aspect that has led to speculation are the small representations like spurs or peaked arches that appear in groups of four around the circle in question. The first interpreter of the sun stone thought they were mountains or hills; whereas for Palacios, they had to do with the revolutions of Venus. To Beyer, on the other hand, they were splattered blood. In my opinion their meaning has not been totally deciphered, although Beyer's idea is interesting when thought of in connection with the sacrificial barbs I mentioned before. The other small arches surrounding the entire circle immediately above the little five-pointed squares, or "quincunxes", are feather ornaments. They are separated from each other by the eight triangular sun rays, four of which I have already mentioned could be pointing to the respective cardinal points, while the bases of the other four are partially covered by the circle of quincunxes or quinternions.

Bibliography of Selected Works

Abadiano, Dionisio. 1889. *Estudio arqueológico y jeroglífico del calendario o gran libro astronómico histórico y cronológico de los antiguos indios.* Mexico City: Secretaría de Fomento.

Aguilera, Carmen. 1977. *El arte oficial tenochca: Su significación social.* Mexico City: Universidad Nacional Autónoma de México.

Álbum de antigüedades. 1902. *Álbum de antigüedades indígenas que se conservan en el Museo Nacional de México.* Mexico City: Impr. del Museo Nacional.

Alcina Franch, José. 1983. *Pre-Columbian Art.* New York: Abrams.

Alcocer, Ignacio. 1935. *Apuntes sobre la antigua México-Tenochtitlan.* Tacubaya, Mexico: Instituto Panamericano de Geografía e Historia.

Alva Ixtlilxóchitl, Fernando de. 1891–92. *Obras históricas de don Fernando de Alva Ixtlilxóchitl.* Annotated by Alfredo Chavero. 2 vols. Mexico City: Secretaría de Fomento.

———. 1965. *Obras históricas de don Fernando de Alva Ixtlilxóchitl publicadas y anotadas por Alfredo Chavero.* Annotated by Alfredo Chavero. 2 vols. Mexico City: Editora Nacional.

Alvarado Tezozómoc, Fernando. 1853. *Histoire du Mexique par Don Alvaro Tezozómoc.* Translated by H. Ternaux Compans. 2 vols. Paris: P. Jannet.

———. 1878. *Crónica mexicana, escrita por d. Hernando Alvarado Tezozómoc hácia el año de MDCXCVIII.* . . . Edited by José M. Vigil. Mexico City: I. Paz.

———. 1944. *Crónica mexicana.* Mexico City: Secretaría de Educación Pública.

———. 1949. *Crónica mexicayotl.* Translated by Adrián León. Mexico City: Impr. Universitaria.

———. 1975a. *Crónica mexicana, escrita por Hernando Alvarado Tezozómoc hácia el año de MDCXCVIII; anotada por Manuel Orozco y Berra, y precedida del Códice Ramírez, manuscrito del siglo XVI intitulado: Relación del origen de los indios que habitan esta Nueva España según sus historias, y de un examen de ambas obras, al cual va anexo un estudio de cronología mexicana por el mismo Orozco y Berra.* Annotated by Manuel Orozco y Berra. 2nd ed. Mexico City: Porrúa.

———. 1975b. *Crónica mexicayotl.* Mexico City: Universidad Nacional Autónoma de México.

Alzate y Ramírez, José Antonio de. 1791. *Descripción de las antigüedades de Xochicalco.* Mexico City: D. Felipe de Zúñiga y Ontiveros.

———. 1831. *Gacetas de literatura de México.* 4 vols. Puebla: Manuel Buen Abad.

Archives de la Commission scientifique du Mexique. 1865–67. 3 vols. Paris: Imprimerie impériale.

Aveni, Anthony F. 1980. *Skywatchers of Ancient Mexico.* Austin: Univ. of Texas Press.

Aveni, Anthony F. 2001. *Skywatchers.* Rev. ed. Austin: Univ. of Texas Press.

Avilés Solares, José. 1939. *Los sistemas calendáricos del Anáhuac.* Mexico City: Taller Autográfico, Secretaría de la Defensa Nacional.

———. 1957. *Descifración de la piedra del calendario.* Mexico City.

Baedeker, Karl. 1893. *The United States, with an Excursion into Mexico: Handbook for Travellers.* Leipzig: Karl Baedeker.

Bahnson, Kristian. 1889. "Ethnographical Museums." *The Archaeological Review* 2:1–18, 73–90, 145–63, 217–36, 289–311.

Bandelier, Adolph F. 1879. "The National Museum of Mexico and the Sacrificial Stones." *American Antiquarian* 2 (1): 15–29.

———. 1884. *Report of an Archaeological Tour in Mexico in 1881.* Boston: Published for the [Archaeological] Institute [of America] by Cupples, Upham.

Baquedano, Elizabeth. 1984. *Aztec Sculpture.* London: Published for the Trustees of the British Museum.

Barlow, Robert H. 1945. "La *Crónica X.*" *Revista mexicana de estudios antropológicos* 7:65–87.

Barnet-Sánchez, Holly. 1993. "The Necessity of Pre-Columbian Art in the United States: Appropriations and Transformations of Heritage, 1933–1945." In Elizabeth Hill Boone, ed., *Collecting the Pre-Columbian Past,* 177–208. Washington, D.C.: Dumbarton Oaks Research Library & Collection.

Barton, Benjamin Smith. 1797. *New Views of the Origin of the Tribes and Nations of America.* Philadelphia: Printed for the author by John Bioren.

———. 1803a. *Elements of Botany; or, Outlines of the Natural History of Vegetables.* Philadelphia: Printed for the author.

———. 1803b. *Hints on the Etymology of Certain English Words and on Their Affinity to Words in the Languages of Different European, Asiatic, and American (Indian) Nations.* . . . Philadelphia: n.p.

Batres, Leopoldo. 1888. *IV Tlalpilli, ciclo ó período de 13 años: Piedra del agua.* . . . Mexico City: Impr. del Gobierno Federal en el Ex-arzobispado.

———. 1902. *Exploraciones arqueológicas en la Calle de las Escalerillas.* Mexico City: Tip. & Lit. "La Europea," de J. Aguilar Vera.

———. 1910. *Antigüedades mejicanas falsificadas. Falsificación y falsificadores.* Mexico City: Imprenta de Fidencio S. Soria.

Benson, Elizabeth P., and Michael D. Coe. 1963. *Handbook of the Robert Woods Bliss Collection of Pre-Columbian Art.* Washington, D.C.: Dumbarton Oaks.

Berlin-Neubart, Heinrich, and Robert H. Barlow, eds. 1948. *Anales de Tlatelolco: Unos anales históricos de la nación mexicana y Códice de Tlatelolco.* Mexico City: Antigua Librería Robredo.

Bernal, Ignacio. 1962. "Humboldt y la arqueología mexicana." In Marianne Oeste de Bopp, ed., *Ensayos sobre Humboldt,* 121–32. Mexico City: Universidad Nacional Autónoma de México.

———. 1980. *A History of Mexican Archaeology: The Vanished Civilizations of Middle America.* London: Thames & Hudson.

———. 1994. "Durán's *Historia* and the *Crónica X.*" In Diego Durán, *The History of the Indies of New Spain,* 565–77. Translated and annotated by Doris Heyden. Norman: Univ. of Oklahoma Press.

Bernal, Ignacio, and Mireille Simoni-Abbat. 1986. *Le Mexique: Des origins aux aztèques.* Paris: Gallimard.

Betancourt, Salvador, and Alejandro Sodi. 1923. *Álbum histórico-mexicano.* Mexico City: S. L. Betancourt & A. Sodi.

Beyer, Hermann. 1908a. "Der 'Drache' der Mexikaner." *Globus* 93:157–58.

———. 1908b. "Die Naturgrundlage des mexikanischen Gottes Xiuhtecutli: Ein mythologischer Versuch." *Revue des études ethnographiques et sociologiques* 1:394–97.

———. 1910. "Sobre un jeroglífico de un nombre tomado del códice Humboldt." In Ernst Wittich et al., *Memoria científica para la inauguración de la estatua de Alejandro Humboldt,* 81–93. Mexico City: Müller.

———. 1912. "Sobre algunas representaciones del dios Huitzilopochtli." In *Reseña de la segunda sesión del XVII Congreso Internacional de Americanistas efectuada en la ciudad de México durante el mes de septiembre de 1910,* 364–72. Mexico City: Imp. del Museo Nacional de Arqueología & Etnologia.

———. 1913. "Über die mythologischen Affen der Mexikaner und Maya." *International Congress of Americanists: Proceedings of the XVIII Session, London, 1912,* 1:140–54. London: Harrison & Sons.

———. 1920. "El temalácatl, la 'piedra del sacrificio gladiatorio' del Museo Nacional de Arqueología." *Revista de revistas,* no. 541, 19 September.

———. 1921. *El llamado "Calendario Azteca": Descripción y interpretación del cuauhxicalli de la "Casa de las Águilas."* Mexico City: Verband Deutscher Reichsangehöriger.

———. 1922. "El llamado 'Calendario Azteca' en la historia del P. Sahagún." *Memorias de la Sociedad Científica "Antonio Alzate" = Mémoires de la Societé scientifique "Antonio Alzate"* 40:669–74.

———. 1923. "Algunos datos nuevos sobre el *Calendario Azteca.*" *Memorias y revista de la Sociedad Científica "Antonio Alzate"* 42:405–11.

———. 1931. "Mayan Hieroglyphs: The Variable Element of the Introducing Glyphs as Month Indicator." *Anthropos* 26:99–108.

———. 1932. *The Stylistic History of the Maya Hieroglyphs.* New Orleans: Tulane University of Louisiana, Department of Middle American Research.

———. 1937. *Studies on the Inscriptions of Chichen Itza.* Washington, D.C.: Carnegie Institution of Washington.

———. 1941. "A Discussion of J. Eric Thompson's Interpretations of Chichén Itzá Hieroglyphs." *American Antiquity* 6 (4): 327–38.

———. 1955a. "La 'piedra del sacrificio gladiatorio' del Museo Nacional de Arqueología." *El México antiguo* 8:87–94.

———. 1955b. "La 'procesión de los señores,' decoración del primer teocalli de piedra en México-Tenochtitlán." *El México antiguo* 8:1–42.

———. 1965a. "Algunos datos nuevos sobre el *Calendario Azteca.*" *El México antiguo* 10:261–65.

———. 1965b. "El 'dragón' de los mexicanos." *El México antiguo* 10:436–439.

———. 1965c. "Un jeroglífico onomástico del *Códice Humboldt.*" *El México antiguo* 10:494–505.

———. 1965d. "El llamado 'Calendario Azteca': Descripción e interpretación del cuauhxicalle de la 'Casa de las Águilas.'" *El México antiguo* 10:134–256.

———. 1965e. "El llamado 'Calendario Azteca' en la historia del padre Sahagún." *El México antiguo* 10:257–60.

———. 1965f. "El ojo en la simbología del México antiguo." *El México antiguo* 10:488–93.

———. 1965g. "Sobre algunas representaciones del dios Huitzilopochtli." *El México antiguo* 10:372–80.

The Bhagvat-Gheeta. 1785. *The Bhagvat-Gheeta; or, Dialogues of the Kreeshna and Arjoon; in Eighteen Lectures with Notes.* Translated by Charles Wilkins. London: Printed for C. Nourse.

Blake, W. W. 1891. *The Antiquities of Mexico: As Illustrated by the Archaeological Collections in Its National Museum.* New York: C. G. Crawford's Print.

———. 1906. *The Aztec Calendar.* Mexico City: Blake & Fiske.

Boban, Eugène, et al. 1891. *Documents pour servir à l'histoire du Mexique: Catalogue raisonné de la Collection de M. E.-Eugène Goupil. . . .* 2 vols. Paris: E. Leroux.

Bolaños, Joaquín. 1792. *La portentosa vida de la Muerte: Emperatriz de los sepulcros, vengadora de los agravios del Altísimo, y muy señora de la humana naturaleza. . . .* Mexico City: Impresa en la oficina de los herederos del Lic. D. Joseph de Jauregui.

———. 1992. *La portentosa vida de la Muerte, emperatriz de los sepulcros, vengadora de los agravios del Altísimo y muy señora de la humana naturaleza.* Introduction and notes by Blanca López de Mariscal. Mexico City: El Colegio de México.

Bolton, Theodore. 1921. *Early American Portrait Painters in Miniature.* New York: Frederick Fairchild Sherman.

Boone, Elizabeth Hill. 1973. "A Reevaluation of *Coatlicue.*" Unpublished manuscript in author's possession.

———. 1987. "Templo Mayor Research, 1521–1978." In Elizabeth Hill Boone, ed., *The Aztec Templo Mayor,* 5–69. Washington, D.C.: Dumbarton Oaks Research Library & Collection.

———. 1988. "The Nature and Earlier Versions of Diego Durán's *Historia de las Indias* in Madrid." In J. Kathryn Josserand and Karen Dakin, eds., *Smoke and Mist: Mesoamerican Studies in Memory of Thelma D. Sullivan,* 41–58. Oxford: B.A.R.

Boorstin, Daniel J. 1993. *The Lost World of Thomas Jefferson.* Chicago: Univ. of Chicago Press.

Boturini Benaduci, Lorenzo. 1746. *Idea de una nueva historia general de la América septentrional: Fundada sobre material copioso de figuras, symbolos, caractères, y geroglíficos, cantares, y manuscritos de autores indios, últimamente descubiertos.* Madrid: Imprenta de Juan de Zúñiga.

Bowditch, Charles P., ed. 1904. *Mexican and Central American Antiquities, Calendar Systems, and History.* Washington, D.C.: Government Printing Office.

Brading, David. 1980. *Los orígenes del nacionalismo mexicano.* Mexico City: Ediciones Era.

Broda de Casas, Johanna. 1969. *The Mexican Calendar as Compared to Other Mesoamerican Systems.* Vienna: Engelbert Stiglmayr.

Buffon, Georges-Louis Leclerc. 1749–67. *Histoire naturelle, générale et particuliére, avec la description du Cabinet du Roi. . . .* 15 vols. Paris: Imprimerie royale.

Bullock, William Henry. 1824a. *A Description of the Unique Exhibition Called Ancient Mexico; Collected on the Spot in 1823 with the Assistance of the Mexican Government.* London: Printed for the proprietor.

———. 1824b. *Six Months' Residence and Travels in Mexico. . . .* 2 vols. London: John Murray.

Bullock, William Henry, et al. 1824. *Le Mexique en 1823; ou, Relation d'un voyage dans la Nouvelle-Espagne, contenant des notions exactes et peu connues sur la situation physique, morale et politique de ce pays. . . .* 2 vols. Paris: Alexis-Eymery.

Bullock, William Henry, fils. 1866. *Across Mexico in 1864–5.* London: Macmillan.

Burrus, Ernest J. 1959. "Clavigero and the Lost Sigüenza y Góngora Manuscripts." *Estudios de cultura náhuatl* 1:59–90.

Bustamante, Carlos María de. 1832. "Dedicatoria a Alamán." In Antonio de León y Gama, *Descripción histórica y cronológica de las dos piedras que con ocasión del nuevo empedrado que se está formando en la plaza principal de México, se hallaron en ella el año de 1790 . . . ,* pt. 1:i–iv. Mexico City: A. Valdés.

Buxó, José Pascual. 1994. *Impresos novohispanos en las bibliotecas públicas de los Estados Unidos de América (1543–1800).* Mexico City: Universidad Nacional Autónoma de México.

Calderón de la Barca, Frances Erskine Inglis. 1843. *Life in Mexico during a Residence of Two Years in That Country.* 2 vols. Boston: Little & Brown.

Campbell, Lyle. 2000. *American Indian Languages.* Oxford: Oxford Univ. Press.

Campbell, Reau. 1895. *Campbell's Complete Guide and Descriptive Book of Mexico.* Chicago: Poole Bros.

Campo y Rivas, Manuel Antonio del. 1803. *Compendio histórico de la fundación, progresos, y estado actual de la ciudad de Cartago en la provincia de Popayán en el Nuevo Reyno de Granada de la América Meridional.* 3 vols. in 1. Guadalajara, Mexico: En la oficina de M. Valdés Tellez.

Cañizares-Esguerra, Jorge. 2001. *How to Write the History of the New World: Histories, Epistemologies, and Identities in the Eighteenth-Century Atlantic World.* Stanford: Stanford Univ. Press.

Carbájal Espinosa, Francisco. 1862. *Historia de México: Desde los primeros tiempos de que hay noticia hasta mediados del siglo XIX.* Mexico City: Tip. de J. Abadiano.

Caso, Alfonso. 1927. *El Teocalli de la Guerra Sagrada.* Mexico City: Talleres Gráficos de la Nación.

———. 1928. "Las medidas del *Calendario Azteca.*" *Revista mexicana de estudios históricos* 2 (4): 128–37.

———. 1934. "The *Aztec Calendar Stone.*" *American Anthropologist,* n.s., 36:487.

———. 1938. "The *Aztec Calendar Stone.*" In idem, *Thirteen Masterpieces of Mexican Archaeology,* 9–15. Translated by Edith Mackie and Jorge R. Acosta. Mexico City: Editoriales Cultura & Polis.

———. 1953. *El pueblo del sol.* Mexico City: Fondo de Cultura Económica.

———. 1958. *The Aztecs, People of the Sun.* Norman: Univ. of Oklahoma Press.

———. 1959. "El dios 1 Muerte." In Wilhelm Bierhenke et al., eds., *Amerikanistische Miszellen: Festband Franz Termer in Freundschaft und Verehrung gewidmet von Freunden, Kollegen und Schülern zur Vollendung des 65. Lebenjahres,* 40–43. Hamburg: Kommissionsverlag Ludwig Appel.

———. 1967. *Los calendarios prehispánicos.* Mexico City: Universidad Nacional Autónoma de México.

———. 1969. *El tesoro de Monte Albán.* With an appendix by Daniel F. Rubín de la Borbolla et al. Mexico City: Instituto Nacional de Antropología & Historia.

Castañeda, Daniel, and Vicente T. Mendoza. 1933. "Los pequeños percutores en las civilizaciones precortesianos." *Anales del Museo Nacional de Arqueología, Historia y Etnografía de México,* ser. 4, 8 (3): 449–576.

Castillo, Cristóbal del. 1908. *Fragmentos de la obra general sobre historia de los mexicanos, escrita en lengua náuatl . . . a fines del siglo XVI.* Translated by Francisco del Paso y Troncoso. Florence: Tip. de S. Landi.

Castillo Ledón, Luis. 1924. *El Museo Nacional de Arqueología, Historia y Etnografía.* Mexico City: Imprenta del Museo Nacional de Arqueología, Historia y Etnografía.

Catálogo oficial de las exhibiciones de los E. U. Mexicanos: Exposición Internacional de St. Louis, Mo., 1904. 1904. Mexico City: Comisión Nacional, Exposición Internacional de St. Louis.

Cepeda-Cárdenas, Gerardo, and Raúl-Martín Arana. 1968. "Hueso grabado del centro de México." *Boletín del Instituto Nacional de Antropología e Historia* 31:38–41.

Chanfón Olmos, Carlos. 1978. "La geometría y la *Piedra del Sol.*" *Churubusco* 1:7–72.

Charnay, Desire. 1885. *Les anciennes villes du Nouveau monde; voyages d'explorations au Mexique et dans l'Amérique Centrale.* Paris: Librairie Hachette.

———. 1887. *The Ancient Cities of the New World: Being Voyages and Explorations in Mexico and Central America from 1857–1882.* Translated from the French by J. Gonino and Helen S. Conant. New York: Harper.

Chavero, Alfredo. 1875. "*Calendario Azteca.*" In José María Pérez Hernández, Manuel Orozco y Berra, and Alfredo Chavero, eds., *Diccionario geográfico, estadístico, histórico, biográfico, de industria y comercio de la República Mexicana, escrito en parte y arreglado en otra por el general José María Pérez Hernández, consultando sus tareas con los distinguidos escritores Lics. D. Manuel Orozco y Berra y D. Alfredo Chavero,* vol. 3, app.: 1–16. Mexico City: Impr. de Cinco de Mayo.

———. 1876. "*Calendario Azteca*": Ensayo arqueológico. 2nd ed. Mexico City: Jens & Zapiain.

———. 1877a. "La *Piedra del Sol,* segundo estudio." *Anales del Museo Nacional de México,* ser. 1, 1:353–86.

———. 1877b. *Quetzalcóatl: Ensayo trágico en tres actos y en verso.* México: Jens & Zapiain.

———. 1878a. "Códice Ramírez.—Durán.—Acosta.—Tezozómoc." In Fernando Alvarado Tezozómoc, *Crónica mexicana, escrita por d. Hernando Alvarado Tezozómoc hácia el año de MDCXCVIII . . . ,* 162–67. Edited by José M. Vigil. Mexico City: I. Paz.

———. 1878b. *Xóchitl: Drama en tres actos y en verso.* 3rd ed. Mexico City: G. A. Esteva.

———. 1879. *Los amores de Alarcón: Poema dramático en tres actos y en prosa.* México: Tip. de G. A. Esteva.

———. 1882. "La *Piedra del Sol*: Estudio arqueológico." *Anales del Museo Nacional de México,* ser. 1, 2:2–46, 107–26, 233a–266, 291–310, 402a–430.

———. 1886. "La *Piedra del Sol*: Estudio arqueológico." *Anales del Museo Nacional de México,* ser. 1, 3:3a–26, 37–56, 110–14, 124–26a.

———. 1888. *Historia antigua y de la conquista.* Vol. 1 of D. Vicente Riva Palacio, ed., *México a través de los siglos. . . .* Barcelona: Espasa y Compañia.

———. 1892. *Lienzo de Tlaxcalla.* Mexico City: A. Chavero.

———. 1903. "La *Piedra del Sol*: Estudio arqueológico." *Anales del Museo Nacional de México,* ser. 1, 7:133–36.

———. 1904. *Obras del Lic. don Alfredo Chavero.* Mexico City: V. Agüeros.

Chavero, Alfredo, and Joaquín Baranda, eds. 1892. *Homenaje á Cristóbal Colón: Antigüedades mexicanas.* Mexico City: Oficina tipográfica de la Secretaría de Fomento.

Chavero, Alfredo, and José Lino Fábrega. 1899. *Interpretación del Códice Borgia: Obra póstuma del P. José Lino Fábrega de la Compañía de Jesú. . . .* Mexico City: Impr. del Museo Nacional.

Chimalpahin Cuauhtlehuanitzin, Domingo Francisco de San Antón Muñón. 1958. "Ausgewählte Abschnitte aus der III. Relación." In Walter Lehmann and Gerdt Kutscher, eds. and trans., *Das Memorial breve acerca de la fundación de la ciudad de Culhuacán und weitere ausgewählte Teile aus den "Diferentes historias originales,"* 148–69. Stuttgart: W. Kohlhammer.

———. 1965. *Relaciones originales de Chalco Amaquemecan.* Translated by S. Rendón. Mexico City: Fondo de Cultura Económica.

Clark, James Cooper. 1913. "The Story of 'Eight Deer' in the Codex Colombino." *International Congress of Americanists: Proceedings of the XVIII Session, London, 1912,* 1:135–36. London: Harrison & Sons.

Clavigero, Francesco Saverio. 1780–81. *Storia antica del Messico, cavata da' migliori storici spagnuoli, e da' manoscritti, e dalle pitture antiche degl'Indiani . . . e dissertazioni sulla terra, sugli animali, e sugli abitatori del Messico.* 4 vols. in 2. Cesena: G. Biasini.

Codex Azcatitlan. 1949. *El Códice Azcatítlan.* 2 vols. Published to accompany an article by Robert H. Barlow. [Paris]: Société des Américanistes.

Codex Borbonicus. 1899. *Codex Borbonicus: Manuscrit mexicain de la Bibliothèque du Palais Bourbon.* Edited by E. T. Hamy. Paris: E. Leroux.

———. 1974. *Codex Borbonicus, Bibliothèque de l'Assemblée nationale, Paris (Y 120): Vollständige Faksimile-Ausgabe des Codex im Originalformat.* Graz, Austria: Akademische Druck- & Verlagsanstalt. Facsimile with commentary by Karl Anton Nowotny and Jaqueline de Durand-Forest.

Codex Borgia. 1900. *Códice Borgia: Interpretación del Códice Borgiano.* Translated and edited by Alfredo Chavero and Francisco del Paso y Troncoso, with commentary by José Lino Fábrega. Mexico City: Impr. del Museo Nacional.

———. 1993. *Códice Borgia. Los templos del cielo y de la oscuridad: Oraculos y liturgia, libro explicativo del llamado Códice Borgia.* Edited by Ferdinand Anders. Mexico City: Fondo de Cultura Económica.

Codex Chimalpopoca. 1945. *Códice Chimalpopoca: Anales de Cuauhtitlan y Leyenda de los soles.* Translated by Primo Feliciano Velázquez. Mexico City: Instituto de Historia, Universidad Nacional Autónoma de México.

———. 1975. *Códice Chimalpopoca: Anales de Cuauhtitlan y Leyenda de los soles.* Translated by Primo Feliciano Velázquez. 2nd ed. Mexico City: Universidad Nacional Autónoma de México, Instituto de Investigaciones Históricas.

Codex Cospi. 1968. *Codex Cospi: Calendario messicano 4093; Biblioteca universitaria Bologna.* Introduction and commentary by Karl Anton Nowotny. Graz, Austria: Akademische Druck- & Verlagsanstalt.

Codex Laud. 1937. *Códice Laud, M.S. pictórico mexicano que existe en la Biblioteca Bodleiana, Universidad de Oxford.* Mexico City: G. M. Echaniz.

Codex Magliabechiano. 1970. *Codex Magliabechiano, CL. XIII. 3 (B. R. 232): Biblioteca nazionale centrale di Firenze.* Introduction by Ferdinand Anders. Graz, Austria: Akademische Druck- & Verlagsanstalt.

Codex Mendoza. 1925. *Colección de Mendoza; o, Códice mendocino: Documento mexicano del siglo XVI que se conserva en la Biblioteca Bodleiana de Oxford, Inglaterra; facsimile fototípico.* Edited by Francisco del Paso y Troncoso, with commentary by Jesús Galindo y Villa. Mexico City: Museo Nacional de Arqueología, Historia & Etnografía.

Codex Telleriano Remensis. 1899. *Codex Telleriano-Remensis: Manuscrit mexicain.* Edited by E. T. Hamy. Paris: n.p.

———. 1964. In José Corona Núñez, ed., *Antigüedades de México, basadas en la recopilación de Lord Kingsborough,* 1:152–357. Mexico City: Secretaría de Hacienda & Crédito Público.

Codex Vaticanus A. 1900. *Codex Vaticanus A: Il manoscritto messicano vaticano 3738, detto il Códice Rios.* Rome: Danesi.

Codex Zouche-Nuttall. 1987. *Codex Zouche-Nuttall: British Museum London (Add. MS. 39671); Vollständige Faksimile-Ausgabe des Codex im Originalformat.* Graz, Austria: Akademische Druck- & Verlagsanstalt.

Coe, Michael D. 1992. *Breaking the Maya Code.* New York: Thames & Hudson.

Conder, Josiah. 1830. *A Popular Description, Geographical, Historical, and Topographical of Mexico and Guatimala.* Vol. 6 of *The Modern Traveller: A Description, Geographical, Historical, and Topographical, of the Various Countries of the Globe.* Boston: Wells & Lilly.

Conkling, Alfred R. 1884. *Appletons' Guide to Mexico, Including a Chapter on Guatemala and a Complete English-Spanish Vocabulary.* New York: D. Appleton.

Cordy-Collins, Alana, and Douglas Sharon, eds. 1993. *Current Topics in Aztec Studies: Essays in Honor of Dr. H. B. Nicholson.* San Diego: San Diego Museum of Man.

Cortés, Hernán. 1770. *Historia de Nueva-España, escrita por su esclarecido conquistador Hernán Cortés: Aumentada con otros documentos, y notas, por el illustríssimo Francisco Antonio Lorenzana, arzobispo de México.* Edited by Francisco Antonio Lorenzana. Mexico City: Hogal.

Cosío Villegas, Daniel, et al. 1974. *A Compact History of Mexico.* Mexico City: Colegio de México.

Cossío, José Lorenzo. 1942. *Ruinas arqueológicas de Tolcayuca, Hidalgo.* Mexico City: Editorial Cultura.

Costeloe, Michael P. 2006. "William Bullock and the Mexican Connection." *Mexican Studies = Estudios mexicanos* 22:275–309.

Couch, N. C. Christopher. 1987. "Style and Ideology in the Durán Illustrations: An Interpretative Study of Three Early Colonial Mexican Manuscripts." Ph.D. diss., Columbia University.

Covarrubias, Miguel. 1957. *Indian Art of Mexico and Central America.* New York: Knopf.

Danzel, Theodor-Wilhelm, and Ernst Fuhrmann. 1922. *Mexiko I–III.* 3 vols. Hagen, Germany: Folkwang

Davies, Claude Nigel. 1973. *Los mexicas: Primeros pasos hacia el imperio.* Mexico City: Universidad Nacional Autónoma de México, Instituto de Investigaciones Históricas.

de Jonghe, Édouard. 1905. "Histoyre du mechique: Manuscrit français inédit du XVIe siècle." *Journal de la Société des Américanistes* 2:1–41.

Delhalle, Jean-Claude, and Albert Luykx. 1983. "A Teotihuacán, le dernier Soleil." *Art and Fact: Revue des historiens d'art, des arquéologues, des musicologues et des orientalistes de l'Université de l'Etat à Liège,* no. 2:50–52.

Dellenbaugh. Frederick S. 1933. "The *Aztec Calendar Stone.*" *American Anthropologist,* n.s., 35:791–92.

———. 1935. "The *Aztec Calendar Stone:* A Reply." *American Anthropologist,* n.s., 37:370.

Delpar, Helen. 1992. *The Enormous Vogue of Things Mexican: Cultural Relations between the United States and Mexico, 1920–1935.* Tuscaloosa: Univ. of Alabama Press.

Description de l'Egypte. 1809–28. *Description de l'Egypte; ou, Recueil de observations et des recherches qui ont été faites en Égypte pendant l'éxpédition de l'armée française.* 21 vols. Paris: Imprimerie Impériale.

de Terra, Helmut. 1955. *Humboldt: The Life and Times of Alexander von Humboldt, 1769–1859.* New York: Knopf.

———. 1958a. "Studies of the Documentation of Alexander von Humboldt." *Proceedings of the American Philosophical Society* 102 (2): 136–41.

———. 1958b. "Studies of the Documentation of Alexander von Humboldt: The Philadelphia Abstract of Humboldt's American Travels; Humboldt Portraits and Sculpture in the United States." *Proceedings of the American Philosophical Society* 102 (6): 136–589.

———. 1959. "Alexander von Humboldt's Correspondence with Jefferson, Madison, and Gallatin." *Proceedings of the American Philosophical Society* 103 (6): 783–806.

Díaz del Castillo, Bernal. 1904–5. *Historia verdadera de la conquista de la Nueva España.* Edited by Genaro García. 2 vols. Mexico City: Oficina tipográfica de la Secretaría de Fomento.

———. 1908–16. *The True History of the Conquest of New Spain.…* Edited by Genaro García. Translated by Alfred

Percival Maudslay. 5 vols. London: Printed for the Hakluyt Society.

Díaz y de Ovando, Clementina. 1990. "México en la Exposición Universal de 1889." *Anales del Instituto de Investigaciones Esteticas* 16 (61): 109–71.

Diehl, Richard A. 2004. *The Olmecs: America's First Civilization.* London: Thames & Hudson.

Dieseldorff, Erwin P. 1930. "The *Aztec Calendar Stone* and Its Significance." *Proceedings of the Twenty-third International Congress of Americanists,* 211–22. New York: n.p.

Diplomatic and Consular Instructions of the Department of State, 1791–1801. 1969. Washington, D.C.: National Archives & Records Service, General Services Administration.

Dresden Codex. 1880. *Die Mayahandschrift der Königlichen öffentliches Bibliothek zu Dresden.* Edited by Ernst Wilhelm Förstemann. Leipzig: Naumann.

Dupaix, Guillermo. 1794. "Descripción de monumentos antiguos mexicanos." MS, Museo Nacional de Antropología, Mexico City.

———. 1831–48. "Viages de Guillelmo Dupaix sobre las antigüedades mejicanas." In Edward King, Viscount Kingsborough, ed., *Antiquities of Mexico: Comprising Fac-Similes of Ancient Mexican Paintings and Hieroglyphics, Preserved in the Royal Libraries of Paris, Berlin and Dresden; in the Imperial Library of Vienna; in the Vatican Library; in the Borgian Museum at Rome; in the Library of the Institute at Bologna; and in the Bodleian Library at Oxford: Together with the Monuments of New Spain, by M. Dupaix, with Their Respective Scales of Measurement and Accompanying Descriptions; the Whole Illustrated by Many Valuable Inedited Manuscripts,* 5:207–344. Translated as "The Monuments of New Spain" in the same compilation, 6:421–86. London: Robert Havell…& Colnaghi, Son & Co….printed by James Moyes.

Dupaix, Guillermo, Alexandre Lenoir, and David Bailie Warden. 1834–44. *Antiquités mexicaines: Relation des trois expéditions du colonel Dupaix, ordonnées en 1805, 1806 et 1807, par le roi Charles IV, pour la recherche les antiquites du pays, notamment celles de Mitla et de Palenque: Avec les dessins de Castañeda.* Edited by H. Baradère. 2 vols. Paris: Au Bureau des Antiquités Mexicaines.

Dupuis, Charles. 1806. *Memoire explicatif du Zodiaque chronologique et mythologique: Ouvrage contenant le tableau comparatif des maisons de la lune chez les différens peuples de l'Orient….* Paris: Courcier.

Durán, Diego. 1964. *The Aztecs: The History of the Indies of New Spain.* Translated by Doris Heyden and Fernando Horcasitas. New York: Orion.

———. 1967. *Historia de las Indias de Nueva España e islas de tierra firme.* Edited by Ángel María Garibay Kintana. 2 vols. Mexico City: Editorial Porrúa.

———. 1971. *Book of the Gods and Rites and the Ancient Calendar.* Translated by Fernando Horcasitas and Doris Heyden. Norman: Univ. of Oklahoma Press.

———. 1990–91. *Historia de las Indias de Nueva España e islas de la tierra firme.* 2 vols. Madrid: Banco Santander, Ediciones Equilibrista.

———. 1994. *The History of the Indies of New Spain.* Translated, annotated, and with an introduction by Doris Heyden. Norman: Univ. of Oklahoma Press.

Durán, Diego, et al. 1867–80. *Historia de las Indias de Nueva-España y islas de tierra firme.* 2 vols. in 1. Mexico City: J. M. Andrade & F. Escalante.

Easby, Elizabeth Kennedy, and John F. Scott. 1970. *Before Cortés, Sculpture of Middle America.* Exh. cat. New York: Metropolitan Museum of Art.

Eliade, Mircea. 1949. *Le mythe de l'eternel retour: Archétypes et répétition.* Paris: Gallimard.

———. 1964. *Shamanism: Archaic Techniques of Ecstasy.* Translated by Willard R. Trask. New York: Pantheon.

Elzey, Wayne. 1976. "The Nahua Myth of the Suns: History and Cosmology in Pre-Hispanic Mexican Religions." *Numen* 23:114–35.

Erickson, Raymond, Mauricio A. Font, and Brian Schwartz, eds. 2004. *Alexander von Humboldt: From the Americas to the Cosmos.* New York: City University of New York, Graduate Center.

Escalona y Ramos, Alberto. 1940. *Cronología y astronomía maya-mexica.* Mexico City: Editorial "Fides."

El escenario urbano de Pedro Gualdi, 1808–1857. 1997. Exh. cat. Mexico City: Instituto Nacional de Bellas Artes.

Ewan, Joseph, et al. 2007. *Benjamin Smith Barton: Naturalist and Physician in Jeffersonian America.* Saint Louis: Missouri Botanical Garden Press.

Fernández, Miguel Angel. 1987. *Historia de los museos de México.* Mexico City: Fomento Cultural Banamex.

Fernández del Castillo, Francisco. 1913. *Apuntes para la historia de San Ángel (San Jacinto Tenanitla) y sus alrededores: Tradiciones, historia, leyendas….* Mexico City: Imp. del Museo Nacional de Arqueología, Historia y Etnología.

Florescano, Enrique. 1993. "The Creation of the Museo Nacional de Antropología of Mexico and Its Scientific, Educational, and Political Purposes." In Elizabeth Hill Boone, ed., *Collecting the Pre-Columbian Past,* 81–104. Washington, D.C.: Dumbarton Oaks Research Library and Collection.

Flor y canto del arte prehispánico de México. 1964. Mexico City: Fondo Editorial de la Plástica Mexicana.

Fradcourt, Ariane. 1982. "Le 'Calendrier Aztèque': Monument conserve au Musée National d'Anthropologie de Mexico." Undergraduate thesis, Université Libre de Bruxelles.

———. 1987. "A New Study of the Central Figure on the *Aztec Calendar Stone.* A Contribution to Methodology in Mesoamerican Iconography." Paper presented at "Les Interprétations de l'objet mexicain précolombien,"

European Coordination Center for Research and Documentation in Social Sciences (Vienna Center), Linz, Austria, 7–9 June.

———. 1988a. "New Insights on the Interpretation of the *Aztec Calendar Stone* (with Notes on Skeletonization)." Paper presented at the XLVI International Congress of Americanists, Amsterdam.

———. 1988b. "Les quatre petits glyphs sur la pierre du 'Calendrier Aztèque': Nouvelle interprétation." *Art and Fact: Revue des historiens d'art, des archéologues, des musicologues et des orientalistes de l'Université de l'Etat de Liège,* no. 7:10–17.

———. 1991. "Une nouvelle étude iconographique de la divinité centrale de la pierre du 'Calendrier aztèque.'" *Art and Fact: Revue des historiens d'art, des archéologues, des musicologues et des orientalistes de l'Université de l'Etat de Liège,* no. 10:99–109.

———. 1992. "Nouvelles perspectives dans l'interprétation de la pierre du *Calendrier aztèque* (avec notes sur le décharnement)." *Art and Fact: Revue des historiens de l'art, des archéologues, des musicologues et des orientalistes de l'Université de Liège,* no. 11:111–24.

———. 1993. "New Insights on the Interpretation of the *Aztec Calendar Stone* (with Notes on Skeletonization)." In Jacqueline de Durand-Forest and Marc Eisinger, eds., *The Symbolism in the Plastic and Pictorial Representations of Ancient Mexico: A Symposium of the 46th International Congress of Americanists, Amsterdam 1988,* 203–31. Bonn: Holos.

Furst, Jill Leslie. 1982. "Skeletonization in Mixtec Art: A Re-evaluation." In Elizabeth Hill Boone, ed., *The Art and Iconography of Late Post-Classic Central Mexico,* 207–25. Washington, D.C.: Dumbarton Oaks.

Galindo y Villa, Jesús. 1895. *Catálogo del Departamento de Arqueología del Museo Nacional: Primera parte, Galería de Monolitos.* Mexico City: Impr. del Museo Nacional.

Gallatin, Albert. 1845. "Notes on the Semi-Civilized Nations of Mexico." *Transactions of the American Ethnological Society* 1:1–352.

Gallegos Ruiz, Roberto. 1978. *El señor 9 Flor en Zaachila.* Mexico City: Universidad Nacional Autónoma de México.

García, Rubén. 1934. "Bibliografía razonada del *Calendario Azteca.*" *Anales del Museo Nacional de Arqueología, Historia y Etnografía,* ser. 5, 1:113–48.

García Icazbalceta, Joaquín. 1886–92. *Nueva colección de documentos para la historia de México.* 3 vols. Mexico City: Andrade y Morales.

García Icazbalceta. 1891. *Pomar y Zurita. Pomar, Relación de Tezcoco; Zurita, Breve relación de los señores de la Nueva España. Varias relaciones antiguas. (Siglo XVI).* 3 vols. Mexico City: Francisco Díaz de León.

Gardner, Brant. 1979. "The Aztec Legend of the Suns: A Structural Approach to Ethnohistory." Unpublished manuscript.

Garibay Kintana, Ángel María, ed. 1953–54. *Historia de la literatura náhuatl.* 2 vols. Mexico City: Editorial Porrúa.

———, ed. 1964–68. *Poesía náhuatl.* Translated by Juan Bautista Pomar. 3 vols. Mexico City: Universidad Nacional Autónoma de México, Instituto de Historia, Seminario Cultura Náhuatl.

———, ed. 1965. *Teogonía e historia de los mexicanos: Tres opúsculos del siglo XVI.* Mexico City: Editorial Porrúa.

Garritz Ruiz, Amaya. 1990. *Impresos novohispanos, 1808–1821.* 2 vols. Mexico City: Universidad Nacional Autónoma de México.

Gatschet, A. S. 1899. "Notes and News." Obituary of Philipp Johann Joseph Valentini. *American Anthropologist,* n.s., 1 (2): 391–400.

Gazeta de México. 1791. In Manuel Antonio Valdes, ed., *Gazeta de México: Compendio de noticias de Nueva España,* 4:379 (16 August). Mexico City: En la Imprenta de Don Felipe de Zúñiga y Ontiveros.

———. 1792. In Manuel Antonio Valdes, ed., *Gazeta de México: Compendio de noticias de Nueva España,* 5:117 (26 June). Mexico City: En la Imprenta de Don Felipe de Zúñiga y Ontiveros.

Gerbi, Antonello. 1982. *La disputa del nuevo mundo: Historia de una polémica, 1750–1900.* Translated by Antonio Alatorre. Rev. ed. Mexico City: Fondo de Cultura Económica.

Gibson, Charles, and John B. Glass. 1975. "A Census of Middle American Prose Manuscripts in the Native Historical Tradition." In Howard F. Cline, ed., *Guide to Ethnohistorical Sources,* pt. 4:322–400. Vol. 15 of Robert Wauchope, ed., *Handbook of Middle American Indians.* Austin: Univ. of Texas Press.

Gilreath, James, and Douglas L. Wilson, eds. 1988. *Thomas Jefferson's Library: A Catalog with the Entries in His Own Order.* Washington, D.C.: Library of Congress.

Glass, John B. 1975. "Boturini Collection." In Howard F. Cline, ed., *Guide to Ethnohistorical Sources,* pt. 4:473–86. Vol. 15 of Robert Wauchope, ed., *Handbook of Middle American Indians.* Austin: Univ. of Texas Press.

Gómez, José. 1854. *Diario curioso de México de D. José Gómez, cabo de alabarderos: Está publicado en lo que se creyó conveniente en los primeros números del Museo mexicano del año de 1848, tomo primero.* Mexico City: Antigua Impr. de la Voz de la Religión.

———. 1947. *Cuaderno de las cosas memorables que han sucedido en esta ciudad de México y en otras en el gobierno del Exmo. señor conde de Revilla Gigedo. . . .* Mexico City: Vargas Rea.

———. 1986. *Diario curioso; y, Cuaderno de las cosas memorables en México durante el gobierno de Revillagigedo (1789–1794).* Edited by Ignacio González-Polo. Mexico City: Universidad Nacional Autónoma de México.

Gondra, Isidro Rafael. 1846. *Esplicación de las laminas a la historia Antigua de México.* Vol. 3 of *Historia de la conquista de México con una ojeada preliminar sobre la antigua civilizacion de los mexicanos, y con la vida de su conquistador, Fernando Cortes; escrita en ingles y tr. al español por Joaquín Navarro.* Mexico City: I. Cumplido.

González Torres, Yólotl. 1975. *El culto a los astros entre los mexicas.* Mexico City: Secretaría de Educación Pública… Subdirección de Divulgación.

Gortari, Elí de. 1980. *La ciencia en la historia de México.* Mexico City: Editorial Grijalbo.

Graham, Ian. 1993. "Three Early Collectors in Mesoamerica." In Elizabeth Hill Boone, ed., *Collecting the Pre-Columbian Past,* 49–80. Washington, D.C.: Dumbarton Oaks Research Library & Collection.

Graulich, Michel. n.d. "Reflections on Two Masterpieces of Aztec Art: The *Calendar Stone* and the *Teocalli of Sacred Warfare.*" Unpublished manuscript in author's possession.

———. 1979. "Mythes et rites des vingtaines du Mexique Central préhispanique." Ph.D. diss., Université Libre deBruxelles.

———. 1987. *Mythes et rituels du Mexique ancien préhispanique.* Brussels: Académie Royale de Belgique.

———. 1988. *Quetzalcóatl y el espejismo de Tollan.* Antwerp: Instituut voor Amerikanistiek.

———. 1990. *Mitos y rituales del México antiguo.* Madrid: Itsmo.

———. 1992. "La *Piedra del Sol.*" In José Alcina Franch, Miguel León-Portilla, and Eduardo Matos Moctezuma, eds., *Azteca-mexica: Las culturas del México antiguo,* 291–95. Madrid: Lunwerg.

———. 1997a. *Myths of Ancient Mexico.* Translated by Bernard R. Ortiz de Montellano and Thema Ortiz de Montellano. Norman: Univ. of Oklahoma Press.

———. 1997b. "Reflexiones sobre dos obras maestras del arte azteca: La *Piedra del Calendario* y el *Teocalli de la Guerra Sagrada.*" In Xavier Noguez and Alfredo López Austin, eds., *De hombres y dioses,* 155–207. Michoacán: Colegio de Michoacán.

———. 1999. *Ritos aztecas: Las fiestas de las veintenas.* Mexico City: Instituto Nacional Indigenista.

———. 2005. *Le sacrifice humain chez les Aztèques.* Paris: Fayard.

Griffin, Gillett G. 1974. "Early Travelers to Palenque." In Merle Greene Robertson, ed., *Primera mesa redonda de palenque,* 1:9–33. Pebble Beach, Calif.: Robert Louis Stevenson School.

Gualdi, Pedro. 1841. *Monumentos de Méjico: Tomados del natural y litografiados.* [Mexico City]: Masse & Decaen.

Gutiérrez Haces, Juana. 1995. "Las antigüedades mexicanas en las descripciones de Don Antonio de Léon y Gama." In idem, ed., *Los discursos sobre el arte: XV coloquio internacional de historia del arte,* 121–46. Mexico City: Universidad Nacional Autónoma de México, Instituto de Investigaciones Estéticas.

Hale, Charles A. 1965. "José María Luis Mora and the Structure of Mexican Liberalism." *Hispanic American Historical Review* 45 (2): 196–227.

Hamy, E. T. 1903. "Le joyau du vent." *Journal de la Societé des américanistes de Paris,* o.s., 4: 72–81.

Hastings, James, ed. 1912–27. *Encyclopedia of Religion and Ethics.* 13 vols. New York: Scribner's.

Hernández, Francisco. 1651. *Rerum Medicarum Novae Hispaniae Thesaurus seu Plantarum, Animalium et Mineralium Mexicanorum Historia… Quibus Singula Contemplanda Graphice Exhibentur.* Rome: Ex typographeio Vitalis Mascardi.

Heyden, Doris. 1970. "Deidad del agua encontrado en el Metro." *Boletín del Instituto Nacional de Antropología e Historia* 40:35–40.

———. 1971. "Comentarios sobre la *Coatlicue* recuperada durante las excavaciones realizadas para la construcción del Metro." *Anales del Instituto Nacional de Antropología e Historia* 7 (50): 153–70.

———. 1975. "An Interpretation of the Cave underneath the Pyramid of the Sun in Teotihuacan, Mexico." *American Antiquity* 40 (2): 131–47.

"Historia de los mexicanos por sus pinturas." 1941. In Joaquin García Icazbalceta, ed., *Nueva colección de documentos para la historia de México,* 3:207–40. 2nd ed. Mexico City: Editorial Salvador Chávez Hayhoe.

———. 1965. In Ángel María Garibay Kintana, ed., *Teogonía e historia de los antiguos mexicanos: Tres opúsculos del siglo XVI,* 23–90. Mexico City: Editorial Porrúa.

———. 1973. In Ángel María Garibay Kintana, ed., *Teogonía e historia de los mexicanos: Tres opúsculos del siglo XVI,* 23–66. 2nd ed. Mexico City: Editorial Porrúa.

Historisches Museum Frankfurt am Main. 1960. *Präkolumbische Kunst aus Mexico und Mittelamerika.* Frankfurt am Main: Historisches Museum Frankfurt am Main.

"Histoyre du Mechique." 1965. In Ángel María Garibay Kintana, ed., *Teogonía e historia de los antiguos mexicanos: Tres opúsculos del siglo XVI,* 91–120. Mexico City: Editorial Porrúa.

Holmes, William Henry. 1889. "On Some Spurious Mexican Antiquities and Their Relation to Ancient Art." *Annual Report of the Board of Regents of the Smithsonian Institution… for the Year Ending June 30, 1886,* 319–34. Washington, D.C.: Government Printing Office.

Horcasitas, Fernando, and Doris Heyden. 1971. "Fray Diego Durán: His Life and Works." In Diego Durán, *Book of the Gods and Rites and the Ancient Calendar,* 3–47. Translated by Fernando Horcasitas and Doris Heyden. Norman: Univ. of Oklahoma Press.

Houston, Stephen D., David Stuart, and Karl A. Taube. 2006. *The Memory of Bones: Body, Being, and Experience among the Classic Maya.* Austin: Univ. of Texas Press.

Hulings, William E. 1803. "Near Natchez, October 29, 1802." Letter to the editor, *National Intelligencer and Washington Adviser,* 31 December.

Humboldt, Alexander von. 1810. *Vues des cordillères et monumens des peuples indigènes de l'Amérique.* 2 vols. Paris: F. Schoell.

———. 1811. *Political Essay on the Kingdom of New Spain.* Translated by John Black. 2 vols. New York: I. Riley.

———. 1811–12. *Essai politique sur le royaume de la Nouvelle-Espagne.…* 2 vols. Paris: F. Schoell.

———. 1814. *Researches Concerning the Institutions and Monuments of the Ancient Inhabitants of America, with Descriptions and Views of Some of the Most Striking Scenes in the Cordilleras!* Translated by Helen Maria Williams. 2 vols. in 1. London: Longman, Hurst, Rees, Orme & Brown, J. Murray & H. Colburn.

Humboldt, Alexander von, and Aimé Bonpland. 1814–25. *Voyage aux régions équinoxiales du nouveau continent, fait en 1799, 1800, 1801, 1802, 1803 et 1804.…* 3 vols. Paris: G. Dufour.

Hvidtfeldt, Arild. 1958. *Teotl and Ixiptlatli: Some Central Conceptions in Ancient Mexican Religion, with a General Introduction on Cult and Myth.* Copenhagen: Munksgaard.

Ibarra Grasso, Dick Edgar. 1978. *La verdadera interpretación del calendario azteca.* Buenos Aires: Editorial Kier.

Icaza, Isidro Ignacio de, and Isidro Rafael Gondra. 1827. *Colección de antigüedades que ecsisten en el Museo Nacional… litografiadas por Federico Waldeck.* Mexico City: Impreso por Pedro Robert.

———. 1927. *Colección de las antigüedades mexicanas que existían en el Museo nacional.…* Reprint of edition of 1827. Mexico City: Talleres Gráficos del Museo Nacional de Arqueología, Historia & Etnografía.

Illustrated Catalogue of Mexican Art Goods and Curiousities. Also Indian Goods. For Sale by the Mexican Art and Curiosity Store, W. G. Walz, Proprietor. 1888. El Paso, Texas: W. G. Walz.

Janvier, Thomas A. 1886. *Mexican Guide.* New York: Scribner's Sons.

Jefferson, Thomas. 2004. *The Papers of Thomas Jefferson: Retirement Series.* Vol. 1, *4 March to 15 November 1809.* Edited by J. Jefferson Looney et al. Princeton: Princeton Univ. Press.

Joyce, Thomas Athol. 1912. *A Short Guide to the American Antiquities in the British Museum.* London: Printed by Order of the Trustees.

———. 1914. *Mexican Archaeology.* New York: G. P. Putnam's Sons.

Jurok, Jiří. 1991. "Dominik Bilimek: Un capítulo desconocido de las relaciones culturales Checo-Mexicanas." *Ibero-Americana* 23:195–203.

Kastor, Peter J. 2004. *The Nation's Crucible: The Louisiana Purchase and the Creation of America.* New Haven: Yale Univ. Press.

Keen, Benjamin F. 1971. *The Aztec Image in Western Thought.* New Brunswick, N.J.: Rutgers Univ. Press.

Kelemen, Pál. 1943. *Medieval American Art: A Survey in Two Volumes.* 2 vols. New York: Macmillan.

Kingsborough, Edward King, Viscount, ed. 1831–48. *Antiquities of Mexico: Comprising Fac-Similes of Ancient Mexican Paintings and Hieroglyphics, Preserved in the Royal Libraries of Paris, Berlin and Dresden; in the Imperial Library of Vienna; in the Vatican Library; in the Borgian Museum at Rome; in the Library of the Institute at Bologna; and in the Bodleian Library at Oxford: Together with the Monuments of New Spain, by M. Dupaix, with Their Respective Scales of Measurement and Accompanying Descriptions; the Whole Illustrated by Many Valuable Inedited Manuscripts.* 9 vols. London: Robert Havell… & Colnaghi, Son & Co.… printed by James Moyes.

Kirchhoff, Paul. 1962. "La aportación de Humboldt al estudio de las antiguas civilizaciones americanas: Un modelo y un programa." In Marianne Oeste de Bopp, ed., *Ensayos sobre Humboldt,* 89–103. Mexico City: Universidad Nacional Autónoma de México.

Klein, Cecelia F. 1972. "Frontality in Postclassic Mexican Two-Dimensional Art." Ph.D. diss., Columbia University.

———. 1975. "Post-Classic Mexican Death Imagery as a Sign of Cyclic Completion." In Elizabeth P. Benson, ed., *Death and the Afterlife in Pre-Columbian America,* 69–85. Washington, D.C.: Dumbarton Oaks Research Library & Collection.

———. 1976a. *The Face of the Earth: Frontality in Two-Dimensional Mesoamerican Art.* New York: Garland.

———. 1976b. "The Identity of the Central Deity on the *Aztec Calendar Stone.*" *Art Bulletin* 58:1–12.

———. 1977. "The Identity of the Central Figure on the *Aztec Calendar Stone.*" In Alana Cordy-Collins and Jean Stern, eds., *Pre-Columbian Art History: Selected Readings,* 167–89. Palo Alto, Calif.: Peek.

———. 1980. "Who Was Tlaloc?" *Journal of Latin American Lore* 6:155–204.

———. 1988. "Rethinking Cihuacóatl: Aztec Political Imagery of the Conquered Woman." In Kathryn Josserand and Karen Dakin, eds., *Smoke and Mist: Mesoamerican Studies in Memory of Thelma D. Sullivan,* 237–78. Oxford: B.A.R.

———. 1990/1991. "Snares and Entrails: Mesoamerican Symbols of Sin and Punishment." *Res* 19/20: 81–100.

———. 1993a. "Shield Women: Resolution of an Aztec Gender Paradox." In Alana Cordy-Collins and Douglas Sharon, eds., *Current Topics in Aztec Studies: Essays in Honor of Dr. H. B. Nicholson,* 39–64. San Diego: San Diego Museum of Man.

———. 1993b. "Teocuitlatl, 'Divine Excrement': The Significance of 'Holy Shit' in Ancient Mexico." *Art Journal* 52 (3): 20–27.

———. 1994. "Fighting with Femininity: Gender and War in Aztec Mexico." *Estudios de cultura náhuatl* 24:219–53.

———. 2000. "The Devil and the Skirt: An Iconographic Inquiry into the Pre-Hispanic Nature of the *Tzitzimime.*" *Ancient Mesoamerica* 11:1–26.

———. 2008. "A New Interpretation of the Aztec Statue Called *Coatlicue,* 'Snakes-Her-Skirt.'" *Ethnohistory* 55 (2): 229–50.

Klein, Cecelia F., and Jeffrey Quilter, eds. 2001. *Gender in Pre-Hispanic America.* Washington, D.C.: Dumbarton Oaks Research Library & Collection.

Köhler, Ulrich. 1979. "'Sonnenstein' ohne Sonnengott: Zur Korrektur einer überkommenen Fehldeutung der bekann-testen aztekischen Steinplastik." *Ethnologia Americana* 16 (91): 906–8.

———. 1982. "On the Significance of the Aztec Day Sign 'Ollin.'" In Franz Tichy, ed., *Space and Time in the Cosmovision of Mesoamerica*. Munich: Wilhelm Fink.

Krauze, Enrique. 1997. *Mexico: Biography of Power; A History of Modern Mexico, 1810–1996*. New York: HarperCollins.

Krickeberg, Walter. 1948. "Das mittelamerikanische Ballspiel und seine religiöse Symbolik." *Paideuma: Mitteilungen zur Kulturkunde* 3:118–90.

———. 1956. *Altmexikanische Kulturen*. Berlin: Safari.

———. 1964. *Las antiguas culturas mexicanas*. 2nd ed. Mexico City: Fondo de Cultura Económica.

———. 1969. *Felsbilder Mexikos*. Berlin: Reimer.

Kubler, George. 1943. "The Cycle of Life and Death in Metropolitan Aztec Sculpture." *Gazette des Beaux-Arts*, ser. 6, 23: 257–68.

———. 1954. *The Louise and Walter Arensberg Collection, Pre-Columbian Sculpture*. Philadelphia: Philadelphia Museum of Art.

———. 1962a. *The Art and Architecture of Ancient America: The Mexican, Maya and Andean Peoples*. Baltimore: Penguin.

———. 1962b. *The Shape of Time: Remarks on the History of Things*. New Haven, Conn.: Yale Univ. Press.

———. 1991. *Esthetic Recognition of Ancient Amerindian Art*. New Haven, Conn.: Yale Univ. Press.

Larráinzar, Manuel. 1875–78. *Estudios sobre la historia de América, sus ruinas y antigüedades...remotos y sobre el origen de sus habitantes*. 5 vols. Mexico City: Impr. de Villanueva, Villageliú.

Lehmann, Walter. 1906. "Die *Historia de los Reynos de Colhuacan y de México*." *Zeitschrift für Ethnologie* 38:752–60.

Lehmann, Walter, ed. and trans. 1938. *Die Geschichte der Königreiche von Colhuacan und Mexico*. Berlin: W. Kohlhammer.

León-Portilla, Miguel. 1962. "Humboldt, investigador de los códices y la cosmología náhuatl." In Marianne Oeste de Bopp, ed., *Ensayos sobre Humboldt*, 133–48. Mexico City: Universidad Nacional Autónoma de México.

———. 1963. *Aztec Thought and Culture*. Translated by Jack Emory Davis. Norman: Univ. of Oklahoma Press.

———. 1969. *Pre-Columbian Literatures of Mexico*. Translated by Grace Lobanov and Miguel León-Portilla. Norman: Univ. of Oklahoma Press.

———. 1972. *Trece poetas del mundo azteca*. 2nd ed. Mexico City: Secretaría de Educación Pública.

———, ed. 1992. *The Broken Spears: The Aztec Account of the Conquest of Mexico*. Rev. ed. Boston: Beacon Press.

León y Gama, Antonio de. 1769. *Diario astronómico, y suplemento al calendario para el año de 1770, segundo después de bissexto. En que van expresado los verdaderos lugares del sol, y luna. Declinación de aquél, y latitud de ésta, para el tiempo del verdadero medio día de cada uno de los del año; con más la hora, y minuto assi del Orto y ocaso del sol, como del tránsito de la luna por el meridiano; los eclipses de los cuatro satélites de Júpiter; y los principales aspectos y congresos de éste, y los demás planetas; por D. Antonio de León, y Gama, oficial mayor de uno de los oficios de Cámara de la Real Audiencia de esta corte*. Mexico City: En la Imprenta del Lic. D. Joseph de Jáuregui.

———. 1770. *Calendario dispuesto por D. Antonio de León, y Gama, Oficial Mayor de uno de los Oficios de Cámara de la Real Hacienda en esta Corte. Para el año de la Encarnación del Verbo Divino de 1771. Tercero después de bissexto*. Mexico City: En la Imprenta del Lic. D. Joseph de Jáuregui.

———. 1778. *Descripción orthográfica universal del eclipse de sol del día 24 de junio de 1778, dedicada al señor Don Joaquín Velázquez de León....* Mexico City: Felipe de Zúñiga y Ontiveros.

———. 1782. *Instrucción sobre el remedio de las lagartijas: Nuevamente descubierto para la curación del cancro, y otras enfermedades....* Mexico City: En la Imprenta de D. Felipe de Zúñiga y Ontiveros, Calle del Espíritu Santo.

———. 1783. *Respuesta satisfactoria a la Carta apologética, que escribieron el Lic. D. Manuel Antonio Moreno, y el Br. D. Alejo Ramón Sánchez: Y defensa contra la censura, que en ella se hace, de algunas proposiciones contenidas en la instrucción sobre el remedio de las lagartijas*. Mexico City: D. F. de Zúñiga y Ontiveros.

———. 1789. "Discurso sobre la luz septentrional que se vio en esta ciudad el día de 14 de noviembre de 1789, entre 8 y 9 de la noche." *Gazeta de México* 3, nos. 44–45 (1 y 22 diciembre): 432–35, 444–47.

———. 1790. *Disertación física sobre la materia y formación de las auroras boreales, que con ocasión de la que apareció en México y otros lugares de la Nueva España el día 14 de noviembre de 1789*. Mexico City: Felipe de Zúñiga y Ontiveros.

———. 1792. *Descripción histórica y cronológica de las dos piedras que con ocasión del nuevo empedrado que se esta formando en la plaza principal de México, se hallaron en ella el año de 1790....* Mexico City: Impr. de Don. F. de Zúñiga y Ontiveros.

———. 1804. *Saggio dell'astronomia cronologia e mitologia degli antichi messicani*. Translated by Pedro José Márquez. Rome: Presso il Salomoni.

———. 1832. *Descripción histórica y cronológica de las dos piedras, que con ocasión del nuevo empedrado que se está formando en la plaza principal de México....* 2nd ed. Mexico City: Impr. del Cuidano A. Valdés.

———. 1875. "Calendario mexicano." In José María Pérez Hernández, ed., *Diccionario geográfico, estadístico, histórico, biográfico, de industria y comercio de la República Mexicana, escrito en parte y arreglado en otra parte por el general José María Pérez Hernández, consultando sus tareas con los distinguidos escritores Lics. D. Manuel Orozco y Berra y D. Alfredo Chavero*, 3:82–118. Mexico City: Imp. de Cinco de Mayo.

———. 1927a. "Descripción de la ciudad de México, antes y después de la llegada de los conquistadores españoles."

Revista mexicana de estudios históricos 1 (2), app.: 8–58.

———. 1927b. "Descripción del obispado de Michoacán." *Revista mexicana de estudios históricos* 1 (3), app.: 91–100.

———. 1978. *Descripción histórica y cronológica....* Mexico City: M. A. Porrúa.

Levi-Strauss, Claude. 1990. "Introductory Address." In Dan Eban et al., eds., *Art as a Means of Communication in Pre-Literate Societies,* 1–6. Jerusalem: Israel Museum.

Lewis, James E. 2003. *The Louisiana Purchase: Jefferson's Noble Bargain?* Chapel Hill: Univ. of North Carolina Press.

"Leyenda de los soles." 1945. In *Códice Chimalpopoca: Anales de Cuauhtitlan y Leyenda de los soles,* 119–28. Translated by Primo Feliciano Velázquez. Mexico City: Imprenta Universitaria.

———. 1975. In *Códice Chimalpopoca: Anales de Cuauhtitlán y Leyenda de los soles,* 119–42. Translated by Primo Feliciano Velázquez. 2nd ed. México: Universidad Nacional Autónoma de México, Instituto de Investigaciones Históricas.

Libro de tributos del Marquesado del Valle. 1978. Translated by Ismael Díaz Cadena. Mexico City: Biblioteca Nacional de Antropología & Historia.

Little, Carol Morris. 1996. *A Comprehensive Guide to Outdoor Sculpture in Texas.* Austin: Univ. of Texas Press.

Lockhart, James. 1993. *We People Here: Nahua Accounts of the Conquest of Mexico.* Berkeley: Univ. of California Press.

Lombardo de Ruiz, Sonia, ed., 1994. *El pasado prehispánico en la cultura nacional: Memoria hemerográfica, 1877–1911.* Mexico City: Insituto Nacional de Antropología e Historia.

López Austin, Alfredo. 1973. *Hombre-dios: Religión y política en el mundo náhuatl.* Mexico City: Universidad Nacional Autónoma de México, Instituto de Investigaciones Históricas.

———. 1983. "Nota sobre la fusión y la fisión de los dioses en el panteón mexica." *Anales de antropología* 20 (2): 75–87. Mexico City: Universidad Nacional Autónoma de México.

López Casillas, Mercurio. 2008. *La muerte en el impreso mexicano = Images of Death in Mexican Prints.* Translated by Gregory Dechant. Mexico City: Editorial RM.

López de Gómara, Francisco. 1554. *Cronica de la nueva España: Con la conquista de México y otras cosas notables; Hechas por el valeroso Hernando Cortes, marques del valle, capitan de su magestad en aquellas partes.* Zaragoza: Augustin Millan.

López Hernández, Haydeé. 2006. "Leyendo cosmogonías en piedra: Enrique Juan Palacios (1881–1953) y los estudios iconográficos." Paper presented at the Society for American Archaeology 71st Annual Meeting, San Juan, Puerto Rico, 29 April.

López Luján, Leonardo. 2005. *Aztèques: La collection de sculptures du Musée du Quai Branly.* Paris: Musée du Quai Branly.

———. 2008a. "'El adiós y triste queja del gran *Calendario Azteca*': El incesante peregrinar de la *Piedra del Sol.*" *Arqueología mexicana* 16 (91): 78–83.

———. 2008b. "El Tajín en el siglo XVIII: Dos exploraciones pioneras en Veracruz." *Arqueología mexicana* 15 (89): 74–81.

López Luján, Leonardo, et al. 2006. "The Destruction of Images in Teotihuacan: Anthropomorphic Sculpture, Elite Cults, and the End of a Civilization." *Res* 49/50:13–39.

Lorenzo, Antonio. 1979. *Uso e interpretación del "Calendario Azteca."* Mexico City: M. A. Porrúa.

Louisiana Historical Society. 1917. "Meeting of December, 1917." *Publications of the Louisiana Historical Society* 10:113.

Lozano, Francisco Xavier. 1794. *Verdades eternas, confirmadas con la Sagrada Escritura, y expuestas en décimas castellanas para conservarlas fácilmente en la memoria.* Mexico City: En la Oficina de los Herederos de Lic. D. Joseph de Jauregui.

Luhnow, Chris. 1976. *Traveler's Guide to Mexico 1976–77: The Most Current Guide to the Major Attractions of Mexico, Including Recommendations as to What to See and Do, Where to Shop, Where to Dine and Where to Stay.* 6th ed. Mexico City: Luhnow.

Luhnow, Christopher. 1980. *Travelers Guide to Mexico.* Mexico City: Secretaría del Turismo.

Lundberg, Magnus. 2002. *Unification and Conflict: The Church Politics of Alonso de Montúfar OP, Archbishop of Mexico, 1554–1572.* Uppsala: Swedish Institute of Missionary Research.

MacCurdy, George Grant. 1910. "An Aztec 'Calendar Stone' in Yale University Museum." *American Anthropologist,* n.s., 12:481–96.

Madison, James. 1998. *The Papers of James Madison.* Vol. 4, *8 October 1802–15 May 1803.* Edited by Mary A. Hackett. Charlottesville: Univ. Press of Virginia.

Madsen, William. 1960. *The Virgin's Children: Life in an Aztec Village Today.* Austin: Univ. of Texas Press.

Manero, Vicente E. 1878. *Guide for Mexico.* Mexico City: Tip. de Gonzalo A. Esteva.

Margáin, Carlos R. 1964. "Don Antonio León y Gama (1735–1802). El primer arqueólogo mexicano: Análisis de su vida y obra." In Enrique Beltrán, ed., *Memorias del primer coloquio mexicano de historia de la ciencia,* 2:149–83. 2 vols. Mexico City: Sociedad Mexicana de Historia de la Ciencia & la Tecnología.

Márquez, Pedro. 1804. *Due antichi monumenti di architettura messicana.* Rome: Presso il Salomoni.

———. 1832. "Biografía de Don Antonio Gama." In Antonio de León y Gama, *Descripción histórica y cronológica de las dos piedras, que con ocasión del nuevo empedrado que se está formando en la plaza principal de México, se hallaron en ella el año de 1790...,* v–viii. 2nd ed. Mexico City: Impr. del ciudadano Alejandro Valdés.

Marquina, Ignacio. 1964. *Arquitectura prehispánica.* 2nd ed. Mexico City: Instituto Nacional de Antropología & Historia, Secretaría de Educación Pública.

Martínez Hernández, José Luis. 1995. "Lorenzo Boturini y su Museo Histórico Indiano." *Arqueología mexicana* 3 (15): 64–70.

Mathes, W. Michael, and María Isabel Grañen Porrúa. 2001. *La ilustración en México colonial: El grabado en madera y cobre en Nueva España, 1539–1821.* Zapopán, Jalisco: El Colegio de Jalisco.

Matos Moctezuma, Eduardo. 1969. "Humboldt y la arqueología americana." *Boletín bibliográfico de antropología americana* 32:133–38.

———. 1981a. *Mexique d'hier et d'aujourd'hui: Découverte du Templo Mayor de Mexico, artistes contemporains.* Exh. cat. Paris: Ministère des Relations Extérieures, Association française d'action artistique.

———. 1981b. *Una visita al Templo Mayor de Tenochtitlan.* Mexico City: Instituto Nacional de Antropología & Historia.

———. 1982. *El Templo Mayor: Excavaciones y estudios.* Mexico City: Instituto Nacional de Antropología & Historia.

———. 1984. "The Templo Mayor of Tenochtitlan, Economics and Ideology." Translated by Kay Brazo. In Elizabeth Hill Boone, ed., *Ritual Human Sacrifice in Mesoamerica,* 133–64. Washington, D.C.: Dumbarton Oaks Research Library & Collection.

———. 1987. "Symbolism of the Templo Mayor." Translated by Patricia Netherly. In Elizabeth Hill Boone, ed., *The Aztec Templo Mayor,* 185–209. Washington, D.C.: Dumbarton Oaks Research Library & Collection.

———. 1988a. *The Great Temple of the Aztecs: Treasures of Tenochtitlan.* Translated by Doris Heyden. New York: Thames & Hudson.

———. 1988b. *Obras maestras del Templo Mayor.* Mexico City: Fomento Cultural Banamex.

———. 1990. *Teotihuacán: The City of the Gods.* Translated by Andrew Ellis. New York: Rizzoli.

———. 1992. *La "Piedra del Sol": "Calendario Azteca."* Mexico City: Grupo Impresa.

———. 1993. "Tríptico del pasado (Discurso de ingreso a El Colegio Nacional)." *Memoria: El Colegio Nacional,* 86–116. Mexico City: El Colegio Nacional.

———. 1997a. "Don Antonio de León y Gama y los comienzos de la arqueología mexicana." In Leonardo Manrique Castañeda and Noemí Castillo Tejero, eds., *Homenaje al doctor Ignacio Bernal,* 71–79. Mexico City: Instituto Nacional de Antropología & Historia.

———. 1997b. "Tlaltecuhtli: Señor de la tierra." *Estudios de cultura náhuatl,* no. 27:15–40.

———. 1998a. "Don Antonio de León y Gama (1735–1802)." *Arqueología mexicana* 5 (30): 20.

———. 1998b. *Las piedras negadas: De la Coatlicue al Templo Mayor.* Mexico City: Consejo Nacional para la Cultura & las Artes.

———. 1999. "La *Piedra del Sol (Calendario Azteca)."* In idem, *Obras: Estudios mexicas,* vol. 1, pt. 2:85–128. Mexico City: Colegio Nacional.

———. 2002a. "La arqueología y la ilustración (1750–1810)." *Arqueología mexicana* 9 (53): 18–25.

———. 2002b. *Los comienzos de la arqueología mexicana: En respuesta de Carlos Navarrete.* Mexico City: El Colegio Nacional.

Matos Moctezuma, Eduardo, and Leonardo López Luján. 2007. "La diosa Tlaltecuhtli de la Casa de las Ajaracas y el rey Ahuízotl." *Arqueología mexicana* 14 (83): 22–29.

Matos Moctezuma, Eduardo, and Felipe R. Solís Olguín. 2002. *Aztecs.* London: Royal Academy of Arts.

———. 2004. *The Aztec Calendar and Other Solar Monuments.* Translated by H. J. Drake. Mexico City: Conaculta-Instituto Nacional de Antropología & Historia, Grupo Azabache.

Matrícula de tributos. 1980. *Matrícula de tributos (Códice de Moctezuma): Museo Nacional de Antropología, México (Cód. 35–52).* Edited by Frances Berdan and Jacqueline de Durand-Forest. Graz, Austria: Akademische Druck- & Verlagsanstalt.

Maudslay, Alfred P. 1889–1902. *Archaeology.* Edited by F. Ducane Godman and Osbert Salvin. 6 vols. in 5. London: R. H. Porter, Dulau.

Mayer, Brantz. 1844. *Mexico as It Was and as It Is.* New York: J. Winchester.

———. 1847. *Mexico as It Was and as It Is.* 3rd ed. Philadelphia: G. B. Zieber.

———. 1852. *Mexico, Aztec, Spanish and Republican: A Historical, Geographical, Political, Statistical and Social Account of That Country from the Period of the Invasion by the Spaniards to the Present Time.* 2 vols. in 1. Hartford: S. Drake.

———. 1853. *Mexico, Aztec, Spanish and Republican: A Historical, Geographical, Political, Statistical and Social Account of That Country from the Period of the Invasion by the Spaniards to the Present Time; with a View of the Ancient Aztec Empire and Civilization; a Historical Sketch of the Late War; and Notices of New Mexico and California.* 2 vols. Hartford: S. Drake.

McCullough, David. 1992. *Brave Companions: Portraits in History.* New York: Prentice Hall Press.

Mena, Ramón. 1928. "Piedra ciclográfica de Motecuhzoma Xocoyotzin." In *Atti del XXII Congresso internazionale degli Americanisti, Roma, settembre 1926,* 1:605–24. Rome: Stab. Tip. R. Garroni.

Mendieta, Gerónimo de. 1870. *Historia eclesiástica indiana.* Mexico City: F. Díaz de León y Santiago White.

———. 1945. *Historia eclesiástica indiana.* Edited by Joaquín García Icazbalceta. 4 vols. Mexico City: Editorial Salvador Chávez Hayhoe.

———. 1971. *Historia eclesiástica indiana: Obra escrita a fines del siglo XVI.* Edited by Joaquín García Icazbalceta.

2nd ed. Mexico City: Editorial Porrúa.

Mendoza, Eufemio, and Manuel A. Romo. 1874. *Nociones de cronología universal extractadas de los mejores autores, para los alumnos de las escuelas de instrucción secundaria*. Mexico City: Imprenta del Gobierno.

Mendoza, Gumesindo, and Jesús Sánchez. 1882. *Catálogo de las colecciones históricas y arqueológicas del Museo Nacional de México*. Mexico City: Impr. de I. Escalante.

Meyer, Michael C., and William L. Sherman. 1979. *The Course of Mexican History*. New York: Oxford Univ. Press.

Milbrath, Susan. 1980. "Star Gods and Astronomy of the Aztecs." In *La antropología americanista en la actualidad: Homenaje a Raphael Girard*, 1:289–305. 2 vols. Mexico City: Editores Mexicanos Unidos.

Miller, Mary Ellen. 1986. *The Art of Mesoamerica: From Olmec to Aztec*. New York: Thames & Hudson.

———. 2006. *The Art of Mesoamerica: From Olmec to Aztec*. 4th ed. New York: Thames & Hudson.

Minguet, Charles. 2003. *Alejandro de Humboldt: Historiador y geógrafo de la América española (1799–1804)*. Translated by Jorge Padín Videla. Mexico City: Universidad Nacional Autónoma de México, UNAM. http://132.248.9.9/libroe_2007/0414631/A01.pdf (7 June 2009).

Miranda, José. 1962. *Humboldt y México*. Mexico City: Universidad Nacional Autónoma de México, Instituto de Historia.

Moor, Edward. 1810. *The Hindu Pantheon*. London: J. Johnson.

Morales Moreno, Luis. 1994. *Orígenes de la museología mexicana: Fuentes para el estudio histórico del Museo Nacional, 1780–1940*. Mexico City: Universidad Iberoamericana, Departamento de Historia.

Moreno, Roberto. 1970. "Ensayo biobibliográfico de Antonio de León y Gama." *Boletín del Instituto de Investigaciones Bibliográficas* 2 (1): 43–135.

———. 1971. "La colección Boturini y las fuentes de la obra de Antonio de León y Gama." *Estudios de cultura náhuatl* 9:253–70.

———. 1972. "Las notas de Alzáte a la *Historia antigua* de Clavigero." *Estudios de cultura náhuatl* 10:359–92.

———. 1976. "Las notas de Alzáte a la *Historia antigua* de Clavigero (Addenda)." *Estudios de cultura náhuatl* 12:85–120.

———. 1981. "La *Historia antigua de México* de Antonio de León y Gama." *Estudios de historia novohispana* 7:49–78.

Moreno de los Arcos, Roberto. 1967. "Los cinco soles cosmogónicos." *Estudios de cultura náhuatl* 7:183–210.

Morgan, Lewis Henry. 1876. "Montezuma's Dinner." *North American Review* 122 (251): 265–309.

Morley, Sylvanus Griswold. 1920. *The Inscriptions at Copan*. Washington, D.C.: Carnegie Institute of Washington.

———. 1937–38. *Inscriptions of Petén*. 5 vols. in 6. Washington, D.C.: Carnegie Institute of Washington.

Motolinía, Toribio. 1971. *Memoriales; o, Libro de las cosas de Nueva España y de los naturales de ella*. Edited by Edmundo O'Gorman. 2nd ed. Mexico City: Universidad Nacional Autónoma de México, Instituto de Investigaciones Históricas.

Moxó, Benito María de. 1839. *Cartas mejicanas, escritas por D. Benito Maria de Moxó, año de 1805*. 2nd ed. Genoa: Tip. de L. Pellas.

Muirhead, James F. 1893. *United States, with an Excursion into Mexico: Handbook for Travellers*. Edited by Karl Baedeker. New York: C. Scribner's Sons.

Muñoz, Juan Bautista. 1793. *Historia del Nuevo-Mundo*. Madrid: Por la viuda de Ibarra.

Muñoz Camargo, Diego. 1892. *Historia de Tlaxcala*. Annotated by Alfredo Chavero. Mexico City: Oficina Tip. de la Secretaría de Fomento.

Navarrete, Carlos. 1968. *La Piedra del Sol = The Stone of the Sun*. Mexico City: Museo Nacional de Antropología & Historia, Servicios Educativos.

———. 1992. "Los ladrillos grabados de Comalcalco, Tabasco." In Elizabeth Mejía Pérez Campos and Lorena Mirambell, eds., *Comalcalco*, 219–36. Mexico City: Instituto Nacional de Antropología & Historia.

———. 2000. *Palenque, 1784: El inicio de la aventura arqueológica maya*. Mexico City: Centro de Estudios Mayas, Universidad Nacional Autónoma de México.

Navarrete, Carlos, and Doris Heyden. 1974. "La cara central de la *Piedra del Sol*: Una hipótesis." *Estudios de cultura náhuatl* 11:355–76.

Navarrete, Carlos, and Luis Luján Muñoz. 1963. *Reconocimiento arqueológico del sitio de 'Dos Pilas,' Petexbatún, Guatemala*. Guatemala City: Universidad de San Carlos, Facultad de Humanidades.

Nebel, Carl. 1836. *Voyage pittoresque et archéologique dans la partie la plus intéressante du Mexique*. Paris: M. Moench.

———. 1963. *Viaje pintoresco y arqueológico sobre la parte más interesante de la República Mexicana.... Mexico City: Librería de M. Porrúa.

Nicholson, H. B. 1955. "The Temalacatl of Tehuacan." *El México antiguo* 8:95–134.

———. 1957. "Topiltzin Quetzalcoatl of Tollan: A Problem in Mesoamerican Ethnohistory." Ph.D. diss., Harvard University.

———. 1958. "An Aztec Monument Dedicated to Tezcatlipoca." In *Miscellanea Paul Rivet*, 1:592–607. Mexico City: Universidad Nacional Autónoma de México.

———. 1959. "The Chapultepec Cliff Sculpture of Motecuhzoma Xocoyotzin." *El México antiguo* 9:379–444.

———. 1966. "The Significance of the 'Looped Cord' Year Symbol in Pre-Hispanic Mexico: An Hypothesis." *Estudios de cultura náhuatl* 6:135–48.

———. 1967a. "A Fragment of an Aztec Relief Carving of the Earth Monster." *Journal de la Société des Américanistes* 56 (1): 81–94.

———. 1967b. "The 'Royal Headband' of the Tlaxcalteca." *Revista mexicana de estudios antropológicos* 21:71–106.

———. 1971a. "Major Sculpture in Pre-Hispanic Central Mexico." In G. F. Ekhom and I. Bernal, eds., *Archaeology of Northern Mesoamerica,* pt. 1:92–134. Vol. 10 of Robert Wauchope, ed., *Handbook of Middle American Indians.* Austin: Univ. of Texas Press.

———. 1971b. "Religion in Pre-Hispanic Central Mexico." In G. F. Ekhom and I. Bernal, eds., *Archaeology of Northern Mesoamerica,* pt. 1:395–446. Vol. 10 of Robert Wauchope, ed., *Handbook of Middle American Indians.* Austin: Univ. of Texas Press.

———. 1973a. "Eduard Georg Seler, 1849–1922." In Howard F. Cline, ed., *Guide to Ethnohistorical Sources,* pt. 2:348–69. Vol. 13 of Robert Wauchope, ed., *Handbook of Middle American Indians.* Austin: Univ. of Texas Press.

———. 1973b. "The Late Pre-Hispanic Central Mexican (Aztec) Iconographic System." In Ignacio Bernal and Elizabeth Kennedy Easby, eds., *The Iconography of Middle American Sculpture,* 72–97. New York: Metropolitan Museum of Art.

———. 1973c. "Phoneticism in the Late Pre-Hispanic Central Mexican Writing System." In Elizabeth P. Benson, ed., *Mesoamerican Writing Systems,* 1–46. Washington, D.C.: Dumbarton Oaks Research Library & Collection.

———. 1982. "The Mixteca-Puebla Concept Revisited." In Elizabeth Hill Boone, ed., *The Art and Iconography of Late Post-Classic Central Mexico,* 227–54. Washington, D.C.: Dumbarton Oaks, Trustees for Harvard University.

———. 1993. "The Problem of the Identification of the Central Image of the *Aztec Calendar Stone.*" In Alana Cordy-Collins and Douglas Sharon, eds., *Current Topics in Aztec Studies: Essays in Honor of Dr. H. B. Nicholson,* 3–15. San Diego: Museum of Man.

———. 1996. "*Aztec Calendar Stone.*" In Barbara A. Tenenbaum, ed., *Encyclopedia of Latin American History and Culture,* 1:254–55. New York: Charles Scribner's Sons.

———. 2001. *Topiltzin Quetzalcoatl: The Once and Future Lord of the Toltecs.* Boulder: Univ. Press of Colorado.

Nicholson, H. B., and Eloise Quiñones Keber. 1983. *Art of Aztec Mexico: Treasures of Tenochtitlan.* Exh. cat. Washington, D.C.: National Gallery of Art.

———, eds., 1994. *Mixteca-Puebla: Discoveries and Research in Mesoamerican Art and Archaeology.* Culver City, Calif.: Labyrinthos.

Nieremberg, Juan Eusebio. 1635. *Historia Naturae, maxime Peregrinae, Libris XVI Distincta: In Quibus Rarissimae Natura Arcana, etiam Astronomica, et Ignota Indiarum Animalia…Enodantur; Accedunt de Miris et Miraculosis Naturis in Europa Libri Duo, Item de Iisdem in Terra Hebraeis Promissa Liber Vnus.* Antwerp: Ex Officina Plantiniana Balthasaris Moreti.

Noriega, Raúl. n.d. *El "Calendario Azteca."* Mexico City: Vargas Rea.

———. 1954. *Tres estudios sobre la Piedra del Sol.…* Mexico City: n.p.

———. 1955. *La Piedra del Sol y 16 monumentos astronómicos del México antiguo: Símbolos y claves.* Mexico City: Editorial Superación.

———. 1959. "Sabiduria matemática, astronómica y cronológica." In Carmen Cook de Leonard, ed., *Esplendor del México antiguo,* 1:263–94. Mexico City: Centro de Investigaciones Antropológicas de México.

Núñez de la Vega, Francisco. 1702. *Constituciones diocesanas del obispado de Chiappa.* Rome: Caetano Zenobi.

Nuttall, Zelia. 1886. "Preliminary Note of an Analysis of the Mexican Codices and Graven Inscriptions." *Proceedings of the American Association for the Advancement of Science* 35:325–27.

———. 1901. *The Fundamental Principles of Old and New World Civilizations: A Comparative Research Based on a Study of the Ancient Mexican Religious, Sociological and Calendrical Systems.* Cambridge, Mass.: Peabody Museum of American Archaeology & Ethnology.

Ober, Frederick A. 1884. *Travels in Mexico and Life among the Mexicans.* Boston: Estes & Lauriat.

Oles, James. 1993. *South of the Border: Mexico in the American Imagination, 1914–1947 = México en la Imaginación Norteamericana, 1914–1947.* Translated by Marta Ferragut. Washington, D.C.: Smithsonian Institution.

Ordóñez, Ezequiel. 1892. "La roca del *Calendario Azteca.*" *Memorias y revista de la Sociedad Científica "Antonio Alzate"* 6:327–32.

Orozco y Berra, Manuel. 1877. "El *cuauhxicalli* de Tizoc." *Anales del Museo Nacional de México,* ser. 1, 1:3–36.

———. 1880. *Historia antigua y de la conquista de México.* 4 vols. Mexico City: Tip. de G. A. Esteva.

———. 1975. "Ojeada sobre cronología mexicana." In Fernando Alvarado Tezozómoc, *Crónica mexicana,* 151–222. 2nd ed. Mexico City: Editorial Porrúa.

Ortega y Medina, Juan Antonio. 1960. *Humboldt desde México.* Mexico City: Universidad Nacional Autónoma de México.

Pagden, Anthony. 1993. *European Encounters with the New World: From Renaissance to Romanticism.* New Haven, Conn.: Yale Univ. Press.

Palacios, Enrique Juan. 1917. *Puebla: Su territorio y sus habitantes.* 2 vols. Mexico City: Secretaría de Fomento.

———. 1918. "La *Piedra del Sol* y el primer capítulo de la historia de México." *Memorias y revista de la Sociedad Científica "Antonio Alzate"* 38:1–100.

———. 1922. *Páginas de la historia de México: La "Piedra del Calendario" mexicano, su simbolismo.* Mexico City: Zamorano.

———. 1924. *Interpretaciones de la "Piedra del Calendario."* Mexico City: Tall. Gráf. del Museo Nacional de Arqueología, Historia & Etnografía.

——. 1928. *En los confines de la selva Lacandona: Exploraciones en el estado de Chiapas: Mayo–agosto 1926.* Mexico City: Direcciones Editorial & de Arqueología, Secretaría de Educación Pública.

——. 1929. *La piedra del escudo nacional de México.* Mexico City: Talleres Gráficos de la Nación.

——. 1932. *Maya-Christian Synchronology or Calendrical Correlation.* Translated by Dolores Morgadanes. New Orleans: Tulane University of Louisiana, Department of Middle American Research.

——. 1933. *El calendario y los jeroglíficos cronográficos mayas.* Mexico City: Editorial "Cultura."

——. 1935a. *Guía arqueológica de Chichén Itzá: Aspectos arquitectónicos, cronológicos y de interpretación.* Mexico City: Talleres Gráficos de la Nación.

——. 1935b. "Más gemas del arte maya en Palenque." *Anales del Museo Nacional de Arqueología, Historia y Etnografía,* ser. 5, 2:193–225.

——. 1936. "Inscripción recientemente descubierta en Palenque." *Maya Research* 3 (1): 2–17.

——. 1937. "El relieve del *Calendario Azteca:* Su elucidación arqueológica." *Anales de la Sociedad de Geografía e Historia de Guatemala* 14:71–89.

——. 1940. "El simbolismo del Chac-Mool: Su interpretación." *Revista mexicana de estudios antropológicos* 4:43–56.

——. 1943. *Los yugos y su simbolismo: Estudio analítico.* Mexico City: Universidad Nacional Autónoma de México.

——. 1945. "Guía arqueológica de Chacmultún, Labná, Sayil, Kabah, Uxmal, Chichén Itzá, y Tulum." In Carlos A. Echánove Trujillo, ed., *Enciclopedia Yucatanense…,* 2:405–554. Mexico City: Edición Oficial del Gobierno de Yucatán.

Palacios, Enrique Juan, and Enrique E. Meyer. 1932. *La ciudad arqueológica del Tajín: Sus revelaciones.* Mexico City: La Impresora.

Paso y Troncoso, Francisco del. 1882. "Ensayo sobre los símbolos cronográficos de los mexicanos." *Anales del Museo Nacional de México,* ser. 1, 2:323–402.

——. 1892–93. *Catálogo de la sección de México.* Exh. cat. 2 vols. Madrid: Est. Tip. "Sucesores de Rivadeneyra."

——. 1903. *Leyenda de los soles: Continuada con otras leyendas y noticias, relación anónima escrita en lengua mexicana el año 1558….* Florence: Tipografía de Salvador Landi.

Pasztory, Esther. 1976. *Aztec Stone Sculpture.* Exh. cat. New York: Center for Inter-American Relations.

——. 1983. *Aztec Art.* New York: Harry N. Abrams.

Pauw, Cornelius de. 1768–69. *Recherches philosophiques sur les Américains; ou, Mémoires intéressantes pour servir à l'histoire de l'espèce humaine.* 2 vols. Berlin: George Jaques Decker.

Paz, Octavio. 1991. *Sunstone = Piedra del Sol.* Translated by Eliot Weinberger. New York: New Directions.

Peñafiel, Antonio. 1890. *Monumentos del arte mexicano antiguo: Ornamentación, mitología, tributos y monumentos.* 3 vols. in 1. Berlin: A. Asher.

——. 1910. *Principio de la época colonial: Destrucción del Templo Mayor de México antiguo.* Mexico City: Imp. de la Secretaria de Fomento.

Pérez Hernández, José María, ed. 1874–75. *Diccionario geográfico, estadístico, histórico, biográfico, de industria e comercio de la República Mexicana,* 4 vols. Mexico City: Impr. de Cinco de Mayo.

Phillips, Henry. 1884. "Notes upon the Codex Ramirez, with a Translation of the Same." *Proceedings of the American Philosophical Society* 21 (116): 616–51.

Pijoán, José. 1928. *History of Art.* Translated by Ralph L. Roys. 3 vols. New York: Harper & Brothers.

——. 1931. *Summa Artis: Historia generale del arte.* Madrid: Espasa Calpe.

——. 1952. *Arte precolombino: Mexicano y maya.* 2nd ed. Madrid: Espasa-Calpe.

——. 1958. *Arte precolombino: Mexicano y maya.* 3rd ed. Madrid: Espasa-Calpe.

Pinzón y Baeza, Manuel. 1797. *Logicae et metaphysicae assertiones quas Emmanuel Pinzon et Baeza…defendet.* Mexico City: apud Marianum Zunnigam Ontiverium. University thesis defense.

Poinsett, Joel. 1825. *Notes on Mexico Made in the Autumn of 1822: Accompanied by an Historical Sketch of the Revolution, and Translations of Official Reports on the Present State of That Country.* London: J. Miller.

Pratt, Mary Louise. 1992a. "Humboldt and the Reinvention of America." In René Jara and Nicholas Spadaccini, eds., *Amerindian Images and the Legacy of Columbus,* 584–606. Minneapolis: Univ. of Minnesota Press.

——. 1992b. *Imperial Eyes: Travel Writing and Transculturation.* New York: Routledge.

Prescott, William Hickling. 1843. *History of the Conquest of Mexico, with a Preliminary View of the Ancient Mexican Civilization, and the Life of the Conqueror, Hernando Cortés.* 3 vols. New York: Harper.

Prescott, William [Guillermo] Hickling. 1844. *Historia de la conquista de Méjico, con un bosquejo preliminar de la civilización de los antiguos mejicanos, y la vida del conquistador Hernando Cortés.* Translated by D. José María González de la Vega and annotated by D. Lucas Almán. Mexico City: V. G. Torres.

Preuss, Konrad T. 1931. "Nueva interpretación de la llamada piedra del calendario mexicano." *Anales del Museo Nacional de Arqueología, Historia y Etnografía,* ser. 4, 7:426–34.

Proceedings of the American Antiquarian Society. 1888. "Biographical Note on Gumesindo Mendoza, in Report from the Council." *Proceedings of the American Antiquarian Society,* n.s., vol. 5:172–74.

Proceedings of the American Philosophical Society. 1875. "Stated Meeting, October 1st, 1875." *Proceedings of the American Philosophical Society* 14 (95): 642.

Proskouriakoff, Tatiana. 1968. "The Jog and the Jaguar Signs in Maya Writing." *American Antiquity* 33 (2): 247–251.

Quiñones Keber, Eloise. 1992. "(Re)discovering Aztec Images." In René Jara and Nicholas Spadaccini, eds., *Amerindian*

Images and the Legacy of Columbus, 132–62. Minneapolis: Univ. of Minnesota Press.

———. 1996. "Humboldt and Aztec Art." *Colonial Latin American Review* 5 (2): 277–297.

Ramírez, José Fernando. 1844–46. "Descripción de cuatro lápidas monumentales conservadas en el Museo Nacional de México, seguida de un ensayo sobre su interpretación." In William Hickling Prescott, *Historia de la conquista de México: Con una ojeada preliminar sobre la antigua civilización de los mexicanos, y con la vida de su conquistador Fernando Cortés,* vol. 2, app., 106–24. Mexico City: Impreso por Ignacio Cumplido.

———. 1855–56. "Antigüedades mexicanas conservadas en el Museo Nacional de México." In *México y sus alrededores. Colección de monumentos, trajes y paisajes. Dibujados al natural y litografiados pos los artistas mexicanos C. Castro, J. Campillo, L. Auda y G. Rodríguez, bajo la dirección de Decaen,* 33–36. Mexico City: Establecimiento litográfico de Decaen.

———. 1857. *Descripción de algunos objetos del Museo Nacional de Antigüedades de México.* Mexico City: Impr. de J. M. Andrade & F. Escalante.

———. 1903. "Cronología de Boturini." *Anales del Museo Nacional de México* 7:167–94.

Raynal, Guillaume-Thomas. 1774. *Histoire philosophique et politique, des éstablissements et du commerce des Européens dans les deux Indes.* 7 vols. Maastricht: Chez Jean-Edmé Dufour.

Riley, Luisa. 1997. "La piedra sin sosiego." *Luna Córnea* 13:16–23.

Río, Antonio del. 1822. *Description of the Ruins of an Ancient City, Discovered near Palenque, in the Kingdom of Guatemala in Spanish America… Followed by Teatro Critico Americano; or, A Critical Investigation and Research into the History of the Americans, by Doctor Paul Felix Cabrera.* London: Henry Berthoud & Suttaby, Evance & Fox.

Rivera Cambas, Manuel. 1880–83. *México pintoresco, artístico y monumental: Vistas, descripción, anécdotas y episodios de los lugares mas notables de la capital y de los estados, aun de las poblaciones cortas, pero de importancia geográfica ó histórica… las descripciones contienen datos científicos histórico y estadístico.* 3 vols. Mexico City: Imprenta de la Reforma.

Robertson, William. 1777. *The History of America.* 2 vols. London: Printed for W. Strahan.

———. 1803. *The History of America.* 10th ed. 4 vols. London: Printed by A. Strahan…for A. Strahan, T. Cadell, and W. Davies…and E. Balfour, Edinburgh.

Romero de Terreros, Manuel. 1948. *Grabados y grabadores en la Nueva España.* Mexico City: Ediciones Arte, Mexicano.

Russell, Philip L. 1977. *Mexico in Transition.* Austin: Colorado River.

Sabin, Joseph, Wilberforce Eames, and R. W. G. Vail, eds. 1868–1936. *A Dictionary of Books Relating to America, from Its Discovery to the Present Time.* 29 vols. New York: Joseph Sabin [&] Bibliographical Society of America.

Sáenz, César A. 1967. *El fuego nuevo.* Mexico City: Instituto Nacional de Antropología & Historia.

Sahagún, Bernardino de. 1829–30. *Historia general de las cosas de Nueva España, que en doce libros y dos volumenes excribió, el R. P. Fr. Bernardino de Sahagún…Dala á luz con notas y suplementaos Carlos María de Bustamante.* 3 vols. Mexico City: Imp. de la ciudadano Valdés.

———. 1950–82. *Florentine Codex: General History of the Things of New Spain.* Edited and translated by Charles E. Dibble and Arthur J. O. Anderson. 13 vols. Santa Fe, N.M.: School of American Research.

———. 1969. *Rhetoric and Moral Philosophy.* Vol. 6 of Charles E. Dibble and Arthur J. O. Anderson, eds. and trans., *Florentine Codex: General History of the Things of New Spain.* Santa Fe, N.M.: School of American Research.

———. 1979. *Códice Florentino.* 3 vols. Florence: Giunti Barbèra.

———. 1981. *The Ceremonies.* Vol. 2 of Charles E. Dibble and Arthur J. O. Anderson, eds. and trans., *Florentine Codex: General History of the Things of New Spain.* 2nd ed. Santa Fe, N.M.: School of American Research.

———. 1988. *Historia general de las cosas de Nueva España.* Edited by Alfredo López Austin and Josefina García Quintana. 2 vols. Madrid: Alianza.

Sala, Rafael. 1925. *Marcas de fuego de las antiguas bibliotecas mexicanas.* Mexico City: Imp. de la Secretaría de Relaciones Exteriores.

Sánchez, Jesús. 1886a. "Fragmentos de la obra de Gama titulada 'Las Dos Piedras,' etc. con una advertencia y notas." *Anales del Museo Nacional de México,* ser. 1, 3:245–57.

———. 1886b. "Notas arqueológicas: Vaso para contener los corazones de las víctimas humanas sacrificadas en ciertas solemnidades religiosas." *Anales del Museo Nacional de México,* ser. 1, 3:296–99.

Saville, Marshall H. 1919. "A Sculptured Vase from Guatemala." *Leaflets of the Museum of the American Indian, Heye Foundation,* no. 1:n.p.

———. 1921. "A Sculptured Vase from Guatemala." *Art and Archaeology* 11:66–67.

Schmidt, Peter J. 1965. *Der Sonnenstein der Azteken.* Hamburg: Hamburgisches Museum für Völkerkunde & Vorgeschichte.

Seler, Eduard. 1888. "Die Charakter der aztekischen und der Maya-Handschriften." *Zeitschrift für Ethnologie* 20:1–97.

———. 1899. "*Quauhxicalli:* Die Opferblutschale der Mexikaner." *Ethnologisches Notizblatt* 2, pt. 1:14–21.

———. 1900. *Das Tonalamatl der Aubin'schen Sammlung: Eine altmexikanische Bilderhandschrift aus der Bibliothèque nationale in Paris (Manuscrits mexicains nr. 18–19).… * Berlin: Druck von Gebrüder Unger.

———. 1900–1901. *The Tonalámatl of the Aubin Collection: An Old Mexican Picture Manuscript in the Paris National Library (Manuscrits mexicains no. 18–19).* Translated by A. H. Keane. Berlin: Printed by Hazell Watson & Viney.

———. 1901. *Codex Fejérváry-Mayer: Eine altmexikanische Bilderhandschrift der Free Public Museums in Liverpool.* Berlin: n.p.

———. 1901–2. *Codex Féjérváry-Mayer: An Old Mexican Picture Manuscript in the Liverpool Free Public Museum.* Translated by A. H. Keane. Berlin: n.p.

———. 1902a. *Codex Vaticanus Nr. 3773 (Codex Vaticanus B): Eine altmexikanische Bilderschrift der Vatikanischen Bibliothek.* Berlin: n.p.

———. 1902b. *Über den Ursprung der mittelamerikanischen Kulturen.* Berlin: Gesellschaft für Erdkunde.

———. 1902–3. *Codex Vaticanus No. 3773 (Codex Vaticanus B): An Old Mexican Pictorial Manuscript in the Vatican Library.* Translated by A. H. Keane. 2 vols. Berlin: n.p.

———. 1902–23. *Gesammelte Abhandlungen zur Amerikanischen Sprach- und Alterthumskunde.* 5 vols. Berlin: A. Asher.

———. 1903a. *Disertaciones,* 6:1–2. Bound manuscript translations of Seler 1902–23. Translated into Spanish by D. de León. Mexico City: M.M.S.S. del Museo Nacional.

———. 1903b. "Las excavaciones en el sitio del Templo Mayor de México." *Anales del Museo Nacional de México* 7:235–59.

———. 1904a. "The Venus Period in the Borgian Codex Group." In Charles Bowditch, ed. and trans., *Mexican and Central American Antiquities, Calendar Systems, and History: Twenty-Four Papers,* 353–91. Washington, D.C.: Government Printing Office.

———. 1904b. "The Wall Paintings of Mitla." In Charles Bowditch, ed. and trans., *Mexican and Central American Antiquities, Calendar Systems, and History: Twenty-Four Papers,* 243–324. Washington, D.C.: Government Printing Office.

———. 1904–9. *Codex Borgia: Eine altmexikanische Bilderschrift der Bibliothek der Congregatio de Propaganda Fide.* 3 vols. Berlin: n.p.

———. 1960a. "Die Ausgrabungen am Orte des Haupttempels in México." In idem, *Gesammelte Abhandlungen zur Amerikanischen Sprach- und Altertumskunde,* 2:767–904. Graz, Austria: Akademische Druck- & Verlagsanstalt.

———. 1960b. "Die holzgeschnitzte Pauke von Malinalco und das Zeichen *atl-tlachinolli.*" In idem, *Gesammelte Abhandlungen zur Amerikanischen Sprach- und Altertumskunde,* 3:221–304. Graz, Austria: Akademische Druck- & Verlagsanstalt.

———. 1960c. "Quauhxicalli: Die Opferblutschale der Mexikaner." In idem, *Gesammelte Abhandlungen zur Amerikanischen Sprach- und Altertumskunde,* 2:704–11. Graz, Austria: Akademische Druck- & Verlagsanstalt.

———. 1960d. "Ueber Steinkisten, Tepetlacalli, mit Opferdarstellungen und andere ähnliche Monumente." In idem, *Gesammelte Abhandlungen zur Amerikanischen Sprach- und Altertumskunde,* 2:717–66. Graz, Austria: Akademische Druck- & Verlagsanstalt.

———. 1960–61. *Gesammelte Abhandlungen zur Amerikanischen Sprach- und Altertumskunde.* 5 vols. Graz, Austria: Akademische Druck- & Verlagsanstalt. Reprint of 1902–23 edition published by A. Asher.

———. 1963. *Comentarios al Códice Borgia.* Translated by Mariana Frenk. 3 vols. Mexico City: Fondo de Cultura Económica.

———. 1990–2002. *Collected Works in Mesoamerican Linguistics and Archaeology.* Edited by Frank E. Comparato. 7 vols. Lancaster, Calif.: Labyrinthos.

Serna, Jacinto de la. 1900. "Manual de ministros de Indios para el conocimiento de sus idolatries, y extirpación de ellas." *Anales del Museo Nacional de México,* ser. 1, 6:261–480.

Siecke, E. 1915. "Zusätze zu dem Ehrenreichsehen Fragment." *Mythologische Bibliothek* 8: 55–60.

Sieck Flandes, Roberto. 1942. "Como estuvo pintada la piedra conocida con el nombre de 'El Calendario Azteca'?" In *Vigesimoséptimo Congreso Internacional de Americanistas: Actas de la primera sesión, celebrada en la ciudad de México en 1939,* 1:550–56. Mexico City: Instituto Nacional de Antropología & Historia.

Sierra, Justo. 1969. *The Political Evolution of the Mexican People.* Edited by Edmundo O'Gorman. Translated by Charles Ramsdell. Austin: Univ. of Texas Press.

———. 1991. "La preparación científica para todas las carreras." In idem, *La educación nacional: Artículos, actuaciones y documentos,* 105–6. Vol. 8 of Agustín Yañez, ed., *Obras completas del maestro Justo Sierra.* Mexico City: Universidad Nacional Autónoma de México.

Smith, Mary Elizabeth. 1973. "The Relationship between Mixtec Manuscript Painting and the Mixtec Language: A Study of Some Personal Names in Codices Muro and Sánchez Solís." In Elizabeth P. Benson, ed., *Mesoamerican Writing Systems,* 47–98. Washington, D.C.: Dumbarton Oaks Research Library & Collection.

Solís, Antonio de. 1783–84. *Historia de la conquista de México, población y progresos de la América septentrional, conocida por el nombre de Nueva España.* 2 vols. Madrid: En la imprenta de D. Antonio de Sancha.

Solís Olguín, Felipe. 1976. *Catálogo de la escultura mexica del Museo de Santa Cecelia Acatitlán.* Mexico City: Instituto Nacional de Antropología & Historia.

———. 1992. "El tamalácatl-cuauhxicalli de Moctezuma Ilhuicamina." In José Alcina Franch, Miguel León-Portilla, and Eduardo Matos Moctezuma, eds., *Azteca-mexica: Las culturas del México antiguo,* 225–32. Madrid: Lunwerg.

———. 1993a. "Aztekische Steinplastik." In Carole Castelli et al., eds., *Die Sammlung vorspanischer Kunst und Kultur aus Mexiko im Museum für Völkerkunde, Berlin = The Precolumbian Collection of Mexico in the Museum of Ethnography, Berlin,* 67–80. Translated by Kurt Hollander et al. Berlin: Staatliche Museen zu Berlin—

Preussischer Kulturbesitz.

———. 1993b. "Las dos piedras de León y Gama." *Arqueología mexicana* 1 (4): 41–43.

———. 1995. "Arte y política en México-Tenochtitlan." *Arqueología mexicana* 3 (15): 42–47.

———. 1997. "Historia de la colección arqueológica del Museo Nacional de Antropología." *Arqueología mexicana* 4 (24): 32–37.

———. 1998. *Tesoros artísticos del Museo Nacional de Antropología.* 2nd ed. Mexico City: Instituto Nacional de Antropología & Historia.

———. 2000. "La *Piedra del Sol.*" *Arqueología mexicana* 7 (41): 32–39.

———, ed. 2004. *The Aztec Empire.* Exh. cat. New York: Guggenheim Museum.

———. 2006. "Imagen de Tonatiuh en el Templo Mayor." In Leonardo López Luján, David Carrasco, and Lourdes Cue, eds., *Arqueología e historia del centro de México: Homenaje a Eduardo Matos Moctezuma,* 567–78. Mexico City: Instituto Nacional de Antropología & Historia.

Solís Olguín, Felipe, and Ted Leyenaar, eds. 2002. *Art Treasures of Ancient Mexico: Journey to the Land of the Gods.* Amsterdam: Waanders.

Solís Olguín, Felipe, et al. 2004. *National Museum of Anthropology, Mexico City.* New York: Harry N. Abrams.

Soustelle, Jacques. 1940. *La pensée cosmologique des anciens Mexicains.* Paris: Hermann.

———. 1975. *Daily Life of the Aztecs on the Eve of the Spanish Conquest.* Translated by Patrick O'Brian. Stanford: Stanford Univ. Press.

Stephens, John Lloyd. 1841. *Incidents of Travel in Central America, Chiapas, and Yucatan.* 2 vols. New York: Harper.

———. 1843. *Incidents of Travel in Yucatan.* 2 vols. New York: Harper.

Stevens, Edward T. 1870. *Flint Chips: A Guide to Pre-Historic Archaeology, as Illustrated by the Collection in the Blackmore Museum, Salisbury.* London: Bell & Daldy.

Stuart, George E. 1992. "Quest for Decipherment: A Historical and Biographical Survey of Maya Hieroglyphic Investigation." In Elin C. Danien and Robert J. Sharer, eds., *New Theories on the Ancient Maya,* 1–64. Philadelphia: University of Pennsylvania, University Museum.

Taube, Karl A. 2000. "The Turquoise Hearth: Fire, Self-Sacrifice, and the Central Mexican Cult of War." In David Carrasco, Lindsay Jones, and Scott Sessions, eds., *Mesoamerica's Classic Heritage: From Teotihuacan to the Aztecs,* 269–340. Boulder: Univ. Press of Colorado.

Tablada, José Juan. 1939. "Fire Marks and Ex-Libris." *Mexican Art and Life,* no. 7.

Teixidor, Felipe. 1931. *Ex Libris y bibliotecas de México.* Mexico City: Imprenta de la Secretaría de Relaciones Exteriores.

Tenorio-Trillo, Mauricio. 1996. *Mexico at the World's Fairs: Crafting a Modern Nation.* Berkeley: Univ. of California Press.

Terry, T. Philip. 1909. *Terry's Mexico: Handbook for Travellers.* Mexico City: Sonora News.

Thompson, J. Eric S. 1934. "Sky Bearers, Colors, and Directions in Maya and Mexican Religion." Publication 436. Washington, D.C.: Carnegie Institution of Washington.

———. 1937. *Mexico before Cortez: An Account of the Daily Life, Religion, and Ritual of the Aztecs.* New York: Charles Scribner's Sons.

———. 1939. *The Moon Goddess in Middle America.* Washington, D.C.: Carnegie Institution of Washington.

———. 1950. *Maya Hieroglyphic Writing: Introduction.* Washington, D.C.: Carnegie Institution of Washington.

———. 1953. "Necrology: Enrique Juan Palacios (1881–1953)." *American Antiquity* 19 (2): 152.

———. 1960. *Maya Hieroglyphic Writing: An Introduction.* 2nd ed. Norman: Univ. of Oklahoma Press.

———. 1962. *A Catalog of Maya Hieroglyphs.* Norman: Univ. of Oklahoma Press.

———. 1970. *Maya History and Religion.* Norman: Univ. of Oklahoma Press.

Torquemada, Juan de. 1723. *Primera [segunda, tercera] parte de los veinte i vn libros rituales i monarchia indiana, con el origen y guerras, de los indios occidentales, de sus poblaçiones descubrimiento, conquista, conuersion, y otras cosas marauillosas de la mesma tierra....* 3 vols. Madrid: N. Rodriquez Franco.

———. 1969. *Monarquía indiana.* 4th ed. 3 vols. Mexico City: Editorial Porrúa.

———. 1975. *Monarquía indiana.* 5th ed. 3 vols. Mexico City: Editorial Porrúa.

Toscano, Salvador. 1944. *Arte precolombino de México y de la América Central.* Mexico City: Instituto de Investigaciones Estéticas, Universidad Nacional Autónoma de México.

Townsend, Richard F. 1979. *State and Cosmos in the Art of Tenochtitlan.* Washington, D.C.: Dumbarton Oaks, Trustees for Harvard University.

Twenty Centuries of Mexican Art = Veinte siglos de arte mexicano. 1940. New York: Museum of Modern Art.

Tylor, Edward B. 1861. *Anahuac; or, Mexico and the Mexicans, Ancient and Modern.* London: Longman, Green, Longman & Roberts.

Umberger, Emily. 1980. "Myth, History, and the *Calendar Stone.*" Unpublished manuscript in author's possession.

———. 1981a. "Aztec Sculptures, Hieroglyphs, and History." Ph.D. diss., Columbia University.

———. 1981b. "The Structure of Aztec History." *Archaeoastronomy* 4 (4): 10–18.

———. 1987a. "Antiques, Revivals, and References to the Past in Aztec Art." *Res* 13:63–105.

———. 1987b. "Events Commemorated by Date Plaques at the Templo Mayor: Further Thoughts on the Solar Metaphor." In Elizabeth Hill Boone, ed., *The Aztec Templo Mayor,* 411–49. Washington, D.C.: Dumbarton Oaks Research Library & Collection.

———. 1988. "A Reconsideration of Some Hieroglyphs on the Mexica *Calendar Stone*." In J. Kathryn Josserand and Karen Dakin, eds., *Smoke and Mist: Mesoamerican Studies in Memory of Thelma D. Sullivan*, 1:345–87. Oxford: B.A.R.

———. 2003. "Aztec Kings and the *Codex Durán*: The Metaphorical Underpinnings of Rulership." *Arara* 6. http://www2.essex.ac.uk/arthistory/arara/issue_six/paper2.html (21 May 2009).

Vaillant, George C. 1941. *Aztecs of Mexico: Origin, Rise and Fall of the Aztec Nation*. New York: Doubleday, Doran.

Valdés, José Francisco. 1808. *Novena consagrada al culto del gloriosísimo proto-martry del Japón el señor San Felipe de Jesús, dirigida a implorar su protección y patrocinio*. Mexico City: Oficina de Doña María Fernández de Jáuregui.

Valdés, Manuel Antonio. 1802. "Elogio histórico de don Antonio de León y Gama." *Gazetas de México* 11 (20): 158–64.

Valentini, E. E. 1939. "The Mexican *Calendar Stone*." *Bulletin of the Pan American Union* 73:712–20.

Valentini, Philipp J. J. 1877. "Discurso acerca de la piedra llamada calendario mexicano pronunciado por el profesor Ph. Valentini, el 30 de abril de 1878 en el 'Republican Hall' (New York), ante una sociedad científico alemana." *Anales del Museo Nacional de México* 1:226–41.

———. 1878a. "The Mexican Calendar Stone." *Proceedings of the American Antiquarian Society*, no. 71:91–108.

———. 1878b. *Vortrag über den Mexikanischen Calender-Stein.…* New York: A. Marrer & Sohn.

———. 1879. "The Mexican Calendar Stone." Translated by Stephen Salisbury Jr. In Stephen Salisbury Jr., comp., *The Mexican Calendar Stone…*, 5–29. Worcester, Mass.: Press of Charles Hamilton.

———. 1880. "'The Landa Alphabet': A Modern Fabrication." *Proceedings of the American Antiquarian Society* 80:59–91.

van Gennep, Arnold. 1909. *Les rites de passage: Études systématique des rites de la porte et du seuil.…* Paris: É. Nourry.

Veytia, Mariano. 1836. *Historia antigua de Méjico*. Edited by Francisco Ortega. 3 vols. Mexico City: J. Ojeda.

———. 1907. *Los calendarios mexicanos*. Mexico City: Museo Nacional de México.

Villegas, Abelardo. 1972. *Positivismo y porfirismo*. Mexico City: Secretaría de Educación Pública.

Villela, Khristaan D. 2001. "Montezuma's Dinner: Precolumbian Art in Nineteenth-Century Mexico, 1821–1876." Ph.D. diss., University of Texas at Austin.

La visita más feliz y compañía misteriosa: Drama místico en tres actos para personajes religiosas, por estar prohibidas en los teatros públicos las comedias de santos. 1811. Mexico City: Don Mariano de Zuñiga y Ontiveros.

Ward, Henry G. 1828. *Mexico in 1827*. 2 vols. London: H. Colburn.

Wehle, Harry Brandeis, and Theodore Bolton. 1927. *American Miniatures, 1730–1850: One Hundred and Seventy-Three Portraits Selected with a Descriptive Account*. Garden City, N.Y.: Published for the Metropolitan Museum of Art by Doubleday, Page.

Wicke, Charles. 1976. "Once More around the *Tizoc Stone*." In José Carlos Chiaramonte, ed., *Actas del XLI Congreso Internacional de Americanistas, México, 2 al 7 de septiembre de 1974*, 2:209–22. Mexico City: Comisión de Publicación de las Actas & Memorias.

Widdifield, Stacie Graham. 1981. "The *Aztec Calendar Stone*: A Critical History." Master's thesis, University of California at Los Angeles.

Wierciński, Andrzej. 1972. "Inter-and-Intrapopulational Racial Differentiation of Tlatilco, Cerro de Las Mesas, Teotihuacan, Monte Alban and Yucatán Maya." In Rosalía Avalos de Matos and Rogger Ravines, eds., *Actas y memorias del XXXIX Congreso Internacional de Americanistas (Lima, 2 9 de agosto 1970)*, 1:231 52. Lima: Instituto de Estudios Peruanos.

———. 1976. "The Dark and Light Side of the Aztec Stone Calendar and Their Symbolical Significance." In *Actas del XLI Congreso Internacional de Americanistas, México, 2 al 7 de septiembre de 1974*, 2:275–78. Mexico City: Comisión de Publicación de las Actas & Memorias.

Willey, Gordon R. 1988. *Portraits in American Archaeology: Remembrances of Some Distinguished Americanists*. Albuquerque: Univ. of New Mexico Press.

Williams, C. A. S. 1960. *Encyclopedia of Chinese Symbolism and Art Motives: An Alphabetical Compendium of Legends and Beliefs as Reflected in the Manners and Customs of the Chinese throughout History*. New York: Julian.

Zantwijk, Rudolph A. M. van. 1977. *Handel en Wandel van de Azteken: De sociale Geschiedenis van voor-Spaans Mexico*. Assen, The Netherlands: Van Gorcum.

Zaremba, Charles W. 1883. *Merchants' and Tourists' Guide to Mexico*. Chicago: Althrop.

Zea, Leopoldo. 1974. *Positivism in Mexico*. Translated by Josephine H. Schulte. Austin: Univ. of Texas Press.

Zea, Leopoldo, and Mario Magallón Anaya, eds. 1999. *Humboldt en México*. Mexico City: Instituto Panamericano de Geografía & Historia.

Zoega, Georg. 1797. *De origine et usu obeliscorum.…* Rome: Typis Lazzarinii.

Biographical Notes on Contributors

Khristaan D. Villela is a visiting professor of art history at the University of New Mexico, a visiting scholar at the New Mexico History Museum, and consulting curator at the Getty Research Institute for the exhibition *Obsidian Mirror Travels* (2010–11). He is consulting curator of arts of the ancient Americas at the Walters Art Museum. From 1998 to 2009, he was Eugene V. Thaw Professor of Art History and director of the Thaw Art History Center at the College of Santa Fe, New Mexico. Villela is a coauthor of *Contemporary Mexican Design and Architecture* (with Ellen Bradbury and Logan Wagner, 2002) and has published numerous articles on Maya inscriptions and culture. He is president of the Association for Latin American Art, an affiliated society of the College Art Association.

Mary Ellen Miller is the dean of Yale College and the Sterling Professor of the History of Art at Yale University. Concentrating on the art of the ancient New World, she has written numerous books, including *The Art of Mesoamerica: From Olmec to Aztec* (1996, 2001, 2006), *Maya Art and Architecture* (1999), and *The Murals of Bonampak* (1986), and coauthored *The Gods and Symbols of Ancient Mexico and the Maya: An Illustrated Dictionary of Mesoamerican Religion* (with Karl Taube, 1993) and *The Blood of Kings: Dynasty and Ritual in Maya Art* (with Linda Schele, 1986, 1992), winner of the Alfred Barr Prize of the College Art Association. In 2004, Miller co-curated *The Courtly Art of the Ancient Maya* exhibition at the National Gallery of Art and the Fine Arts Museums of San Francisco. She is a fellow of the American Academy of Arts and Sciences and the fifty-ninth A. W. Mellon Lecturer in the Fine Arts at the National Gallery of Art, Washington, D.C. (2010).

Matthew H. Robb is the assistant curator of ancient American and Native American art at the Saint Louis Art Museum. From 2007 to 2009, he held an Andrew W. Mellon Postdoctoral Curatorial Fellowship at the same institution. Robb's dissertation on the apartment compounds of Teotihuacan won Yale University's Frances Blanshard Fellowship Fund Prize for an outstanding doctoral dissertation in the history of art. He has conducted extensive research on Teotihuacan and has a particular interest in how sculpture from domestic contexts at Teotihuacan helped shape a collective civic identity. Robb has published on the application of spatial syntax to Teotihuacan's urban plan, as well as on the history of collecting Pre-Columbian art in the postwar period.

Illustration Credits

The following sources have granted permission to reproduce illustrations in this book:

Plates

Pls. 1, 3–10. © Michel Zabé

Pls. 2, 11, 17. Photo: Marco Antonio Pacheco/Arquelogía Mexicana/Raíces

Pl. 12. Library of Congress, Prints and Photographs Division, Detroit Publishing Company Collection, LC-USZC4-6810

Pl. 15. CONACULTA.-INAH.-MEX. Reproduction authorized by the Instituto Nacional de Antropología e Historia

Pl. 16. María Elena Rico Covarrubias

Pls. 18, 19. Photo: Javier Hinojosa. Colección Museo Soumaya. Fundación Carlos Slim, A.C., Mexico City

Pls. 20, 21. © Biblioteca Nacional de España

Introduction

Fig. 1. © The Trustees of the National Museums of Scotland

Figs. 3, 8. Benson Library, University of Texas, Austin

Fig. 6. Musée du Quai Branly/Scala/Art Resource, New York

Fig. 7. Courtesy of George Eastman House, International Museum of Photography and Film

Figs. 12, 15. Collection of Khristaan D. Villela

Fig. 13. DeGolyer Library, Southern Methodist University, Dallas, Texas, fol. 4, E404.K46 1994

Fig. 14. Photo: Courtesy of the Architect of the Capitol

Figs. 18, 19, 24. CONACULTA.-INAH.-MEX. Reproduction authorized by the Instituto Nacional de Antropología e Historia

Fig. 20. Private collection, New York

Fig. 21. Lalo Alcaraz

Fig. 22. From the *New Yorker,* 26 November 1960. © The New Yorker Collection, 1960, A. Kovarsky from cartoonbank.com. All rights reserved

Fig. 23. Brooklyn Museum. 87.182. Modernism Benefit Fund

Leon y Gama

Figs. 1–3. From León y Gama 1832

Seler

Figs. 1–4, 6–9. Tozzer Library of Harvard College Library

Fig. 5. Bildarchiv Preussischer Kulturbesitz/Art Resource, New York

Fig. 10. © Michel Zabé

Beyer

Fig. 8. Museum für Völkerkunde, Vienna

Fig. 18. Bildarchiv Preussischer Kulturbesitz/Art Resource, New York

Fig. 44. © Michel Zabé

Fig. 50. © Peabody Museum of Natural History, Yale University, New Haven, Connecticut

Fig. 53. Michel Zabé/Art Resource, New York

Palacios

Fig. 1. Collection of Khristaan D. Villela

Navarrete and Heyden

Figs. 2, 3, 10. © Michel Zabé

Fig. 4. Courtesy Emily Umberger

Fig. 7. Werner Forman/Art Resource, New York

Fig. 9. Photo: Marco Antonio Pacheco/*Arqueología Mexicana*/Raíces

Fig. 11. Carlos Navarrete

Klein

Fig. 5. Bildarchiv Preussischer Kulturbesitz/Art Resource, New York

Umberger

Figs. 1, 3, 5, 7. Courtesy Emily Umberger

Fig. 2. Michel Zabé/Art Resource, New York

Fig. 4. © Biblioteca Nacional de España

Fig. 8. CONACULTA.-INAH.-MEX. Reproduction authorized by the Instituto Nacional de Antropología e Historia

Fig. 10. CONACULTA.-INAH.-MEX. Reproduction authorized by the Instituto Nacional de Antropología e Historia. Museo Nacional de Antropología, Mexico City

Nicholson

Figs. 2, 4. From *Codex Borbonicus* 1974. ADEVA, Graz, Austria

Fig. 3. Musée des Confluences, Lyon, inv. 81000037

Fig. 5. © The Trustees of the British Museum

Fig. 6. Photo: P. Frankenstein, H. Zwietasch; Landesmuseum Württemberg

Fig. 9. Werner Forman/Art Resource, New York

Fig. 10. CONACULTA.-INAH.-MEX. Reproduction authorized by the Instituto Nacional de Antropología e Historia

Fradcourt

Figs. 1, 3, 8. Ariane Fradcourt

Fig. 2. Ariane Fradcourt. After Graulich 1987, 277

Fig. 4. © The Trustees of the British Museum

Fig. 5. From *Codex Borbonicus* 1974, 16. ADEVA, Graz, Austria

Figs. 7, 10. CONACULTA.-INAH.-MEX. Reproduction authorized by the Instituto Nacional de Antropología e Historia

Fig. 9. Erich Lessing/Art Resource, New York

Index

Note: Page numbers in *italics* refer to illustrations.

Bilimek, Dominik, 102

Bilimek Pulque Vessel, 102, *137, 284*

Blake, William Wilberforce, 39n27

blood, 123, 125, 135, *135*

Boas, Franz, 35

Bolaños, Joaquín: *Portentosa vida de la Muerte, La,* 52

Bonavia y Zapata, Bernardo, 61

Bonpland, Aimé, 81; *Voyage aux régions équinoxiales du nouveau continent,* 81

Boturini Benaduci, Lorenzo, 2, 50, 51, 83, 84, 101; *Idea de una nueva historia general de la América septentrional,* 40n51

Bowditch, Charles, 105

Box of the Sun, 21, 22

Brinton, Daniel, 100n4

Brumidi, Constantino, 27; *Frieze of American History, 28*

Buboso, 67

Bullock, William Henry, 6, 102, 170, 179; cast of *Calendar Stone, 7*

burner, sacred, *137*

Bustamante, Carlos María de, 6, 51, 101

Caballito (Little horse), 18

Calderón de la Barca, Frances, 6

Calendario antiguo, El (Durán), 42

Calendario Azteca (Chavero), 91

"Calendario Azteca" (Chavero), 90

Calendar Stone, 151, 152, 153–56; Abadiano's albumen print of, *31;* Abadiano's lithograph of, *11;* adaptive reuse images of, *33, 33, 34, 35;* Agüera's rendering of, *52, 54, 55;* as anomalous, 19; Axayacatl and, 14, 91; Bullock's cast of, 6, *7;* burial of, 4, 16; as calendar, 3–4; Chanfón's deconstructed drawing of, *36;* Charnay's albumen print of, *25;* Cloquet's engraving of, *85; Coatlicue vs.,* 18, 226–27; color in, 126–27, *157, 161, 162,* 181–84, 297; commissioning of, 45–46; as *cuauhxicalli,* 3, 91, 104, 119–20, 122–25, 149; daguerreotype of, 20, *20;* damage to, 19–20; dating of, 254–55; detail, *154–56;* discovery of, 1; documentary images of, 23–24; flange on, 22; Garcés's lithograph of, *163;* human sacrifice on, 1; importance of, 1; Iriarte's lithograph of, *11;* makeup of, 1, 84; mounting of, at Catedral Metropolitana de la Asunción de María, 4, 18–19; at Museo Nacional, 10, 12; in Museo Nacional catalog, 103; as national symbol, 234–235; position of, 193–94, 294–95; in profile, *153;* publication of, 4–5; reproductions of, 23–36; research, 4–16; scale of, 122; solar disk edge of, 133–35; style

of, 21–22; sun on, 1–2; Templo Mayor and, 16; *Teocalli* and, 17; themes in, 3; transport of, 75–76; as ubiquitous symbol, 1; unearthing of, 4, 58; vandalism of, 58; Velasco's lithograph of, *10;* weight of, 1, 75, 84

calendar wheels, 19, 40n51

Calli, 68, *152,* 197

Camaxtle, 196

Cambas, Manuel Rivera: *México pintoresco, artístico y monumental,* 29

Cantinflas, 29, *32*

Capitol rotunda, United States, 27, *28*

Carnestolendas, 98

Carranza, Venustiano, 29

Carreri, Giovanni Gemelli, 19

Casa de las Ajaracas, La, 16

Casillas, José Bribiesca: *Untitled, 165*

Caso, Alfonso, 12, 24, 118, 181

Castillo, Bernal Díaz del, 16

Castillo, Cristóbal del, 65, 72, 83; *Historia de los mexicanos,* 52

casts, of *Calendar Stone,* 27

Catedral Metropolitana de la Asunción de María, 4, 15, *158*

Cat Eyes—Aztec Calendar Stone (Muñoz), *33*

Cavo, Andrés, 50

Ce Acatl, 67, 173

Ce ácatl. See Ce Acatl

Ce Calli, 67

Ce Cipactli, 71

Ce Ocelotl, 65

Ce Quiahuitl, 70, 71, 114

ce quiauitl. See Ce Quiahuitl

Ce Tecpatl, 67, 70, 113, 175, 176, 178, 179

Ce técpatl. See Ce Tecpatl

Ce Xochitl, 63–64, 78n40

Cexocitl. See Ce Xochitl

Chachame, 64

Chacmool, 9

Chacmool figures, 167

chalchihuitl, 2, 114, 260, 265

Chalchiuhtlicue, 22, 193, 197

Chanfón Olmos, Carlos, 24; *Aztec Calendar Stone, 36*

Chantico, 64, 78n40

Chapultepec cliff carving, 19

Charles III, 59, 227

Charles IV, 81, 227

Charles V, 88

Charnay, Desire, 15; *Aztec Calendar Stone, 25*

Chavero, Alfredo, 6, 8–9, 24, 43, 44, 82, 90; *Los amores de Alarcón,* 90; *Anales del Museo Nacional de México,* 90, 91; *Calendario Azteca,*

Maldonado, Victor Manuel, 15; *Aztec Calendar Stone,* 157

Malinalli, 68, 70, *152,* 197

Mamalhuaztli, 208

mamalhuaztli, 175

Mapa Sigüénza, 52, 81

Marín, Feliciano, 39n48

"Marines' Hymn," 29

Márquez, Pedro, 50

Masonic commemorative medal, *27*

matemecatl, 110

mathematics, 59

matlactli omei acatl. See Matlactli Omey Acatl

Matlactli Omey Acatl, 68, 87, 93, 115

Matlactly Omey Acatl. *See* Matlactli Omey Acatl

Matos Moctezuma, Eduardo, 15, 19, 298

Matrícula de Tributos, 52

Maximilian (emperor), 6, 29, 102

Mayer, Brantz, 102; *Mexico as It Was and Is,* 170

Mazatl, 68, *152*

Mendoza, Gumesindo, 12, 43, 90, 102

methodology, of source selection, 37

Metzlapohualiztli, 74

Metztli, 74

Mexican-American War, 27, *28*

México Antiguo, El (journal), 118

Mexico as It Was and Is (Mayer), 170

México a través de los siglos (Chavero), 8, 90

México pintoresco, artístico y monumental (Cambas), 29

Meztli, 86

Michoacán, 50, 95

Mictlantecuhtli, *129,* 299

Milky Way galaxy, 65, 67, 69, 99

Miquiztli, 68, 86, *152*

Mixcoamazátzin, 178

Mixcoatl, 99, 288

Monarquía Indiana (Torquemada), 78n36, 83

"Montezuma's Dinner" (Morgan), 91

"Montezuma's watch," 38n15

Montúfar, Alonso de, 3, 4, 16, 93

Monumentos del arte mexicano antiguo (Peñafiel), 9

moon, 74, 86, 216n16

Morgan, Lewis Henry, 9; "Montezuma's Dinner," 91

Morley, Sylvanus G.: *Inscriptions at Copan,* 27; *Inscriptions at Petén,* 27

morning star, 144

Motecuhçoma. *See* Motecuhzoma

Motecuhzoma I, 2, 42, 144, *245*

Motecuhzoma II, *244;* in creation of *Calendar Stone,* 46–48; large-scale commissions by, 42; as patron of *Calendar Stone,* 1, 45–46; *Teocalli* and, 17

Motecuhzoma Ilhuicamina. *See* Motecuhzoma I

Motion. *See* Nahui Ollin; Ollin

Movement. *See* Nahui Ollin; Ollin

Muñoz, Juan: *Historia del Nuevo-Mundo,* 51

Muñoz, Maurio: *Cat Eyes—Aztec Calendar Stone,* 33

Musée d'ethnographie du Trocadéro, 38n24

Museo de la Ciudad de México, 101

Museo Nacional. *See* Museo Nacional de Antropología

Museo Nacional de Antropología, 1, 6–8, 10, 12, 13, 15, 21, 101

Museo Público de Historia Natural, Arqueología e Historia, 102

Museum of Modern Art, 13

Nahui Atl, 2, 60, 66, 67, 70, 114, *152, 155*

Nahui Calli, 70

Nahui Ehecatl, 2, 67, 114, *152, 154*

Nahui Ocelotl, 2, 66, 67, 70, 72, *152, 155*

Nahui Ollin, 2, 45, 64–65, 66, 67, 99, 113, *130,* 149

Nahui Ollin Tonatiuh, 5, 86

Nahui Quiahuitl, 2, 66, 67, 72, 114, *152, 154*

Nahui Tonatiuh, 72

Nanahuatzin, 186

Napoleon III, 29

Nation (newspaper), 91

Nauholin. *See* Nahui Ollin

naui atl. *See* Nahui Atl

naui eecatl. *See* Nahui Ehecatl

naui olin. *See* Nahui Ollin

naui quiauitl. *See* Nahui Quiahuitl

Navarrete, Carlos, 13, 185

Nebel, Carl, 6, *21, 28,* 92, 102

Netonatiuh Caoalo. *See* Netonatiuhqualo

Netonatiuhqualo, 64, 86, 96

New Fire ceremony, 246

Newton, Isaac, 3

New Yorker cartoon (Kovarsky), *34*

New York Times, 91

Nezahualpilli, 246

Nicholson, H. B., 15, 263

Nieremberg, Eusebio, 86, 96; *Historia Naturae maxime peregrinae,* 78n36

Noriega, Raúl, 13, 24; *Aztec Calendar Stone,* 264

North American Review, 91

"Notes on the Semi-Civilized Nations of Mexico" (Gallatin), 24

Nuttall, Zelia, 8, 33

Ocelotl, 65, 68, 87, *152*

Ocelotonatiuh, 131

Ochpaniztli, 70

sacred burner, *137*

sacrifice: adoption of practice, 82; autosacrifice, 123, *124;* in Beyer, *119,* 120, *120;* on *Calendar Stone,* 1; *cuauhxicalli* in, 106–7; of deities, 37n2, 78n41; in *Durán Codex, 166;* reason for, 123; in Seler, 113

Sahagún, Bernardino de, 8, 52, 78n36, 83; *Historia de las cosas de la Nueva España, 141*

Saldaña, Mateo A., 181

Salón de Monolitos, 12, *30*

San Antón Chimalpaín, Domingo de, 52

Sánchez, Jesús, 12, 90, 102, 110

Santa Elena Poco Uinic, 167

Santelizes, Juan Eugenio, 73

"scientific" images, 23–24

Scott, Winfield, 27, *28*

selection, of sources, 37

Seler, Eduard, 12, 90, *137;* priest drawing by, *142;* Tlaltecuhtli drawing by, *186*

self-sacrifice, 123, *124*

Sieck Flandes, Roberto, 13, 181; *Aztec Calendar Stone, 161*

Siguenza, Carlos de. *See* Sigüenza y Góngora, Carlos

Sigüenza y Góngora, Carlos, 83, 84, 101

sky band, 144–47

Snake. *See* Coatl

solar disk, on *Calendar Stone,* 133–35

Solares, José Aviles, 212

solar year, 51, 82, 215n5

Solís, Antonio de: *Historia de la conquista de México,* 51

Solís, Felipe, 15, 24, 293

solstice, 68, 73, 82

source selection, 37

souvenirs, 33, 35

speech attributed to *Calendar Stone,* 46–47

Starr, Frederick, *168,* 169

Steinen, Wilhelm von: Plan of the main temple of Mexico and its buildings (after Sahagún), *112*

Stephens, John Lloyd, 6

stone, of *Calendar Stone,* 46–48

stonemasons, in creation of *Calendar Stone,* 46

Stone of Motecuhzoma I, 3, 15, 16

Stone of the Five Suns, 21, 115, *116,* 117

Stone of the Gladiators, 100n22

"*Stone of the Sun* and the First Chapter of the History of Mexico" (Palacios), *168*

Stone of Tiçoc. *See Stone of Tizoc*

Stone of Tizoc, 3, 4, 16, 22, 49, 113, 194, *242;* daytime sky on, *147;* sun disk on, *133*

Storia antica del Messico (Clavigero), 51

style, of *Calendar Stone,* 21–22

Sumaria relación (Alva Ixtlilxóchitl), 52, 60

sun: on *Calendar Stone,* 1–2; in *Dresden Codex, 106;* eagle as, *120;* fables about, 67, 72–73, 79n51, 131–32; Fifth, 2; moon and, 216n16

sundial, 65

Syphilitic One. *See* Buboso; Nanahuatzin

tableaus, 17

Tablet of the Cross, 9

Tablet of the 96 Glyphs, 167

Techichco, 47

Tecpatl, 68, 70, 87, 152

Tecuccizcalco, 74

Tecucciztecatl, 74

temalacatitlan, 17

temalacatl, 3, 16, 17, 46, 104

Temoctzin, 186

Temple of Sacred Warfare. See *Teocalli de la Guerra Sagrada*

Temple Stone. See *Teocalli de la Guerra Sagrada*

Templo Mayor, 2, 12, 16–17, *112*

teoamoxtli, 57–58

teocalli, 96

Teocalli de la Guerra Sagrada, 15, 17, 167, 194, *246, 249, 285*

Teotecpatl, 70

Teoyamiqui, 18

Tepan Temoctzin, 186

Tepepulla, 46

Tepeyólotl, 186, 197

Tepictoton, 186

Tepoztecatl, 67

Tetlacmancalmecac, 64

Tetlanman, 63, 78n40

tezcacuitlapilli, 110

Tezcatlipoca, 105, 243, *286*

Thompson, J. Eric S., 15, 105

three-dimensional reproductions, 27

Tibet, 82

Tiçoc. See *Stone of Tizoc*

Tiffany & Co.: Tray, *35*

Tizoc, *249*

Tlacaxipehualiztli, 87

Tlacchitonatiuh. See Tlalchitonatiuh

tlachco, 105

Tlachtemalacatl, *148*

tlachtemalácatl, 115

tlachtli, 115

Tlahuizcalpantecuhtli, *146*

Tlalchitonatiuh, 176, 178, *192,* 193, 202, *280, 281,* 281–82, *282*

Tlalloque. *See* Tlaloque

Tlaloc, 22, 66, 68, 69, 87, 186, 212

Designed by Kurt Hauser

Coordinated by Stacy Miyagawa

Type composed by Diane Franco

Printed in China through Asia Pacific Offset, Inc.